Architecting Microsoft® .NET Solutions for the Enterprise

Dino Esposito

Andrea Saltarello

PUBLISHED BY
Microsoft Press
A Division of Microsoft Corporation
One Microsoft Way
Redmond, Washington 98052-6399

Library of Congress Control Number: 2008935425

Printed and bound in the United States of America.

1 2 3 4 5 6 7 8 9   QWT   3 2 1 0 9 8

Distributed in Canada by H.B. Fenn and Company Ltd.

A CIP catalogue record for this book is available from the British Library.

Microsoft Press books are available through booksellers and distributors worldwide. For further information about international editions, contact your local Microsoft Corporation office or contact Microsoft Press International directly at fax (425) 936-7329. Visit our Web site at www.microsoft.com/mspress. Send comments to mspinput@microsoft.com.

Acquisitions Editor: Ben Ryan
Project Editor: Lynn Finnel
Editorial Production: S4Carlisle Publishing Services
Technical Reviewer: Kenn Scribner ; Technical Review services provided by Content Master, a member of CM Group, Ltd.
Cover: Tom Draper Design

Body Part No. X15-12272

"Any sufficiently advanced technology is indistinguishable from magic."

—Arthur C. Clarke

Contents at a Glance

Table of Contents

Part I   Principles

What do you think of this book? We want to hear from you!

Microsoft is interested in hearing your feedback so we can continually improve our books and learning resources for you. To participate in a brief online survey, please visit:

www.microsoft.com/learning/booksurvey/

What do you think of this book? We want to hear from you!

Microsoft is interested in hearing your feedback so we can continually improve our books and learning resources for you. To participate in a brief online survey, please visit:

www.microsoft.com/learning/booksurvey/

Acknowledgments

For at least two years, Andrea didn't miss any opportunity to remind Dino about the importance of a .NET-focused architecture book covering the horizontal slice of a multitier enterprise system. And for two years Dino strung Andrea along with generic promises, but absolutely no commitment. Then, suddenly, he saw the light. During a routine chat over Messenger, we found out that we repeatedly made similar statements about architecture—too many to mark it down as a simple coincidence. So we started thinking, and this time seriously, about this book project. But we needed a team of people to do it right, and they were very good people, indeed.

Ben Ryan was sneakily convinced to support the project on a colorful Las Vegas night, during an ethnic dinner at which we watched waiters coming up from and going down to the wine-cellar in transparent elevators.

Lynn Finnel just didn't want to let Dino walk alone in this key project after brilliantly coordinating at least five book projects in the past.

Kenn Scribner is now Dino's official book alter ego. Kenn started working with Dino on books back in 1998 in the age of COM and the Active Template Library. How is it possible that a book with Dino's name on the cover isn't reviewed and inspired (and fixed) by Kenn's unique and broad perspective on the world of software? The extent to which Kenn can be helpful is just beyond human imagination.

Roger LeBlanc joined the team to make sure that all these geeks sitting together at the same virtual desktop could still communicate using true English syntax and semantics.

We owe you all the (non-rhetorically) monumental "Thank you" for being so kind, patient, and accurate.

Only two authors and a small team for such a great book? Well, not exactly. Along the project lifetime, we had the pleasure to welcome aboard a good ensemble of people who helped out in some way. And we want to spend a word or two about each of them here.

Raffaele Rialdi suggested and reviewed our section in Chapter 3 about design for security. **Roy Osherove** was nice enough to share his enormous experience with testing and testing tools. **Marco Abis** of ThoughtWorks had only nice words for the project and encouraged us to make it happen. **Alex Homer** of Microsoft helped with Unity and Enterprise Library. And the whole team at Managed Design (our Italian company) contributed tips and ideas—special thanks go to **Roberto Messora**.

It's really been a pleasure!

—*Andrea and Dino*

Dino's Credits

This is the first book I have co-authored in 8 or 9 years. I think the last was a multi-author book on data access involving COM and OLE DB. In the past, co-authoring a book for me meant accepting to write a few chapters on specific topics, while having only a faint idea of what was coming before and after my chapters.

This book is different.

This book has really been written by a virtual author: a human with the hands of Dino and the experience of Andrea. I actually did most of the writing, but Andrea literally put concepts and

ideas into my keyboard. If it were a song, it would be described as lyrics by Dino and music by Andrea.

This book wouldn't exist, or it wouldn't be nearly as valuable, without Andrea. Andrea has been my personal Google for a few months—the engine to search when I need to understand certain principles and design issues. The nicest part of the story is that I almost always asked about things I (thought I) knew enough about. My "enough" was probably really enough to be a very good architect in real life. But Andrea gave me a new and broader perspective on virtually everything we covered in the book—ISO standards, UML, design principles, patterns, the user interface, business logic, services, and persistence. I've been the first hungry reader of this book. And I've been the first to learn a lot.

It was so fun that I spent the whole summer on it. And in Italy, the summer is a serious matter. I smile when I get some proposals for consulting or training in mid-August. There's no way I can even vaguely hint to my wife about accepting them.

So, on many days, I reached 7 p.m. so cloudy minded that running, running, and running—which was more soothing than my favorite pastime of trying to catch up to and hit a bouncing tennis ball—was the only way to recover a decent state of mind. On other days, my friends at **Tennis Club Monterotondo** helped a lot by just throwing at me tons of forehands and passing shots. One of them, **Fabrizio**—a guy who played Boris Becker and Stefan Edberg and who now wastes his time with my hopeless backhand slice—has been my instructor for a while. He also tried to learn some basic concepts of Web programming during what often became long conversations while changing ends of the court. But just as I keep on twirling the wrist during the execution of a backhand slice, he still keeps on missing the whole point of HTTP cookies.

My friend **Antonio** deserves a very special mention for organizing a wonderful and regenerative vacation in the deep blue sea of Sardinia, and for being kind enough to lose all the matches we played. It was just the right medicine to rejuvenate a fatigued spirit after a tough book project. He tried to initiate me into the sport of diving, too, but all I could do was snorkel while the kids got their Scuba Diver certification.

My kids, **Francesco** and **Michela**, grow taller with every book I write, and not because they just hop on the entire pile of dad's books. They're now 10 and 7, and Michela was just a newborn baby when I started working on my first .NET book for Microsoft Press. I really feel a strong emotion when attendees of conferences worldwide come by and ask about my kids—loyal readers of my books have been seeing their pictures for years now.

For me, this book is not like most of the others that I have written—and I do write about one book per year. This book marks a watershed, both personal and professional. I never expressed its importance in this way with **Silvia**, but she understood it anyway and supported me silently and effectively. And lovingly. And with great food, indeed!

Life is good.

—Dino

Andrea's Credits

This is my first book. More precisely, this is my first serious publication. The seeds for this book were sowed in November 2004 when a rockstar like Dino approached me and proposed that we work together.

We started a successful business partnership, and we delivered a number of classes and some articles—including one for MSDN Magazine—and took a number of industry projects home to ensure our customers were happy.

In all these years, Dino impressed me especially with his unique ability of going straight to the point, and being a terrifically quick learner of the fundamentals of any topics we touched on. More, he also showed an unparalleled ability to express any concept precisely and concisely. Countless times during this book project, I found my own wording hard to read, nebulous, and even cryptic. A few days later, instead, massaged by Dino, the same text looked to me magically fluent and perfectly understandable—just like any technical text should always be.

(OK, I admit. Sometimes I thought "I hate this man," but it was an unusual and unconfessed way to look up to Dino with admiration.)

More than everything else, what initially was a simple although successful professional collaboration turned into friendship. This book, therefore, is not a finish line. It is, instead, the starting point of a common path. I really don't know either where we're going or how long it will take, but I'm going to be happy to take the walk.

Being a full-time consultant, it was very hard for me to set aside the time needed for writing this book. So I had to start living a double life, resorting to writing in what you would define as "spare time": evenings and weekends, and suddenly the summer also became standard working time. Every now and then, it has been a little frustrating, but I found new strength and inspiration due to the love and support I was blessed with by my guardian angels: my **mom** and **Laura**. I'd like to say to them that words cannot express how precious your caring is. I love you.

Now, this is fun.

—*Andrea*

Introduction

Good judgment comes from experience, and experience comes from bad judgment.

—*Fred Brooks*

Every time we are engaged on a software project, we create a solution. We call the process *architecting*, and the resulting concrete artifact is the *architecture*. Architecture can be implicit or explicit.

An *implicit* architecture is the design of the solution we create mentally and persist on a bunch of Microsoft Office Word documents, when not on handwritten notes. An implicit architecture is the fruit of hands-on experience, the reuse of tricks learned while working on similar projects, and an inherent ability to form abstract concepts and factor them into the project at hand. If you're an expert artisan, you don't need complex drawings and measurements to build a fence or a bed for your dog; you can implicitly architect it in a few moments. You just proceed and easily make the correct decision at each crossroad. When you come to an end, it's fine. All's well that ends well.

An *explicit* architecture is necessary when the stakeholder concerns are too complex and sophisticated to be handled based only on experience and mental processes. In this case, you need vision, you need guidance, and you need to apply patterns and practices that, by design, take you where you need to be.

What Is Architecture?

The word *architecture* has widespread use in a variety of contexts. You can get a definition for it from the Oxford English Dictionary or, as far as software is concerned, from the American National Standards Institute/Institute of Electrical and Electronics Engineers (ANSI/IEEE) library of standards. In both cases, the definition of architecture revolves around planning, designing, and constructing something—be it a building or a software program. Software architecture is the concrete artifact that solves specific stakeholder concerns—read, *specific user requirements*.

An architecture doesn't exist outside of a context. To design a software system, you need to understand how the final system relates to, and is embedded into, the hosting environment. As a software architect, you can't ignore technologies and development techniques for the environment of choice—for this book, the .NET platform.

Again, what is architecture?

We like to summarize it as the art of making hard-to-change decisions correctly. The architecture is the skeleton of a system, the set of pillars that sustain the whole construction.

The architect is responsible for the architecture. The architect's job is multifaceted. She has to acknowledge requirements, design the system, ensure the implementation matches the expectation, and overall ensure that users get what they really need—which is not necessarily what they initially accept and pay for.

Software architecture has some preconditions—that is, design principles—and one post condition—an implemented system that produces expected results. Subsequently, this book is divided into two parts: principles and the design of the system.

The first part focuses on the role of the architect: what he does, who he interacts with and who he reports to. The architect is primarily responsible for acknowledging the requirements, designing the system, and communicating that design to the development team. The communication often is based on Unified Modeling Language (UML) sketches; less often, it's based on UML blueprints. The architect applies general software engineering principles first, and object-oriented design principles later, to break down the system into smaller and smaller pieces in an attempt to separate what is architecture (points that are hard to change) and what is not. One of the purposes of object-oriented design is to make your code easy to maintain and evolve—and easy to read and understand. The architect knows that maintainability, security, and testability need to be built into the system right from the beginning, and so he does that.

The second part of the book focuses on the layers that form a typical enterprise system—the presentation layer, business layer, and data access layer. The book discusses design patterns for the various layers—including Domain Model, Model-View-Presenter, and Service Layer—and arguments about the evolution of technologies and summaries of the new wave of tools that have become a common presence in software projects—O/R mappers and dependency injection containers.

So, in the end, what's this book about?

It's about the things you need to do and know to serve your customers in the best possible way as far as the .NET platform is concerned. Patterns, principles, and techniques described in the book are valid in general and are not specific to particularly complex line-of-business applications. A good software architecture helps in controlling the complexity of the project. And controlling the complexity and favoring maintainability are the sharpest tools we have to fight the canonical Murphy's Law of technology: "Nothing ever gets built on schedule or within budget."

The expert is the one who knows how to handle complexity, not the one who simply predicts the job will take the longest and cost the most—just to paraphrase yet another popular Murphy's Law.

Who This Book Is For

In the previous section, we repeatedly mentioned architects. So are software architects the ideal target audience for this book? Architects and lead developers in particular are the target audience, but any developers of any type of .NET applications likely will find this book beneficial. Everyone who wants to be an architect may find this book helpful and worth the cost.

What about prerequisites?

Strong object-oriented programming skills are a requirement, as well as having a good foundation of knowledge of the .NET platform and data access techniques. We point out a lot of design patterns, but we explain all of them in detail in nonacademic language with no weird formalisms. Finally, we put in a lot of effort into making this book read well. It's not a book about abstract design concepts; it is not a classic architecture book either, full of cross-references and fancy strings in square brackets that hyperlink to some old paper listed in the bibliography available at the end of the book.

This is (hopefully) a book you'll want to read from cover to cover, and maybe more than once—not a book to keep stored on a shelf for future reference. We don't expect readers to pick up this book at crunch time to find out how to use a given pattern. Instead, our ultimate goal is transferring some valuable knowledge that enables you to know what to do at any point. In a certain way, we would happy if, thanks to this book, you could do more *implicit* architecture design on your own.

Companion Content

In the book, we present several code snippets and discuss sample applications, but with the primary purpose of illustrating principles and techniques for readers to apply in their own projects. In a certain way, we tried to teach fishing, but we don't provide some sample fish to take home. However, there's a CodePlex project that we want to point out to you. You find it at *http://www.codeplex.com/nsk*.

This book also features a companion Web site where you can also find the CodePlex project. You can download it from the companion site at this address: *http://www.microsoft.com/mspress/companion/9780735626096*.

The Northwind Starter Kit (NSK) is a set of Microsoft Visual Studio 2008 projects that form a multitier .NET-based system. Produced by Managed Design (*http://www.manageddesign.it*), NSK is a reference application that illustrates most of the principles and patterns we discuss in the book. Many of the code snippets in the book come directly from some of the projects in the NSK solution. If you're engaged in the design and implementation of a .NET layered application, NSK can serve as a sort of blueprint for the architecture.

Refer to the Managed Design Web site for the latest builds and full source code. For an overview of the reference application, have a look at the Appendix, "The Northwind Starter Kit," in this book.

Hardware and Software Requirements

You'll need the following hardware and software to work with the companion content included with this book:

- Microsoft Windows Vista Home Premium Edition, Windows Vista Business Edition, or Windows Vista Ultimate Edition

- Microsoft Visual Studio 2008 Standard Edition, Visual Studio 2008 Enterprise Edition, or Microsoft Visual C# 2008 Express Edition and Microsoft Visual Web Developer 2008 Express Edition

- Microsoft SQL Server 2005 Express Edition, Service Pack 2

- The Northwind database of Microsoft SQL Server 2000 is used by the Northwind Starter Kit to demonstrate data-access techniques. You can obtain the Northwind database from the Microsoft Download Center (http://www.microsoft.com/downloads/details.aspx?FamilyID=06616212-0356-46A0-8DA2-EEBC53A68034&displaylang=en).

- 1.6 GHz Pentium III+ processor, or faster

- 1 GB of available, physical RAM.

- Video (800 by 600 or higher resolution) monitor with at least 256 colors.

- CD-ROM or DVD-ROM drive.

- Microsoft mouse or compatible pointing device

Find Additional Content Online

As new or updated material becomes available that complements this book, it will be posted online on the Microsoft Press Online Developer Tools Web site. The type of material you might find includes updates to book content, articles, links to companion content, errata, sample chapters, and more. This Web site is available at *www.microsoft.com/learning/books/online/developer* and is updated periodically.

Support for This Book

Every effort has been made to ensure the accuracy of this book and the contents of the companion CD. As corrections or changes are collected, they will be added to a Microsoft Knowledge Base article.

Microsoft Press provides support for books and companion CDs at the following Web site:

http://www.microsoft.com/learning/support/books

Questions and Comments

If you have comments, questions, or ideas regarding the book or the companion content, or questions that are not answered by visiting the sites above, please send them to Microsoft Press via e-mail to

mspinput@microsoft.com

Or via postal mail to

Microsoft Press
Attn: *Microsoft .NET: Architecting Applications for the Enterprise* Editor
One Microsoft Way
Redmond, WA 98052-6399

Please note that Microsoft software product support is not offered through the above addresses.

Part I
Principles

You know you've achieved perfection in design, not when you have nothing more to add, but when you have nothing more to take away.

—*Antoine de Saint-Exupery, "Wind, Sand and Stars"*

Chapter 1
Architects and Architecture Today

The purpose of software engineering is to control complexity, not to create it.

—*Dr. Pamela Zave*

At the beginning of the computing age, in the early 1960s, the costs of hardware were largely predominant over the costs of software. Some 40 years later, we find the situation to be radically different.

Hardware costs have fallen dramatically because of the progress made by the industry. Software development costs, on the other hand, have risen considerably, mostly because of the increasing complexity of custom enterprise software development. Cheaper computers made it worthwhile for companies to add more and more features to their information systems. What in the beginning was a collection of standalone applications with no connection to one another that barely shared a database has grown over years into a complex system made of interconnected functions and modules, each with a particular set of responsibilities.

This situation has created the need for a set of precepts to guide engineers in the design of such systems. The modern software system—or the software-intensive system, as it is referred to in international standards papers—can be compared quite naturally to any construction resulting from a set of detailed blueprints.

Appropriated from the construction industry, the term *architecture* has become the appropriate way to describe the art of planning, designing, and implementing software-intensive systems. In software, though, architecture needs less artistry than in building. Well-designed buildings are pleasing to the eye and functional. Software architecture is less subjective. It either functions as required or it does not. There is less room for artistry and interpretation, unless you want to consider the artistry of a well-crafted algorithm or a piece of user interface.

One of this book's authors had, in the past, frequent interaction with an architecture studio. One day, a question popped up for discussion: What's architecture? Is it an art? Or is it just building for a client?

In software, the term *architecture* precisely refers to building a system for a client.

In this first chapter, we'll look at some papers from the International Organization for Standardization (ISO), the International Electrotechnical Commission (IEC), and the Institute of Electrical and Electronics Engineers (IEEE) that provide an architectural description of software-intensive systems. From there, we'll give our own interpretation of software architecture and voice our opinions about the role and responsibilities of software architects.

Note While some definitions you find in this book come from ISO standards, others reflect our personal opinions, experiences, and feelings. Although the reader might not agree with all of our personal reflections, we all should agree that software systems that lack strong architectural design and support are nearly guaranteed to fail. So having good architects on the team is a necessity. What's a "good" architect? It is one who is experienced, educated, and qualified.

Modern systems need more engineering and understanding, and less artistry and subjective guesswork. This is the direction we need to move toward as good software architects.

What's a Software Architecture, Anyway?

Herman Melville, the unforgettable author of *Moby Dick*, once said that men think that by mouthing hard words they can understand hard things. In software, the "hard" word *architecture* was originally introduced into the field to simplify the transmission and understanding of a key and "hard" guideline. The guideline was this: Care (much) more about the design of software systems than you have in the past; care about it to the point of guiding the development of a software system similar to guiding the development of a building.

It's a hard thing to do and probably beyond many developers' capabilities. But let's give it a try. Let's try to clarify what a "software architecture" is or, at least, what we intend it to be.

Applying Architectural Principles to Software

The word "architecture" is indissolubly bound to the world of construction. It was first used in the software industry to express the need to plan and design before building computer programs. However, a fundamental difference exists between designing and building habitable structures and designing and building usable software systems.

Intuitively, we care if the building falls on people. But software? There is always plenty of money to rewrite things, right? In construction, the design must be completed entirely up front and based on extremely detailed calculations and blueprints. In software, you tend to be more agile. A few decades ago, the up-front design methodology was common and popular in software, too. But, over the years, that approach increased development costs. And because software can be efficiently (and safely) tested before deployment, agility got the upper hand over up-front design.

Today the architectural parallelism between construction and software is not as close as it was a few years ago. However, many dictionaries currently list a software-related definition of the term "architecture." And a software architecture is described as "the composition, integration, and interaction of components within a computer system." It is certainly a definition that everybody would agree on. But, in our opinion, it is rather abstract.

We think that software professionals should agree on a more detailed explanation that breaks down that definition into smaller pieces and puts them into context.

Defining the Architecture from a Standard Viewpoint

Many seem to forget that a standard definition for software architecture exists. More precisely, it is in ANSI/IEEE standard 1471, "Recommended Practice for Architectural Description of Software-intensive Systems." The document was originally developed by IEEE and approved as a recommended practice in September 2000.

The document focuses on practices to describe the architecture of software-intensive systems. Using the definition in the standard, a *software-intensive system* is any system in which software is essential to implementation and deployment.

Stakeholders are defined as all parties interested or concerned about the building of the system. The list includes the builders of the system (architects, developers, testers) as well as the acquirer, end users, analysts, auditors, and chief information officers (CIOs).

In 2007, the ANSI/IEEE document was also recognized as a standard through ISO/IEC document 42010. Those interested in reading the full standard can navigate their browser to the following URL: *http://www.iso.org/iso/iso_catalogue/catalogue_tc/catalogue_detail.htm?csnumber=45991*.

Examining Key Architecture-Related Points in ANSI/IEEE 1471

The key takeaway from the ANSI/IEEE standard for software architecture is that a software system exists to meet the expectations of its stakeholders. Expectations are expressed as functional and nonfunctional requirements. Processed by the architect, requirements are then communicated to the development team and finally implemented. All the steps occur and exist to ensure the quality of the software. Skipping any step introduces the possibility for less software quality and the potential to not meet the stakeholders' expectations.

To design a software system that achieves its goals, you need to devise it using an architectural metaphor. Accepting an architectural metaphor means that you recognize the principle that some important decisions regarding the system might be made quite early in the development process; just like key decisions are made very early in the development of civil architecture projects. For example, you wouldn't build a skyscraper when a bridge was required. Similarly, requirements might steer you to a Web-oriented architecture rather than a desktop application. Decisions this major must be made very early.

A software architecture, therefore, is concerned with the organization of a system and lays out the foundations of the system. The system, then, has to be designed—which entails making some hard decisions up front—and described—which entails providing multiple views of the system, with each view covering a given set of system responsibilities.

Defining the System from a Standard Viewpoint

As mentioned, a software system is universally understood to be a collection of components composed and integrated to accomplish a specific set of functions.

A system lives in a context; and this context influences the design of the system by driving some developmental and operational decisions. A system exists to solve a problem and achieve its mission in full respect of the stakeholders' concerns. Stakeholders' concerns include functional and nonfunctional requisites as well as system aspects such as security, testability, performance, reliability, and extensibility.

Although it envisions the system as a composition of interconnected components, an architecture also establishes some firm points that are hard to modify later. In a way, expressing software development in terms of an architecture boils down to making some key decisions that affect the development life cycle and, ultimately, the quality of the resulting system.

Figure 1-1 illustrates the relationships between the system, architecture, and stakeholders as identified by ANSI/IEEE standard 1471. The content of Figure 1-1 is actually an adaptation of one of the figures in the document.

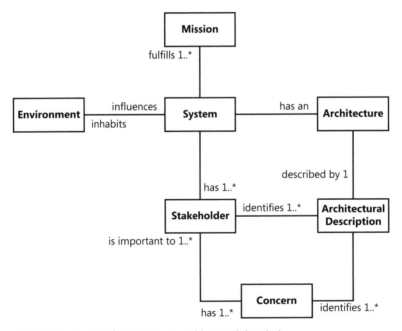

FIGURE 1-1 A model for creating an architectural description

The figure uses the notation of the Unified Modeling Language (UML) to express its concepts. We'll offer a refresher of UML in the next chapter. Even if you're new to UML, you should be able to read the figure quite comfortably. Each connector indicates an action (with a specified name) that is executed by the element where the connector starts and that affects the target. So, for example, the System fulfills one or more Missions; the Environment (context) influences the System; a Concern is important to one or more Stakeholders; the System has an Architecture.

Describing the Architecture

As you can see in Figure 1-1, the Architecture is described by one Architectural Description. How would you describe the architecture to stakeholders?

The key messages about an architecture are its components and classes, their mapping onto binaries, their relationships and dependencies, usage scenarios, and detailed work flows for key operations. How would you render all these things?

A very popular choice is UML diagrams.

UML is also a recognized international standard—precisely, ISO/IEC 19501 released in 2005. You create UML *class diagrams* to show relationships between classes; you employ *use-case diagrams* to present usage scenarios; you create *component diagrams* to capture the relationships between reusable parts of a system (components) and see more easily how to map them onto binaries. In some cases, you can also add some *sequence diagrams* to illustrate in more detail the workflow for some key scenarios. These terms are defined and discussed in more detail in Chapter 2, "UML Essentials."

At the end of the day, you serve different and concurrent views of the same architecture and capture its key facts.

> **Note** The same principle of offering multiple views from distinct viewpoints lies behind another vendor-specific model for architectural description—IBM/Rational's *4+1 views* model. The model defines four main views—nearly equivalent to UML diagrams. These views are as follows:
>
> The *logical view*, which describe components
>
> The *process view*, which describes mapping and dependencies
>
> The *development view*, which describes classes
>
> The *physical view*, which (if necessary) describes mapping onto hardware
>
> The fifth, partially redundant, view is the scenario view, which is specific to use cases.

Validating the Architecture

How would you validate the design to ensure that stakeholders' concerns are properly addressed?

There's no magic wand and no magic formulas that take a more or less formal definition of an architecture as input and tells you whether it is appropriate for the expressed requirements. To validate the design of a system, you can only test it—in various ways and at various levels.

So you will perform unit tests to validate single functionalities, and you will perform integration tests to see how the system coexists with other systems and applications. Finally, you'll run acceptance tests to verify how users actually feel about the application and whether the application provides the services it was created for. (Testing is one of the key topics of Chapter 3, "Design Principles and Patterns.")

What's Architecture and What's Not

When you think about creating or defining the architecture of a software system, you first try to identify a possible collection of interacting components that, all together, accomplish the requested mission. In international standards, there's no mention for any methodology you should use to decompose the system into more detailed pieces. Let's say that in the first step you a get a conceptual architecture and some different views of it. In a second step, you need to get closer to a functional and physical architecture. How you get there is a subjective choice, although a top-down approach seems to be a very reasonable strategy. You decompose components into smaller and smaller pieces, and from there you start building.

No System Is a Monolith

We've been told that, once upon a time, any piece of software was a monolith with an entry point and finish point. The introduction of structured programming, and the concept of a *subroutine*, in the early 1970s started shouldering such monoliths out of the way.

Since then, many software systems have been designed as a graph of components communicating in various ways and having various levels of dependency. In practical terms, designing a system consists of expanding the System element that was shown in Figure 1-1 into a graph of subsystems and defining communication policies and rules for each of them.

The process of breaking down these details should ideally continue until you have described in detail the structure and relationships for the smallest part of the system. Although fully completing the breakdown process up front is key for constructing habitable buildings, it is not that necessary for building software.

The actual implementation of the breakdown process depends on the methodology selected for the project—the more you are *agile*, the more the breakdown process is iterative and articulated in smaller and more frequent steps. (We'll return to the topic of methodologies later in the chapter.)

The output of the breakdown process is a set of specifications for the development team. Also, the content and format of the specifications depend on the methodology. The more you are agile, the more freedom and independence you leave to developers when implementing the architecture.

Defining the Borderline Between Architecture and Implementation

The constituent components you identified while breaking down the system represent logical functions to be implemented in some way. The design of components, their interface, their responsibilities, and their behavior are definitely part of the architecture. There's a border, though, that physically separates architecture from implementation.

This border is important to identify because, to a large extent, it helps to define roles on a development team. In particular, it marks the boundary between architects and developers. Over the years, we learned that architects and developers are not different types of fruit, like apples and oranges. They are the same type of fruit. However, if they are apples, they are like red apples and green apples. Distinct flavors, but not a different type of fruit. And neither flavor is necessarily tastier.

You have arrived at the border between architecture and implementation when you reach a *black box of behavior*. A black box of behavior is just a piece of functionality that can be easily replaced or refactored without significant regression and with zero or low impact on the rest of the architecture. What's above a black box of behavior is likely to have architectural relevance and might require making a hard-to-change decision.

What's our definition of a good architecture? It is an architecture in which all hard-to-change decisions turn out to be right.

Dealing with Hard-to-Change Decisions

There are aspects and features of a software system that are hard (just *hard*, not *impossible*) to change once you have entered the course of development. And there are aspects and features that can be changed at any time without a huge effort and without having a wide impact on the system.

In his book *Patterns of Enterprise Application Architecture* (Addison-Wesley, 2002), Martin Fowler puts it quite simply:

> If you find that something is easier to change than you once thought, then it's no longer architectural. In the end architecture boils down to the important stuff—whatever that is.

To sum it up, we think that under the umbrella of the term *architecture* falls everything you must take seriously at quite an early stage of the project. Architecture is ultimately about determining the key decisions to make and then making them correctly.

Architecture Is About Decisions

When we talk about hard architectural decisions, we are not necessarily referring to irreversible decisions about design points that can be difficult and expensive to change later. Hard-to-change decisions are everywhere and range from the definition of a conceptual layers to the attributes of a class.

To illustrate our point, let's go through a few different examples of architectural points that can run into budget limits and deadlines if you have to touch them in the course of the project.

Changing the Organization of the Business Logic

In Chapter 4, "The Business Layer," we'll examine various approaches to organizing the business logic in the context of a layered system. Possible approaches for the design of the business logic include transaction script, table module, active record, and domain model. The selection of a pattern for the business logic is an excellent example of a design choice to be made very, very carefully. Once you have opted for, say, table module (which means, essentially, that you'll be using typed *DataSets* to store an application's data in the business logic layer), moving to an object model (for example, using the LINQ-to-SQL or Entity Framework object model) is definitely hard and requires nontrivial changes in the data access layer and in the application (service) layer, and probably also in the presentation layer. If you need to change this decision later in the project, you enter into a significant refactoring of the whole system.

Switching to a Different Library

Suppose you developed some functionality around a given library. One day, the client pops up and lets you know that a new company policy prevents the IT department from buying products from a given vendor. Now you have a new, unexpected nonfunctional requirement to deal with.

A change in the specifications might require a change in the architecture, but at what cost? In such a case, you have to comply with the new list of requirements, so there's not much you can do.

In the best case, you can get a similar tool from an authorized vendor or, perhaps, you can build a similar tool yourself. Alternatively, you can consider introducing a radical change into the architecture that makes that library unnecessary.

We faced an analogous situation recently, and the type of library was an Object/Relational mapping tool. With, say, a UI control library, it would have been much simpler to deal with. Replacing an Object/Relational mapping tool is not easy; it is a task that can be accomplished *only* by getting another tool from another vendor. Unfortunately, this wasn't possible. In other words, we were left to choose between either of two unpleasant and painful options: writing our own Object/Relational mapping tool, or rearchitecting the middle tier to use a different (and much simpler) object model.

With over 500 presenters in the Model View Presenter–based user interface directly consuming the object model, having to make this decision was our worst nightmare. We knew it would require a huge amount of work on the middle tier, consuming both financial resources and time. We lobbied for more time and successfully stretched the deadline. Then we built our own tailor-made data access layer for a domain model. (After you've read Chapter 6, "The Data Access Layer," you'll have a clear picture of what this all means.)

Changing the Constructor's Signature

Don't think that architecture is only about high-level decisions like those involving the design and implementation of parts of the middle tier. A requested change in the signature of a class constructor might get you in a fine mess, too.

Imagine a scenario where you handle an *Order* class in your application's object model. You don't see any reason to justify the introduction of a factory for the *Order* class. It is a plain class and should be instantiated freely. So you scatter tons of *new Order()* instructions throughout your code. You don't see, though, that *Order* has some logical dependency on, say, *Customer*.

At some point, a request for change hits you—in the next release, an order will be created only in association with a customer. What can you do?

If you only add a new constructor to the *Order* class that accepts a *Customer* object, you simply don't meet the requirement, because the old constructor is still there and only new code will follow the new pattern. If you drop or replace the old constructor, you have tons of *new* statements to fix that are scattered throughout the entire code base.

If only you had defined a factory for the *Order* class, you would have met the new requirement without the same pain. (By the way, domain-driven design methodology in fact suggests that you always use a factory for complex objects, such as aggregates.)

Changing a Member's Modifiers

When you design a class, you have to decide whether the class is public or internal and whether it is sealed or further inheritable. And then you decide whether methods are virtual or nonvirtual. Misusing the *virtual* and *sealed* modifiers might take you along an ugly route.

In general, when you use the *sealed* and *virtual* modifiers you take on a not-so-small responsibility. In C#, by default each class is unsealed and each method on a class is nonvirtual. In Java, for example, things go differently for methods, which are all virtual by default.

Now what should you do with your .NET classes? Make them sealed, or go with the default option?

The answer is multifaceted—maintenance, extensibility, performance, and testability all might factor into your decision. We're mostly interested in maintenance and extensibility here, but we'll return to this point in Chapter 3 when we touch on design for testability and make some performance considerations.

From a design perspective, sealed classes are preferable. In fact, when a class is sealed from the beginning you know it—and you create your code accordingly. If something happens later to justify inheritance of that class, you can change it to unsealed without breaking changes and without compromising compatibility. Nearly the same can be said for virtual methods, and the visibility of classes and class members, which are always private by default.

The opposite doesn't work as smoothly. You often can't seal a class or mark a virtual method as nonvirtual without potentially breaking some existing code. If you start with most-restrictive modifiers, you can always increase the visibility and other attributes later. But you can never tighten restrictions without facing the possibility of breaking existing dependencies. And these broken dependencies might be scattered everywhere in your code.

To contrast these statements, some considerations arise on the theme of testability. A nonsealed class and virtual methods make testing much easier. But the degree of ease mostly depends on the tool you use for testing. For example, TypeMock is a tool that doesn't suffer from these particular limitations.

It's hard to make a choice as far as the *sealed* and *virtual* keywords are concerned. And whatever choice you make in your context, it doesn't have to be a definitive choice that you blindly repeat throughout your code for each class and member. Make sure you know the testability and performance implications, make sure you know the goals and scope of your class, and then make a decision. And, to the extent that it's possible, make the right decision!

Requirements and Quality of Software

The mission of the system is expressed through a set of requirements. These requirements ultimately drive the system's architecture.

In rather abstract terms, a *requirement* is a characteristic of the system that can either be functional or nonfunctional. A *functional* requirement refers to a behavior that the system must supply to fulfill a given scenario. A *nonfunctional* requirement refers to an attribute of the system explicitly requested by stakeholders.

Are the definitions of functional and nonfunctional requirements something standard and broadly accepted? Actually, an international standard to formalize quality characteristics of software systems has existed since 1991.

Examining the ISO/IEC 9126 Standard

As a matter of fact, failure to acknowledge and adopt quality requirements is one of the most common causes that lead straight to the failure of software projects. ISO/IEC 9126 defines a general set of quality characteristics required in software products.

The standard identifies six different families of quality characteristics articulated in 21 subcharacteristics. The main families are functionality, reliability, usability, efficiency, maintainability, and portability. Table 1-1 explains them in more detail and lists the main subcharacteristics associated with each.

TABLE 1-1 Families of Quality Characteristics According to ISO/IEC 9126

Family	Description
Functionality	Indicates what the software does to meet expectations. It is based on requirements such as suitability, accuracy, security, interoperability, and compliance with standards and regulations.
Reliability	Indicates the capability of the software to maintain a given level of performance when used under special conditions. It is based on requirements such as maturity, fault tolerance, and recoverability. Maturity is when the software doesn't experience interruptions in the case of internal software failures. Fault tolerance indicates the ability to control the failure and maintain a given level of behavior. Recoverability indicates the ability to recover after a failure.
Usability	Indicates the software's ability to be understood by, used by, and attractive to users. It dictates that the software be compliant with standards and regulations for usability.
Efficiency	Indicates the ability to provide a given level of performance both in terms of appropriate and timely response and resource utilization.
Maintainability	Indicates the software's ability to support modifications such as corrections, improvements, or adaptations. It is based on requirements such as testability, stability, ability to be analyzed, and ability to be changed.
Portability	Indicates the software's ability to be ported from one platform to another and its capability to coexist with other software in a common environment and sharing common resources.

Subcharacteristics are of two types: external and internal. An external characteristic is user oriented and refers to an external view of the system. An internal characteristic is system oriented and refers to an internal view of the system. External characteristics identify functional requirements; internal characteristics identify nonfunctional requirements.

As you can see, features such as security and testability are listed as requirements in the ISO standard. This means that an official paper *states* that testability and security are an inherent part of the system and a measure of its quality. More importantly, testability and security should be planned for up front and appropriate supporting functions developed.

Important If you look at the ISO/IEC 9126 standard, you should definitely bury the practice of first building the system and then handing it to a team of network and security experts to make it run faster and more securely. You can't test quality in either. Like security, quality has to be designed in. You can't hope to test for and find all bugs, but you can plan for known failure conditions and use clean coding practices to prevent (or at least minimize) bugs in the field.

It's surprising that such a practice has been recommended, well, since 1991. To give you an idea of how old this standard is, consider that at the time it was written both Windows 3.0 and Linux had just been introduced, and MS-DOS 5.0 was the rage, running on blisteringly fast Intel i486 processors. It was another age.

In the context of a particular system, the whole set of general quality requirements set by the ISO/IEC 9126 standard can be pragmatically split into two types of requirements: functional and nonfunctional.

Functional Requirements

Functional requirements indicate *what* the system is expected to do and provide an appropriate set of functions for such specified tasks and user objectives. Generally, a function consists of input, behavior, and output. A team of analysts is responsible for collecting functional requirements and communicating them to the architect. Another common source of functional requirements are meetings organized with users, domain experts, and other relevant stakeholders. This process is referred to as *elicitation*.

Requirements play a key role in the generation of the architecture because they are the raw input for architects to produce specifications for the development team. Needless to say, it is recommended by ISO/IEC that software requirements be "clear, correct, unambiguous, specific, and verifiable."

However, this is only how things go in a perfect world.

Nonfunctional Requirements

Nonfunctional requirements specify overall requirements of the final system that do not pertain specifically to functions. Canonical examples of nonfunctional requirements are using (or not using) a particular version of a framework and having the final product be interoperable with a given legacy system.

Other common nonfunctional requirements regard support for accessibility (especially in Web applications developed for the public sector) or perhaps the provision of a given level of security, extensibility, or reliability.

In general, a nonfunctional requirement indicates a constraint on the system and affects the quality of the system. Nonfunctional requirements are set by some of the system stakeholders and represent a part of the contract.

Gathering Requirements

The analyst is usually a person who is very familiar with the problem's domain. He gathers requirements and writes them down to guarantee the quality and suitability of the system. The analyst usually composes requirements in a document—even a Microsoft Office Word document—in a format that varies with the environment, project, and people involved.

Typically, the analyst writes requirements using casual language and adds any wording that is specific to the domain. For example, it is acceptable to have in a requirement words such as *Fund*, *Stock*, *Bond*, and *Insurance Policy* because they are technical terms. It is less acceptable for a requirement to use terms such as *table* or *column* because these technical terms are likely to be foreign terms in the problem's domain.

Again, requirements need to be clear and verifiable. Most importantly, they must be understandable, without ambiguity, to all stakeholders—users, buyers, analysts, architects, testers, documentation developers, and the like.

> **Note** It is not uncommon that analysts write functional requirements using relatively abstract use cases. As we'll see in a moment, a use case is a document that describes a form of interaction between the system and its clients. Use cases created by the analysis team are not usually really detailed and focus on *what* the system does rather than *how* the system does it. In any case, it must come out in a form that stakeholders can understand. In this regard, a use case describes all the possible ways for an actor to obtain a value, or achieve a goal, and all possible exceptions that might result from that.

Specifications

Based on functional and nonfunctional requirements, specifications offer a development view of the architecture and are essentially any documentation the architect uses to communicate details about the architecture to the development team. The main purpose of specifications is to reach an understanding within the development team as to how the program is going to perform its tasks.

> **Note** Typically, an architect won't start working on specifications until some requirements are known. In the real world, it is unlikely that requirements will be entirely known before specifications are made. The actual mass of requirements that triggers the generation of specifications depends mostly on the methodology selected for the process. In an agile context, you start working on specifications quite soon, even with a largely incomplete set of requirements.

Specifications for functional requirements are commonly expressed through *user stories* or *use cases*.

A user story is an informal and very short document that describes, in a few sentences, what should be done. Each story represents a single feature and ideally describes a feature that stands on its own. User stories work especially well in the context of an agile methodology, such as Extreme Programming (XP), and are not designed to be exhaustive. A typical user story might be as simple as, *"The user places an order; the system verifies the order and accepts it if all is fine."* When, and if, that user story gets implemented, developers translate it into tasks. Next, through teamwork, they clarify obscure points and figure out missing details.

A use case is a document that describes a possible scenario in which the system is being used by a user. Instead of *user*, here, we should say *actor*, actually. An *actor* is a system's user and interacts with the system. An actor can be a human as well as a computer or another piece of software. When not human, an actor is not a component of the system; it is an external component. When human, actors are a subset of the stakeholders.

When used to express a functional requirement, a use case fully describes the interaction between actors and the system. It shows an actor that calls a system function and then illustrates the system's reaction. The collection of all use cases defines all possible ways of using the system. In this context, a use case is often saved as a UML diagram. (See Chapter 2 for detailed UML coverage.) The scenario mentioned a bit earlier in this section, described through a use case, might sound like this: *"The user creates an order and specifies a date, a shipment date, customer information, and order items. The system validates the information, generates the order ID, and saves the order to the database."* As you can see, it is a much more detailed description.

The level of detail of a specification depends on a number of factors, including company standards currently in use and, particularly, the methodology selected to manage the project. Simplifying, we can say that you typically use user stories within the context of an agile methodology; you use the use cases otherwise.

> **Note** Note that use cases you might optionally receive from analysts are not the same as use cases that you, as an architect, create to communicate with the development team. More often than not, use cases received by analysts are plain Microsoft Office Word documents. Those that get handed on to the development team are typically (but not necessarily) UML diagrams. And, more importantly, they are much more detailed and oriented to implementation.

Methodology and the Use of Requirements

Collected and communicated by analysts, requirements are then passed down the chain to the design team to be transformed into something that could lead to working code. The architect is the member on the design team who typically receives requirements and massages them into a form that developers find easy to manage.

The architect is the point of contact between developers and stakeholders, and she works side by side with the project manager. It is not unusual that the two roles coincide and the same person serves simultaneously as an architect and a project manager.

The project manager is responsible for choosing a methodology for developing the project. To simplify, we could say that the project manager decides whether or not an agile methodology is appropriate for the project.

The choice of methodology has a deep impact on how requirements are used in defining the architecture.

In the case of using an agile methodology, user stories are the typical output generated from requirements. For example, consider that a typical XP iteration lasts about two weeks. (An XP iteration is a smaller and faster version of a classic software development cycle.) In two weeks, you can hardly manage complex specifications; you would spend all the time on the specifications, thus making no progress toward the implementation of those specifications. In this context, user stories are just fine.

In the case of using a traditional, non-agile methodology with much longer iterations, the architect usually processes a large share of the requirements (if not all of them) and produces exhaustive specifications, including classes, sequences, and work flows.

Who's the Architect, Anyway?

As we've seen, architecture is mostly about expensive and hard-to-change decisions. And someone has to make these decisions.

The design of the architecture is based on an analysis of the requirements. Analysis determines *what* the system is expected to do; architecture determines *how* to do that. And someone has to examine the *what*s to determine the *how*s.

The architect is the professional tying together requirements and specifications. But what are the responsibilities of an architect? And skills?

An Architect's Responsibilities

According to the ISO/IEC 42010 standard, an architect is the person, team, or organization responsible for the system's architecture. The architect interacts with analysts and the project manager, evaluates and suggests options for the system, and coordinates a team of developers.

The architect participates in all phases of the development process, including the analysis of requirements and the architecture's design, implementation, testing, integration, and deployment.

Let's expand on the primary responsibilities of an architect: acknowledging the requirements, breaking the system down into smaller subsystems, identifying and evaluating technologies, and formulating specifications.

Acknowledging the Requirements

In a software project, a few things happen before the architect gets involved. Swarms of analysts, IT managers, and executives meet, discuss, evaluate, and negotiate. Once the need for a new or updated system is assessed and the budget is found, analysts start eliciting requirements typically based on their own knowledge of the business, company processes, context, and feedback from end users.

When the list of requirements is ready, the project manager meets with the architect and delivers the bundle, saying more or less, "This is what we (*think we*) want; now you build it."

The architect acknowledges the requirements and makes an effort to have them adopted and fulfilled in the design.

Breaking Down the System

Based on the requirements, the architect expresses the overall system as a composition of smaller subsystems and components operating within processes. In doing so, the architect envisions logical layers and/or services. Then, based on the context, the architect decides about the interface of layers, their relationships to other layers, and the level of service orientation the system requires.

> **Note** At this stage, the architect evaluates various architectural patterns. Layering is a common choice and the one we are mostly pursuing in this book. Layering entails a vertical distribution of functionality. Partitioning is another approach, where all parts are at the same logical level and scattered around some shared entities—such as an object model or a database. Service-oriented architecture (SOA) and hexagonal architecture (HA) are patterns that tend to have components (services in SOA, adapters in HA) operating and interacting at the same logical level.

The overall design will be consistent with the enterprise goals and requirements. In particular, the overall design will be driven by requirements; it will not lead requirements.

The resulting architecture is ideally inspired by general guidelines, such as minimizing the coupling between modules, providing the highest possible level of cohesion within modules, and giving each module a clear set of responsibilities.

The resulting architecture is also driven by nonfunctional requirements, such as security, scalability, and technologies allowed or denied. All these aspects pose further constraints and, to some extent, delimit the space where the architect can look for solutions.

Finally, the architect also strategizes about tasking individual developers, or teams of developers, with each of the components resulting from the breakdown of the system.

> **Note** There are no absolute truths in software architecture. And no mathematical rules (or building codes like in structural engineering) to help in making choices. Company X might find architecture A successful at the same time company Y is moving away from it to embrace architecture B. The nice fact is that both might be totally right. The context is king, and so is *gut* feeling.

Identifying and Evaluating Technologies

After acknowledging requirements and designing the layers of the system, the next step for the architect entails mapping logical components onto concrete technologies and products.

The architect typically knows the costs and benefits of products and technologies that might be related to the content of the project. The architect proposes the use of any technologies and products that he regards as beneficial and cost-effective for the project.

The architect doesn't choose the technology; based on his skills, the architect just makes proposals.

The architect might suggest using, say, Microsoft Windows 2008 Server for the Web server and a service-oriented architecture with services implemented through Windows Communication Foundation (WCF). The architect might suggest NHibernate over Entity Framework and Microsoft SQL Server 2008 over Oracle. And he might suggest a particular rich control suite for the Web presentation layer instead of, perhaps, an entirely in-house developed Silverlight client.

Who does make the final decision about which technologies and products are to be used?

Typically, it is the project manager or whoever manages the budget. The architect's suggestions might be accepted or rejected. If a suggestion is rejected, using or not using a given product or technology just becomes a new nonfunctional requirement to fulfill, and that might influence, even significantly, the architecture.

Formulating Specifications

The architect is ultimately responsible for the development of the system and coordinates the work of a team of developers. Technical specifications are the means by which the architect communicates architectural decisions to the developers.

Specifications can be rendered in various forms: UML sketches, Word documents, Microsoft Visio diagrams or, even, working prototypes.

Communication is key for an architect. Communication happens between the architect and developers, and it also happens between architects and project managers and analysts, if not users. A great skill for an architect is the clarity of language.

The interaction between architects and developers will vary depending on the methodology chosen. And also the involvement of project managers, analysts, and users varies based, essentially, on the level of agility you accept.

We'll return to the topic of methodologies in a moment.

How Many Types of Architects Do You Know?

There are many possible definitions of "architect." Definitions vary depending on how they factor in different roles and different responsibilities. In this book, we work with the ISO/IEC definition of an architect, which is the "person, team, or organization responsible for the system's architecture."

According to ISO/IEC, there are not various types of architects. An architect is an architect. Period.

Microsoft, however, recognizes four types of architects: enterprise architect (EA), infrastructure architect (IA), technology-specific architect (TSA), and solution architect (SA). The list is taken from the job roles recognized by the Microsoft Certified Architect Program. You can read more about the program and job roles at *http://www.microsoft.com/learning/mcp/architect/ specialties/default.mspx*.

In our opinion, the distinctions offered by Microsoft are misleading because they attempt to break into parts what is ultimately an atomic, yet complex, role. It creates unnecessary categorization and lays the groundwork for confusing, who-does-what scenarios.

For example, who's responsible for security? Is it the SA or the IA? Ultimately, security is an ISO-recognized quality attribute of a software architecture and, as such, it should be planned from the beginning. Security should grow with the system's design and implementation. It cannot be added at a later time, by a separate team. Not if you really want security in the system.

Who's ultimately responsible for picking out a technology? Is it the SA? Is it the EA? Do both accept suggestions from a swarm of different TSAs? At the end of the day, it's not the architect who makes this decision. Instead, it's the customer, who holds the purse strings, that decides.

It is fine to have multiple architects on the same project team. Likewise, it is fine, if not desirable, that different architects have slightly different skills. But they remain just architects, working on the same team on the design of the same system. And architects also have a significant exposure to code. They work out the design of the system but then work closely with developers to ensure proper implementation.

As we see things, an architect is, among other things, a better and more experienced developer. We don't believe there's value in having architects who just speak in UML and Visio and leave any implementation details to developers. At least, we've never found it easy to work with these people when we've crossed paths with them.

> **Note** This said, we recognize that titles like *enterprise architect, solution architect,* and perhaps *security architect* look much better than a plain *software architect* when printed out on a business card. But the terms are only a way to more quickly communicate your skills and expertise. When it comes to the actual role, either you're an architect or you're not.

Common Misconceptions About Architects

Although international ISO standards exist to define requirements, architecture, and architects, they seem not to be taken into great account by most people. Everybody seems to prefer crafting her own (subtly similar) definition for *something*, rather than sticking to (or reading) the ISO definition for the same *something*.

Try asking around for the definition of terms such as *architect, architecture,* or *project manager.* You can likely get distinct, and also unrelated and contrasting, answers.

Quite obviously, a set of misconceptions have grown out of the mass of personalized definitions and interpretations. Let's go through a few of them and, we hope, clear up a few of them.

The Architect Is an Analyst

This is a false statement. An architect is simply not an analyst.

At times, an architect might assist analysts during elicitations to help clarify obscure requirements or smooth improbable requirements. At times, an architect might participate in meetings with stakeholders. But that's it.

In general, an analyst is a person who is an expert on the domain. An architect is not (necessarily) such an expert. An analyst shares with an architect his own findings about how the system should work and what the system should do.

This common misconception probably originates from the incorrect meaning attributed to the word *analyst.* If the word simply indicates someone who does some analysis on a system, it is quite hard to deny the similarities between architects and analysts. Some 30 years ago, the term *system analyst* was used to indicate a professional capable of making design considerations about a system. But, at the time, the software wasn't as relevant as it is today, and it was merely a (small) part of an essentially hardware-based system.

Today, the roles of an analyst and an architect are commonly recognized as being different. And hardly ever does an architect play the role of an analyst.

> **Note** Given that roles are neatly separated, anyway, in small companies, it can happen that the same person serves as an analyst and architect. It simply means that there's a person in the company who knows the business and processes well enough to come up with functional requirements and translate them into specifications for developers. The roles and responsibilities are still distinct, but the distinct skills for each can be found in the same individual.

The Architect Is a Project Manager

Is this another false statement? It depends.

The architect is responsible for the system's architecture and coordinates and guides the development of the system. The project manager represents stakeholders and manages the project by choosing, in the first place, a methodology. The project manager is then responsible for ensuring that the project adheres to the architecture while proceeding within the limits of the timeline and budget.

If we look at the role of the architect and the role of the project manager, we find out that they are distinct. Period.

However, it is not unusual that one actor ends up playing two roles. Like in the theater, this hardly happens in large companies, but it happens quite frequently in small companies.

In summary, if you want to be a software architect when you grow up, you don't necessarily have to develop project management skills. If you have skills for both roles, though, you can try to get double pay.

The Architect Never Writes Any Code

This is definitely an ongoing debate: Should architects write code? There are essentially two schools of thought.

One school thinks that architects live on the upper floor, maybe in an attic. Architects then step down to the developers' floor just for the time it takes them to illustrate, using UML diagrams, what they have thought about the system. After this, they take the elevator up, collect their things, and go out to play golf. When on the course, they switch off their cell phones and focus on the game. When done, if they missed a call or two, they call back and explain to dummy developers what was so clear in the diagram that nobody on the developers' floor could understand. According to this school of thought, architects never, ever dirty their hands with even the simplest C# statement. C#? Oh no, the latest language they've been exposed to is probably Pascal while in college and Borland Turbo Pascal at home.

Another school of thought thinks, instead, that every architect is a born developer. To take the metaphor one step further, we could say that the class *Architect* inherits from the class *Developer* and adds some new methods (skills) while overriding (specializing) a few others. Becoming an architect is the natural evolution in the career of some developers. The basic differences between an architect and a developer are experience and education. You gain experience by spending time on the job; you earn your education from studying good books and taking the right classes. In addition, an architect has the ability to focus her vision of the system from a higher level than an average developer. Furthermore, an architect has good customer-handling skills.

An architect might not write much production code. But she writes a lot of code; she practices with code every day; she knows about programming languages, coding techniques, libraries, products, tools, Community Technology Previews (CTPs); and she uses the latest version of Visual Studio or Team Foundation Server. In certain areas of programming, an architect knows even more than many developers. An architect might be able to write tools and utilities to help developers be more productive. And, more often than you might think at first, the architect is just a member of the development team. For example, an architect writing production code is an absolutely normal occurrence in an agile context. It is also a normal occurrence in small companies regardless of the methodology. At the same time, an architect who writes production code might be an absolutely weird occurrence in some large-company scenarios, especially if a traditional and non-agile methodology is used.

What about the two of us? To which school do we belong?

Well, Andrea is more of an architect than Dino because he lives on the fifth floor. Dino, on the other hand, is closer to development because he has quite a few highly technical ASP .NET books on his record and, more importantly, lives on the second floor. We don't play golf, though. Dino plays tennis regularly, whereas Andrea likes squash better. We just have been denied access to the first school of thought.

Note In no other area of engineering is the distinction between *those-who-design* and *those-who-build* as poorly accepted as it is in software. The distinction exists mostly through postulation rather than flowing from a public recognition of skills.

The canonical comparison is with civil architecture. Bricklayers have their own unique skills that engineers lack. No bricklayer, though, will ever dream of questioning designs or calculations, simply because the bricklayer lacks the skill to make the decisions himself. Bricklayers do their own work the best they can, taking full advantage of having the building work delegated to them.

In software, the situation is different because architects and developers have common roots. The more skilled a developer is, the more he feels encouraged to discuss design choices—and often with reason. The more the architect loses contact with everyday programming, the more he loses the respect of other developers. This generates a sort of vicious circle, which magically becomes better as you switch to an agile methodology.

Overview of the Software Development Process

For quite a few years, we've been highly exposed to the idea that writing software is easy, pleasant, and fun. You click this, you drag that, and the tool will write the code for you. You "declare" what you want, and the award-winning tool will do it for you. Admittedly, in this scenario everybody could gain the rank of architect, and the burden of writing code can be entirely delegated to the tool—aptly named the *wizard*.

Not all software is the same.

Writing a filing system to track the movies you've rented from Blockbuster is different from writing a line-of-business application to run a company. You probably don't need to work on an architecture to build a syndication reader; you probably need more than just architecture if you're working on the control system for, say, a chemical plant.

In some sectors of the industry (for example, in the defense sector), the need for a systematic approach to the various aspects of software—development, testing, operation, maintenance—was recognized long ago, as early as the 1960s. In fact, the term *software engineering* was first coined by Professor Friedrich L. Bauer during the NATO Software Engineering Conference in 1968.

Today, software engineering is a broad term that encompasses numerous aspects of software development and organizes them into a structured process ruled by a methodology.

The Software Life Cycle

Software development is a process created and formalized to handle complexity and with the primary goal of ensuring (expected) results. As in the quote at the top of the chapter, the ultimate goal is controlling complexity, not creating it.

To achieve this goal, a methodology is required that spans the various phases of a software project. Over the years, an international standard has been developed to formalize the software life cycle in terms of processes, activities, and tasks that go from initial planning up to the retirement of the product.

This standard is ISO/IEC 12207, and it was originally released in 1995. The most recent revision, however, was in March 2008.

Processes

According to the ISO/IEC 12207 standard, the software life cycle is articulated in 23 processes. Each process has a set of activities and outcomes associated with it. Finally, each activity has a number of tasks to complete.

Processes are classified in three types: primary, supporting, and organizational. The production of the code pertains to the primary process. Supporting processes and organizational processes refer to auxiliary processes, such as configuration, auditing, quality assurance, verification, documentation, management, and setup and maintenance of the infrastructure (hardware, software, tools). Figure 1-2 offers a graphical view of the software life cycle, showing specific processes.

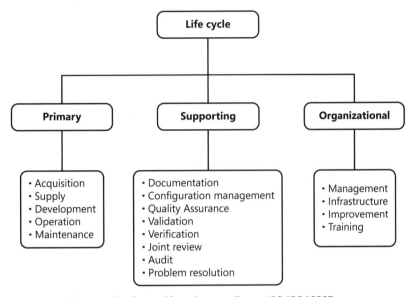

FIGURE 1-2 The overall software life cycle according to ISO/IEC 12207

Activities

The primary processes are those more directly concerned with the design and implementation of software. Let's briefly have a look at some of the activities for the primary processes.

The Acquisition process includes elicitation of requirements and evaluation of options, negotiations, and contracts. The Supply process is concerned with the development of a project management plan. Usually, architects are not involved in these steps unless they are also serving to some extent as project managers.

The Development process deals with the analysis of requirements, design of the system as well as its implementation, testing, and deployment. This is really all within the realm of the architect.

The Operation process essentially involves making the software operative within the company, integrating it with the existing systems, running pilot tests, and assisting users as they familiarize themselves with the software. Finally, the Maintenance process aims to keep the system in shape by fixing bugs and improving features. This includes a set of activities that might require the architect to be involved to some extent.

Models for Software Development

Before starting on a software project, a methodology should be selected that is appropriate for the project and compatible with the skills and attitude of the people involved. A *methodology* is a set of recommended practices that are applied to the process of software development. The methodology inspires the realization and management of the project.

There are two main developmental models: traditional methodologies and agile methodologies. We'll also touch on a third model—the Microsoft Solutions Framework.

Traditional Methodologies

The best-known and oldest methodology is the *waterfall* model. It is a model in which software development proceeds from one phase to the next in a purely sequential manner. Essentially, you move to step N+1 only when step N is 100% complete and all is perfect with it. Figure 1-3 shows a sample of the waterfall model.

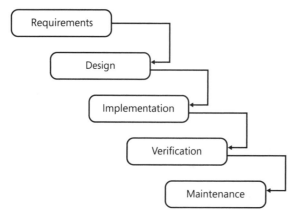

FIGURE 1-3 The waterfall model

After the team has completed the analysis of requirements, it proceeds with the design of the architecture. Next, coding begins. Next, testing is started, and it continues until the system is shipped.

The waterfall model goes hand in hand with the idea of software development paired to civil architecture. The primary characteristic of a waterfall model is BDUF—Big Design Up Front— which means essentially that the design must be set in stone before you start coding.

Waterfall is a simple and well-disciplined model, but it is unrealistic for nontrivial projects. Why? Because you almost never have all requirements established up front.

So you inevitably must proceed to the next step at some point while leaving something behind you that is incomplete.

For this reason, variations of the waterfall method have been considered over the years, where the design and implementation phases overlap to some extent. This leads us to a key consideration.

Ultimately, we find that all methodologies share a few common attributes: a number of phases to go through, a number of iterations to produce the software, and a typical duration for a single iteration. All phases execute sequentially, and there's always at least one iteration that ends with the delivery of the software.

The difference between methodologies is all in the order in which phases are entered, the number of iterations required, and the duration of each iteration.

After buying into this consideration, the step to adopting the agile methods is much smaller than you might think at first.

> **Note** We could even say that when you move to an agile methodology, you have a much smaller *waterfall*, one that is less abundant and doesn't last as long. But it's more frequent and occurs nearly on demand. Not a waterfall…maybe a *shower*?

Agile Methodologies

Iterative development is a cyclic process that was developed in response to the waterfall method, and it emphasizes the incremental building of the software. After the initial startup, the project goes through a series of iterations that include design, coding, and testing. Each iteration produces a deliverable but incomplete version of the system. At each iteration, the team enters design changes and adds new functions until the full set of specifications are met. Figure 1-4 provides a graphical view of the iterative process.

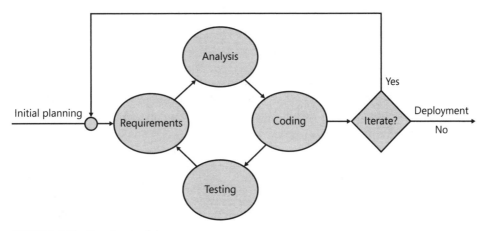

FIGURE 1-4 The iterative model

Iterative development forms the foundation of agile methodologies. The term *agile* was deliberately selected to symbolize a clear opposition to heavyweight methods such as the waterfall model. The principles behind agile methods are listed in the "Agile Manifesto," which you can find at *http://agilemanifesto.org*. The agile manifesto was first published in 2001.

Agile methodologies put individuals at the center of the universe. As stated on the home page of the manifesto, agile methods *focus on people* working together and communicating rather than on software building and processes. Change and refactoring are key in an agile methodology. User feedback is valued over planning, and feedback is driven by regular tests and frequent releases of the software. In fact, one of the agile principles states, "Working software is the primary measure of progress."

So in the end, how is an agile methodology different? And how does it work? Let's look at an example.

The project starts and only a few requirements are known. You know for a fact that many more will show up between now and the end. With an agile mindset, this is not an issue. You take a subset of the existing requirements that you can implement in a single iteration. And you go with the first iteration. During the iteration, you focus on a single requirement at a time and implement it. At the end of the iteration, you deliver a working piece of software. It might be incomplete, but it works.

Next, you go with another iteration that focuses on another set of requirements. If something changed in the meantime or proved to be wrong, refactoring is in order. And the process continues until there's nothing more to add.

Customers and developers work together daily; feedback is solicited and delivered on a timely basis; results are immediately visible; the architect is just one of the developers; and the team is highly skilled and motivated. The length of an iteration is measured in weeks—often, two weeks. In a word, an agile process is agile to react to changes. And changes in the business are the rule, not the exception.

Agile methodologies is a blanket term. When you refer to an agile methodology, you aren't talking very precisely. Which methodology do you mean, actually?

The most popular agile methodology for software development is Extreme Programming (XP). In XP, phases are carried out in extremely short iterations that take two weeks to terminate. Coding and design proceed side by side. For more information on XP, visit the site *http://www.extremeprogramming.org*.

Scrum is another popular agile methodology, but it is aimed at managing projects rather than developing code. Scrum is not prescriptive for any software development model, but it works very well with XP as the method to develop code. For more information on Scrum, have a look at *Agile Project Management with Scrum* by Ken Schwaber (Microsoft Press, 2004).

Microsoft Solutions Framework

Microsoft Solutions Framework (MSF) is another methodology for software development, like XP or waterfall. Like XP, MSF has its own principles, roles, and vocabulary. In particular, the roles in MSF are Program Manager, Architect, Developer, Tester, Release Manager, DBA, and Business Analyst. Typical terms are iteration, release, phase, and work item (to indicate an activity within the project).

MSF is a methodology that Microsoft developed and has used internally for the past ten years. Since 2006, it has also been supported by Team Foundation Server (TFS).

TFS is essentially a collection of Web services within an Internet Information Server (IIS) Web server that provide business logic specific to project management. Either through the TFS console (if you have proper administrative rights) or through a Visual Studio plug-in, you can create a TFS project and use TFS services to manage your project. Great, but what is the methodology being used?

TFS provides only one methodology out of the box: MSF. However TFS plug-ins exist to add other methodologies to TFS. In particular, plug-ins exist for the Rational Unified Process (RUP), Feature Driven Development (FDD), and Scrum.

When the project manager creates a TFS project, he is first asked to pick up an available methodology (say, MSF). When MSF is picked up, the project manager is also asked to choose which flavor of MSF he likes. There are two flavors: MSF for Agile, and MSF for CMMI.

> **Note** CMMI is an acronym for Capability Maturity Model Integration. CMMI is a general methodology for improving processes within a company. CMMI focuses on processes and fights common misconceptions such as "good people are enough" and "processes hinder agility." CMMI proposes a set of best practices and a framework for organizing and prioritizing activities, with the purpose of improving processes related to the building of a product.

In essence, you opt for a model that is more agile or more rigorous. In the context of MSF, the word *agile* has exactly the meaning it has in an English dictionary. It is not necessarily related to agile methodologies.

For example, in MSF for Agile you don't give work items an explicit duration in terms of hours; instead, you use an integer to indicate the level of effort (order of magnitude) required. You have to use hours in MSF for CMMI, instead. In MSF for Agile, a Developer can assign a task to another Developer; in MSF for CMMI, only the project manager has a similar right. In an agile process, therefore, it is *assumed* that such an action is accomplished with due forethought. In MSF for Agile, a work item can be moved from one project area to another without problems. This might not be true for another methodology.

In general, MSF for Agile is designed for small teams working iteratively on a project. MSF for CMMI is more appropriate for large and heterogeneous teams, working on long iterations and particularly concerned with control of quality.

Summary

Architecture is a widely used term that has quite a few definitions. If you read between the lines, though, you mostly find variations of the same concept: architecture refers to identifying the software components that, when interacting, make the program work.

In the process of identifying these components, you encounter points of decision making. When you design an architecture, not all decisions you make have the same impact. The approach to the design of the business logic, for example, is something you can hardly change at a later time in an inexpensive way. So architecture is about components and hard-to-change decisions.

The design of an architecture is qualified by a number of quality parameters that are part of an international standard. The design of the architecture comes out of functional and nonfunctional requirements, gathered by business analysts and acknowledged by architects.

Who's the architect and what are his responsibilities? The role of the architect is different from that of an analyst or a project manager, but sometimes the same individual can play both roles in the context of a specific project. Does an architect write code? Oh, yes. In our vision, an architect is a born developer, and even if the architect doesn't write much, or any, production code, he definitely practices with deep code.

The role of the architect, and the way in which the architect and the development team work with requirements, largely depends on the methodology in use—whether it is agile or traditional.

In this chapter, we mentioned in some places the Unified Modeling Language (UML) as the primary notation to describe architectural aspects of a system. In the next chapter, we'll take a closer look at the UML language.

Murphy's Laws of the Chapter

Murphy's laws are the portrait of the real world. If anything happens repeatedly in the real world, it is then captured in a law. Software projects are a part of the real world and it is not surprising that laws exist to describe software-related phenomena. In all chapters, therefore, we'll be listing a few Murphy's laws.

- Adding manpower to a late software project makes it later.
- Program complexity grows until it exceeds the capability of the programmers who must maintain it.
- If builders built buildings the way programmers wrote programs, the first woodpecker that came along would destroy civilization.

See *http://www.murphys-laws.com* for an extensive listing of other computer-related (and non-computer-related) laws and corollaries.

Chapter 2
UML Essentials

All models are wrong, but some models are useful.

—George E. P. Box

To design a system—any system in any scientific field—you first need to create an *abstraction* of it. An abstraction is essentially a *model* that provides a conceptual representation of the system in terms of views, structure, behavior, participating entities, and processes.

A model exists to be shared among the stakeholders of the system, including developers, architects, owners, and customers. Stakeholders should be able to understand the model in order to provide feedback, spot wrong assumptions, and suggest improvements. To share a model, though, you need to express it in a formal way using a common, and possibly broadly accepted, notation. For this, you need a *modeling language*.

Typically, a modeling language is a graphical or textual language based on a set of rules, symbols, diagrams, and keywords. All together, the language elements are used to express the structure and behavior of the model in a way that transmits clear knowledge and information to anybody familiar with the language.

There are several well-known examples of modeling languages—for example the Integrated DEFinition (IDEF) family of modeling languages used for functional modeling, information modeling, simulation, and more. There's also the Virtual Reality Modeling Language (VRML), which is used to represent 3D graphics, and EXPRESS (textual) and EXPRESS-G (graphical) for data modeling.

However, when it comes to modeling languages, the most popular one is Unified Modeling Language (UML). UML is a general-purpose graphical modeling language that, over the years, has become the industry standard for modeling software systems. Based on a family of graphical notations, UML is particularly suited to creating models in *object-oriented scenarios*. It might not be as effective when another paradigm is used, such as a functional or perhaps a relational paradigm, but it's a good fit for object-oriented systems.

Although UML is a general-purpose modeling language for software-centric systems, it also provides tools to customize the language to a specific domain. This is accomplished through *UML profiles*, which we'll discuss later in the chapter.

In this book and its companion source code, we'll use some UML here and there to describe scenarios and design solutions. For this reason, we decided to include this brief chapter that summarizes the essential facts you have to know about UML. The chapter serves as a primer for readers with limited exposure to UML, or no exposure at all, and as a quick refresher for more experienced readers.

We should add the following disclaimer: This chapter doesn't claim to be an exhaustive and in-depth guide to UML. Instead, it is merely intended to provide a foundation for understanding diagrams that might appear later in the book. At the same time, it should also communicate to you the gist of UML and allow you to form an idea about the capabilities of UML to serve as a language for modeling object-oriented systems—a key preliminary step toward the design of the system layers that we cover in chapters 4 through 7.

Note If you're serious about learning UML, we recommend two main routes to gaining that knowledge. The first route entails downloading the UML specifications from the Object Modeling Group Web site. You can get any papers from *http://www.uml.org*. However, we anticipate that running through the official UML papers might take you quite a bit of time. One of the sharpest criticisms of UML is its inherent tendency to be unnecessarily large and complex. As we'll see later, UML (especially in the latest version) contains many diagrams that are infrequently used and often redundant. Clearly, this issue creates problems in both learning and adopting the language. The problem gets even more acute if you're relatively new to UML.

This leads us to the second suggested route. If you would really like to put a "UML-Expert" pin on your shirt before you retire—and, more importantly, if your goal is to use UML skills in real projects as soon as possible—we recommend that you get a copy of some digestible books that focus on the topic. An excellent resource is *UML Distilled: A Brief Guide to the Standard Object Modeling Language (Third Edition)* by Martin Fowler (Addison-Wesley, 2003). Also, tutorials and other resources are available online—for example, at *http://www.uml.org*.

If you are an experienced UML designer, you might consider skipping this chapter and moving directly to the next one. Before you do, however, consider the following anecdote from Dino's early public-speaking days: Ten years ago, when he was about to deliver one of his first speeches in English, Dino was shocked to find out that Don Box was peacefully sitting in the audience. Dino approached Don to ask what he was expecting to learn from a talk covering COM and OLE DB stuff—exactly the areas in which Don was the recognized expert at the time. Don smiled and said, "Hey Dino, it's all about perspective."

So, again, it's all about perspective. Even if you know UML very well, you might still find this chapter to be an interesting read.

UML at a Glance

Modeling is a key stage in any software project, but it is crucial for large, enterprise-class applications—exactly the class of applications that keep companies up and running. A model is essential where complexity is high. It helps to check correctness and adherence to specifications, and it helps to build and maintain the software more easily. A clear and well-designed model also helps developers—at any time—find the right place to intervene to fix a bug. In software, a model should be viewed the same as site maps, blueprints, and physical models in the construction of houses: a definite need more than an optional tool.

Like it or not, years of real-world experience demonstrate that large projects normally exceed their budgets, their deadlines, or both. This is just the real world, baby. Proper modeling is not a guarantee of success for the project. However, it can be seen as your insurance against a dramatic failure.

UML addresses this need for an effective modeling language—a need that arose back in the early days of object-orientated development.

Motivation for and History of Modeling Languages

The need for modeling languages is tightly related to the broad adoption of the object-oriented paradigm, which started in the early 1990s. Object-orientation led developers to abandon subroutines and structured programming and, instead, embrace a vision in which an application is seen as a collection of interacting objects. Each object can receive and send messages, process data, and invoke and control the behavior of other objects.

Quite naturally, the object-oriented paradigm led to devising systems as a web of related components rather than as something that could be represented with start-to-finish flowcharts. Describing and documenting the behavior of such systems became harder and required appropriate tools and methodologies for modeling.

UML Predecessors

In 1991, the need for a modeling language produced Object Modeling Technique (OMT). Developed by James Rumbaugh, OMT was a language for software modeling and analysis. More or less at the same time, Grady Booch of Rational Software (now part of IBM) created the so-called "Booch method," which was an object modeling language and methodology tailor-made for object-oriented design.

Around 1994, Booch, Rumbaugh, and Ivar Jacobson (the *Three Amigos*) set up the group that unified different but related modeling languages and methodologies into a single language. After that, an international consortium—the Object Modeling Group (OMG)—was created under the technical leadership of the *amigos* to formalize the Unified Modeling Language specification. This eventually happened in 1997.

Today, OMG governs the development of UML and has more than 800 organizations associated as members. You can learn more about OMG roles and initiatives at *http://www.omg.org*.

Versions and Standards of UML

Currently, there are two main versions of UML, only one of which is officially ratified as an international standard. Back in 2005, the International Organization for Standardization (ISO) appointed version 1.4.2 of UML with the rank of a recognized ISO standard with ISO/IEC

19501:2005. You can find out more about the UML ISO standard at *http://www.iso.org/iso/ iso_catalogue/catalogue_tc/catalogue_detail.htm?csnumber=32620.*

> **Note** ISO is an international organization whose primary goal is reaching a general consensus on solutions that span an entire industry including, but not limited to, the software industry. Usually, ISO doesn't actually define its own standards from scratch; rather, it draws on specifications from other organizations. However, once ratified as an ISO standard, a given specification is an effective standard worldwide. This has been the case for UML (as of version 1.4.2) since 2005.

ISO/IEC 19501:2005 officially presents UML to the world as a graphical language for visualizing, specifying, constructing, and documenting the artifacts of a software-intensive system. As a result, today UML is the standard way to write the blueprints for software systems.

Currently, the progress of UML within OMG has reached version 2.1.2. You can download the full paper at *http://www.omg.org/technology/documents/modeling_spec_catalog.htm#UML.* You should note, though, that this version has not been ratified as an ISO standard just yet.

So how does UML 2.*x* improve upon the previous, and standard, version?

In a nutshell, UML 1.*x* is a simpler language centered around the idea of modeling classes and objects. UML 2.*x* goes beyond this threshold and adds the capability to present not only behavioral models but also architectural models, as well as business process and rules. With version 2.*x*, UML ceases to be an object-oriented modeling language and begins to target models used in other areas of the computing world and even in noncomputing disciplines. UML 2.*x* reorganizes the contents of version 1.*x* in a broader perspective and introduces many new tools, including new types of diagrams. (We'll say more about this in a moment.)

The Strengths and Weaknesses of UML

In the real world, nothing draws criticism like recognized standards built from a generalized consensus. It's really hard to keep everybody happy. UML is no exception. Although it is by far the most widely used modeling language, UML lays itself open to criticism for being essentially a bloated language. Not surprisingly, the ISO standard version 1.*x* was seen as needing improvement, and improvement came in version 2.*x*. Some people, though, now consider UML 2.*x* as being too bloated and complex as well as significantly harder to learn.

We feel that the strengths and weaknesses of UML descend from the U in the name, which stands for *Unified*. In other words, UML attempts to be too many things to too many people. Because of its declared generality, UML can be used in nearly all areas of computing, but not always with the same effectiveness. The bottom line is that UML generates a model, whereas working and functional code is all that customers want—to start off, at least. Managing the gap between the model and the code is up to the team, and that is the natural habitat in which general criticism toward the language as a whole springs up.

Initially, the *U* in UML had a positive overtone—unifying different, but similar, approaches to object-oriented modeling. Now, the *U* in UML is more the crux of the problem. To turn the general feeling about the *U* back to positive, we should be able to easily and effectively restrict UML to a particular domain. How can we easily transform a model into another model without loss of information? How can we automa(g)ically start working with UML and end up with code? If you look around, you'll see a number of ideas and some implementations, but no widely accepted and adopted solutions.

Today, *profiles* in UML 2.*x* offer a first formulation to adapt UML to a specific domain. Likewise, the idea of programming on the UML diagram is precisely the vision behind the model-driven architecture (MDA)—a design methodology launched by OMG a few years ago. MDA is being talked about a lot, but it is not yet in widespread use. A domain-specific language (DSL) is a possible alternative to UML and MDA, as far as generating code out of a model is concerned. (For more information, see the "Domain-Specific Languages and UML" sidebar later in this chapter.)

In summary, there are a lot of good things in UML. In particular, UML is primarily a standard language for modeling object-oriented systems through a graphical notation. Based on this key milestone (essentially achieved with version 1.*x*), other features have been added to build a richer modeling platform. And here's where most of the shades begin to appear.

UML should be conceptually split in two parts: *U* and *ML*. A unified approach to modeling is welcome, but context-specific modeling languages that are really close to implementation languages and that have domain-specific expressivity are an unavoidable requirement.

> **Note** UML is merely a modeling language; it is *not* a software development process. However, a few software development processes exist that fully and rigorously integrate UML modeling techniques. Examples are Agile Modeling and Unified Process.

UML in Practice

As mentioned, in this chapter we are basically providing the tools to read any UML you find in the remaining chapters and any diagrams scattered throughout the source code. That's great, but how would you use UML in practice? And how do we use UML ourselves?

Abstractly speaking, to use UML you need a methodology to gather and analyze requirements and then a modeling tool to turn them into a designed model. Usually, UML modeling tools incorporate their own methodology so that, in the end, you just pick up the best tool for you. So, which tool?

You basically have two options—pick up a plain drawing tool that "does" UML, or pick up a comprehensive tool that offers a team-based modeling environment and embraces the full software development life cycle.

Microsoft Visio Professional is certainly a tool that belongs in the first category. There are several free, shareware tools and commercial tools that just draw UML diagrams. A nonexhaustive list can be found at *http://en.wikipedia.org/wiki/List_of_UML_tools*.

In the second category, we find tools such as Rational Rose XDE from IBM, Enterprise Architect from Sparx Systems and, last but not least, Microsoft Visio for Enterprise Architects. Microsoft Visio for Enterprise Architects is included in MSDN Premium Subscription. It extends Microsoft Visio Professional to perform round-trip engineering on software and databases, thus enabling you to generate code from your UML diagrams and generate databases from your database model diagrams. You can get the same capabilities, and even more, from the other products mentioned, which have different pricing models and scopes.

Note, though, that the *round-trip engineering* description here is a bit emphatic and might look like an excerpt from some commercial pamphlet. An effective implementation of round-trip engineering is the key to effective use of UML in the real world. The description here is definitely alluring; however, we admit the reality might be a bit different. To understand why, we need to introduce typical UML working modes first.

> **Note** Even though UML 2.*x* is the current version of the language, not all modeling tools fully support it. In particular, if you use Microsoft Visio Professional, you might want to add some external stencils such as those from Pavel Hruby, which are available through the Web site *http://www.softwarestencils.com*. Note that these stencils and Visio vanilla stencils are mutually exclusive. In addition, the Pavel Hruby stencils are purely graphics tools and, unlike Visio standard stencils, do not perform any validation of the model being created.

UML Modes and Usage

Over time, three modes of using UML have emerged and gained more or less wide adoption. They are referred to as *sketch* mode, *blueprint* mode, and *programming language* mode. Let's dig out more details about each.

UML as a Sketch

We're pretty sure that every reader of this book, at least once in his or her life, has drawn something on a paper napkin to record the basics of an idea. This is pretty common among geeks, isn't it? When drawing or writing on a sticky note, a napkin, a whiteboard, or the back of a paid bill, you are sketching an idea.

> **Note** Did you know the venerable B-52 was in fact designed the evening before Boeing presented it to the US Air Force, and it was designed on a napkin? This is a true story. It still flies today, 50 years after its design. Now this is exactly the difference between recording the basics of an idea on a napkin and saving a napkin design!

"UML as a sketch" works in the same way, except that you sketch out a preliminary model for a software system and commonly use a file rather than a piece of paper. Used in this way, UML is merely a formal and visual language to express and communicate an early and incomplete vision of the system. Tools such as Microsoft Visio Professional and Microsoft Office PowerPoint are commonly used to sketch out UML diagrams. (We have also seen handmade UML-like paper drawings scanned to files and incorporated in the project documentation as Microsoft Office Word files.)

"UML as a sketch" allows you to render incomplete diagrams with the simplest form—for example, diagrams with limited details and covering only the principal aspects of a system. More often than not, UML sketches are collaboratively created by architects and developers during both forward-engineering and reverse-engineering phases.

In general, *forward engineering* is classic engineering—that is, an engineering approach wherein, to build a system, you start by formally defining how it should be done and how it should work. In forward engineering, you employ UML as the language to express ideas to be shared and discussed. Through UML high-level diagrams, you typically weigh alternatives, plan activities, and assign tasks.

In general, *reverse engineering* is when you take an existing system and figure out how it works. In reverse engineering, you get a UML model out of the actual source code of the system. The optimum situation is when the diagram you get from reverse engineering matches the diagram you created with forward engineering. Hitting this goal is the essence of round-trip engineering.

Do not be too surprised to see UML in action looking like the diagram shown in Figure 2-1.

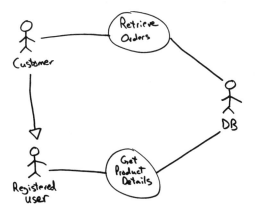

FIGURE 2-1 A sketch representing a use case

You might reasonably wonder if there's any benefit and added value in this approach. At first, you might think that it is a waste of time or, worse yet, clear evidence of poor professionalism. A sketched-out piece of UML like the one in the figure clearly has no formal value, and we are *not* saying that we would present it at a formal meeting with the customer.

However, designing a system is far too serious a thing to pretend you can sit down on day one, have a look at standardized requirements, and start producing fully detailed diagrams. As disappointing as it seems, things just don't go this way. In the early stages of development, using UML as a sketch is highly productive because it provides a common, visual, and formal language to express ideas and brainstorm about the design. Getting the specifications of a system is an iterative process, and each iteration might require creating a number of informal and approximate sketches, whether drawn on napkins or saved digitally to a Visio or PowerPoint file.

With a "UML as a sketch" approach, your goal as an architect is communicating information about the system being created and gathering good input for developers to code up. Using "UML as a sketch" lets the proper design *emerge* progressively and collaboratively, in an agile manner. To enhance communication, you don't need and don't want to use UML at its fullest. You need a formal language for sure, but one used in a more loose fashion—just like sketches.

> **Note** On the topic of UML, we gladly note Microsoft's commitment to significantly improve UML support in the next version of Microsoft Visual Studio. According to the latest product Community Technology Preview (CTP), we'll find a bunch of designers for UML diagrams integrated into the next version of Visual Studio, such as use-case, sequence, and class diagrams. Unlike Microsoft Visio for Enterprise Architects, UML support in the upcoming version of Visual Studio (codenamed Rosario at the time of this writing) will be limited to modeling and separated from code generation. This switch basically enables you to use "UML as a sketch" scenarios in the next version of Visual Studio—a quantum leap in the right direction, we feel.

UML as a Blueprint

UML is as good at brainstorming the system design (a sketch) as it is good at realizing a formal and full description of the system that is ready for coders (a blueprint). In any case, UML is the tool that architects leverage to communicate with the development team.

"UML as a sketch" and "UML as a blueprint" are two distinct modes of using UML that refer to different views of the design process. There are radically different philosophies underlying each approach. With a "UML as a blueprint" approach, your goal is to deliver a complete and exhaustive set of specifications to the development team. You need to have a maximum level of detail and accuracy in this type of UML diagram. The design is essentially done entirely up front.

We like to summarize the differences between the two approaches by using the following contrasts: *emerging vs. up front,* or perhaps *collaborative vs. ipse dixit*. We also tried to capture these differences between "UML as a sketch" and "UML as a blueprint" in Table 2-1.

TABLE 2-1 UML Sketches vs. UML Blueprints

	UML as a Sketch	UML as a Blueprint
Philosophy	Emerging, collaborative	Up front, ipse dixit
Focus	Communication	Completeness of design
Goals	Help communicate ideas and alternatives about design choices, and focus on selected issues. Iteratively come to a stable, but still incomplete, design of the system that is meaningful to developers.	Neat separation between design and coding. Leave little or nothing to developer's discretion. Development must be a manual translation of UML into a programming language.
Level of detail in UML documents	Low	High
Formal value of UML documents	Low/medium	High
Tool	Lightweight designers, PowerPoint, whiteboards, napkins, backs of paid bills, and so forth	Ad hoc rich, specific, and often expensive tools

In forward engineering, the team first writes the UML blueprints and then produces the related implementation code in the language of choice. Blueprints should be detailed enough to leave as little as possible to the developer's discretion.

In reverse engineering, a blueprint is generated from the source code to describe the effective behavior of the system, typically in a graphical fashion.

With a "UML as a blueprint" approach, you need a specialized modeling tool. Ideally, the tool should assist the architect during the forward-engineering stage to generate a set of detailed and unambiguous diagrams that are easy to turn into code without open points and gaps for developers to fill. Likewise, the tool should also be able to minimize over time the costs of synchronization between the UML model and the software artifact. Tools that support both forward engineering and reverse engineering are said to be *round-trip* tools.

As you proceed with coding and refactoring, it is crucial that you keep the UML model in sync with the evolution of the code. As you refactor the code, you want an updated UML returned that reflects your changes (reverse engineering). The tool should provide this ability, and this is mostly what makes "UML as a blueprint" tools extremely sophisticated and also expensive.

Does the "perfect" tool exist? This is hard to say.

For sure, tools such as Rational Rose and Enterprise Architect give it a try and do roundtrips. The tools vary in the way in which they store internal information to sync up the model and the code. It is not unusual, though, that after a certain number of roundtrips the chain breaks up and you are left with the model and code out of sync. Manual intervention to restore synchronization is then required.

For sure, Microsoft Visio for Enterprise Architect does not provide much help in this regard. For sure, the upcoming Visual Studio version will not be of much help either, but probably for a different reason. In the upcoming version of Visual Studio, the focus is on the "UML as a sketch" approach.

> **Note** "UML as a sketch" and "UML as a blueprint" are based on different philosophies and have different goals. We summarized this using the contrast of emerging vs. up front. This might lead you to believe that the "UML as a sketch" approach is agile and "UML as a blueprint" is not. Agile is a methodology, and the project manager is responsible for the methodology. A project manager can certainly require detailed UML blueprints in the context of an agile methodology—and vice versa. You can pick up a waterfall-like methodology and still communicate sketched specifications to the development team.

UML as a Programming Language

The more you can come up with a detailed model, the closer you get to a new programming language. You have a formal, yet graphical, language and fully detailed behavior. What really keeps you from compiling that source into executable code? Nothing in theory. But, in practice, graphical programming is not manna from heaven.

Can UML ever replace C#? Or, better, will there ever come a day when you model your application using UML and then just pass it on to a tool to generate code? Does this really mean that all applications will be written in a fraction of the time they take today?

Honestly, we currently don't think so. But we like the idea that this might be (effectively) possible one day. Everybody has a secret dream, don't they?

In a certain way, "UML as a programming language" is just the next step past "UML as a blueprint." The highest hurdle on the way to "UML as a blueprint" is the availability of tools that can perform loss-less roundtrips. A second, and nearly as high, hurdle exists on the way to "UML as a programming language": the absence of a UML graphical language with a pseudocode syntax.

We don't know what the future has in store, but in our humble opinion the general technology outlook is not favorable for the success of a pure model-driven architecture—the methodology that pushes the idea of using just UML as your programming language. But we probably will get to use UML in a much more powerful way than it's used today and significantly reduce the impedance between the model and the code artifact.

> **Note** OK, we just made a bold statement about MDA here and took a clear and reasoned stand. Only those who make predictions can make wrong ones. As the ancient Romans used to say, "The future is held on Jupiter's knees." So only time will tell. However, if we're wrong about MDA's poor prospects for success, it will likely be because of significant technical innovations. If MDA fulfills its promise within a few years, we'll be among the first to adopt it.

How We Use UML in Our Own Real World

So we got to know the three main modes of using UML exist in the industry. But what mode is the best? This is so hard to measure that we prefer to rephrase the question for clarity and to avoid misunderstandings. So what, *in our humble opinion*, is the best way to use UML? And how are we using it in our real-world projects?

We essentially iterate through cycles of UML sketches up to the point of reaching a sort of blueprint. More often than not, though, the blueprint is not as perfect and detailed as it should ideally be. What we deliver as architects is normally a model that is clear enough to communicate some key architectural details and can be easily understood by developers. The model contains at least the most significant use cases and class diagrams. It doesn't usually contain all possible sequence and activity diagrams. Let's say that we tend to put in all the most important sequences, especially those for which we don't want to leave any doubt about the intended behavior. On the other hand, when you have well-written use cases, the risk of creating a misunderstanding with developers is really low.

What about reverse engineering? Most of the time, we always end up keeping the UML and code in sync through some doses of manual intervention.

Which tools do we use? Because we strongly believe in "UML as a sketch," we stick to Microsoft Visio for Enterprise Architects. (And we are eagerly awaiting the next version of Visual Studio.)

Finally, some notes about UML in the industry. There's a growing consensus in the industry toward using "UML as a sketch." And the announced set of features slated for the next version of Visual Studio reflects this. We think that "UML as a sketch" delivers an excellent cost/benefit ratio—a good specification created in a small amount of time, with no need to spend money to license ad hoc tools.

In our experience, "UML as a blueprint" is a sort of chimera. And the same holds true for "UML as a programming language" and the related MDA approach. The UML we have today suggests that the best we can do is sketch out models iteratively, reach a good blueprint-like specification, and then start coding. This has worked well for us to date.

UML Diagrams

UML 2.0 has 13 different types of diagrams, articulated in two groups: *structural* and *behavioral*. Structural diagrams define classes as well as their attributes, operations, and relationships. Behavioral diagrams show collaborations among objects as required by the system. Table 2-2 lists all UML diagrams available.

TABLE 2-2 **Diagrams in UML 2.0**

Diagram	Category	Purpose
Activity	Behavior	Shows the flow of operations in an activity
Class	Structure	Shows classes, interfaces, and relationships within a system
Communication	Behavior	Shows the interaction between objects
Component	Structure	Shows components and their dependencies
Composite structure	Structure	Shows the internal structure of a class
Deployment	Structure	Shows how components are mapped to hardware resources
Interaction overview	Behavior	Shows sequences and activities
Object	Structure	Shows a view of the system at a particular time
Package	Structure	Shows how classes are split into logically related groups
Sequence	Behavior	Shows the interaction between objects
State machine	Behavior	Shows how the state of objects changes after events
Timing	Behavior	Shows the behavior of objects in a period of time
Use case	Behavior	Shows what actors perform which action in the system

Figure 2-2, on the other hand, offers a hierarchical view of the UML diagrams.

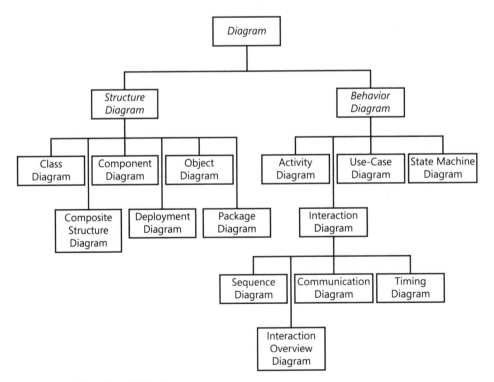

FIGURE 2-2 Hierarchy of UML diagrams

Note that a UML document can contain multiple instances of the same diagram type—for example, multiple use-case diagrams. At the same time, the same element (that is, the same use case or the same actor) can appear in multiple instances of the same diagram. This is normally done to augment clarity and readability.

As an example, imagine a scenario where you have 10 use cases (essentially, interactions with the system) and 4 actors (essentially, people or objects that interact with the system). Putting everything in a single use-case diagram will likely make the diagram overly complex and hard to read. For this reason, you might want to create three distinct use-case diagrams. In doing so, though, it might happen that one actor or two use cases appear in different diagrams.

As mentioned, this chapter is not attempting to cover all aspects of UML. For a more comprehensive explanation of UML, we recommend our favorite book on the topic, Martin Fowler's *UML Distilled: A Brief Guide to the Standard Object Modeling Language (Third Edition)*, which we referenced earlier in the chapter. If a UML-related topic is not covered there, it is probably not all that necessary to cover it.

Let's learn more about the three most commonly used diagrams: use-case diagrams, class diagrams, and sequence diagrams.

Use-Case Diagrams

A use-case diagram provides a graphical representation of use cases. As mentioned, a use case is an interaction between the system and one of its actors. A use case shows which actors do what. An actor can be a user or any other external system (for example, a database) that interacts with the system being described. An actor cannot be controlled by the system; an actor is defined outside the system itself. Let's start getting familiar with the notation.

A Look at the Notation

The main elements of a use-case diagram are the following:

- The system
- The actors
- The use cases
- The relationships

As you can see, the diagram employs a small number of graphical elements. This means that a use-case diagram is often readable and understandable at first sight. Have a look at Figure 2-3.

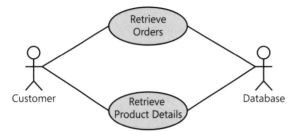

FIGURE 2-3 A sample use-case diagram

The diagram in Figure 2-3 contains a couple of use cases. A use case is graphically represented with an oval that contains a sufficiently evocative name for the action and actors that participate in the action. An actor is commonly represented using a basic stick man with a name depicted nearby.

 Note Alternative representations exist for the actor. Sometimes the actor is rendered as a rectangle with the word "actor" inside; other times, it is an icon that transmits the idea of someone or something executing an action. However, these notations are extremely rare.

Sometimes the system, or a part of it, might be represented using a rectangle. Within the rectangle, you find use cases, while actors are placed outside of it. The rectangle represents the boundary of the system. (See Figure 2-4.)

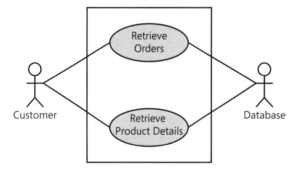

FIGURE 2-4 The system's boundary in a use-case diagram

Actors and use cases can be connected using lines. The connecting line indicates a relationship. A relationship can exist in the following forms:

- Between an actor and a use case
- Between two actors
- Between two use cases

As you can imagine, UML allows you to specify in a more precise manner the semantics of relationships. Relationships can be of three types: *inclusion*, *extension*, and *generalization*.

Plus, a fourth type exists that is not formally listed in the specification that indicates a form of interaction. We'll call this fourth type a *generic* relationship. Let's just start with this type.

Generic Relationships

A generic relationship is established between an actor and a use case. It is rendered with a solid line not ending in any arrow. Figure 2-3 demonstrates a generic relationship between the actor Customer and the use case Retrieve Orders.

A generic relationship merely indicates that some sort of interaction is expected between the connected parts. Of course, there's always an active part and a passive part that you normally figure out based on the context.

In the UML standard, there's no notation to indicate essentially whether the actor has an active or passive role, whether it triggers the use case or it incurs the use case. As mentioned, this is normally clear from the use case itself. For example, in Figure 2-3, the actor Customer is active as it triggers the use case Retrieve Orders. The actor Database is passive as it incurs the effect of retrieving orders.

Inclusion

An *include* relationship is rendered through a directed line that connects two use cases. It indicates that the use case where the line starts contains the behavior defined in the use case where the line ends.

The line is dashed and ends with an open arrow. The line is also labeled with the word *include*. Figure 2-5 shows an example.

FIGURE 2-5 An *include* relationship between two use cases

In the preceding example, the use case Cart Checkout incorporates the behavior associated with the Verify User Credentials use case. The message for the developer is clear: when it comes to implementing the checkout process, ask the user to provide credentials and verify them against the membership system.

Extension

The *extend* relationship indicates that one use case extends the behavior of the target use case. The notation employed is very similar to the include relationship—a connecting dashed line ending with an open arrow. In this case, though, the arrow is labeled with the word "extend."

What's the real difference between inclusion and extension? Could you just reverse the arrow in Figure 2-5 and change the label? What's the point of having both forms of relationships? Formally, the key difference is that an extension relationship indicates an optional dependency. Hence, the message is this: there's a use case that optionally might be used to decorate and extend another use case.

The developer should include the behavior of the extender use case in the implementation of the extended use case. However, it should also provide for some triggers because the extension relationship is triggered only under certain specific run-time conditions. (See Figure 2-6.)

FIGURE 2-6 An extend relationship between two use cases

In the diagram in Figure 2-6, the Cart Checkout use case is extended by the Online Help use case. This additional behavior is optional, and the inclusion happens whenever, say, the user hits F1 during the execution of the Cart Checkout use case. Note that the extender and extended use cases (Cart Checkout and Online Help, in this case) are defined independent of one another.

Generalization

The *generalization* relationship can exist between homogeneous pairs of actors and use cases. It indicates that a specialized form of a use case (or actor) exists. The generalization relationship identifies a child and a parent in a sort of inheritance mechanism.

The notation is a solid line ending with a hollow triangle. The triangle touches on the parent element and the lines originates in the child element. The child actor or use case inherits the functionality of the parent and extends it through more specific and specialized features. (See Figure 2-7.)

The diagram in Figure 2-7 indicates that the actor Registered User triggers the Retrieve Product Details use case. The Retrieve Orders use case can be triggered only by a Customer actor. In the end, the Customer actor is a special type of a registered user. This diagram can be further extended by defining a new actor—say, the Backoffice User—who inherits Registered User to represent all users within the company.

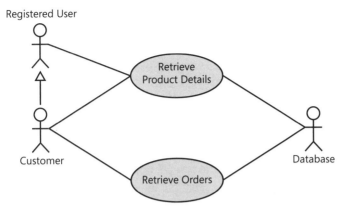

FIGURE 2-7 Generalization between two actors: a Customer is a special type of Registered User

Class Diagrams

Class diagrams are probably the most widely used UML diagram. You don't have to be a a a huge fan of UML, or an experienced UML user, to have seen and to recognize a class diagram. A class diagram represents the static structure of a system. The static structure of a system is composed of classes and their relationships. Classes are exactly the classes (and interfaces) to be implemented by the development team. Let's start with a look at the notation.

A Look at the Notation

From a notational perspective, the class is a rectangle that is usually vertically partitioned in three areas. The top-most rectangle contains the name of the class. The second area lists the *attributes* of the class. By attributes, we mean properties and fields you want to see defined in the body of the class. Finally, the bottom area contains class *operations*. By operations, we mean essentially class methods. (See Figure 2-8.)

Table
+Name:string
+Clear() +WriteToFile(in fileName:string):int

FIGURE 2-8 A class description in a class diagram

The name of the class can also be qualified by a namespace. In UML, the concept of a namespace (as we know it from the Microsoft .NET Framework) is expressed through the package. To indicate that a class should be defined within a package, you concatenate the names using double colons (::)—for example, *System.Data::DataTable*.

Characteristics of the class, attributes, and operations are associated with a modifier. Feasible symbols are listed in Table 2-3.

TABLE 2-3 UML Modifiers

Symbol	Meaning
+	The attribute or operation is public.
-	The attribute or operation is private.
#	The attribute or operation is protected.

In Figure 2-8, you see a sample class *Table* with a property *Name* and a couple of methods: *Clear* and *WriteToFile*. All properties and methods are public.

Note that when you define a UML class, you also specify the type of a property and the signature of a method. The class *Table* schematized in Figure 2-8 can be expressed in pure C# as follows:

```
class Table
{
    public string Name;

    public void Clear()
    {
    }

    public int WriteToFile(string fileName)
    {
    }
}
```

Special font styles indicate a special meaning, too. In particular, if you use the Italic style with an attribute or operation, you indicate you want it to be a virtual member of the class. The Underlined style indicates a static member.

Finally, UML supplies a specific symbol to refer to *parameterized types*—that is, .NET generic types. The symbol is similar to a conventional class and includes an extra overlapped dashed rectangle with a placeholder for types. (See Figure 2-9.)

Let's delve a bit deeper into the syntax and sematics of attributes and relationships.

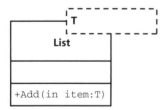

FIGURE 2-9 A generic List<T> class in UML

UML, Java, and the Two of Us

Like it or not, UML is a bit biased by the Java language. You might have suspected this already from the aforementioned use of the term *package* instead of *namespace*. But there's more to the story.

According to UML and the Java language, class attributes should be limited to defining fields. So what about properties? In Java, you don't even have properties; in the .NET Framework, properties are a pinch of syntactic sugar. As you might know, in the .NET Framework properties are implemented through a pair of *getter* and *setter* methods. So UML suggests that you use the same approach for properties.

This is the theory; but what about the practice? In our projects, we use attributes for both properties and fields. We employ a sort of de facto standard notation to distinguish fields from properties. Property names are *PascalCase*, whereas field names are *camelCase*. And in general, everything we mark as public is a property.

Likewise, in both UML and the Java language you don't have events. In Java, a different eventing model is used based on your own implementation of the publish/subscribe pattern. In the .NET Framework, events are merely a system-provided implementation of the same pattern, made even simpler by idiomatic language features such as the *event* keyword in C#.

So in UML, you have no syntax element to define an event as a class attribute. Yet, our .NET classes might require events. What do we do? We simply use attributes of type *EventHandler* or any other more specific event delegate type. Developers will understand.

Attributes

As mentioned, attributes indicate fields of a class, but in a pure .NET context we loosely use them to define properties and events, too. Attributes are made of a line of text. The full notation includes the following:

- Access modifier.
- Name of the attribute.
- Type of the attribute. The type can be either a primitive type or a custom type.
- Multiplicity of the attribute—that is, the number of objects used to define a value for the attribute.
- Default value (if any) for the attribute.

Here's a more complete definition for the *Name* attribute in a *Table* class:

```
+ Name: String = String.Empty
```

This UML definition might become the following C# code:

```
public string Name = String. Empty;
```

The multiplicity is a single number, or an interval, that indicates how many values are required to set the attribute. Numbers appear in square brackets. A single number indicates that a single value or instance is required. The previous example can be rewritten as shown here:

```
+ Name: String [1] = string.Empty
```

A collection of values is represented with the following notation:

```
+ Rows: Row [0..5]
```

In this case, to initialize the *Rows* attribute, up to six instances of the *Row* object are required. In C#, you might have the following:

```
public Row[6] Rows;
```

You use the asterisk (*) symbol to indicate an unlimited number, as shown here:

```
+ Rows: Row[0..*] = List<Row>
```

This corresponds to the following C# code:

```
public IList<Row> Rows = new List<Row>();
```

Operations

In general, operations in a UML class diagram indicate the actions that instances of a class can take. Operations are essentially methods. Here's the full notation:

- Access modifier
- Name of the operation
- Parameter list (using the comma as the separator)
- Return type

Each parameter in the list is represented with a notation close to that of attributes, but with an extra prefix, as shown in Table 2-4.

TABLE 2-4 Direction of a Parameter

Prefix	Meaning
In	Input parameter
Out	Output parameter
Inout	Input and output parameter

If unspecified, the direction is assumed to be *in*. Look at the following operation:

```
+ WriteToFile(fileName: string, overwriteIfExisting: bool): int
```

It corresponds to the following C# code:

```
public int WriteToFile(string filename, bool overwriteIfExisting)
{
}
```

The UML's *out* prefix corresponds to the C#'s out keyword, whereas UML's *inout* matches C#'s *ref* keyword. Note that not all languages can accommodate this. Visual Basic .NET. for example, can't deal with UML's *out* prefix directly. To define an output parameter in Visual Basic .NET you have to use the keyword *ByRef*, which actually corresponds to UML's *inout*. In the end, in Visual Basic .NET an output parameter always has to be promoted to an input and output parameter.

Associations

An association indicates a relationship existing between classes. You can use an association as an alternative syntax to list the properties of a class. In terms of notation, an association is a solid line between classes. Figure 2-10 and Figure 2-11 express equivalent content.

Order
+Customer:Customer +Items[1..*]:OrderItem

FIGURE 2-10 Attributes in the *Order* class are expressed with a simple notation.

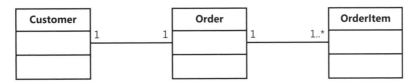

FIGURE 2-11 Attributes on the *Order* class expressed via associations

With associations, you can indicate the multiplicity at both ends, and this might make the resulting diagram clearer to read. Because they are logically equivalent, the diagrams in both Figure 2-10 and Figure 2-11 can be expressed with the following C# code:

```
class Order
{
    public Customer Customer;
    public List<OrderItem> Items;
}
```

Two special types of associations are *aggregation* and *composition*.

Aggregation specifies a whole/part relationship between two objects, or in other words a *has-a* relationship. Graphically, it is represented using a connecting line ending with a clear diamond shape on the container class. Figure 2-12 shows an aggregation where the *Order* class has a *Customer* using a one-to-one multiplicity.

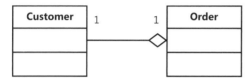

FIGURE 2-12 Aggregation: the class *Order* relates to one instance of the *Customer* class.

Note that in the case of aggregation the contained object is not entirely dependent on the container. If you destroy the container, this might not affect the contained objects. In Figure 2-12, *Order* has one and only one *Customer*, but if the *Customer* disappears (perhaps goes out of business), the *Order* remains (perhaps as historical information).

Composition is perhaps a stronger form of aggregation. It specifies that you have a compound object where the container entirely owns the contained object. If you destroy the parent, the children are destroyed as well. You indicate a composition using a connecting line ending with a black diamond shape on the container class. The line can be adorned with multiplicity. (See Figure 2-13.)

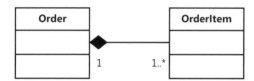

FIGURE 2-13 Composition: the class *Order* owns multiple order items.

Generalization

The *generalization* relationship occurs between two classes and indicates that one specializes the other, thus making it a subtype. As you can see, this relationship corresponds to inheritance in C# and other object-oriented languages. The relationship is rendered using a line that ends with a hollow triangle. The line connects the involved classes, and the triangle touches on the parent class, as illustrated in Figure 2-14.

Generalization defines a relationship of type *is-a*. With an eye on Figure 2-14; therefore, we can say that "supplier is a company" and, likewise, that "customer is a company."

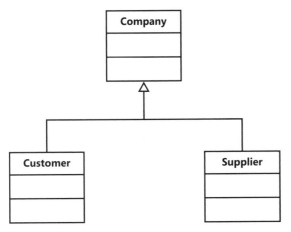

FIGURE 2-14 The relationship generalization between company classes

Dependency

A dependency relationship exists between two classes when one class requires another class in order to be implemented. You have a dependency when a change in one class affects the other class.

The notation for a dependency is a dashed line going from the dependent class to the independent class. The line ends with an open arrow touching on the independent class. For example, you might have a line connecting a client to a supplier. This indicates a dependency of the client on the supplier. If you modify the supplier, the client might be broken. (See Figure 2-15.)

FIGURE 2-15 A dependency between a *Client* class and a *Supplier* class: the *Client* depends on the *Supplier*.

> **Note** Many UML relationships imply a dependency. For example, a class derived from a parent class is dependent on its base class. Although dependencies between classes (static dependencies) are easy to discover at design time, other forms of dependencies (such as transient relationships) require code inspection or analysis to be discovered.

Sequence Diagrams

Sequence diagrams illustrate any interactions within a group of objects that implement a given scenario. A sequence diagram is aimed at showing the exact flow of control that one could observe within a system. With a sequence diagram, any observer knows exactly how the system implements a given use case.

A Look at the Notation

In a sequence diagram, participating objects are rendered with rectangles containing the object's name. The full UML syntax dictates that you use the notation *instance : class* to name an object. More commonly, though, you use an informal name (for example, *an Order*) that indicates the nature and role of the object in the sequence. The name is usually underlined. (Note that we are not taking the UML standard literally here. Ours is a loose interpretation that is much more practical in the real world.)

A vertical and dashed line departs from each object that participates in the sequence. This line is called the *lifeline* and represents the passing of time and, contextually, the life span of the object. An interaction between two objects in the sequence is rendered by drawing a solid line ending with a filled arrow between the lifelines of the objects. The solid line starts from the lifeline of the caller and ends at the lifeline of the callee. The line is also decorated with text that commonly indicates the method invoked or the data returned.

> **Note** Generally, the line is decorated with the name of the message sent or received. However, it is common that the message corresponds to a method. Therefore, the name of the message matches the name of the method. If you want to be rigorous, you should detail the signature of the method being called.

You indicate that an object is active and gains control of the operation by showing what is known as an *activation bar*. An activation bar is a part of the lifeline that is rendered using a narrow rectangle. (See Figure 2-16.)

The sequence in Figure 2-16 illustrates the retrieval of a little piece of information—the price of an ordered item. As you can see, four different objects participate in the operation—Order, Order Item, Customer, and Product. It all begins when the *GetPrice* method is invoked on an *Order* object.

Internally, the *Order* object figures out the ordered item and attempts to retrieve the price. In turn, the *Order Item* finds a reference to the ordered product and gets the related price. At some point, when the activation bar of the *Product* object terminates, the *Order Item* knows about the standard price of the product. However, it also needs to check any applicable discount for the customer who actually ordered it. So the *GetDiscountRate* method is invoked on a *Customer* object. At the end, the price of the ordered item is carried back to the original caller.

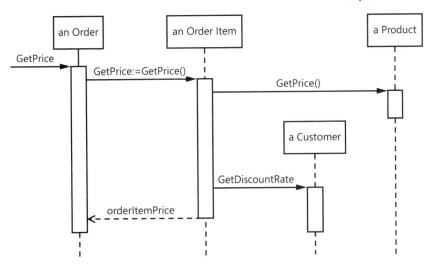

FIGURE 2-16 A simple sequence diagram

When the invoked method returns a value, you typically draw a return line (dashed this time) that connects callee and caller. This line is decorated with the logical name assigned to the returned value. This optional item increases the readability of the diagram and also gives you a chance to express conditions by using interaction frames. (We'll say more about this in a moment.) Return values are optional, however.

> **Note** An object can invoke a method on the same instance—for example, an *Order* object invokes a method on itself. This situation is represented by drawing an arrow (in a semicircular shape) that starts and ends on the same activation bar.

Life and Death of an Object

The lifeline notation in a UML sequence diagram merely shows the passing of time, but it says nothing about the creation and destruction of objects. A special notation exists to indicate explicitly the lifetime of an object. (See Figure 2-17.)

To indicate the creation of an object, the creator sends a message labeled with a *new* keyword. The message moves from the activation bar of the creator up to the box of the created object. The destruction of an object is represented with an X symbol placed at the end of the lifeline at the precise moment you want the object to be removed from memory.

What the expression "remove the object from memory" exactly means depends on the language you use. In C++, the developer needs to personally take care of the destruction of any previously created objects. In this case, the *X* symbol indicates an explicit call to the object's destructor using the C++ *delete* keyword. In Java and .NET managed languages, conversely, objects are removed automatically from memory when they go out of scope (garbage collection). In this case, the *X* symbol on the lifeline simply indicates when the object is expected to be no longer available for use.

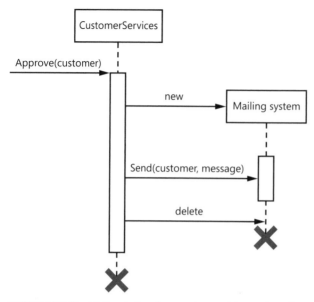

FIGURE 2-17 The UML notation for creating and destroying objects

When an external object is responsible for destroying a given object, and the object supports a deterministic disposal model, you place a *delete* message that ends at the *X* on the lifeline of the object being destroyed.

> **Note** In particular, in the .NET Framework an object that implements the *IDisposable* interface supports a more deterministic model for destruction. Through the interface, the object exposes a method for callers to explicity clean up the internal state and mark the instance for future deletion care of the garbage collector.

In general, it is acceptable that as an architect you just don't bother with also modeling the destruction of objects. It is reasonable that you leave the burden of this to the development team and trust their skills.

Asynchronous Messages

So far, we haven't distinguished between synchronous and asynchronous messages in a sequence diagram. All the messages you have seen so far—those represented with a solid line ending in a filled arrow—are synchronous messages. In the case of a synchronous message, the caller waits until the operation terminates. For example, the caller waits until a given routine ends. An asynchronous message indicates that the processing continues without the caller needing to stop and wait for a response. How does UML represent an asynchronous message?

In UML 2.*x*, a filled arrowhead shows a synchronous message, whereas a stick arrowhead shows an asynchronous message, as you can see in Figure 2-18.

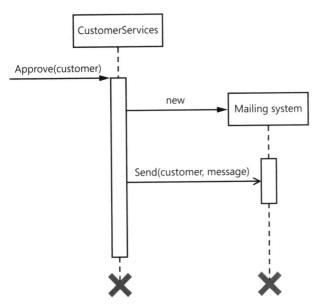

FIGURE 2-18 Synchronous and asynchronous messages

Figure 2-18 updates Figure 2-17 by using an asynchronous UML message to indicate that after a new customer has been approved an e-mail message should be sent to the customer through the mailing system. The *CustomerServices* object, though, doesn't have to wait until the e-mail is delivered. You typically use asynchronous messages for all interactions with hardware devices and shared subsystems.

You should pay attention to the subtle difference existing between the notation used for synchronous and asynchronous messages. The difference is all in the arrowhead: a filled one for synchronous messages, and a stick one for asynchronous messages. Also note that this is the latest notation used with UML 2.*x*. In earlier versions of UML, the notation for asynchronous messages was different: a half-stick arrowhead. Table 2-5 summarizes the notations.

TABLE 2-5 Notations for Messages in UML Sequence Diagrams

Notation	Version	Meaning
⟶	**All**	Synchronous message
⟶	**Up to UML 1.3**	Asynchronous message
⟶	**Starting with UML 1.4**	Asynchronous message

Standing in the Way of Control

Sequence diagrams are essentially a tool to render how objects interact. They do not lend themselves very well to model control logic. However, if in a sequence you need to put some conditions, you can use *interaction frames*. Interaction frames are a new feature of UML 2.*x* aimed at expressing conditions and controlling flow in a sequence. Let's start with the C# code shown here:

```
class OrderServices
{
    public void Create(Order order)
    {
        // Calculate the total of all orders received from this customer
        decimal total = order.Customer.GetAllOrdersAmount();

        // Ask the system to suggest a discount rate for existing customers
        if (total > 0)
        {
            string customerID = order.Customer.ID;
            CustomerServices svc = new CustomerServices();
            decimal rate = svc.SuggestDiscountRate(customerID);
            order.SetDiscountRate(rate);
        }

        // Get the updated total for the order and proceed
        decimal orderTotal = order.GetOrderTotal();
        :
        :

        // Save the order back to storage
        using(DataContext ctx = new DataContext())
        {
            ctx.Save(order);
        }
    }
}
```

The requirement behind this piece of code is that before processing an order, you check whether the customer who placed it is a known customer. If the customer has already placed orders in the past, it is eligible for a discount. The system suggests an appropriate discount rate that is set within the *Order* object. Next, the order is processed by the system and then saved back to storage. How would you render this logic in UML? In particular, how would you render the condition? (See Figure 2-19.)

An interaction frame delimits a region of a sequence diagram and marks it with an operator and a Boolean guard. The operator indicates the behavior you expect, whereas the guard indicates whether or not the sequence in the frame executes or not. Table 2-6 lists the most commonly used operators for interaction frames.

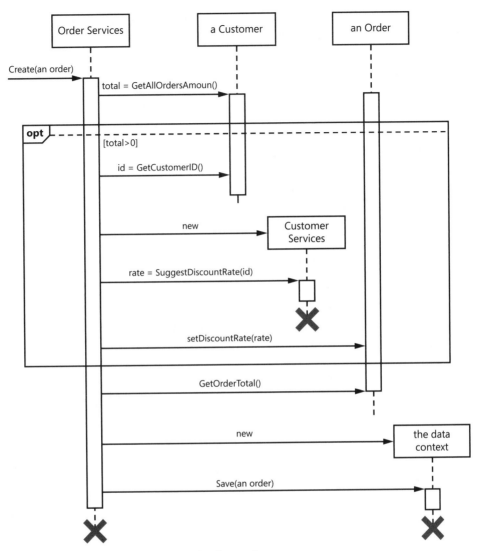

FIGURE 2-19 A sequence diagram including interactions

TABLE 2-6 Common Operators for Interaction Frames

Operator	Meaning
alt	Indicates alternative branches. The frame hosts multiple sequences, but only those with a true Boolean guard execute. Multiple sequences in a frame are separated with a dashed line.
opt	The sequence in the frame will execute only if the guard is true.
par	The frame hosts multiple sequences; all sequences will run in parallel.
loop	The sequence in the frame will be executed multiple times, based on the guard expression.
region	Indicates a critical section, and requires that only one thread executes it at a time.

Finally, note that interaction frames can be nested if this is really necessary. The point here is that nested frames augment the complexity, and decrease the readability, of the resulting diagram. If you have really complex control logic to express, we suggest that you opt for an activity diagram—essentially, an object-oriented version of flowcharts—or even code snippets. The best you can do, though, is break the sequence down into smaller pieces so that a standard sequence diagram with simple interaction frames is readable enough.

Domain-Specific Languages and UML

UML is a general-purpose modeling language with incorporated concepts and tools that can be easily applied to a variety of contexts. Adapting the model to a particular domain might require additional and more specific tools and elements. For this reason, UML 2.*x* defines a standard mechanism, known as *profiles*, to extend the language. When you create a custom UML profile, you essentially extend the base metamodel by adding new elements with specific properties suitable to a given domain.

However, a UML profile is still a piece of a fixed model. A domain-specific language (DSL) is something different. A DSL is a domain-specific programming language created to solve problems in a particular domain. A DSL can be a visual language or a textual language. In general, it falls somewhere in between a small programming language and a scripting language. A DSL doesn't usually compile to binary code; rather, it is rendered to some intermediate language. Although it was not created to be a DSL, all in all SQL can be considered a realistic example of a DSL—it is a language specific to a domain (database access), and it is invoked by other applications.

To model your domain effectively, should you use UML extensions or switch to a DSL? In our way of looking at things, UML is a general-purpose language, meaning that it is good at describing any sort of domain, but only approximately. Or, put another way, it can't be used to describe any domain precisely. In the imperfect world where we live, no universal language can be used to solve all sorts of problems with the same level of effectiveness. Enter DSLs. A DSL is a language for just one domain and scenario: it's a made-to-measure, straight-to-the-point, and ad hoc language. Its elements come from the domain, not from a fixed metamodel.

By extending UML with a profile, you transform a general language into something specific and, in doing so, you use the set of tools the general language makes available. Sure, it works. But is it effective? By using DSLs, you create your own language using ad hoc DSL tools, such as those integrated in Visual Studio. (See *http://msdn.microsoft.com/ en-us/library/bb126235.aspx*.) This language might not be reusable outside the domain, but it is direct. And, by the way, are you sure that your profile is reusable as well?

Because a DSL language is tailor-made for a domain, generating compile code out of it is easier. And the DSL tool does it for you. We see the future of model-driven development passing through DSL rather than using UML as the modeling tool.

Summary

UML is a standard language for object modeling. It is independent from any programming language. This is a key attribute, in both a good way and a bad way. It is a good attribute because it makes UML an extremely versatile tool for modeling and communicating any business process. At the same time, all that it can produce is a generic model using a fixed metamodel. This is far from the compiled code that forms a system.

Based on a metamodel, UML can be extended using profiles and a set of custom tools and elements. But still, you need to write code based upon your UML model. It is debatable whether extensions to UML or domain-specific languages are the optimal solution to model applications at the highest possible level. All in all, we reckon that DSLs are a more direct approach, but we still like UML when a modeling tool is required. And it is required in most real projects. We feel that UML and DSL are complementary and one doesn't exclude the other. But they are different things, with each one being good at different things.

In this chapter, we mostly presented UML as a modeling language. We discussed the three main modes of using UML, including the emerging "UML as a sketch" mode. In our vision, this sketching model is ideal to communicate ideas within and around the team; then manual coding, or DSLs integrated into the development environment, will be responsible for the actual production of compiled code.

UML is all about diagrams. The latest version of UML supports up to 13 types of diagrams. In this overview chapter, we covered only the most important of these diagram types—use-case, class, and sequence diagrams. For a complete reference for UML, you should look elsewhere. And we recommend Martin Fowler's excellent book *UML Distilled: A Brief Guide to the Standard Object Modeling Language (Third Edition)*.

Murphy's Laws of the Chapter

Communication is important in a software project, like in any other aspect of life. Communication, though, requires notation and models, if not formal specifications. The UML we presented in this chapter is all about supplying a model for communicating key ideas about design. Communication and modeling are the subject of the following Murphy's laws:

- Real programmers don't comment their code. If it was hard to write, it should be hard to understand.

- Ninety percent of a programmer's errors come from data from other programmers.

- Walking on water and developing software to specification are easy as long as both are frozen.

See *http://www.murphys-laws.com* for an extensive listing of other computer-related (and non-computer-related) laws and corollaries.

Chapter 3
Design Principles and Patterns

Experienced designers evidently know something inexperienced others don't. What is it?

—*Erich Gamma*

In Chapter 1, "Architects and Architecture Today," we focused on the true meaning of architecture and the steps through which architects get a set of specifications for the development team. We focused more on the process than the principles and patterns of actual design. In Chapter 2, "UML Essentials," we filled a gap by serving up a refresher (or a primer, depending on the reader's skills) of Unified Modeling Language (UML). UML is the most popular modeling language through which design is expressed and communicated within development teams.

When examining the bundle of requirements, the architect at first gets a relatively blurred picture of the system. As the team progresses through iterations, the contours of the picture sharpen. In the end, the interior of the system unveils a web of interrelated classes applying design patterns and fulfilling design principles.

Designing a software system is challenging because it requires you to focus on today's requested features while ensuring that the resulting system be flexible enough to support changes and addition of new features in the future.

Especially in the past two decades, a lot has been done in the Information Technology (IT) industry to make a systematic approach to software development possible. Methodologies, design principles, and finally patterns have been developed to help guide architects to envision and build systems of any complexity in a disciplined way.

This chapter aims to provide you with a quick tutorial about software engineering. It first outlines some basic principles that should always inspire the design of a modern software system. The chapter then moves on to discuss principles of object-oriented design. Along the way, we introduce patterns, idioms, and aspect-orientation, as well as pearls of wisdom regarding requirement-driven design that affect key areas such as testability, security, and performance.

Basic Design Principles

It is one thing to write code that just works. It is quite another to write *good* code that works. Adopting the attitude of "writing good code that works" springs from the ability to view the system from a broad perspective. In the end, a top-notch system is not just a product of writing instructions and hacks that make it all work. There's much more, actually. And it relates, directly or indirectly, to design.

The attitude of "writing good code that works" leads you, for example, to value the maintainability of the code base over any other quality characteristics, such as those defined by International Organization for Standardization (ISO) and International Electrotechnical Commission (IEC) standard 9126. (See Chapter 1.) You adopt this preference not so much because other aspects (such as extensibility or perhaps scalability) are less important than maintainability—it's just that maintenance is expensive and can be highly frustrating for the developers involved.

A code base that can be easily searched for bugs, and in which fixing bugs is not problematic for anyone, is open to any sort of improvements at any time, including extensibility and scalability. Thus, maintainability is the quality characteristic you should give the highest priority when you design a system.

Why is software maintenance so expensive?

Maintenance becomes expensive if essentially you have produced unsatisfactory (should we say, sloppy?) software, you haven't tested the software enough, or both. Which attributes make software easier to maintain and evolve? Structured design in the first place, which is best applied through proper coding techniques. Code readability is another fundamental asset, which is best achieved if the code is combined with a bunch of internal documentation and a change-tracking system—but this might occur only in a perfect world.

Before we proceed any further with the basic principles of structured design, let's arrange a brief cheat-sheet to help us catch clear and unambiguous symptoms of bad code design.

Note Unsatisfactory software mostly springs from a poor design. But what causes a poor design? A poor design typically has two causes that are not mutually exclusive: the architect's insufficient skills, and imprecise or contradictory requirements. So what about the requirements problem, then? Contradictory requirements usually result from bad communication. Communication is king, and it is one of the most important skills for an architect to cultivate and improve.

Not surprisingly, fixing this communication problem drives us again straight to agile methodologies. What many people still miss about the agile movement is that the primary benefit you get is not so much the iterative method itself. Instead, the major benefit comes from the continuous communication that the methodology promotes within the team and between the team and the customers. Whatever you get wrong in the first iteration will be fixed quite soon in the next (or close to the next) iteration because the communication that is necessary to move forward will clarify misunderstood requirements and fix bad ones. And it will do so quite early in the process and on a timely basis. This iterative approach simply reduces the entry point for the major cause of costly software maintenance: poor communication. And this is the primary reason why, one day, a group of (perfectly sane) developers and architects decided to found the agile movement. It was pragmatism that motivated them, not caprice.

This said, you should also keep in mind that that agile methodologies also tend to increase development costs and run the risk of scope/requirements creep. You also must make sure everyone in the process is on board with it. If the stakeholders don't understand their role or are not responsive, or can't review the work between iterations, the agile approach fails. So the bottom line is that the agile approach isn't a magic wand that works for everyone. But when it works, it usually works well.

For What the Alarm Bell Should Ring

Even with the best intentions of everyone involved and regardless of their efforts, the design of a system at some point can head down a slippery slope. The deterioration of a good design is generally a slow process that occurs over a relatively long period of time. It happens by continually studding your classes with hacks and workarounds, making a large share of the code harder and harder to maintain and evolve. At a certain point, you find yourself in serious trouble.

Managers might be tempted to call for a complete redesign, but redesigning an evolving system is like trying to catch a runaway chicken. You need to be in a very good shape to do it. But is the team really in shape at that point?

> **Note** Have you ever seen the movie *Rocky*? Do you remember the scene where Rocky, the boxer, finally catches the chicken, thus providing evidence that he's ready for the match? By the way, the scene is on *http://www.youtube.com/watch?v=o8ZkY7tnpRs*. During the movie, Rocky attempts several times to get the chicken, but he gets the chicken only when he has trained well enough.

Let's identify a few general signs that would make the alarm bell ring to warn of a problematic design.

Rigid, Therefore Fragile

Can you bend a piece of wood? What do you risk if you insist on doing it? A piece of wood is typically a stiff and rigid object characterized by some resistance to deformation. When enough force is applied, the deformation becomes permanent and the wood breaks.

What about rigid software?

Rigid software is characterized by some resistance to changes. Resistance is measured in terms of regression. You make a change in one module, but the effects of your change cascade down the list of dependent modules. As a result, it's really hard to predict how long making a change—any change, even the simplest—will actually take.

If you pummel glass or any other fragile material, you manage only to break it into several pieces. Likewise, when you enter a change in software and break it in various places, it becomes quite apparent that software is definitely fragile.

As in other areas of life, in the software world fragility and rigidity go hand in hand. When a change in a software module breaks (many) other modules because of (hidden) dependencies, you have a clear symptom of a bad design that needs to be remedied as soon as possible.

Easier to Use Than to Reuse

Imagine you have a piece of software that works in one project; you would like to reuse it in another project. However, copying the class or linking the assembly in the new project just doesn't work.

Why is it so?

If the same code doesn't work when moved to another project, it's because of dependencies. The real problem isn't just dependencies, but the number and depth of dependencies. The risk is that to reuse a piece of functionality in another project, you have to import a much larger set of functions. Ultimately, no reuse is ever attempted and code is rewritten from scratch.

This is not a good sign for your design. This negative aspect of a design is often referred to as *immobility*.

Easier to Work Around Than to Fix

When applying a change to a software module, it is not unusual that you figure out two or more ways to do it. Most of the time, one way of doing things is nifty, elegant, coherent with the design, but terribly laborious to implement. The other way is, conversely, much smoother, quick to code, but sort of a hack.

What should you do?

Actually, you can solve it either way, depending on the given deadlines and your manager's direction about it.

In summary, it is not an ideal situation when a workaround is much easier and faster to apply than the right solution. And it doesn't make a great statement about your overall design, either. It is a sign that too many unnecessary dependencies exist between classes and that your classes do not form a particularly cohesive mass of code.

This aspect of a design—that it invites or accommodates workarounds more or less than fixes—is often referred to as *viscosity*. High viscosity is bad, meaning that the software resists modification just as highly viscous fluids resist flow.

Structured Design

When the two of us started programming, which was far before we started making a living from it, the old BASIC language was still around with its set of GOTO statements. Like many others, we wrote toy programs jumping from one instruction to the next within the same monolithic block of code. They worked just fine, but they were only toy programs in the end.

> **Note** Every time we looked at the resulting messy BASIC code we wrote, continually referring to other instructions that appeared a bunch of lines up or down in the code, we didn't really like it and we weren't really proud of it. But, at the time, we just thought we were picking up a cool challenge that only a few preordained souls could take on. Programming is a darned hard thing—we thought—but we are going to like it.

It was about the late 1960s when the complexity of the average program crossed the significant threshold that marked the need for a more systematic approach to software development. That signaled the official beginning of software engineering.

From Spaghetti Code to Lasagna Code

Made of a messy tangle of jumps and returns, GOTO-based code was soon belittled and infamously labeled as *spaghetti code*. And we all learned the first of a long list of revolutionary concepts: structured programming. In particular, we learned to use *subroutines* to break our code into cohesive and more reusable pieces. In food terms, we evolved from *spaghetti* to *lasagna*. If you look at Figure 3-1, you will spot the difference quite soon. Lasagna forms a layered block of noodles and toppings that can be easily cut into pieces and just exudes the concept of structure. Lasagna is also easier to serve, which is the food analogy for reusability.

FIGURE 3-1 From a messy tangle to a layered and ordered block

> **Note** A small note (and some credits) about the figure is in order. First, as Italians we would have used the term *lasagne*, which is how we spell it, but we went for the international spelling of *lasagna*. However, we eat it regardless of the spelling. Second, Dino personally ate all the food in the figure in a sort of manual testing procedure for the book's graphics. Dino, however, didn't cook anything. Dino's mother-in-law cooked the spaghetti; Dino's mom cooked the lasagna. Great stuff—if you're in Italy, and want to give it a try, send Dino an e-mail.

What software engineering really has been trying to convey since its inception is the need for some design to take place before coding begins and, subsequently, the need for some basic design principles. Still, today, when someone says "structured programming," immediately many people think of subroutines. This assumption is correct, but it's oversimplifying the point and missing the principal point of the structured approach.

Behind structured programming, there is structured design with two core principles. And these principles are as valid today as they were 30 and more years ago. Subroutines and Pascal-like programming are gone; the principles of *cohesion* and *coupling*, instead, still maintain their effectiveness in an object-oriented world.

These principles of structured programming, coupling and cohesion, were first introduced by Larry Constantine and Edward Yourdon in their book *Structured Design: Fundamentals of a Discipline of Computer Program and Systems Design* (Yourdon Press, 1976).

Cohesion

Cohesion indicates that a given software module—be it a subroutine, class, or library—features a set of responsibilities that are strongly related. Put another way, cohesion measures the distance between the logic expressed by the various methods on a class, the various functions in a library, and the various actions accomplished by a method.

If you look for a moment at the definition of cohesion in another field—chemistry—you should be able to see a clearer picture of software cohesion. In chemistry, cohesion is a physical property of a substance that indicates the attraction existing between like molecules within a body.

Cohesion measurement ranges from low to high and is preferably in the highest range possible.

Highly cohesive modules favor maintenance and reusability because they tend to have no dependencies. Low cohesion, on the other hand, makes it much harder to understand the purpose of a class and creates a natural habitat for rigidity and fragility in the software. Low cohesive modules also propagate dependencies through modules, thus contributing to the immobility and high viscosity of the design.

Decreasing cohesion leads to creating modules (for example, classes) where responsibilities (for example, methods) have very little in common and refer to distinct and unrelated activities. Translated in a practical guideline, the principle of cohesion recommends creating extremely specialized classes with few methods, which refer to logically related operations. If the logical distance between methods grows, you just create a new class.

Ward Cunningham—a pioneer of Extreme Programming—offers a concise and pragmatic definition of cohesion in his wiki at *http://c2.com/cgi/wiki?CouplingAndCohesion*. He basically says that two modules, A and B, are cohesive when a change to A has no repercussion for B so that both modules can add new value to the system.

There's another quote we'd like to use from Ward Cunningham's wiki to reinforce a concept we expressed a moment ago about cohesion. Cunningham suggests that we define cohesion as inversely proportional to the number of responsibilities a module (for example, a class) has. We definitely like this definition.

> **Important** Strongly related to cohesion is the Single Responsibility Principle (SRP). In the formulation provided by Robert Martin (which you can see at *http://www.objectmentor.com/ resources/articles/srp.pdf*), SRP indicates that each class should always have just one reason to change. In other words, each class should be given a single responsibility, where a responsibility is defined as "a reason to change." A class with multiple responsibilities has more reasons to change and, subsequently, a less cohesive interface. A correct application of SRP entails breaking the methods of a class into logical subsets that configure distinct responsibilities. In the real world, however, this is much harder to do than the opposite—that is, aggregating distinct responsibilities in the same class.

Coupling

Coupling measures the level of dependency existing between two software modules, such as classes, functions, or libraries. An excellent description of coupling comes, again, from Cunningham's wiki at *http://c2.com/cgi/wiki?CouplingAndCohesion*. Two modules, A and B, are said to be coupled when it turns out that you have to make changes to B every time you make any change to A.

In other words, B is not directly and logically involved in the change being made to module A. However, because of the underlying dependency, B is forced to change; otherwise, the code won't compile any longer.

Coupling measurement ranges from low to high and the lowest possible range is preferable.

Low coupling doesn't mean that your modules are to be completely isolated from one another. They are definitely allowed to communicate, but they should do that through a set of well-defined and stable interfaces. Each module should be able to work without intimate knowledge of another module's internal implementation.

Conversely, high coupling hinders testing and reusing code and makes understanding it nontrivial. It is also one of the primary causes of a rigid and fragile design.

Low coupling and high cohesion are strongly correlated. A system designed to achieve low coupling and high cohesion generally meets the requirements of high readability, maintainability, easy testing, and good reuse.

> **Note** Introduced to support a structured design, cohesion and coupling are basic design principles not specifically related to object orientation. However, it's the general scope that also makes them valid and effective in an object-oriented scenario. A good object-oriented design, in fact, is characterized by low coupling and high cohesion, which means that self-contained objects (high cohesion) are interacting with other objects through a stable interface (low coupling).

Separation of Concerns

So you know you need to cook up two key ingredients in your system's recipe. But is there a supermarket where you can get both? How do you achieve high cohesion and low coupling in the design of a software system?

A principle that is helpful to achieving high cohesion and low coupling is separation of concerns (SoC), introduced in 1974 by Edsger W. Dijkstra in his paper "On the Role of Scientific Thought." If you're interested, you can download the full paper from *http://www.cs.utexas.edu/users/EWD/ ewd04xx/EWD447.PDF*.

Identifying the Concerns

SoC is all about breaking the system into distinct and possibly nonoverlapping features. Each feature you want in the system represents a *concern* and an *aspect* of the system. Terms such as feature, concern, and aspect are generally considered synonyms. Concerns are mapped to software modules and, to the extent that it is possible, there's no duplication of functionalities.

SoC suggests that you focus on one particular concern at a time. It doesn't mean, of course, that you ignore all other concerns of the system. More simply, after you've assigned a concern to a software module, you focus on building that module. From the perspective of that module, any other concerns are irrelevant.

Note If you read Dijkstra's original text, you'll see that he uses the expression "separation of concerns" to indicate the general principle, but switches to the word "aspect" to indicate individual concerns that relate to a software system. For quite a few years, the word "aspect" didn't mean anything special to software engineers. Things changed in the late 1990s when *aspect-oriented programming* (AOP) entered the industry. We'll return to AOP later in this chapter, but we make the forward reference here to show Dijkstra's great farsightedness.

Modularity

SoC is concretely achieved through using modular code and making heavy use of *information hiding*.

Modular programming encourages the use of separate modules for each significant feature. Modules are given their own public interface to communicate with other modules and can contain internal chunks of information for private use.

Only members in the public interface are visible to other modules. Internal data is either not exposed or it is encapsulated and exposed in a filtered manner. The implementation of the interface contains the behavior of the module, whose details are not known or accessible to other modules.

Information Hiding

Information hiding (IH) is a general design principle that refers to hiding behind a stable interface some implementation details of a software module that are subject to change. In this way, connected modules continue to see the same fixed interface and are unaffected by changes.

A typical application of the information-hiding principle is the implementation of properties in C# or Microsoft Visual Basic .NET classes. (See the following code sample.) The property name represents the stable interface through which callers refer to an internal value. The class can obtain the value in various ways (for example, from a private field, a control property, a cache, the view state in ASP.NET) and can even change this implementation detail without breaking external code.

```
// Software module where information hiding is applied
public class Customer
{
    // Implementation detail being hidden
    private string _name;

    // Public and stable interface
    public string CustomerName
    {
        // Implementation detail being hidden
        get {return _name;}
    }
}
```

Information hiding is often referred to as *encapsulation*. We like to distinguish between the principle and its practical applications. In the realm of object-oriented programming, encapsulation is definitely an application of IH.

Generally, though, the principle of SoC manifests itself in different ways in different programming paradigms, and so it is for modularity and information hiding.

SoC and Programming Paradigms

The first programming paradigm that historically supported SoC was *Procedural Programming* (PP), which we find expressed in languages such as Pascal and C. In PP, you separate concerns using functions and procedures.

Next—with the advent of object-oriented programming (OOP) in languages such as Java, C++, and more recently C# and Visual Basic .NET—you separate concerns using classes.

However, the concept isn't limited to programming languages. It also transcends the realm of pure programming and is central in many approaches to software architecture. In a service-oriented architecture (SOA), for example, you use services to represent concerns. Layered architectures are based on SoC, and within a middle tier you can use an Object/ Relational Mapping tool (O/RM) to separate persistence from the domain model.

Note In the preceding section, we basically went back over 40 years of computer science, and the entire sector of software engineering. We've seen how PP, OOP, and SOA are all direct or indirect emanations of the SoC principle. (Later in this chapter, we'll see how AOP also fits this principle. In Chapter 7, "The Presentation Layer," we'll see how fundamental design patterns for the presentation layer, such as Model-View-Controller and Model-View-Presenter, also adhere to the SoC principle.)

You really understand the meaning of the word *principle* if you look at how SoC influenced, and still influences, the development of software. And we owe this principle to a great man who passed away in 2002: Edsger W. Dijkstra. We mention this out of respect for this man.

For more information about Dijkstra's contributions to the field, pay a visit to *http://www.cs.utexas .edu/users/ewd*.

Naming Conventions and Code Readability

When the implementation of a line-of-business application is expected to take several months to complete and the final application is expected to remain up and running for a few years, it is quite reasonable to expect that many different people will work on the project over time.

With such significant personnel turnover in sight, you must pay a lot of attention to system characteristics such as readability and maintainability. To ensure that the code base is manageable as well as easily shared and understood, a set of common programming rules and conventions should be used. Applied all the way through, common naming conventions, for example, make the whole code base look like it has been written by a single programmer rather than a very large group of people.

The most popular naming convention is Hungarian Notation (HN). You can read more about it at *http://en.wikipedia.org/wiki/Hungarian_Notation*. Not specifically bound to a programming language, HN became quite popular in the mid-1990s, as it was largely used in many Microsoft Windows applications, especially those written directly against the Windows Software Development Kit (SDK).

HN puts the accent on the type of the variable, and it prefixes the variable name with a mnemonic of the type. For example, *szUserName* would be used for a zero-terminated string that contains a user name, and *iPageCount* would be used for an integer that indicates the number of pages. Created to make each variable self-explanatory, HN lost most of its appeal with the advent of object-oriented languages.

In object-oriented languages, everything is an object, and putting the accent on the value, rather than the type, makes much more sense. So you choose variable names regardless of the type and look only at the value they are expected to contain. The choice of the variable name happens in a purely evocative way. Therefore, valid names are, for example, *customer*, *customerID*, and *lowestPrice*.

Finally, an argument against using HN is that a variable name should be changed every time the type of the variable changes during development. In practice, this is often difficult or overlooked, leading developers to make incorrect assumptions about the values contained within the variables. This often leads directly to bugs.

You can find detailed design guidelines for the .NET Framework classes and applications at *http://msdn.microsoft.com/en-us/library/ms229042.aspx*.

Object-Oriented Design

Before object orientation (OO), any program resulted from the interaction of modules and routines. Programming was procedural, meaning that there was a main stream of code determining the various steps to be accomplished.

OO is a milestone in software design.

OO lets you envision a program as the result of interacting objects, each of which holds its own data and behavior. How would you design a graph of objects to represent your system? Which principles should inspire this design?

We can recognize a set of core principles for object-oriented design (OOD) and a set of more advanced and specific principles that descend from, and further specialize, the core principles.

Basic OOD Principles

To find a broadly accepted definition of OOD, we need to look at the Gang of Four (Erich Gamma, Richard Helm, Ralph Johnson, and John Vlissides) and their landmark book *Design Patterns: Elements of Reusable Object-Oriented Software*, (Addison-Wesley, 1994). (We'll make further references to this book as GoF, which is the universal acronym for "Gang of Four.")

The entire gist of OOD is contained in this sentence:

> *You must find pertinent objects, factor them into classes at the right granularity, define class interfaces and inheritance hierarchies, and establish key relationships among them.*

In GoF, we also find another excerpt that is particularly significant:

> *Your design should be specific to the problem at hand but also general enough to address future problems and requirements.*

Wouldn't you agree that this last sentence is similar to some of the guidelines resulting from the ISO/IEC 9126 standard that we covered in Chapter 1? Its obvious similarity to that standard cannot be denied, and it is not surprising at all.

The basics of OOD can be summarized in three points: find pertinent objects, favor low coupling, and favor code reuse.

Find Pertinent Objects First

The first key step in OOD is creating a crisp and flexible abstraction of the problem's domain. To successfully do so, you should think about things instead of processes. You should focus on the *whats* instead of the *hows*. You should stop thinking about algorithms to focus mostly on interacting entities. Interacting entities are your pertinent objects.

Where do you find them?

Requirements offer the raw material that must be worked out and shaped into a hierarchy of pertinent objects. The descriptions of the use cases you receive from the team of analysts provide the foundation for the design of classes. Here's a sample use case you might get from an analyst:

> To view all **orders** placed by a **customer**, the **user** indicates the **customer ID**. The program displays an error message if the customer does not exist. If the customer exists, the program displays **name**, **address**, **date of birth**, and all outstanding **orders**. For each order, the program gets **ID**, **date**, and all **order items**.

A common practice for finding pertinent objects is tagging all nouns and verbs in the various use cases. Nouns originate classes or properties, whereas verbs indicate methods on classes. Our sample use case suggests the definition of classes such as *User*, *Customer*, *Order*, and *OrderItem*. The class *Customer* will have properties such as *Name*, *Address*, and *DateOfBirth*. Methods on the class *Customer* might be *LoadOrderItems*, *GetCustomerByID*, and *LoadOrders*.

Note that finding pertinent objects is only the first step. As recommended in the statement that many consider to be the emblem of OOD, you then have to factor pertinent objects into classes and determine the right level of granularity and assign responsibilities.

In doing so, two principles of OOD apply, and they are listed in the introduction of GoF.

Favor Low Coupling

In an OO design, objects need to interact and communicate. For this reason, each object exposes its own public interface for others to call. So suppose you have a logger object with a method *Log* that tracks any code activity to, say, a database. And suppose also that another object at some point needs to log something. Simply enough, the caller creates an instance of the logger and proceeds. Overall, it's easy and effective. Here's some code to illustrate the point:

```
class MyComponent
{
  void DoSomeWork()
  {
    // Get an instance of the logger
    Logger logger = new Logger();

    // Get data to log
    string data = GetData();

    // Log
    logger.Log(data);
  }
}
```

The class *MyComponent* is tightly coupled to the class *Logger* and its implementation. The class *MyComponent* is broken if *Logger* is broken and, more importantly, you can't use another type of logger.

You get a real design benefit if you can separate the interface from the implementation.

What kind of functionality do you really need from such a logger component? You essentially need the ability to log; where and how is an implementation detail. So you might want to define an *ILogger* interface, as shown next, and extract it from the *Logger* class:

```
interface ILogger
{
    void Log(string data);
}

class Logger : ILogger
{
    :
}
```

At this point, you use an intermediate factory object to return the logger to be used within the component:

```
class MyComponent
{
  void DoSomeWork()
  {
    // Get an instance of the logger
    ILogger logger = Helpers.GetLogger();
```

```
    // Get data to log
    string data = GetData();

    // Log
    logger.Log(data);
  }
}

class Helpers
{
  public static ILogger GetLogger()
  {
    // Here, use any sophisticated logic you like
    // to determine the right logger to instantiate.

    ILogger logger = null;
    if (UseDatabaseLogger)
    {
        logger = new DatabaseLogger();
    }
    else
    {
        logger = new FileLogger();
    }
    return logger;
  }
}
class FileLogger : ILogger
{
    :
    :
}

class DatabaseLogger : ILogger
{
    :
    :
}
```

The factory code gets you an instance of the logger for the component to use. The factory returns an object that implements the *ILogger* interface, and the component consumes any object that implements the contracted interface.

The dependency between the component and the logger is now based on an interface rather than an implementation.

If you base class dependencies on interfaces, you minimize coupling between classes to the smallest possible set of functions—those defined in the interface. In doing so, you just applied the first principle of OOD as outlined in GoF:

> *Program to an interface, not an implementation.*

This approach to design is highly recommended for using with the parts of your code that are most likely to undergo changes in their implementation.

Note Should you use an interface? Or should you perhaps opt for an abstract base class? In object-oriented languages that do not support multiple inheritance—such as Java, C#, and Visual Basic .NET—an interface is always preferable because it leaves room for another base class of your choice. When you have multiple inheritance, it is mostly a matter of preference. You should consider using a base class in .NET languages in all cases where you need more than just an interface. If you need some hard-coded behavior along with an interface, a base class is the only option you have. ASP.NET providers, for example, are based on base classes and not on interfaces.

An interesting possibility beyond base classes and interfaces are mixins, but they are an OOP feature not supported by .NET languages. A mixin is a class that provides a certain functionality that other classes can inherit, but it is not meant to be a standalone class. Put another way, a mixin is like an interface where some of the members might contain a predefined implementation. Mixins are supported in some dynamic languages, including Python and Ruby. No .NET languages currently support mixins, but mixins can be simulated using ad hoc frameworks such as Castle. DynamicProxy. With this framework, you first define a class that contains all the methods you want to inject in an existing class—the mixin. Next, you use the framework to create a proxy for a given class that contains the injected methods. Castle.DynamicProxy uses *Reflection.Emit* internally to do the trick.

Real-World Example: *IButtonControl* in ASP.NET

In ASP.NET 1.*x*, there was no support for cross-page postbacks. Every time the user clicked a button, he could only post to the same page. Starting with ASP.NET 2.0, buttons (and only buttons) were given the ability to trigger the post of the current form to an external page.

To support this feature, the *Page* class needs to know whether the control that caused the postback is a button or not. How many types of buttons do you know? There's the *Button* class, but also *LinkButton* and finally *ImageButton*. Up until ASP.NET 2.0, these classes had very little in common—just a few properties, but nothing that could be officially perceived as a contract or a formal link.

Having the *Page* class check against the three types before posting would have limited the extensibility of the framework: only those three types of control would have ever been able to make a cross-page post.

The ASP.NET team extracted the core behavior of a button to the *IButtonControl* interface and implemented that interface in all button classes. Next, they instructed the *Page* class to check the interface to verify the suitability of a posting control to make a cross-page post.

In this way, you can write custom controls that implement the interface and still add the ability to make your own cross-page posts.

Favor Code Reuse

Reusability is a fundamental aspect of the object-oriented paradigm and one of the keys to its success and wide adoption. You create a class one day, and you're happy with that. Next, on another day, you inherit a new class, make some changes here and there, and come up with a slightly different version of the original class.

Is this what code reuse is all about? Well, there's more to consider.

With class inheritance, the derived class doesn't simply inherit the code of the parent class. It really inherits the context and, subsequently, it gains some visibility of the parent's state. Is this a problem?

For one thing, a derived class that uses the context it inherits from the parent can be broken by future changes to the parent class.

In addition, when you inherit from a class, you enter into a polymorphic context, meaning that your derived class can be used in any scenarios where the parent is accepted. It's not guaranteed, however, that the two classes can really be used interchangeably. What if the derived class includes changes that alter the parent's context to the point of breaking the contract between the caller and its expected (base) class? (Providing the guarantee that parent and derived classes can be used interchangeably is the goal of Liskov's principle, which we'll discuss later.)

In GoF, the authors recognize two routes to reusability—white-box and black-box reusability. The former is based on class inheritance and lends itself to the objections we just mentioned. The latter is based on *object composition*.

Object composition entails creating a new type that holds an instance of the base type and typically references it through a private member:

```
public CompositeClass
{
  private MyClass theObject;

  public CompositeClass()
  {
    // You can use any lazy-loading policy you want for instantiation.
    // No lazy loading is being used here ...
    theObject = new MyClass();
  }

  public object DoWork()
  {
    object data = theObject.DoSomeWork();

    // Do some other work
    return Process(data);
  }
```

```
    private object Process(object data)
    {
        :
    }
}
```

In this case, you have a wrapper class that uses a type as a black box and does so through a well-defined contract. The wrapper class has no access to internal members and cannot change the behavior in any way—it uses the object as it is rather than changing it to do its will. External calls reach the wrapper class, and the wrapper class delegates the call internally to the held instance of the class it enhances. (See Figure 3-2.)

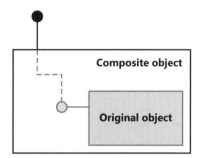

FIGURE 3-2 Object composition and delegation

When you create such a wrapper object, you basically apply the second principle of OOD:

> *Favor object composition over class inheritance.*

Does all this mean that classic class inheritance is entirely wrong and should be avoided like the plague? Using class inheritance is generally fine when all you do is add new functions to the base class or when you entirely unplug and replace an existing functionality. However, you should never lose track of the Liskov principle. (We'll get to the details of the Liskov principle in a moment.)

In many cases, and especially in real-world scenarios, object composition is a safer practice that also simplifies maintenance and testing. With composition, changes to the composite object don't affect the internal object. Likewise, changes to the internal object don't affect the outermost container as long as there are no changes to the public interface.

By combining the two principles of OOD, you can refer to the original object through an interface, thus further limiting the dependency between composite and internal objects. Composition doesn't provide polymorphism even if it will provide functionality. If polymorphism is key for you, you should opt for a white-box form of reusability. However, keep the Liskov principle clearly in mind.

> **Note** In addition to composition, another approach is frequently used to contrast class inheritance—*aggregation*. Both aggregation and composition refer to a *has-a* relationship between two classes, whereas inheritance implies an *is-a* relationship. The difference between composition and aggregation is that with composition you have a static link between the container and contained classes. If you dispose of the container, the contained classes are also disposed of. With aggregation, the link is weaker and the container is simply associated with an external class. As a result, when the container is disposed of, the child class blissfully survives.

Advanced Principles

You cannot go to a potential customer and sing the praises of your software by mentioning that it is modular, well designed, and easy to read and maintain. These are internal characteristics of the software that do not affect the user in any way. More likely, you'll say that your software is correct, bug free, fast, easy to use, and perhaps extensible. However, you can hardly write correct, bug-free, easy-to-use, and extensible software without paying a lot of attention to the internal design.

Basic principles such as low coupling, high cohesion (along with the single responsibility principle), separation of concerns, plus the first two principles of OOD give us enough guidance about how to design a software application. As you might have noticed, all these principles are rather old (but certainly not outdated), as they were devised and formulated at least 15 years ago.

In more recent years, some of these principles have been further refined and enhanced to address more specific aspects of the design. We like to list three more advanced design principles that, if properly applied, will certainly make your code easier to read, test, extend, and maintain.

The Open/Closed Principle

We owe the Open/Closed Principle (OCP) to Bertrand Meyer. The principle addresses the need of creating software entities (whether classes, modules, or functions) that can happily survive changes. In the current version of the fictional product "This World," the continuous changes to software requirements are a well-known bug. Unfortunately, although the team is working to eliminate the bug in the next release, we still have to face reality and deal with frequent changes of requirements the best we can.

Essentially, we need to have a mechanism that allows us to enter changes where required without breaking existing code that works. The OCP addresses exactly this issue by saying the following:

> *A module should be open for extension but closed for modification.*

Applied to OOD, the principle recommends that we never edit the source code of a class that works in order to implement a change. In other words, each class should be conceived to be stable and immutable and never face change—the class is closed for modification.

How can we enter changes, then?

Every time a change is required, you enhance the behavior of the class by adding new code and never touching the old code that works. In practical terms, this means either using composition or perhaps safe-and-clean class inheritance. Note that OCP just reinforces the point that we made earlier about the second principle of OOD: if you use class inheritance, you add only new code and do not modify any part of the inherited context.

Today, the most common way to comply with the OCP is by implementing a fixed interface in any classes that we figure are subject to changes. Callers will then work against the interface as in the first principle of OOD. The interface is then closed for modification. But you can make callers interact with any class that, at a minimum, implements that interface. So the overall model is open for extension, but it still provides a fixed interface to dependent objects.

Liskov's Substitution Principle

When a new class is derived from an existing one, the derived class can be used in any place where the parent class is accepted. This is polymorphism, isn't it? Well, the Liskov Substitution Principle (LSP) restates that this is the way you should design your code. The principle says the following:

> *Subclasses should be substitutable for their base classes.*

Apparently, you get this free of charge from just using an object-oriented language. If you think so, have a look at the next example:

```
public class ProgrammerToy
{
    private int _state = 0;

    public virtual void SetState(int state)
    {
        _state = state;
    }

    public int GetState()
    {
        return _state;
    }
}
```

The class *ProgrammerToy* just acts as a wrapper for an integer value that callers can read and write through a pair of public methods. Here's a typical code snippet that shows how to use it:

```
static void DoSomeWork(ProgrammerToy toy)
{
    int magicNumber = 5;
    toy.SetState(magicNumber);
    Console.WriteLine(toy.GetState());
    Console.ReadLine();
}
```

The caller receives an instance of the *ProgrammerToy* class, does some work with it, and then displays any results. So far, so good. Let's now consider a derived class:

```
public class CustomProgrammerToy : ProgrammerToy
{
    public override void SetState(int state)
    {
        // It inherits the context of the parent but lacks the tools
        // to fully access it. In particular, it has no way to access
        // the private member _state.
        // As a result, this class MAY NOT be able to
        // honor the contract of its parent class. Whether or not, mostly
        // depends on your intentions and expected goals for the overridden
        // SetState method. In any case, you CAN'T access directly the private member
        // _state from within this override of SetState.

        // (In .NET, you can use reflection to access a private member,
        // but that's a sort of a trick.)
        :
        :
    }
}
```

From a syntax point of view, *ProgrammerToy* and *CustomProgrammerToy* are just the same and method *DoSomeWork* will accept both and successfully compile.

From a behavior point of view, though, they are quite different. In fact, when *CustomProgrammerToy* is used, the output is 0 instead of 5. This is because of the override made on the *SetState* method.

This is purely an example, but it calls your attention to Liskov's Principle. It *doesn't* go without saying that derived classes (subclasses) can safely replace their base classes. You have to ensure that. How?

You should handle keywords such as *sealed* and *virtual* with extreme care. Virtual (overridable) methods, for example, should never gain access to private members. Access to private members can't be replicated by overrides, which makes base and derived classes not semantically equivalent from the perspective of a caller. You should plan ahead of time which members are private and which are protected. Members consumed by virtual methods must be protected, not private.

Generally, virtual methods of a derived class should work out of the same preconditions of corresponding parent methods. They also must guarantee at least the same postconditions.

Classes that fail to comply with LSP don't just break polymorphism but also induce violations of OCP on callers.

> **Note** OCP and LSP are closely related. Any function using a class that violates Liskov's Principle violates the Open/Close Principle. Let's reference the preceding example again. The method *DoSomeWork* uses a hierarchy of classes (*ProgrammerToy* and *CustomProgrammerToy*) that violate LSP. This means that to work properly *DoSomeWork* must be aware of which type it really receives. Subsequently, it has to be modified each time a new class is derived from *ProgrammerToy*. In other words, the method *DoSomeWork* is not closed for modification.

The Dependency Inversion Principle

When you create the code for a class, you represent a behavior through a set of methods. Each method is expected to perform a number of actions. As you specify these actions, you proceed in a top-down way, going from high-level abstractions down the stack to more and more precise and specific functions.

As an illustration, imagine a class, perhaps encapsulated in a service, that is expected to return stock quotes as a chunk of HTML markup:

```
public class FinanceInfoService
{
  public string GetQuotesAsHtml(string symbols)
  {
    // Get the Finder component
    IFinder finder = ResolveFinder();
    if (finder == null)
      throw new NullReferenceException("Invalid finder.");

    // Grab raw data
    StockInfo[] stocks = finder.FindQuoteInfo(symbols);

    // Get the Renderer component
    IRenderer renderer = ResolveRenderer();
    if (renderer == null)
        throw new NullReferenceException("Invalid renderer.");

    // Render raw data out to HTML
    return renderer.RenderQuoteInfo(stocks);
  }
    ⋮
}
```

The method *GetQuotesAsHtml* is expected to first grab raw data and then massage it into an HTML string. You recognize two functionalities in the method: the finder and the renderer. In a top-down approach, you are interested in recognizing these functionalities, but you don't need to specify details for these components in the first place. All that you need to do is hide details behind a stable interface.

The method *GetQuotesAsHtml* works regardless of the implementation of the finder and renderer components and is not dependent on them. (See Figure 3-3.) On the other hand, your purpose is to reuse the high-level module, not low-level components.

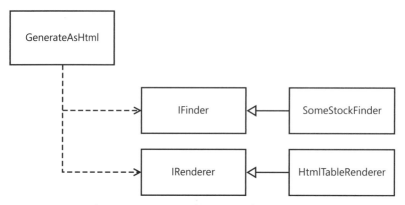

FIGURE 3-3 Lower layers are represented by an interface

When you get to this, you're in full compliance with the Dependency Inversion Principle (DIP), which states the following:

> *High-level modules should not depend upon low-level modules. Both should depend upon abstractions. Abstractions should not depend upon details. Details should depend upon abstractions.*

The *inversion* in the name of the principle refers to the fact that you proceed in a top-down manner during the implementation and focus on the work flow in high-level modules rather than focusing on the implementation of lower level modules. At this point, lower level modules can be injected directly into the high-level module. Here's an alternative implementation for a DIP-based module:

```
public class FinanceInfoService
{
  // Inject dependencies through the constructor. References to such external components
  // are resolved outside this module, for example by using an inversion-of-control
  // framework (more later).
  IFinder _finder = null;
  IRenderer _renderer = null;

  public FinanceInfoService(IFinder finder, IRenderer renderer)
  {
    _finder = finder;
    _renderer = renderer;
  }

  public string GetQuotesAsHtml(string symbols)
  {
    // Get the Finder component
    if (_finder == null)
      throw new NullReferenceException("Invalid finder.");
```

```
  // Grab raw data
  StockInfo[] stocks = _finder.FindQuoteInfo(symbols);

  // Get the Renderer component
  if (_renderer == null)
    throw new NullReferenceException("Invalid renderer.");

  // Render raw data out to HTML
  return _renderer.RenderQuoteInfo(stocks);
}

   ⋮
}
```

In this case, the lower level modules are injected through the constructor of the DIP-based class.

The DIP has been formalized by Robert Martin. You can read more about it at *http://www.objectmentor.com/resources/articles/dip.pdf.*

> **Important** In literature, the DIP is often referred to as *inversion of control* (IoC). In this book, we use the DIP formulation by Robert Martin to indicate the principle of dependency inversion and consider IoC as a pattern. In this regard, IoC and dependency injection are, for us, synonyms. The terminology, however, is much less important than the recognition that there's a principle about inversion of control and a practical pattern. We'll return on this in a moment with a more detailed explanation of our perspective.

From Principles to Patterns

It is guaranteed that by fulfilling all the OOD principles just discussed, you can craft a good design that matches requirements and is maintainable and extensible. A seasoned development team, though, will not be limited to applying effective design principles over and over again; members of the team, in fact, will certainly draw from the well of their experience any solutions for similar problems that worked in the past.

Such building blocks are nothing more than hints and the skeleton of a solution. However, these very same building blocks can become more refined day after day and are generalized after each usage to become applicable to a wider range of problems and scenarios. Such building blocks might not provide a direct solution, but they usually help you to find your (right) way. And using them is usually more effective and faster than starting from scratch.

By the way, these building blocks are known as *patterns*.

What's a Pattern, Anyway?

The word *pattern* is one of those overloaded terms that morphed from its common usage to assume a very specific meaning in computer science. According to the dictionary, a pattern is a template or model that can be used to generate things—any things. In computer science, we use patterns in design solutions at two levels: implementation and architecture.

At the highest level, two main families of software patterns are recognized: *design patterns* and *architectural patterns*. You look at design patterns when you dive into the implementation and design of the code. You look at architectural patterns when you fly high looking for the overall design of the system.

Let's start with design patterns.

> **Note** A third family of software patterns is also worth a mention—*refactoring patterns*. You look at these patterns only when you're engaged in a refactoring process. Refactoring is the process of changing your source code to make it simpler, more efficient, and more readable while preserving the original functionality. Examples of refactoring patterns are "Extract Interface" and "Encapsulate Field." Some of these refactoring patterns have been integrated into Visual Studio 2008 on the Refactor menu. You find even more patterns in ad hoc tools such as Resharper. (For more information, see *http://www.jetbrains.com/resharper*.)
>
> A good book to read to learn about refactoring patterns is *Refactoring to Patterns* by Joshua Kerievsky (Addison-Wesley, 2004).

Design Patterns

We software professionals owe design patterns to an architect—a *real* architect, not a software architect. In the late 1970s, Christopher Alexander developed a pattern language with the purpose of letting individuals express their innate sense of design through a sort of informal grammar. From his work, here's the definition of a pattern:

> *Each pattern describes a problem which occurs over and over again in our environment, and then describes the core solution to that problem, in such a way that you can use the solution a million times over, without ever doing it the same way twice.*

Nicely enough, although the definition was not written with software development in mind, it applies perfectly to that. So what's a design pattern?

A design pattern is a known and well-established *core* solution applicable to a family of concrete problems that might show up during implementation. A design pattern is a core solution and, as such, it might need adaptation to a specific context. This feature becomes a major strength when you consider that, in this way, the same pattern can be applied many times in many slightly different scenarios.

Design patterns are not created in a lab; quite the reverse. They originate from the real world and from the direct experience of developers and architects. You can think of a design pattern as a package that includes the description of a problem, a list of actors participating in the problem, and a practical solution.

The primary reference for design patterns is GoF. Another excellent reference we want to recommend is *Pattern-Oriented Software Architecture* by Frank Buschmann, et al. (Wiley, 1996).

How to Work with Design Patterns

Here is a list of what design patterns are *not*:

- Design patterns are not the verb and should never be interpreted dogmatically.

- Design patterns are not Superman and will never magically pop up to save a project in trouble.

- Design patterns are neither the dark nor the light side of the Force. They might be with you, but they won't provide you with any special extra power.

Design patterns are just helpful, and that should be enough.

You don't choose a design pattern; the most appropriate design pattern normally emerges out of your refactoring steps. We could say that the pattern is buried under your classes, but digging it out is entirely up to you.

The wrong way to deal with design patterns is by going through a list of patterns and matching them to the problem. Instead, it works the other way around. You have a problem and you have to match the problem to the pattern. How can you do that? It's quite simple to explain, but it's not so easy to apply.

You have to understand the problem and generalize it.

If you can take the problem back to its roots, and get the gist of it, you'll probably find a tailor-made pattern just waiting for you. Why is this so? Well, if you really reached the root of the problem, chances are that someone else did the same in the past 15 years (the period during which design patterns became more widely used). So the solution is probably just there for you to read and apply.

This observation prompts us to mention the way in which all members of our teams use books on design patterns. (By the way, there are always plenty of such books scattered throughout the office.) Design patterns books are an essential tool. But we never *read* such books. We *use* them, instead, like cookbooks.

What we normally do is stop reading after the first few pages precisely where most books list the patterns they cover in detail inside. Next, we put the book aside and possibly within reach. Whenever we encounter a problem, we try to generalize it, and then we flip through the pages of the book to find a pattern that possibly matches it. We find one much more often than not. And if we don't, we repeat the process in an attempt to come to a better generalization of the problem.

When we've found the pattern, we start working on its adaptation to our context. This often requires refactoring of the code which, in turn, might lead to a more appropriate pattern. And the loop goes on.

> **Note** If you're looking for an online quick reference about design patterns, you should look at *http://www.dofactory.com*. Among other things, the site offers .NET-specific views of most popular design patterns.

Where's the Value in Patterns, Exactly?

Many people would agree in principle that there's plenty of value in design patterns. Fewer people, though, would be able to indicate what the value is and where it can be found.

Using design patterns, per se, doesn't make your solution more valuable. What really matters, at the end of the day, is whether or not your solution works and meets requirements.

Armed with requirements and design principles, you are up to the task of solving a problem. On your way to the solution, though, a systematic application of design principles to the problem sooner or later takes you into the immediate neighborhood of a known design pattern. That's a certainty because, ultimately, patterns are solutions that others have already found and catalogued.

At that point, you have a solution with some structural likeness to a known design pattern. It is up to you, then, to determine whether an explicit refactoring to that pattern will bring some added value to the solution. Basically, you have to decide whether or not the known pattern you've found represents a further, and desirable, refinement of your current solution. Don't worry if your solution doesn't match a pattern. It means that you have a solution that works and you're happy with that. You're just fine. You never want to change a winning solution!

In summary, patterns might be an *end* when you refactor according to them, and they might be a *means* when you face a problem that is clearly resolved by a particular pattern. Patterns are not an added value for your solution, but they are valuable for you as an architect or a developer looking for a solution.

Applied Design Patterns

We said a lot about design patterns, but we haven't shown a single line of code or a concrete example. Patterns are everywhere, even if you don't realize it. As we'll see in a moment, sometimes patterns are buried in the language syntax—in which case, we'll call them *idioms*.

Have you ever needed to use a global object (or a few global objects) to serve all requests to a given class? If you have, you used the Singleton pattern. The Singleton pattern is described as a way to ensure that a class has only one instance for which a global point of access is required. Here's an example:

```
public class Helpers
{
  public static Helpers DefaultInstance = new Helpers();

  protected Helpers() {}

  public void DoWork()
  {
    :
  }

  public void DoMoreWork()
  {
    :
  }
}
```

In a consumer class, you take advantage of *Helpers* through the following syntax:

```
Helpers.DefaultInstance.DoWork();
```

Swarms of Visual Basic 6 developers have used the Singleton pattern for years probably without ever realizing it. The Singleton pattern is behind the default instance of Visual Basic 6 forms, as shown here:

```
Form1.Show()
```

The preceding code in Visual Basic 6 invokes the *Show* method on the default instance of the type *Form1*. In the source, there's no explicit mention of the default instance only because of the tricks played by the Visual Basic runtime.

> **Tip** Admittedly, the Singleton pattern on a class is similar to defining the same class with only static methods. Is there any difference?
>
> With a Singleton pattern, you can actually control the number of instances because you're not actually limited to just one instance. In addition, you can derive a new (meaningful) class because the Singleton pattern has some instance-level behavior and is not a mere collection of static functions. Finally, you have more freedom to control the creation of the actual instance. For example, you can add a static method, say, *GetInstance*, instead of the static field and add there any logic for the factory.

Another interesting pattern to briefly mention is the Strategy pattern. The pattern identifies a particular functionality that a class needs and can be hot-plugged into the class. The functionality is abstracted to an interface or a base class, and the Strategy-enabled class uses it through the abstraction, as shown here:

```
public class MyService
{
  // This is the replaceable strategy
  ILogger _logger;

  public MyService(ILogger logger)
  {
    this._logger = logger;
  }

  public void DoWork()
  {
    this._logger.Log("Begin method ...");
    :
    this._logger.Log("End method ...");
  }
}
```

The Strategy pattern is the canonical example used to illustrate the power of composition. The class *MyService* in the example benefits from the services of a logger component, but it depends only on an abstraction of it. The external logger component can be changed with ease and without risking breaking changes. Moreover, you can even change the component (for example, the strategy) on the fly. Try getting the same flexibility in a scenario where the implementation of the strategy object is hard-coded in the *MyService* class and you have to inherit a new class to change strategy. It's just impossible to change strategy in that case without recompilation and redeployment.

Architectural Patterns

Architectural patterns capture key elements of software architecture and offer support for making hard-to-change decisions about the structure of the system. As we saw in Chapter 1, software architecture is mostly about decisions regarding design points that, unlike code design, are not subject to refactoring.

Architectural patterns are selected and applied very early in the course of design, and they influence various quality characteristics of the system, such as performance, security, maintenance, and extensibility.

Examples of architectural patterns are Layers and SOA for modeling the application structure, Model-View-Controller for the presentation, Domain Model and Service Layer for the business logic, and Peer-to-Peer for the network topology.

Antipatterns

In physics, we have matter and antimatter. Just as matter is made of particles, antimatter is made of antiparticles. An antiparticle is identical to a particle except for the charge—positive in the particles of normal matter, and negative in an element of antimatter.

Likewise, in software we have patterns made of solutions, and antipatterns made of antisolutions. What's the difference? It is all in the "charge" of the solution. Patterns drive us to good solutions, whereas antipatterns drive us to bad solutions. The clearest definition for antipatterns we could find comes (again) from Ward Cunningham's wiki, at *http://c2.com/cgi/wiki?AntiPattern*:

> *An anti-pattern is a pattern that tells how to go from a problem to a bad solution.*

Put this way, one could reasonably wonder why antipatterns are worth the effort of defining them. For matter and antimatter, it's all about the thirst for knowledge. But developers and architects are usually more pragmatic and they tend to prefer knowledge with a practical application to their everyday work. What's the link that relates antipatterns to the real-world of software development?

The keystone of antipatterns is that they might, at first, look like good ideas that can add new power and effectiveness to your classes. An antipattern, though, is devious and insidious and adds more trouble than it removes. From Cunningham's wiki again:

> *In the old days, we used to just call these* bad ideas. *The new name is much more diplomatic.*

Designers and antipatterns, in some way, attract each other, but the experienced designer recognizes and avoids antipatterns. (This is definitely a characteristic that marks the difference between expert and nonexpert designers.) Because of the fatal attraction designers generally have toward antipatterns, a catalog of antipatterns is as valuable as a catalog of good design patterns.

A long list of antipatterns can be found at *http://c2.com/cgi/wiki?AntiPatternsCatalog* and also at *http://en.wikipedia.org/wiki/anti-pattern*. We like to briefly address a couple of them—one relates to architecture and the other relates to development.

The *Architecture-As-Requirements* antipattern refers to situations where a prominent and influential member of the design team has a pet technology or product and absolutely wants to use it in the project—even when there is no clear evidence of its usefulness and applicability in the customer's context.

The *Test-By-Release* antipattern refers to releasing a software product without paying much attention to all those boring and time-consuming chores related to unit and integration testing. Are users the final recipients of the product? Great, let's give them the last word on whether the software works or not.

Patterns vs. Idioms

Software patterns indicate well-established solutions to recurring design problems. This means that developers end up coding their way to a given solution over and over again. And they might be repeatedly writing the same boilerplate code in a given programming language.

Sometimes specific features of a given programming language can help significantly in quickly and elegantly solving a recurring problem. That specific set of features is referred to as an *idiom*.

What's an Idiom, Anyway?

An *idiom* is a pattern hard-coded in a programming language or implemented out of the box in a framework or technology.

Like a design pattern, an idiom represents a solution to a recurring problem. However, in the case of idioms, the solution to the problem doesn't come through design techniques but merely by using the features of the programming language. Whereas a design pattern focuses on the object-oriented paradigm, an idiom focuses on the technology of the programming language.

An idiom is a way to take advantage of the language capabilities and obtain a desired behavior from the code. In general, an idiom refers to a very specific, common, and eye-catching piece of code that accomplishes a given operation—as simple as adding to a counter or as complex as the implementation of a design pattern.

In C#, for example, the ++ operator can be considered a programming idiom for the recurring task of *adding to a counter variable*. The same can be said for the *as* keyword when it comes to *casting to a type and defaulting to null in case of failure*.

Let's see some more examples of programming idioms in C#.

Sample Idioms

Events are the canonical example of a programming idiom. Behind events, you find the Observer pattern. The pattern refers to a class that has the ability to notify registered observers of some internal states. Whenever a particular state is reached, the class loops through the list of registered observers and notifies each observer of the event. It does that using a contracted observer interface.

In languages such as C# or Visual Basic .NET that support event-driven programming, you find this pattern natively implemented and exposed through keywords. Consider the following code:

```
Button1.Click += new EventHandler(Button1_Click);
```

When it runs, a new "observer for the *Click* event" is added to the list maintained by object *Button1*. The observer in this case is a *delegate*—a special class wrapping a class method.

The interface through which observer and object communicate is the signature of the method wrapped by the delegate.

Similarly, the *foreach* keyword in C# (and *For…Each* in Visual Basic .NET) is a hard-coded version of the Iterator pattern. An iterator object accomplishes two main tasks: it retrieves a particular element within a collection and jumps to the next element. This is exactly what happens under the hood of the following code:

```
foreach(Customer customer in dataContext.Customers)
{
    // The variable customer references the current element in the collection.
    // Moving to the next element is implicit.
}
```

Finally, the most recent versions of C# and Visual Basic .NET—those shipping with the .NET Framework 3.5—also support a set of contextual keywords for Language Integrated Query (LINQ): *from, select, in, orderby.* When you apply the set of LINQ keywords to a database-oriented object model, you have LINQ-to-SQL. With LINQ-to-SQL, you ultimately use language keywords to query the content of a database. In other words, you programmatically define an object that represents a query and run it. This behavior is described by the Query Object pattern. And LINQ-to-SQL is a programming idiom for the pattern.

Idiomatic Design

We spent a lot of time pondering OOD principles and showing their benefits and applicability. We did it by reasoning in a general context and looking at the OO paradigm rather than by examining the concrete technology and platform. General principles are always valid and should always be given due consideration.

However, when you step inside the design, at some point you meet the technology. When this happens, you might need to review the way you apply principles in the context of the specific technology or platform you're using. This is called *idiomatic design.*

As far as the .NET Framework is concerned, a set of idiomatic design rules exists under the name of Framework Design Guidelines. You can access them online from the following URL: *http://msdn.microsoft.com/en-us/library/ms229042.aspx.*

 Note *Framework Design Guidelines* is also the title of a book written by Krzysztof Cwalina and Brad Abrams from Microsoft (Addison-Wesley, 2008). Cwalina's blog is also an excellent source for tidbits and more details on guidelines. We definitely recommend it. The blog is *http://blogs.msdn.com/kcwalina.*

As an example, let's go through a couple of these guidelines.

Idiomatic Design: Structures or Classes?

When defining a type in a C# .NET application, should you use *struct* or *class*? To start out, a *struct* is not inheritable. So if you need to derive new classes from the type, you must opt for a class rather than a structure. This said, a class is a reference type and is allocated on the heap. Memorywise, a reference type is managed by the garbage collector. Conversely, a *struct* is a value type; it is allocated on the stack and deallocated when it goes out of scope. Value types are generally less expensive than reference types to work with, but not when boxing is required. In the .NET Framework, *boxing* is the task of storing a value type in an object reference so that it can be used wherever an object is accepted. As an example, consider the *ArrayList* class. When you add, say, an *Int32* (or a *struct*) to an *ArrayList*, the value is automatically boxed to an object. Done all the time, this extra work might change the balance between class and *struct*. Hence, the need of an official guideline on the theme shows up.

The guideline suggests that you always use a class unless the footprint of the type is below 16 bytes and the type is immutable. A type is immutable if the state of its instances never changes after they've been created. (The *System.String* type in the .NET Framework is immutable because a new string is created after each modification.) However, if the *struct* is going to be boxed frequently you might want to consider using a class anyway. (If you're looking for the list of differences between *struct*s and classes go here: *http://msdn.microsoft.com/en-us/library/saxz13w4.aspx*.)

Idiomatic Design: Do Not Use *List<T>* in Public Signatures

Another guideline we want to point out has to do with the *List<T>* type. Their use in the signature of public members is not recommended, as you can see in this blog post: *http://blogs.gotdotnet.com/kcwalina/archive/2005/09/26/474010.aspx*.

Why is this so?

One of the reasons behind the guideline is that *List<T>* is a rather bloated type with many members that are not relevant in many scenarios. This means that *List<T>* has low cohesion and to some extent violates the Single Responsibility Principle.

Another reason for not using *List<T>* in public signatures is that the class is unsealed, yes, but not specifically designed to be extended. This doesn't mean, though, that the class is not LSP-safe. If you look at the source of the class, you can see that using *List<T>* is absolutely safe in any polymorphic context. The issue is that the class has no protected and virtual methods for inheritors to do something significant that alters the behavior of the class while preserving the core interface. The class is just not designed to be extended.

It is therefore recommended that you use *IList<T>*, or derived interfaces, in public signatures. Alternatively, use custom classes that directly implement *IList<T>*.

Dependency Injection

As a design principle, DIP states that higher level modules should depend on abstractions rather than on the concrete implementation of functionalities. *Inversion of control* (IoC) is an application of DIP that refers to situations where generic code controls the execution of more specific and external components.

In an IoC solution, you typically have a method whose code is filled with one or more stubs. The functionality of each stub is provided (statically or dynamically) by external components invoked through an abstract interface. Replacing any external components doesn't affect the high-level method, as long as LSP and OCP are fulfilled. External components and the high-level method can be developed independently.

A real-world example of IoC is Windows shell extensions. Whenever the user right-clicks and selects Properties, Windows Explorer prepares a standard dialog box and then does a bit of IoC. It looks up the registry and finds out whether custom property page extensions have been registered. If any are registered, it talks to these extensions through a contracted interface and adds pages to the user dialog box.

Another real-world example of IoC is event-driven programming as originally offered by Visual Basic and now supported by Windows Forms and Web Forms. By writing a *Button1_Click* method and attaching it to the *Click* event of, say, the *Button1* control, you essentially instruct the (reusable and generic) code of the *Button* class to call back your *Button1_Click* method any time the user clicks.

What is dependency injection (DI), then?

From DIP to Inversion of Control

For the purpose of this discussion, IoC and DI are synonyms. They are not always considered synonyms in literature, as sometimes you find IoC to be the principle and DI the application of the principle—namely, the pattern. In reality, IoC is historically a pattern based on DIP. The term *dependency injection* was coined by Martin Fowler later, as a way to further specialize the concept of inversion of control.

IoC/DI remains essentially a pattern that works by letting you pass high-level method references to helper components. This injection can happen in three ways. One way is via the constructor of the class to which the method belongs. We did just this in the implementation of the *FinanceInfoService* class. Another way consists of defining a method or a setter property on the class to which the method belongs. Finally, the class can implement an interface whose methods offer concrete implementations of the helper components to use.

Today, IoC/DI is often associated with special frameworks that offer a number of rather advanced features.

IoC Frameworks

Table 3-1 lists some of the most popular IoC frameworks available.

TABLE 3-1 **Main IoC Frameworks**

Framework	More Information
Castle Windsor	*http://www.castleproject.org/container/index.html*
Ninject	*http://www.ninject.org*
Spring.NET	*http://www.springframework.net*
StructureMap	*http://structuremap.sourceforge.net/Default.htm*
Unity	*http://codeplex.com/unity*

Note that Ninject is also available for Silverlight and the Compact Framework. In particular, Microsoft's Unity Application Block (*Unity* for short) is a lightweight IoC container with support for constructor, property, and method call injection. It comes as part of the Enterprise Library 4.0. Let's use that for our demos.

All IoC frameworks are built around a container object that, bound to some configuration information, resolves dependencies. The caller code instantiates the container and passes the desired interface as an argument. In response, the IoC/DI framework returns a concrete object that implements that interface.

IoC Containers in Action

Suppose you have a class that depends on a logger service, such as the class shown here:

```
public class Task
{
  ILogger _logger;
  public Task(ILogger logger)
  {
    this._logger = logger;
  }
  public void Execute()
  {
    this._logger.Log("Begin method ...");
      :
    this._logger.Log("End method ...");
  }
}
```

The *Task* class receives the logger component via the constructor, but how does it locate and instantiate the logger service? A simple and static *new* statement certainly works, and so does a factory. An IoC container is a much richer framework that supports a configuration section:

```
<configuration>
  <configSections>
    <section name="unity"
            type="Microsoft.Practices.Unity.Configuration.UnityConfigurationSection,
                Microsoft.Practices.Unity.Configuration" />
  </configSections>
    :
```

```
<unity>
  <containers>
    <container>
      <types>
        <type type="ILogger, mdUtils"
              mapTo="ManagedDesign.Tools.DbLogger, mdTools" />
      </types>
    </container>
  </containers>
</unity>
</configuration>
```

The configuration file (*app.config* or *web.config*) contains mapping between interfaces and concrete types to be injected. Whenever the container gets a call for *ILogger*, it'll return an instance of *DbLogger*:

```
IUnityContainer container = new UnityContainer();
UnityConfigurationSection section = (UnityConfigurationSection)
                             ConfigurationManager.GetSection("unity");
section.Containers.Default.Configure(container);
ILogger logger = container.Resolve<ILogger>();
Task t = new Task(logger);
⋮
```

IoC/DI is extremely useful for testing purposes and for switching between implementations of internal components. Frameworks just make it simple and terrific. In Chapter 6, "The Data Access Layer," we'll return to IoC/DI to show how to inject a data access layer (DAL) in the middle tier of a layered system.

To finish, here are a couple of brief remarks about IoC/DI containers. Through the configuration script, you can instruct the container to treat injected objects as singletons. This means, for example, that the container won't create a new instance of *DbLogger* every time, but will reuse the same one. If the *DbLogger* class is thread safe, this is really a performance boost.

In addition, imagine that the constructor of *DbLogger* needs a reference to another type registered with the IoC/DI framework. The container will be able to resolve that dependency, too.

Applying Requirements by Design

In Chapter 1, we saw that international standard ISO/IEC 9126 lists testability and security as key quality characteristics for any software architecture. This means that we should consider testability and security as nonfunctional requirements in any software architecture and start planning for them very early in the design phase.

Testability

A broadly accepted definition for testability in the context of software architecture describes it as the ease of performing testing. And testing is the process of checking software to ensure that it behaves as expected, contains no errors, and satisfies its requirements.

A popular slogan to address the importance of software testing comes from Bruce Eckel and reads like this:

> *If it ain't tested, it's broken.*

The key thing to keep in mind is that you can state that your code works only if you can provide evidence for that it does. A piece of software can switch to the status of *working* not when someone states it works (whether stated by end users, the project manager, the customer, or the chief architect), but only when its correctness is proven beyond any reasonable doubt.

Software Testing

Testing happens at various levels. You have *unit tests* to determine whether individual components of the software meet functional requirements. You have *integration tests* to determine whether the software fits in the environment and infrastructure and whether two or more components work well together. Finally, you have *acceptance tests* to determine whether the completed system meets customer requirements.

Unit tests and integration tests pertain to the development team and serve the purpose of making the team confident about the quality of the software. Test results tell the team if the team is doing well and is on the right track. Typically, these tests don't cover the entire code base. In general, there's no clear correlation between the percentage of code coverage and quality of code. Likewise, there's also no agreement on what would be a valid percentage of code coverage to address. Some figure that 80 percent is a good number. Some do not even instruct the testing tool to calculate it.

The customer is typically not interested in the results of unit and integration tests. Acceptance tests, on the other hand, are all the customer cares about. Acceptance tests address the completed system and are part of the contract between the customer and the development team. Acceptance tests can be written by the customer itself or by the team in strict collaboration with the customer. In an acceptance test, you can find a checklist such as the following one:

```
1)  Insert a customer with the following data ...;

2)  Modify the customer using an existing ID;

3)  Observe the reaction of the system and verify specific expected results;
```

Another example is the following:

```
1)  During a batch, shut down one nodes on the application server;

2)  Observe the reaction of the system and the results of the transaction;
```

Run prior to delivery, acceptance tests, if successful, signal the termination of the project and the approval of the product. (As a consultant, you can issue your final invoice at this point.)

Tests are a serious matter.

Testing the system by having end users poke around the software for a few days is not a reliable (and exhaustive) test practice. As we saw earlier in the chapter, it is even considered to be an antipattern.

> **Note** Admittedly, in the early 1990s Dino delivered a photographic Windows application using the *test-by-poking-around* approach. We were a very small company with five developers, plus the boss. Our (patented?) approach to testing is described in the following paragraph.
>
> The boss brings a copy of the program home. The boss spends the night playing with the program. Around 8 a.m. the next day, the team gets a call from the boss, who is going to get a few hours of very well-deserved sleep. The boss recites a long list of serious bugs to be fixed instantly and makes obscure references to alleged features of the program, which are unknown to the entire team. Early in the afternoon, the boss shows up at work and discusses improvements in a much more relaxed state of mind. The list of serious bugs to be fixed instantly morphs into a short list of new features to add.
>
> In this way, however, we delivered the application and we could say we delivered a reliable and fully functioning piece of software. It was the 1994, though. The old days.

Software Contracts

A software test verifies that a component returns the correct output in response to given input and a given internal state. Having control over the input and the state and being able to observe the output is therefore essential.

Your testing efforts greatly benefit from detailed knowledge of the software contract supported by a method. When you design a class, you should always be sure you can answer the following three questions about the class and its methods in particular:

- Under which conditions can the method be invoked?
- Which conditions are verified after the method terminates?
- Which conditions do not change before and after the method execution?

These three questions are also known, respectively, as preconditions, postconditions, and invariants.

Preconditions mainly refer to the input data you pass; specifically, data that is of given types and values falling within a given range. Preconditions also refer to the state of the object required for execution—for example, the method that might need to throw an exception if an internal member is null or if certain conditions are not met.

When you design a method with testability in mind, you pay attention to and validate input carefully and throw exceptions if any preconditions are not met. This gets you clean code, and more importantly, code that is easier to test.

Postconditions refer to the output generated by the method and the changes produced to the state of the object. Postconditions are not directly related to the exceptions that might be thrown along the way. This is not relevant from a testing perspective. When you do testing, in fact, you execute the method if preconditions are met (and if no exceptions are raised because of failed preconditions). The method might produce the wrong results, but it should not fail unless really exceptional situations are encountered. If your code needs to read a file, that the file exists is a precondition and you should throw a *FileNotFoundException* before attempting to read. A *FileIOException*, say, is acceptable only if during the test you lose connection to the file.

There might be a case where the method delegates some work to an internal component, which might also throw exceptions. However, for the purpose of testing, that component will be replaced with a fake one that is guaranteed to return valid data by contract. (You are testing the outermost method now; you have tested the internal component already or you'll test it later.) So, in the end, when you design for testability the exceptions you should care about most are those in the preconditions.

Invariants refer to property values, or expressions involving members of the object's state, that do not change during the method execution. In a design for testability scenario, you know these invariants clearly and you assert them in tests. As an example of an invariant, consider the property *Status* of *DbConnection*: it has to be *Open* before you invoke *BeginTransaction*, and it must remain *Open* afterward.

Software contracts play a key role in the design of classes for testability. Having a contract clearly defined for each class you write makes your code inherently more testable.

Unit Testing

Unit testing verifies that individual units of code are working properly according to their software contract. A *unit* is the smallest part of an application that is testable—typically, a method.

Unit testing consists of writing and running a small program (referred to as a *test harness*) that instantiates classes and invokes methods in an automatic way. In the end, running a battery of tests is much like compiling. You click a button, you run the test harness and, at the end of it, you know what went wrong, if anything.

In its simplest form, a test harness is a manually written program that reads test-case input values and the corresponding expected results from some external files. Then the test harness calls methods using input values and compares results with expected values. Needless to say, writing such a test harness entirely from scratch is, at the very minimum, time consuming and error prone. But, more importantly, it is restrictive in terms of the testing capabilities you can take advantage of.

At the end of the day, the most effective way to conduct unit testing passes through the use of an automated test framework. An automated test framework is a developer tool that normally includes a runtime engine and a framework of classes for simplifying the creation of test programs. Table 3-2 lists some of the most popular ones.

TABLE 3-2 Popular Testing Tools

Product	Description
MSTest	The testing tool incorporated into Visual Studio 2008 Professional, Team Tester, and Team Developer. It is also included in Visual Studio 2005 Team Tester and Team Developer.
MBUnit	An open-source product with a fuller bag of features than MSTest. However, the tight integration that MSTest has with Visual Studio and Team Foundation Server largely makes up for the smaller feature set. For more information on MBUnit, pay a visit to *http://www.mbunit.com.*
NUnit	One of the most widely used testing tools for the .NET Framework. It is an open-source product. Read more at *http://www.nunit.org.*
xUnit.NET	Currently under development as a CodePlex project, this tool builds on the experience of James Newkirk—the original author of NUnit. It is definitely an interesting tool to look at, with some interesting and innovative features. For more information, pay a visit to *http://www.codeplex.com/xunit.*

A nice comparison of testing tools, in terms of their respective feature matrix, is available at *http://www.codeplex.com/xunit/Wiki/View.aspx?title=Comparisons.*

Unit Testing in Action

Let's have a look at some tests written using the MSTest tool that comes with Visual Studio 2008. You start by grouping related tests in a *text fixture*. Text fixtures are just test-specific classes where methods typically represent tests to run. In a text fixture, you might also have code that executes at the start and end of the test run. Here's the skeleton of a text fixture with MSTest:

```
using Microsoft.VisualStudio.TestTools.UnitTesting;
:

[TestClass]
public class CustomerTestCase
{
  private Customer customer;

  [TestInitialize]
  public void SetUp()
  {
    customer = new Customer();
  }

  [TestCleanup]
```

```
  public void TearDown()
  {
    customer = null;
  }

  // Your tests go here
  [TestMethod]
  public void Assign_ID()
  {
     .
     .
     .
  }
     .
     .
     .
}
```

It is recommended that you create a separate assembly for your tests and, more importantly, that you have tests for each class library. A good practice is to have an *XxxTestCase* class for each *Xxx* class in a given assembly.

As you can see, you transform a plain .NET class into a test fixture by simply adding the *TestClass* attribute. You turn a method of this class into a test method by using the *TestMethod* attribute instead. Attributes such as *TestInitialize* and *TestCleanup* have a special meaning and indicate code to execute at the start and end of the test run. Let's examine an initial test:

```
[TestMethod]
public void Assign_ID()
{
  // Define the input data for the test
  string id = "MANDS";

  // Execute the action to test (assign a given value)
  customer.ID = id;

  // Test the postconditions:
  // Ensure that the new value of property ID matches the assigned value.
  Assert.AreEqual(id, customer.ID);
}
```

The test simply verifies that a value is correctly assigned to the *ID* property of the *Customer* class. You use methods of the *Assert* object to assert conditions that must be true when checked.

The body of a test method contains plain code that works on properties and methods of a class. Here's another example that invokes a method on the *Customer* class:

```
[TestMethod]
public void TestEmptyCustomersHaveNoOrders()
{
  Customer c = new Customer();
  Assert.AreEqual<decimal>(0, c.GetTotalAmountOfOrders());
}
```

In this case, the purpose of the test is to ensure that a newly created *Customer* instance has no associated orders and the total amount of orders add up to zero.

Dealing with Dependencies

When you test a method, you want to focus only on the code within *that* method. All that you want to know is whether *that* code provides the expected results in the tested scenarios. To get this, you need to get rid of all dependencies the method might have. If the method, say, invokes another class, you assume that the invoked class will *always* return correct results. In this way, you eliminate at the root the risk that the method fails under test because a failure occurred down the call stack. If you test method A and it fails, the reason has to be found *exclusively* in the source code of method A—given preconditions, invariants, and behavior—and not in any of its dependencies.

Generally, the class being tested must be *isolated* from its dependencies.

In an object-oriented scenario, class A depends on class B when any of the following conditions are verified:

- Class A derives from class B.

- Class A includes a member of class B.

- One of the methods of class A invokes a method of class B.

- One of the methods of class A receives or returns a parameter of class B.

- Class A depends on a class that, in turn, depends on class B.

How can you neutralize dependencies when testing a method? This is exactly where manually written test harnesses no longer live up to your expectations, and you see the full power of automated testing frameworks.

Dependency injection really comes in handy here and is a pattern that has a huge impact on testability. A class that depends on interfaces (the first principle of OOD), and uses dependency injection to receive from the outside world any objects it needs to do its own work, is inherently more testable. Let's consider the following code snippet:

```
public class Task
{
  // Class Task depends upon type ILogger
  ILogger _logger;

  public Task(ILogger logger)
  {
    this._logger = logger;
  }

  public int Sum(int x, int y)
  {
    return x+y;
  }
```

```
  public void Execute()
  {
    // Invoke an external "service"; not relevant when unit-testing this method
    this._logger.Log("Begin method ...");

    // Method specific code; RELEVANT when unit-testing this method
    :

    // Invoke an external "service"; not relevant when unit-testing this method
    this._logger.Log("End method ...");
  }
}
```

We want to test the code in method *Execute,* but we don't care about the logger. Because the class *Task* is designed with DI in mind, testing the method *Execute* in total isolation is much easier.

Again, how can you neutralize dependencies when testing a method?

The simplest option is using *fake* objects. A fake object is a relatively simple clone of an object that offers the same interface as the original object but returns hard-coded or programmatically determined values. Here's a sample fake object for the *ILogger* type:

```
public class FakeLogger : ILogger
{
    public void Log(string message)
    {
        return;
    }
}
```

As you can see, the behavior of a fake object is hard-coded; the fake object has no state and no significant behavior. From the fake object's perspective, it makes no difference how many times you invoke a fake method and when in the flow the call occurs. Let's see how to inject a fake logger in the *Task* class:

```
[TestMethod]
public void TestIfExecuteWorks()
{
  // Inject a fake logger to isolate the method from dependencies
  FakeLogger fake = new FakeLogger();
  Task task = new Task(fake);

  // Set preconditions
  int x = 3;
  int y = 4;
  int expected = 7;

  // Run the method
  int actual = task.Sum(x, y);

  // Report about the code's behavior using Assert statements
  Assert.AreEqual<int>(expected, actual);
  :
}
```

In a test, you set the preconditions for the method, run the method, and then observe the resulting postconditions. The concept of *assertion* is central to the unit test. An assertion is a condition that might or might not be verified. If verified, the assertion passes. In MSTest, the *Assert* class provides many static methods for making assertions, such as *AreEqual*, *IsInstanceOfType*, and *IsNull*.

In the preceding example, after executing the method *Sum* you are expected to place one or more assertions aimed at verifying the changes made to the state of the object or comparing the results produced against expected values.

> **Note** In some papers, terms such as *stub* and *shunt* are used to indicate slight variations of what we reference here as a *fake*. A broadly accepted differentiation is based on the fact that a stub (or a shunt) merely provides the implementation of an interface. Methods can just throw or, at most, return canned values.
>
> A fake, on the other hand, is a slightly more sophisticated object that, in addition to implementing an interface, also usually contains more logic in the methods. Methods on a fake object can return canned values but also programmatically set values. Both fakes and stubs can provide a meaningful implementation for some methods and just throw exceptions for other methods that are not considered relevant for the purpose of the test.
>
> A bigger and juicier differentiation, however, is the one that exists between fakes (or stubs) and mock objects, which is discussed next.

From Fakes to Mocks

A *mock* object is a more evolved and recent version of a fake. A mock does all that a fake or a stub does, plus something more. In a way, a mock is an object with its own personality that mimics the behavior and interface of another object. What more does a mock provide to testers?

Essentially, a mock allows for verification of the context of the method call. With a mock, you can verify that a method call happens with the right preconditions and in the correct order with respect to other methods in the class.

Writing a fake manually is not usually a big issue—all the logic you need is for the most part simple and doesn't need to change frequently. When you use fakes, you're mostly interested in verifying that some expected output derives from a given input. You are interested in the state that a fake object might represent; you are not interested in interacting with it.

You use a mock instead of a fake only when you need to interact with dependent objects during tests. For example, you might want to know whether the mock has been invoked or not, and you might decide within the text what the mock object has to return for a given method.

Writing mocks manually is certainly a possibility, but is rarely an option you really want to consider. For the level of flexibility you expect from a mock, you should be updating its source code every now and then or you should have (and maintain) a different mock for each test case in which the object is being involved. Alternatively, you might come up with a very generic mock class that works in the guise of any object you specify. This very generic mock class also exposes a general-purpose interface through which you set your expectations for the mocked object. This is exactly what mocking frameworks do for you. In the end, you never write mock objects manually; you generate them on the fly using some mocking framework.

Table 3-3 lists and briefly describes the commonly used mocking frameworks.

TABLE 3-3 Some Popular Mocking Frameworks

Product	Description
NMock2	An open-source library providing a dynamic mocking framework for .NET interfaces. The mock object uses strings to get input and reflection to set expectations. Read more at *http://sourceforge.net/projects/nmock2*.
TypeMock	A commercial product with unique capabilities that basically don't require you to (re)design your code for testability. TypeMock enables testing code that was previously considered untestable, such as static methods, nonvirtual methods, and sealed classes. Read more at *http://www.typemock.com*.
Rhino Mocks	An open-source product. Through a wizard, it generates a static mock class for type-safe testing. You set mock expectations by accessing directly the mocked object, rather than going through one more level of indirection. Read more at *http://www.ayende.com/projects/rhino-mocks.aspx*.

Let's go through a mocking example that uses NMock2 in MSTest.

Imagine you have an *AccountService* class that depends on the *ICurrencyService* type. The *AccountService* class represents a bank account with its own currency. When you transfer funds between accounts, you might need to deal with conversion rates, and you use the *ICurrencyService* type for that:

```
public interface ICurrencyService
{
  // Returns the current conversion rate: how many "fromCurrency" to
  // be changed into toCurrency
  decimal GetConversionRate(string fromCurrency, string toCurrency);
}
```

Let's see what testing the *TransferFunds* method looks like:

```
[TestClass]
public class CurrencyServiceTestCase
{
  private Mockery mocks;
  private ICurrencyService mockCurrencyService;
  private IAccountService accountService;
```

```
[TestInitialize]
public void SetUp()
{
  // Initialize the mocking framework
  mocks = new Mockery();

  // Generate a mock for the ICurrencyService type
  mockCurrencyService = mocks.NewMock<ICurrencyService>();

  // Create the object to test and inject the mocked service
  accountService = new AccountService(mockCurrencyService);
}

[TestMethod]
public void TestCrossCurrencyFundsTransfer()
{
  // Create two test accounts
  Account eurAccount = new Account("12345", "EUR");
  Account usdAccount = new Account("54321", "USD");
  usdAccount.Deposit(1000);

  // Set expectations for the mocked object:
  //    When method GetConversionRate is invoked with (USD,EUR) input
  //    the mock returns 0.64
  Expect.Once.On(mockCurrencyService)
            .Method("GetConversionRate")
            .With("USD", "EUR")
            .Will(Return.Value(0.64));

  // Invoke the method to test (and transfer $500 to an EUR account)
  accountService.TransferFunds(usdAccount, eurAccount, 500);

  // Verify postconditions through assertions
  Assert.AreEqual<int>(500, usdAccount.Balance);
  Assert.AreEqual<int>(320, eurAccount.Balance);
  mocks.VerifyAllExpectationsHaveBeenMet();
}
}
```

You first create a mock object for each dependent type. Next, you programmatically set expectations on the mock using the static class *Expect* from the NMock2 framework. In particular, in this case you establish that when the method *GetConversionRate* on the mocked type is invoked with a pair of arguments such as "USD" and "EUR", it has to return 0.64. This is just the value that the method *TransferFunds* receives when it attempts to invoke the currency services internally.

There's no code around that belongs to a mock object, and there's no need for developers to look into the implementation of mocks. Reading a test, therefore, couldn't be easier. The expectations are clearly declared and correctly passed on the methods under test.

Note A mock is generated on the fly using .NET reflection to inspect the type to mimic and the CodeDOM API to generate and compile code dynamically.

Security

Located at Carnegie Mellon University in Pittsburgh, Pennsylvania, the CERT Coordination Center (CERT/CC) analyzes the current state of Internet security. It regularly receives reports of vulnerabilities and researches the inner causes of security vulnerabilities. The center's purpose is to help with the development of secure coding practices.

Figure 3-4 shows a statistic about the number of identified vulnerabilities in the past ten years. As you can see, the trend is impressive. Also, you should consider that the data includes only the first two quarters of 2008. (See *http://www.cert.org/stats/vulnerability_remediation.html*.)

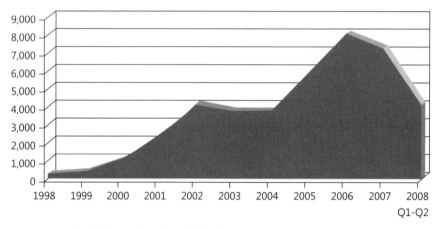

FIGURE 3-4 Identified security vulnerabilities in past ten years

It is broadly accepted that these numbers have a common root—they refer to software created through methodologies not specifically oriented to security. On the other hand, the problem of security is tightly related to the explosion in the popularity of the Internet. Only ten years ago, the big bubble was just a tiny balloon.

In sharp contrast with the ISO/IEC 9126 standard, all current methodologies for software development (agile, waterfall, MSF, and the like) hardly mention the word *security*. Additionally, the use of these methodologies has not resulted (yet?) in a measurable reduction of security bugs. To accomplish this, you need more than these methodologies offer.

Security as a (Strict) Requirement

We can't really say whether this is a real story or an urban legend, but it's being said that a few years ago, in the early days of the .NET Framework, a consultant went to some CIA office for a training gig. When introducing Code Access Security—the .NET Framework mechanism to limit access to code—the consultant asked students the following question: "Are you really serious about security here?"

Can you guess the answer? It was sort of like this: "Not only yes, but HELL YES. And you'll experience that yourself when you attempt to get out of the building."

Being serious about (software) security, though, is a subtle concept that goes far beyond even your best intentions. As Microsoft's senior security program manager Michael Howard points out:

> If your engineers know nothing about the basic security tenets, common security defect types, basic secure design, or security testing, there really is no reasonable chance they could produce secure software. I say this because, on the average, software engineers don't pay enough attention to security. They may know quite a lot about security features, but they need to have a better understanding of what it takes to build and deliver secure features.

Security must be taken care of from the beginning. A secure design starts with the architecture; it can't be something you bolt on at a later time. Security is by design. To address security properly, you need a methodology developed with security in mind that leads you to design your system with security in mind. This is just what the Security Development Lifecycle (SDL) is all about.

Security Development Lifecycle

SDL is a software development process that Microsoft uses internally to improve software security by reducing security bugs. SDL is not just an internal methodology. Based on the impressive results obtained internally, Microsoft is now pushing SDL out to any development team that wants to be really serious about security.

SDL is essentially an iterative process that focuses on security aspects of developing software. SDL doesn't mandate a particular software development process and doesn't preclude any. It is agnostic to the methodology in use in the project—be it waterfall, agile, spiral, or whatever else.

SDL is the incarnation of the SD^3+C principle, which is a shortcut for "Secure by Design, Secure by Default, Secure in Deployment, plus Communication." *Secure by Design* refers to identifying potential security risks starting with the design phase. *Secure by Default* refers to reducing the attack surface of each component and making it run with the least possible number of privileges. *Secure in Deployment* refers to making security requirements clear during deployment. *Communication* refers to sharing information about findings to apply a fix in a timely manner.

Foundations of SDL: Layering

The foundations of SDL are essentially three: layering, componentization, and roles.

Decomposing the architecture to layers is important because of the resulting separation of concerns. Having functionality organized in distinct layers makes it easier to map functions to physical tiers as appropriate. This is beneficial at various levels.

For example, it is beneficial for the data server.

You can isolate the data server at will, and even access it through a separate network. In this case, the data server is much less sensitive to denial of service (DoS) attacks because of the firewalls scattered along the way that can recognize and neutralize DoS packets.

You move all security checks to the business layer running on the application server and end up with a single user for the database—the data layer. Among other things, this results in a bit less work for the database and a pinch of additional scalability for the system.

Layers are beneficial for the application server, too.

You use Code Access Security (CAS) on the business components to stop untrusted code from executing privileged actions. You use CAS imperatively through *xxxPermission* classes to decide what to do based on actual permissions. You use CAS declaratively on classes or assemblies through *xxxPermission* attributes to prevent unauthorized use of sensitive components. If you have services, the contract helps to delimit what gets in and what gets out of the service.

Finally, if layering is coupled with thin clients, you have fewer upgrades (which are always a risk for the stability of the application) and less logic running on the client. Securitywise, this means that a possible dump of the client process would reveal much less information, so being able to use the client application in partial trust mode is more likely.

Foundations of SDL: Componentization

Each layer is decomposed to components. Components are organized by functions *and* required security privileges. It should be noted that performance considerations might lead you to grouping or further factorizing components in successive iterations.

Componentization here means identifying the components to secure and not merely breaking down the logical architecture into a group of assemblies.

For each component, you define the public contract and get to know exactly what data is expected to come in and out of the component. The decomposition can be hierarchical. From a security point of view, at this stage you are interested *only* in components within a layer that provide a service. You are not interested, for example, in the object model (that is, the domain model, typed *DataSets*, custom DTOs) because it is shared by multiple layers and represents only data and behavior on the data.

For each component, you identify the least possible set of privileges that make it run. From a security perspective, this means that in case of a successful attack, attackers gain the minimum possible set of privileges.

Components going to different processes run in total isolation and each has its own access control list (ACL) and Windows privileges set. Other components, conversely, might require their own AppDomain within the same .NET process. An AppDomain is like a virtual process within a .NET application that the Common Language Runtime (CLR) uses to isolate code within a secure boundary. (Note, however, that an AppDomain doesn't represent a security barrier for applications running in full-trust mode.) An AppDomain can be sandboxed to have a limited set of permissions that, for example, limit disk access, socket access, and the like.

Foundation of SDL: Roles

Every application has its own assets. In general, an asset is any data that attackers might aim at, including a component with high privileges. Users access assets through the routes specified by use cases. From a security perspective, you should associate use cases with categories of users authorized to manage related assets.

A *role* is just a logical attribute assigned to a user. A role refers to the logical role the user plays in the context of the application. In terms of configuration, each user can be assigned one or more roles. This information is attached to the .NET identity object, and the application code can check it before the execution of critical operations. For example, an application might define two roles—Admin and Guest, each representative of a set of application-specific permissions. Users belonging to the Admin role can perform tasks that other users are prohibited from performing.

Assigning roles to a user account doesn't add any security restrictions by itself. It is the responsibility of the application—typically, the business layer—to ensure that users perform only operations compatible with their role.

With roles, you employ a unique model for authorization, thus unifying heterogeneous security models such as LDAP, NTFS, database, and file system. Also, testing is easier. By impersonating a role, you can test access on any layer.

In a role-based security model, total risks related to the use of impersonation and delegation are mitigated. Impersonation allows a process to run using the security credentials of the impersonated user but, unlike delegation, it doesn't allow access to remote resources on behalf of the impersonated user. In both cases, the original caller's security context can be used to go through computer boundaries from the user interface to the middle tier and then all the way down to the database. This is a risk in a security model in which permissions are restricted by object. However, in a role-based security model, the ability to execute a method that accesses specific resources is determined by role membership, not credentials. User's credentials might not be sufficient to operate on the application and data server.

Authorization Manager (AzMan) is a separate Windows download that enables you to group individual operations together to form tasks. You can then authorize roles to perform specific tasks, individual operations, or both. AzMan offers a centralized console (an MMC snap-in) to define manager roles, operations, and users.

Note AzMan is a COM-based component that has very little to share with the .NET Framework. The .NET-based successor to AzMan is still in the works somewhere in Redmond. The community of developers expects something especially now that Microsoft has unveiled a new claims-based identity model that essentially factors authentication out of applications so that each request brings its own set of claims, including user name, e-mail address, user role, and even more specific information.

Threat Model

Layering, componentization, and roles presuppose that, as an architect, you know the assets (such as sensitive data, highly privileged components) you want to protect from attackers. It also presupposes that you understand the threats related to the system you're building and which vulnerabilities it might be exposed to after it is implemented. Design for security means that you develop a threat model, understand vulnerabilities, and do something to mitigate risks.

Ideally, you should not stop at designing this into your software, but look ahead to threats and vulnerabilities in the deployment environment and to those resulting from interaction with other products or systems. To this end, understanding the threats and developing a threat model is a must. For threats found at the design level, applying countermeasures is easy. Once the application has been developed, applying countermeasures is much harder. If an application is deployed, it's nearly impossible to apply internal countermeasures—you have to rely on external security practices and devices. Therefore, it's better to architect systems with built-in security features.

You can find an interesting primer on threat models at the following URL: *http://blogs.msdn. com/ptorr/archive/2005/02/22/GuerillaThreatModelling.aspx.*

Threat modeling essentially consists of examining components for different types of threats. STRIDE is a threat modeling practice that lists the following six types of threats:

- **Spoofing of user identity**   Refers to using false identities to get into the system. This threat is mitigated by filtering out invalid IP addresses.

- **Tampering**   Refers to intercepting/modifying data during a module's conversation. This threat is mitigated by protecting the communication channel (for example, SSL or IPSec).

- **Repudiation**   Refers to the execution of operations that can't be traced back to the author. This threat is mitigated by strong auditing policies.

- **Information disclosure**   Refers to unveiling private and sensitive information to unauthorized users. This threat is mitigated by enhanced authorization rules.

- **Denial of service**   Refers to overloading a system up to the point of blocking it. This threat is mitigated by filtering out requests and frequently and carefully checking the use of the bandwidth.

- **Elevation of privilege**   Refers to executing operations that require a higher privilege than the privilege currently assigned. This threat is mitigated by assigning the least possible privilege to any components.

If you're looking for more information on STRIDE, you can check out the following URL: *http://msdn.microsoft.com/en-us/magazine/cc163519.aspx*.

After you have the complete list of threats that might apply to your application, you prioritize them based on the risks you see associated with each threat. It is not realistic, in fact, that you address all threats you find. Security doesn't come for free, and you should balance costs with effectiveness. As a result, threats that you regard as unlikely or not particularly harmful can be given a lower priority or not covered at all.

How do you associate a risk with a threat? You use the DREAD model. It rates the risk as the probability of the attack multiplied by the impact it might have on the system. You should focus on the following aspects:

- **Discoverability**   Refers to how high the likelihood is that an attacker discovers the vulnerability. It is a probability attribute.

- **Reproducibility**   Refers to how easy it could be to replicate the attack. It is a probability attribute.

- **Exploitability**   Refers to how easy it could be to perpetrate the attack. It is a probability attribute.

- **Affected users**   Refers to the number of users affected by the attack. It is an impact attribute.

- **Damage potential**   Refers to the quantity of damage the attack might produce. It is an impact attribute.

You typically use a simple High, Medium, or Low scale to determine the priority of the threats and decide which to address and when. If you're looking for more information on DREAD, you can check out the following URL: *http://msdn.microsoft.com/en-us/library/aa302419.aspx*.

> **Note** STRIDE and DREAD is the classic analysis model pushed by the Security Development Lifecycle (SDL) team and is based on the attacker's viewpoint. It works great in an enterprise scenario, but it requires a security specialist because the resulting threat model is large and complex. Another, simplified, model is emerging—the CIA/PI model, which stands for Confidentiality Integrity Availability/Probability Impact. This model is simplified and focuses on the defender's point of view. An interesting post is this one: *http://blogs.msdn.com/ threatmodeling/archive/2007/10/30/a-discussion-on-threat-modeling.aspx*.

Security and the Architect

An inherently secure design, a good threat model, and a precise analysis of the risk might mean very little if you then pair them with a weak and insecure implementation. As an architect, you should intervene at three levels: development, code review, and testing.

As far as development is concerned, the use of strong typing should be enforced because, by itself, it cuts off a good share of possible bugs. Likewise, knowledge of common security patterns (for example, the "all input is evil" pattern), application of a good idiomatic design, and static code analysis (for example, using FxCop) are all practices to apply regularly and rigorously.

Sessions of code review should be dedicated to a careful examination of the actual configuration and implementation of security through CAS, and to spot the portions of code prone to amplified attacks, such as cross-site scripting, SQL injection, overflows, and similar attack mechanisms.

Unit testing for security is also important if your system receives files and sequences of bytes. You might want to consider a technique known as *fuzzing*. Fuzzing is a software testing technique through which you pass random data to a component as input. The code might throw an appropriate exception or degrade gracefully. However, it might also crash or fail some expected assertions. This technique can reveal some otherwise hidden bugs.

Final Security Push

Although security should be planned for from the outset, you can hardly make some serious security tests until the feature set is complete and the product is close to its beta stage. It goes without saying that any anomalies found during security tests lead the team to reconsidering the design and implementation of the application, and even the threat model.

The final security push before shipping to the customer is a delicate examination and should preferably be delegated to someone outside the team, preferably some other independent figure.

Releasing to production doesn't mean the end of the security life cycle. As long as a system is up and running, it is exposed to possible attacks. You should always find time for penetration testing, which might lead to finding new vulnerabilities. So the team then starts the cycle again with the analysis of the design, implementation, and threat model. Over and over again, in an endless loop.

Performance Considerations

You might wonder why we're including a sidebar on performance rather than a full "Design for Performance" section. Performance is something that results from the actual behavior of the system, not something you can put in. If you're creating a standalone, small disconnected program, you can optimize it almost at will. It is radically different when we move up in scope to consider an enterprise-class system.

Performance is not something absolute.

What is performance? Is it the response time the end user perceives? Is it resource utilization that might or might not penalize the middle tier? Is it network latency or database I/O latency? Is it related to caching or smarter algorithms? Is it a matter of bad design? Is it merely horsepower?

Too often, a design decision involves a tradeoff between performance and scalability. You release some performance-oriented improvement to achieve better scalability—that is, a better (read, faster) response when the workload grows. Performance is never something absolute.

In an enterprise-class system, efficiency and performance are certainly requirements to take into account, but they are not fundamental requirements.

In our opinion, a bad design influences performance, but there's no special suggestion we can share to help you to come up with a high-performance design. The design is either good or bad; if it's good, it sets the groundwork for good performance.

As we've seen in this chapter, a good design is based on interfaces, has low coupling, and allows for injection of external functionalities. Done in this way, the design leaves a lot of room for replacing components with others that might provide a better performance.

As Donald Knuth used to say, "Premature optimization is the root of all evil." So optimizing is fine and necessary, but you should care about it only when you have evidence of poor performance. And only when you know what is doing poorly and that it can be improved. Optimization is timely—it is never premature, never late.

Performance is hardly something that works (or doesn't work) in theory. You can hardly say from a design or, worse yet, from a specification whether the resulting system will perform poorly or not. You build the system in the best and simplest way you can. You adhere to OOD principles and code your way to the fullest. Then you test the system.

If it works, but it doesn't work as fast as it should, you profile the system and figure out what can be improved—be it a stored procedure, an intermediate cache, or a dynamic proxy injection. If the design is flexible enough and leaves room for changes, you shouldn't have a hard time applying the necessary optimization.

From Objects to Aspects

No doubt that OOP is currently a mainstream programming paradigm. When you design a system, you decompose it into components and map the components to classes. Classes hold data and deliver a behavior. Classes can be reused and used in a polymorphic manner, although you must do so with the care we discussed earlier in the chapter.

Even with all of its undisputed positive qualities, though, OOP is not the perfect programming paradigm.

The OO paradigm excels when it comes to breaking a system down into components and describing processes through components. The OO paradigm also excels when you deal with the *concerns* of a component. However, the OO paradigm is not as effective when it comes to dealing with *cross-cutting concerns*.

A cross-cutting concern is a concern that affects multiple components in a system, such as logging, security, and exception handling. Not being a specific responsibility of a given component or family of components, a cross-cutting concern looks like an *aspect* of the system that must be dealt with at a different logical level, a level beyond application classes. Enter a new programming paradigm: *aspect-oriented programming* (AOP).

Aspect-Oriented Programming

The inherent limitations of the OO paradigm were identified quite a few years ago, not many years after the introduction of OOP. However, today AOP still is not widely implemented even though everybody agrees on the benefits it produces. The main reason for such a limited adoption is essentially the lack of proper tools. We are pretty sure the day that AOP is (even only partially) supported by the .NET platform will represent a watershed in the history of AOP.

The concept of AOP was developed at Xerox PARC laboratories in the 1990s. The team also developed the first (and still most popular) AOP language: AspectJ. Let's discover more about AOP by exploring its key concepts.

> **Note** We owe to the Xerox PARC laboratories many software-related facilities we use every day. In addition to AOP (which we don't exactly use every day), Xerox PARC is "responsible" for laser printers, Ethernet, and mouse-driven graphical user interfaces. They always churned out great ideas, but failed sometimes to push their widespread adoption—look at AOP. The lesson that everybody should learn from this is that technical excellence is not necessarily the key to success, not even in software. Some good commercial and marketing skills are always (strictly) required.

Cross-Cutting Concerns

AOP is about separating the implementation of cross-cutting concerns from the implementation of core concerns. For example, AOP is about separating a logger class from a task class so that multiple task classes can use the same logger and in different ways.

We have seen that dependency injection techniques allow you to inject—and quite easily, indeed—external dependencies in a class. A cross-cutting concern (for example, logging) can certainly be seen as an external dependency. So where's the problem?

Dependency injection requires up-front design or refactoring, which is not always entirely possible in a large project or during the update of a legacy system.

In AOP, you wrap up a cross-cutting concern in a new component called an *aspect*. An aspect is a reusable component that encapsulates the behavior that multiple classes in your project require.

Processing Aspects

In a classic OOP scenario, your project is made of a number of source files, each implementing one or more classes, including those representing a cross-cutting concern such as logging. As shown in Figure 3-5, these classes are then processed by a compiler to produce executable code.

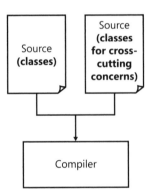

FIGURE 3-5 The classic OOP model of processing source code

In an AOP scenario, on the other hand, aspects are not directly processed by the compiler. Aspects are in some way merged into the regular source code up to the point of producing code that can be processed by the compiler. If you are inclined to employ AspectJ, you use the Java programming language to write your classes and the AspectJ language to write aspects. AspectJ supports a custom syntax through which you indicate the expected behavior for the aspect. For example, a logging aspect might specify that it will log before and after a certain method is invoked and will validate input data, throwing an exception in case of invalid data.

In other words, an aspect describes a piece of standard and reusable code that you might want to inject in existing classes without touching the source code of these classes. (See Figure 3-6.)

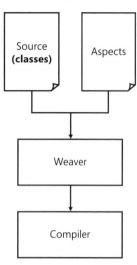

FIGURE 3-6 The AOP model of processing source code

In the AspectJ jargon, the *weaver* is a sort of preprocessor that takes aspects and weaves their content with classes. It produces output that the compiler can render to an executable.

In other AOP-like frameworks, you might not find an explicit weaver tool. However, in any case, the content of an aspect is always processed by the framework and results in some form of code injection. This is radically different from dependency injection. We mean that the code declared in an aspect will be invoked at some specific points in the body of classes that require that aspect.

Before we discuss an example in .NET, we need to introduce a few specific terms and clarify their intended meaning. These concepts and terms come from the original definition of AOP. We suggest that you do not try to map them literally to a specific AOP framework. We suggest, instead, that you try to understand the concepts—the pillars of AOP—and then use this knowledge to better and more quickly understand the details of a particular framework.

Inside AOP Aspects

As mentioned, an aspect is the implementation of a cross-cutting concern. In the definition of an aspect, you need to specify *advice* to apply at specific *join points*.

A *join point* represents a point in the class that requires the aspect. It can be the invocation of a method, the body of a method or the getter/setter of a property, or an exception handler. In general, a join point indicates the point where you want to inject the aspect's code.

A *pointcut* represents a collection of join points. In AspectJ, pointcuts are defined by criteria using method names and wildcards. A sample pointcut might indicate that you group all calls to methods whose name begins with *Get*.

An *advice* refers to the code to inject in the target class. The code can be injected before, after, and around the join point. An advice is associated with a pointcut.

Here's a quick example of an aspect defined using AspectJ:

```
public aspect MyAspect
{
  // Define a pointcut matched by all methods in the application whose name begins with
  // Get and accepting no arguments. (There are many other ways to define criteria.)
  public pointcut allGetMethods ():
        call (* Get*() );

  // Define an advice to run before any join points that matches the specified pointcut.
  before(): allGetMethods()
  {
    // Do your cross-cutting concern stuff here
    // for example, log about the method being executed
    :
  }
}
```

The weaver processes the aspect along with the source code (regular class-based source code) and generates raw material for the compiler. The code actually compiled ensures that an advice is invoked automatically by the AOP runtime whenever the execution flow reaches a join point in the matching pointcut.

AOP in .NET

When we turn to AOP, we essentially want our existing code to do extra things. And we want to achieve that without modifying the source code. We need to specify such extra things (advice) and where we want to execute them (join points). Let's briefly go through these points from the perspective of the .NET Framework.

How can you express the semantic of aspects?

The ideal option is to create a custom language *a là* AspectJ. In this way, you can create an ad hoc aspect tailor-made to express advice at its configured pointcuts. If you have a custom language, though, you also need a tool to parse it—like a weaver.

A very cost-effective alternative is using an external file (for example, an XML file) where you write all the things you want to do and how to do it. An XML file is not ideal for defining source code; in such a file, you likely store mapping between types so that when a given type is assigned an aspect, another type is loaded that contains advice and instructions about how to join it to the execution flow. This is the approach taken by Microsoft's Policy Injection Application Block (PIAB) that we'll look at in a moment.

How can you inject an aspect's advice into executable code?

There are two ways to weave a .NET executable. You can do that at compile time or at run time. Compile-time weaving is preferable, but in our opinion, it requires a strong commitment from a vendor. It can be accomplished by writing a weaver tool that reads the content of the aspect, parses the source code of the language (C#, Visual Basic .NET, and all of the other languages based on the .NET common type system), and produces modified source code, but source code that can still be compiled. If you want to be language independent, write a weaver tool that works on MSIL and apply that past the compilation step. Alternatively, you can write a brand new compiler that understands an extended syntax with ad hoc AOP keywords.

If you want to weave a .NET executable at run time, you have to review all known techniques to inject code dynamically. One is emitting JIT classes through *Reflection.Emit*; another one is based on the CLR's Profiling API. The simplest of all is perhaps managing to have a proxy sitting in between the class's aspects and its caller. In this case, the caller transparently invokes a proxy for the class's aspects. The proxy, in turn, interweaves advice with regular code. This is the same mechanism used in .NET Remoting and Windows Communication Foundation (WCF) services.

Using a transparent proxy has the drawback of requiring that to apply AOP to the class, the class must derive from *ContextBoundObject* or *MarshalByRefObject*. This solution is employed by PIAB.

AOP in Action

To finish off our AOP overview, let's proceed with a full example that demonstrates how to achieve AOP benefits in .NET applications. We'll use Microsoft's Policy Injection Application Block in Enterprise Library 3.0 and higher to add aspects to our demo. For more information on PIAB, see *http://msdn.microsoft.com/en-us/library/cc511729.aspx*.

Enabling Policies

The following code demonstrates a simple console application that uses the Unity IoC container to obtain a reference to a class that exposes a given interface—*ICustomerServices*:

```
public interface ICustomerServices
{
    void Delete(string customerID);
}

static void Main(string[] args)
{
    // Set up the IoC container
    UnityConfigurationSection section;
    section = ConfigurationManager.GetSection("unity") as UnityConfigurationSection;
    IUnityContainer container = new UnityContainer();
    section.Containers.Default.Configure(container);
```

```
      // Resolve a reference to ICustomerServices. The actual class returned depends
      // on the content of the configuration section.
      ICustomerServices obj = container.Resolve<ICustomerServices>();

      // Enable policies on the object (for example, enable aspects)
      ICustomerServices svc = PolicyInjection.Wrap<ICustomerServices>(obj);

      // Invoke the object
      svc.Delete("ALFKI");

      // Wait until the user presses any key
      Console.ReadLine();
}
```

After you have resolved the dependency on the *ICustomerServices* interface, you pass the object to the PIAB layer so that it can wrap the object in a policy-enabled proxy. What PIAB refers to here as a *policy* is really like what many others call, instead, an aspect.

In the end, the *Wrap* static method wraps a given object in a proxy that is driven by the content of a new section in the configuration file. The section *policyInjection* defines the semantics of the aspect. Let's have a look at the configuration file.

Defining Policies

PIAB is driven by the content of an ad hoc configuration section. There you find listed the policies that drive the behavior of generated proxies and that ultimately define aspects to be applied to the object within the proxy.

```
<policyInjection>
  <policies>
    <add name="Policy">
      <matchingRules>
        <add type="EnterpriseLibrary.PolicyInjection.MatchingRules.TypeMatchingRule ..."
            name="Type Matching Rule">
          <matches>
            <add match="ArchNet.Services.ICustomerServices" ignoreCase="false" />
          </matches>
        </add>
      </matchingRules>
      <handlers>
        <add order="0"
            type="ManagedDesign.Tools.DbLogger, mdTools"
            name="Logging Aspect" />
      </handlers>
    </add>
  </policies>
</policyInjection>
```

The *matchingRules* section expresses type-based criteria for a pointcut. It states that whenever the proxy wraps an object of type *ICustomerServices* it has to load and execute all listed handlers. The attribute *order* indicates the order in which the particular handler has to be invoked.

From this XML snippet, the result of this is that *ICustomerServices* is now a log-enabled type.

Defining Handlers

All that remains to be done—and it is the key step, indeed—is to take a look at the code for a sample handler. In this case, it is the *DbLogger* class:

```
public interface ILogger
{
    void LogMessage(string message);
    void LogMessage(string category, string message);
}

public class DbLogger : ILogger, ICallHandler
{
    // ILogger implementation
    public void LogMessage(string message)
    {
        Console.WriteLine(message);
    }
    public void LogMessage(string category, string message)
    {
        Console.WriteLine(string.Format("{0} - {1}", category, message));
    }

    // ICallHandler implementation
    public IMethodReturn Invoke(IMethodInvocation input, GetNextHandlerDelegate getNext)
    {
        // Advice that runs BEFORE
        this.LogMessage("Begin ...");

        // Original method invoked on ICustomerServices
        IMethodReturn msg = getNext()(input, getNext);

        // Advice that runs AFTER
        this.LogMessage("End ...");

        return msg;
    }
    public int Order{ get; set; }
}
```

The class *DbLogger* implements two interfaces. One is its business-specific interface *ILogger*; the other (*ICallHandler*) is a PIAB-specific interface through which advice code is injected into the class's aspect list. The implementation of *ICallHandler* is fairly standard. In the *Invoke* method, you basically redefine the flow you want for any aspect-ed methods.

In summary, whenever a method is invoked on a type that implements *ICustomerServices*, the execution is delegated to a PIAB proxy. The PIAB proxy recognizes a few handlers and invokes them in a pipeline. Each handler does the things it needs to do before the method executes. When done, it yields to the next handler delegate in the pipeline. The last handler in the chain yields to the object that executes its method. After that, the pipeline is retraced and each registered handler has its own chance to execute its postexecution code. Figure 3-7 shows the overall pipeline supported by PIAB.

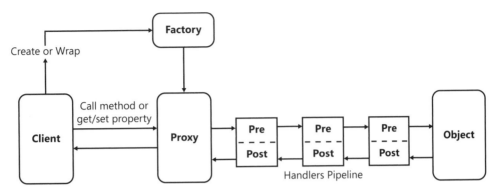

FIGURE 3-7 The PIAB handler pipeline

Note For completeness, we should mention that there are other AOP alternatives available for you to use, the most notable of which is COM+, although WCF exhibits AOP behavior as well. With COM+, you modify your aspects using Component Services. This assumes, of course, that you've taken the necessary steps to register the components by using *System.EnterpriseServices* or are using "services without components." (See *http://msdn.microsoft.com/en-us/library/ms686921(VS.85).aspx*.) Both COM+ and WCF AOP discussions are beyond the scope of this chapter, but by all means investigate the possibilities. (For a bit more information on WCF, see *http://msdn.microsoft.com/en-us/magazine/cc136759.aspx*.)

Practical Advice for the Software Practitioner

To design good software, general principles are enough. You don't strictly need patterns; but patterns, if recognized in a problem, are an effective and proven shortcut to get to the solution. Today, reinventing the wheel is a great sin, for yourself and your team.

Patterns are not essential to the solution of a problem. Using patterns won't make your code necessarily better or faster. You can't go to a customer and say "Hey, my product uses the composite pattern, a domain model, inversion of control, and strategy *à gogo*. So it's really great." Patterns, if correctly applied, ensure that a problem will be solved. Take an easy approach to patterns, and don't try to match a given pattern to a problem regardless of the costs of doing so.

Having mixed basic and OOD principles for years, we think we have now arranged our own few pearls of software design wisdom. These guide us every day, and we communicate them to all people we work with:

- Group logically related responsibilities and factor them out to classes. In the factoring process, pay attention to forming extremely specialized classes.

- Create concise and flexible abstractions of functionalities in classes. In this context, two other adjectives are commonly used in literature to describe abstractions: crisp and resilient.

- When it comes to implementing classes, keep in mind separation of concerns—essentially, who does what—and make sure that each role is played by just one actor and each actor does the minimum possible; this is not done out of laziness, but just for simplicity and effectiveness.

The emphasis on simplicity is never enough. Andrea has the following motto on a poster in the office, and Dino writes it as a dedication in each book he signs: *Keep it as simple as possible, but no simpler.* It's a popular quotation from Albert Einstein that every software professional should always keep in mind.

Often referred to as KISS (short for *Keep It Simple, Stupid*), the idea of "simplicity above all" emerges in various forms from a number of heuristic principles that populate software design articles and conversations. The most popular principles are these:

- **Don't Repeat Yourself (DRY)** Refers to reducing duplication of any information needed by the application, and suggests you store the same information only in one place.

- **Once and Only Once (OAOO)** Refers to reducing the number of times you write the code that accomplishes a given operation within an application.

- **You Aren't Gonna Need It (YAGNI)** Refers to adding any functionality to an application only when it proves absolutely necessary and unavoidable.

We often like to summarize the "simplicity above all" concept by paraphrasing people's rights in court: everything you write can and will be used against you in a debugging session. And, worse yet, it will be used in every meeting with the customer.

Summary

Just as an architect wouldn't design a house while ignoring the law of gravity, a software architect shouldn't design a piece of software ignoring basic principles such as low coupling and high cohesion. Just as an architect wouldn't design a house ignoring building codes that apply to the context, a software architect working in an object-oriented context shouldn't design a piece of software ignoring OOD principles such as the Open/Closed Principle (OCP), the Liskov Substitution Principle (LSP), and the Dependency Inversion Principle (DIP).

But other quality characteristics (defined in an ISO/IEC standard) exist—in particular, testability and security. These aspects must be taken care of at the beginning of the design process—even though magical testing tools and aspect orientation might partially alleviate the pain that comes from not introducing testability and security from the very beginning.

The fundamentals never go out of style, we can safely say, and they are always useful and essential at whatever level of detail.

Murphy's Laws of the Chapter

This chapter is about design and proving that your design is effective and meets requirements. If you think of acceptance tests, in fact, how can you help but recall the original Murphy's Law: "If anything can go wrong, it will." We selected a few related laws for the chapter.

- The chances of a program doing what it's supposed to do are inversely proportional to the number of lines of code used to write it.

- The probability of bugs appearing is directly proportional to the number and importance of people watching.

- An expert is someone brought in at the last minute to share the blame.

See *http://www.murphys-laws.com* for an extensive listing of other computer-related (and non-computer-related) laws and corollaries.

Part II
Design of the System

First, solve the problem. Then, write the code.

—*John B. Johnson*

Chapter 4
The Business Layer

Any fool can write code that a computer can understand. Good programmers write code that humans can understand.

—Martin Fowler

Any software of any reasonable level of complexity is organized in layers. Each layer represents a logical section of the system. In particular, the modules in the business layer include all the functional algorithms and calculations that make the system work and interact with other layers, including the data access layer (DAL) and presentation layer.

The business layer is the nerve center of any layered system and contains most of its core logic. For this reason, it is often referred to as the *business logic layer* (BLL). In the rest of this chapter, we'll primarily use the BLL acronym to indicate the business layer and all of its logic.

How complex and sophisticated can the BLL be?

This is a very hard question to answer in general. It becomes a much easier question to answer once you know and study the user requirements, rules, and constraints that apply to the specific context. There's virtually no logic to implement in a simple archiving system that barely has some user-interface (UI) forms on top of a database. Conversely, there's quite complex logic to deal with in a financial application or, more generally, in any application that is modeled after some real-world business process.

Where do you start designing the BLL of a real-world system?

When the problem's domain features a few hundred entities to work with, and thousands of business rules to fulfill, you need some structured guidance on how to create components. This guidance comes from two main families of patterns: design and architectural patterns. As we saw in Chapter 3, a *design pattern* is a general solution to a recurring software design problem. An *architectural pattern* is a larger scale pattern that describes the organizational schema of the system and specifies the responsibilities of each constituent subsystem.

In this book, we essentially assume a three-tier architecture with some flavors of service orientation. This chapter, in particular, is dedicated to a set of design patterns that are commonly used to design the business logic of a layered system.

What's the Business Logic Layer, Anyway?

Abstractly speaking, the BLL is the part of the software system that deals with the performance of business-related tasks. Essentially, the BLL consists of an array of operations to execute on some data. Data is modeled after the real entities in the problem's domain— something like invoices, customers, orders, and inventories. Operations, on the other hand, try to model business processes or, more likely, individual steps of a single process—for instance, creating an invoice, adding a customer, or posting an order.

Let's see what the BLL is really made of, where you typically deploy it, and which conceptual models exist to devise the business layer of a multitier system.

Dissecting the Business Layer

If you could take a look at a vertical section of the BLL, what would you see? In the BLL, you find an *object model* that models business entities, *business rules* that express all the customer's policies and requirements, *services* to implement autonomous functionalities, and *workflows* that define how documents and data are passed around from one constituent module to another and to and from other layers.

Security is also a serious matter and must be addressed in all layers, but especially here in the BLL where the code acts as a gatekeeper for the persistence layer. Security in the BLL means essentially role-based security to restrict access to business objects only to authorized users.

The Domain's Object Model

The domain's object model is intended to provide a structural view of the whole system, including a functional description of the entities, their relationships, and their responsibilities. The model is inspired by user requirements and is documented through the Unified Modeling Language (UML) *use cases* and *class diagrams*. (See Chapter 2, "UML Essentials," and Chapter 3, "Design Principles and Patterns" for more information about use cases and class diagrams.) With domain entities, you indicate real-world elements that store some data and expose some operations. Each entity plays a role in the model and provides an overall behavior. Each entity has responsibilities and interacts with other entities according to a domain-specific set of relationships.

Many applications that are commonly labeled as *complex* are, in reality, relatively simple if you look at the technical challenges they ultimately pose. However, the overall perception that these applications are complex is often because of the inherent complexity of the domain in which they originate. Often, the difficulty is all related to the building of an appropriate software model for the business rather than with its implementation. With a well-designed model, you can possibly go everywhere and possibly handle any level of complexity with a reasonable effort.

Object Model and Domain Model

For the sake of clarity, let us formalize what we mean by the terms *object model* and *domain model*. Although the terms are often used interchangeably, they actually address different things—or, at least, the same thing but at different levels of abstraction. What we call an object model is simply a graph of objects. There are no constraints on how the model is designed and implemented. Wherever you have a bunch of interrelated classes, you have an object model. As you can see, the description is quite general and applies to a large number of scenarios.

What we mean by *domain model* is kind of different. We haven't used this term yet, but we'll be using it plenty of times in this chapter and in the rest of the book. A domain model is an object model designed to meet a given set of requirements. Typically, classes in a domain model have no knowledge of the persistence layer and ideally have no dependencies on other classes in some helper framework you might use to create the graph. In addition, the domain model is designed looking at a particular problem's domain and trying to abstract processes and data flows in terms of those entities and relationships.

Note that *Domain Model* is also the name of a specific design pattern that we'll discuss later in this chapter and in the rest of the book. When referring to the pattern, though, we'll use either the term *pattern*, initial caps (as in *Domain Model*), or the acronym *DM*.

The Domain Entities

From the outside, the BLL can be seen as a sort of machinery that operates on business objects. Most of the time, a business object (BO) is just the implementation of a domain entity—namely, a class that encapsulates both data and behavior. When it is not, it will be a helper class performing some special calculations. The BLL determines how business objects interact with one another. It also enforces rules and workflows for participating modules to interact with, and update, business objects.

BLL occupies the middle segment of a layered system and exchanges information with both the presentation layer and DAL. The input and output of the BLL are not necessarily business objects. In many cases, architects prefer to resort to *data-transfer objects* (DTOs) to move data across the layers.

What's the difference between a BO and a DTO?

A business object contains both data and behavior, and it can be considered a full-fledged active object participating in the domain logic. A data-transfer object is a sort of value object—namely, a mere container of data with no attached behavior. The data stored in an instance of a BO is typically copied into a DTO for serialization purposes. The DTO has no logical behavior except for *get* accessors and *set* mutators. There might be multiple DTOs for each domain entity class in the model. Why *multiple* DTOs?

A DTO is not simply a behaviorless copy of a domain object. It is, instead, an object that represents a subset of a particular domain object as you would use it in a particular context. For example, in one method you might need a *Customer* DTO with only the company name and ID; elsewhere, you might need another one with the ID, company name, country, and contact information. Generally, however, a domain object is a graph of objects—for example, the *Customer* includes orders, which include order details, and so forth. A DTO indicates any needed projection of this aggregate.

Important The use of DTOs in conjunction with BOs is one of those topics that can trigger an endless, and sort of pointless, discussion within a team. The theory suggests that DTOs are used in all cases to reduce coupling between layers and to lend the system greater formal neatness. The practice, though, often reminds us that complexity is generally high enough that we should avoid any unnecessary additions. As a practical rule, we suggest that when you deal with a model of a few hundred business objects, you probably don't want to double the number of classes just to be neater in your implementation. In this case, a DTO might likely be the same as a BO.

Business Rules

Any real-world organization is based on a set of business rules. We can probably argue about the level of awareness of these rules within the organization, but you can't just deny that such rules exist. Each organization has strategies to pursue, and business rules are the primary instrument used to codify and implement these strategies. The strategy dictates where you want to go; business rules detail how to get there.

There are various ways to formalize business rules. If we were living and working in a perfect world, we would find out that each organization maintains its own database of rules that is easy to share with any teams active on a project. More often than not, though, the process of collecting business rules starts along with the development project. As a result, rules are shared with architects at quite a late stage of the project.

Depending on the context in which you operate, business rules can be quite fluid and variable. This means that in the BLL, rules should be implemented in a very flexible way, preferably through a *rules engine*. At the highest level of abstraction, a rules engine is a piece of software that accepts rules in some formal format and applies them to business objects.

In more practical terms, business rules are often just a set of IF-THEN-ELSE pseudo-statements that are manually mapped into the methods of business objects, producing what is commonly referred to as the *domain logic* or *business logic*.

In a realistic system, you can easily have thousands of business rules to map over a few hundred business objects. Quite often, as an architect, you are left alone to figure out which business rules were meant in the user requirements, while awaiting for the official papers to shed light and clarify. When the official papers with specifications eventually come in, your rules engine should be flexible enough to accommodate changes and fix misunderstandings.

Validation

The properties of a business object come from the attributes of the mapped entity. The methods of a business object come from its own set of responsibilities and any subset of business rules that apply to the entity.

A significant share of business rules go arm in arm with data validation. Put another way, many of the business rules are ultimately rules for validating the current content of a given business object.

In light of this, it would be desirable if you could come up with your own validation layer that business objects might optionally support—for example, through an interface. Each business object will then expose an interface for other objects to check their current state against the known set of applicable rules. With this model in mind, it shouldn't be hard to devise a system that can be fed externally with rules as they become available.

State validation for business objects is just one aspect of a broader area of BLL that touches on the relationships between objects and the internal flow of information. In addition to business objects, other software components contribute to the BLL.

Business Processes and Workflows

In BLL, you might also find cross-cutting components that perform ad hoc calculations, enforce mandatory flows of data within the system, orchestrate domain-specific processes to manipulate business objects, or do all of these things.

These components manage specific tasks—such as automatic routing of some sort of messages, automated processing of specific pieces of information, and any required integration between the core system and some existing subsystems, perhaps running on a different platform.

For example, suppose you have entities such as the order and the invoice. Does it mean that you have all the pieces you need to manage the full life cycle of an order? You can design the *Order* class with methods such as *Create*, *Post*, and *GetStatus*. But which module will actually call into these methods? The progress in the status of an order depends on a number of factors and triggers. A cross-cutting component that faithfully represents the effective business process, and that internally manages instances of business objects, offers a more manageable solution.

Better yet, this cross-cutting component can be created as a workflow. A workflow differs from a plain class because it allows you to express any required logic through a logical diagram. In addition, many commercial products (including Visual Studio 2008) supply a nice designer to visually create the diagram and a built-in toolbox of activities.

Figure 4-1 provides a high-level view of the software pieces a BLL is made of. The main point of contact with the outside world is represented by a repository of global functions that internally connect to modules doing calculations or running workflows. If you don't use data-transfer objects, your business objects should also be publicly available so that the presentation layer can directly instantiate them.

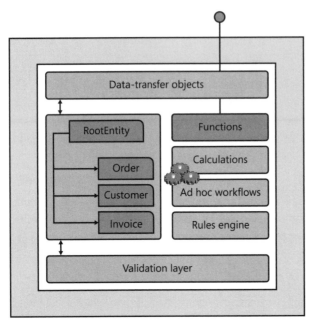

FIGURE 4-1 An interior view of a business layer

Where Would You Fit the BLL?

The BLL represents the logic of the system and is the layer of code that makes decisions and performs operations. Where would you deploy this layer of code? The BLL ideally lives in that part of the software universe known as the *middle tier*. So what would be a good definition for the term *middle tier*?

A widely accepted definition is the following. The middle tier (also referred to as application tier or logic tier) contains any logic that controls the functionality of an application.

When it comes to abstractly discussing the architecture of a complex application, many people tend to use the terms *tier* and *layer* interchangeably. Sometimes this is fair; sometimes it is not. Let's clarify.

Layer vs. Tier

With the term *tier*, we indicate a physical hardware and software section of the system defined by one or more servers that perform the same function. Conversely, the *layer* indicates a logical section of the system that performs a given duty.

A layer is merely a way of organizing your code. When you mention the presentation layer, for instance, you are referring to the functions that you expect from the application's front end. You are not referring to a particular client platform or technology. Or, at least, you shouldn't be.

Likewise, when you talk about layers you make no statements—neither implicitly nor explicitly—about where these layers might run, such as on different computers or in different processes. Equally valid terms that are often used to indicate a layer are *logical tier* and *logical layer*.

A tier, on the other hand, refers to where the code runs. For this reason, a tier is often referred to as a *physical tier*, or perhaps a *physical layer*. More specifically, a tier is the place where architects make logical layers run.

As a result, multiple layers can coexist on the same physical tier. At the same time, a layer should be easily moveable to another tier.

Why Should You Care About Layers?

A layer is normally conceived as a sort of black box with a clear contract (interface) that defines input and output and little, or no, dependency on other layers or physical servers. The main benefits that you get from layering are organizational and revolve around reuse and separation of concerns. Layer reuse allows you to write your layer once but use it within multiple business applications. A data access layer is a good candidate for that. Separation of concerns embodies the notion that layers should be encapsulated, or perhaps better stated, as highly cohesive but loosely coupled. Your business logic layer should not pull information directly from the database any more than your data access layer should present information directly to the user. By properly encapsulating your layers, you gain access to tools such as test-driven design and the use of "mock" layers that serve as temporary substitutes while the actual layer they represent is created. This allows development of dependent layers to continue rather than forcing layers to be created sequentially.

A high degree of reusability, coupled with the proper isolation of functions, makes for better and easier maintenance of the system. In the end, logical layers can significantly shorten the development cycle, allowing different teams to work in parallel.

Logical layering is often a very desirable feature to have in an application, or a system, regardless of real complexity. Mapping logical layers onto physical tiers is a different story, though, and it has different rules and perspectives.

Why Should You Care About Tiers?

Multiple tiers indicate that different physical entities are involved in running the application. A physical entity can be a computer or a process within a computer. In an enterprise scenario, nearly all applications these days have at least two tiers—and one of these tiers is a separate computer hosting the database server. Are multiple physical tiers a desirable feature?

The key point to note about physical tiers is that a tier represents a boundary to cross, whether it is a process boundary or machine boundary. Crossing a boundary is an expensive operation. The cost is higher if you have to reach a physically distant computer rather than just another process within the same machine. One rule of thumb to consider is that a call that crosses the boundaries of a process is about 100 times slower than an equivalent in-process call. And it is even slower if it has to travel over the network to reach the endpoint.

Multiple tiers are not generally a good feature to have in a system. Tiers slow down the overall performance and increase the overall complexity. Both aspects, then, affect the overall cost to build and maintain the application. This said, tiers—some tiers—just can't be avoided. So they're sort of evil, but a necessary evil.

In any system, there might be some physical boundaries that can't just be ignored and must be dealt with. For example, an unavoidable barrier exists between the code that runs on the user's machine and the server-side code. Another typical divide exists between the server-side code (also referred to as the *application server*) and the database server. Web applications mostly fall into this category.

In addition, each application might have its own good reasons to introduce multiple tiers. One reason could be the need to support an external product that requires its own process. Another good reason for multiple tiers is the quest for security. A module that runs in isolation in a process can be more easily protected and accessed if it's used only by authorized callers.

Much less often than commonly reckoned, multiple tiers serve as a trick to increase the scalability of a system. More precisely, a system where certain components can be remoted and duplicated on additional tiers is inherently more scalable than systems that do not have this capability. But scalability is just one aspect of a system. And often the quest for scalability—that is, the need for stabilized performance under pressure—hurts everyday performance.

In summary, the number of physical tiers should be kept as low as possible. And the addition of a new tier should happen only after a careful cost-benefit analysis, where costs are mostly in the area of increased complexity and benefits lie in the area of security, scalability and, perhaps, fault tolerance.

Exposing BLL to the World

So where should you deploy the BLL? Should it go in the same process as its callers? And how should you deal with inherent architectural divides such as client machines and application servers?

Back in 2003, Martin Fowler published a popular article in Dr. Dobb's Journal that is still a milestone for architects, regardless of which specialization and reference platform they use. The article, "Errant Architectures," is available at *http://www.ddj.com/184414966*. Why is it such an interesting read?

In the article, Fowler formalizes his first law of distributed object design. And it couldn't be clearer: *Don't distribute your objects.*

In more recent years, *distributed objects* have become *services*, which makes them significantly simpler, more effective, and more affordable. However, it didn't change a basic fact: whether it is a distributed object or a service, you're placing a call over the wire to a remote piece of software. A software layer that runs remotely is different from a layer that runs in a local process. Remote software is better designed with a coarse-grained interface, whereas in-process software is ideally architected with a fine-grained interface.

Hence, *location transparency* is a concept that works better in demos and presentations than in the real world. We're not saying that you have to change the internal architecture of the BLL if it has to run remotely. However, a remote BLL should always be wrapped by a component with a coarse-grained interface—typically, an implementation of the *Façade* pattern. (We'll return to this point in the next chapter while discussing the service layer of a system.)

Hosting BLL

At least when using the .NET Framework, the BLL is generally a collection of assemblies waiting for a host process. The shape and color of the host process are determined based on the application's context.

In a Web scenario, you typically host the BLL in the same process as ASP.NET. Nothing, if not the concerns expressed earlier in the chapter, prevents you from using separate processes and thus running the BLL in its own application server. Having the BLL on the server side greatly simplifies maintenance.

In a smart-client scenario, the BLL can be bundled with the presentation layer and run entirely on the user's machine within the application process. You still have separation between the presentation and business layers, and gain as much as possible in terms of interactivity and responsiveness. On the down side, maintenance can be problematic, unless you resort to ad hoc deployment technologies such as ClickOnce.

The BLL on the client is a must in the case of occasionally connected applications. With the BLL in place, the user of the application can work at will and save changes for later, when the connection is re-established. In this case, though, it might be sufficient to install only a portion of the BLL on the client. As a result, the BLL is split across the client and server.

Note The BLL, though, should not be considered as a monolithic component or as the composition of disjoint modules. Years of real-world experience taught us that some duplication of the BLL across layers—the classic three layers—is acceptable and realistic. But to the extent that it is possible, it shouldn't be encouraged.

Business and Other Layers

Everybody would agree that the BLL deserves its own module. However, this is not always what happens in reality. More often than not, logic that objectively belongs to the BLL is interwoven with other layers (when not tiers), such as the presentation layer and DAL. Nearly all developers would agree that this is not the right approach to take; yet, it happens more often than you might think.

With this in mind, let's take a look at some numbers that help us to figure out where we are and what we should target.

BLL Distribution and Measurements

Let's assume we have a classic layered system articulated in presentation, business, and data access layers. What percentage of business logic should go in each layer? The canonical answer is 0-100-0.

These numbers, though, are a lot like the ideal gas mileage numbers automobile manufacturers present when you're looking for a new car. How many vehicles ever attain the reported ideal mileage? And how realistic are the mileage figures? What really matters is the car is reliable, relatively fuel efficient, and fun to drive. The same generally holds true for layered architectures too.

When it comes to applications, what really matters is that a system is healthy, easy to maintain, and makes users happy. As an architect, you might find that the only way to get this is to make compromises such as duplicating some logic or moving it around. Honestly, the truth of the matter is often there is no problem with this.

In general, you should try to put everything in the BLL, except create, read, update, and delete (CRUD) operations and user-interface adjustments such as sizing, moving, and binding. Any amount of logic you might find in the presentation and data access layers might be because of some deliberate duplication introduced to capture some bit of extra performance.

Sometimes, though, it is there because of a sort of laziness or because of compromises with other figures. Have you ever heard or said something like, "It's easier this way; we'll rearchitect it later"?

The duplication might also be because of some gray areas in the overall functionality of the system—when, quite simply, it's not clear enough where some function has to go. The following sections describe a few common gray areas, with our thoughts about each.

Gray Area #1: Data Formatting

One of the most common reasons why the amount of logic in the presentation layer is not null is that you end up applying business logic in decisions about input validation and display formatting. Let's look at a concrete example. How would you store and handle some very specific data, such as a phone number or a value that represents money?

Users reasonably demand to see phone numbers or money displayed in a human-readable way—that is, properly formatted. OK, is this business logic or UI? We would tend to choose the first option, but we definitely recognize this as a gray area.

If you format data on the client, the presentation layer might need to know a lot about the context and the logic of the system. If you recognize formatting as part of the business logic, you should equip the BLL with proper methods for the client to retrieve ready-to-display strings.

And how would you store the raw information—in these examples, just numbers? All in all, you have three options:

- Store data twice, in both raw and easy-display format.
- Store data in its raw format, and apply formatting on the fly.
- Store data in the same input format as you receive it.

We would clearly go for option #2, but what if, because of other constraints, that meant adding logic to a stored procedure? This type of decision is where architects consider and work with tradeoffs.

Storing data twice is not an attractive solution because it leads to duplicated data (which might be the least attractive solution) and, more importantly, because it leads to additional update work and increased complexity of the code. Put another way, duplicate data results in more tests, risks of introducing errors, and so forth.

Not using data in its raw format is also problematic because it might hinder you when it comes to sorting, finding, and indexing that data.

Gray Area #2: CRUD Operations

When the logic in the DAL is not empty, it means that you've probably been forced to encode some logic in stored procedures. But this can lead to some interesting behavior. Consider this example: how would you delete a customer record?

You probably agree that in the BLL the customer is a business object whose data is mapped to some record in some database table. Some business logic decisions need to be made to "delete a customer." In particular, you must make a decision about the following issues: Can the customer even be deleted? Historical records such as customer-specific orders might preclude customer deletion. What other dependent records are to be deleted? Do you delete all orders placed by the customer, or contacts where the deleted customer is referenced? What else should be done before and after the deletion? Do you need to notify other processes (say, accounting or customer relations), close accounts, or send notifications to suppliers?

Such complex logic ideally belongs to the behavior of the business object. The code that implements the behavior of the business object knows when and if the object can be deleted and what this means to the rest of the system.

The DAL should only be commanded to proceed with database operations and should not even be aware of an entity named "the customer." All that it needs to know is how to get to the record, that it has to check are data types and nullability, and that it needs to ensure data integrity and indexing.

Other types of records that are different from the customer record, however, might not be so difficult to deal with in a stored procedure. All in all, it is essentially a matter of intelligent application of design principles and an understanding of the domain and context.

Gray Area #3: Stored Procedures

As mentioned, you often deal with stored procedures (SP). This might happen because you're fanatical about stored procedures or because the DBA forced you to use SPs. As a result, sometimes the deletion of data associated with a business object is handled exclusively by a stored procedure. In this case, inevitably, the SP contains logic.

In a nutshell, you should consider SPs to be only a database tool and not the repository for a single ounce of business logic. You should use SPs to return and update data, not to interpret data in any way. Furthermore, SPs should operate only on one table, except when they join tables for the purpose of returning data or when they implement batch updates that loop over data in a way that would generate hundreds of statements if executed from the business logic layer.

Let's be honest: often business logic slips into SPs because it's so quick and easy to do it that way. In a rush, you might decide that it's (temporarily) better to just put a given feature in an SP. But, of course, you promise yourself that you'll fix it later, as soon as you can catch your breath. Often, this moment of pause never happens and the code remains there in the SP forever or until the application is retired or replaced entirely.

Moreover, by moving any business logic out of SPs, you make your logic a lot easier to update, test, and debug. In addition, you increase the database portability of the solution because SPs designed for portability need to be extremely simple. In addition, online transaction processing (OLTP) would also force simple SPs. The more you put in there, the longer the transaction might take, killing OLTP functionality.

A common objection you have to face with regard to this point frequently comes from DBAs: moving logic out of SPs increases the traffic to and from the database.

The validity of this objection is debatable. The concerns of the DBA are not always justified. Databases are often connected over a very high-speed connection, so they can often happily handle any increased traffic. If this issue comes up, whatever decision you make, just be sure it is backed up by numbers. And if you have to resort to SPs, pay close attention so that no logic eventually slips into them.

> **Note** When it comes to database traffic, it's often possible to add more or better hardware to ease the bottlenecks. Furthermore, where possible you'd probably also cache information in the BLL. Sometimes you can't, but other times you can, especially for simple table lookups, which are just the sort of thing you'd be hitting the database for on a frequent basis.

Patterns for Creating the Business Layer

As shown in Figure 4-1, the BLL is centered on the domain's object model—that is, a graph of objects that model the entities in the domain. Each business object has its own data and behavior. After you have a class diagram and know the model, how do you approach the task of actually building this business layer?

There are a few design patterns for organizing the domain logic, each with a different level of complexity and different objectives. We'll go into the details of these patterns in the remainder of the chapter. For now, we'd like to briefly describe them by category.

Why Patterns for the BLL?

In the design of the BLL, we could go ad hoc, but the success rate in doing so isn't all that good, historically speaking. So we leverage patterns because patterns help us understand and deal with complexity. Each pattern has strengths and weaknesses, or probably more precisely, patterns have architectural strengths versus cost.

Which path we choose isn't always based on cost; rather, it's often based on an intimate knowledge of the business domain. The more complex the BLL needs to be to support stakeholders' requirements, the less likely we are to choose a pattern that doesn't handle domain-specific complexity well. Some BLL patterns are great for relatively simple applications, but you wouldn't run large applications on them.

So the focus is on understanding the application's intended domain, understanding the palette of available and known patterns, and selecting the pattern that we believe gives us the best hope of dealing with the complexity of the BLL we anticipate.

Procedural Patterns

Before the long wave of object-oriented development, quite a few years ago, the BLL was simply perceived as a collection of procedures, each handling a single request from the presentation layer. Therefore, a good design was mostly a matter of organizing procedures in a way that minimized code redundancy while fully matching the requirements.

The BLL was seen collectively, as a series of related transactions. Starting from the use cases, each step the system had to carry out was broken down into smaller steps. And each step was then rendered through an operation, generally referred to as a *transaction*.

In this context, however, a transaction indicates a monolithic logical operation and has *no* relationship to a database management system (DBMS) transaction. This pattern is known as a *Transaction Script*.

If you need to submit an order for some goods, your logical transaction is made of steps such as checking for the availability of goods, calculating totals, verifying funds on the user account, updating databases, and perhaps interacting with the shipping service.

Historically, a Transaction Script was the first pattern to appear and gain popularity. Over the years, another approach emerged, built around the notion of a table of data. It goes by the name of *Table Module*. The perspective is similar to a series of transactions, but this time operations are grouped by data. Operations are defined as methods on an object that represents a table of records. From our standpoint, this remains a mostly procedural approach, but one with a more strongly object-oriented vision. In the end, you use the table of data (often a real database table or view) as a factor that helps to organize methods. For example, you might want to set up the BLL as a collection of methods on a table object that contains all orders or customers.

Object-Based Patterns

A fully object-based pattern takes you to organizing the domain logic as a graph of interrelated and interconnected objects each representing an entity or a concern in the business and each object equipped with data and behavior. How close is this object model to the data model represented in the database? It depends on the complexity and, subsequently, on the level of abstraction you need.

A very simple object model looks a lot like the data model expressed by database tables. In this case, the objects that form the model are essentially records with some extra methods. This pattern is generally referred to as the *Active Record pattern*.

The more you add abstraction, the more you move away from the data model. So to create a domain-driven object model, most likely, you start from the vision of the domain you have rather than from the structure of the database. A domain-driven design invariably leads you to having a significant gap between the data model and the resulting domain model. This pattern is generally referred to as the *Domain Model pattern*.

In summary, if you feel the focus should be put on operations, you opt for a Transaction Script. If you find it easier to reason in terms of tables of data, go for a Table Module. If your domain model mimics your data model fairly faithfully, the Active Record pattern might best suit your needs. Finally, if the process you're modeling causes you to start with an abstract schema of interconnected entities and break it down into compositional subsystems, the Domain Model pattern is probably for you.

Is this synopsis correct? Are things really as easy and smooth as schematized here? Well, not really. This wouldn't be the notorious *real world* then. As you might have guessed, each approach has pros, cons, and preferred fields of application. Before we delve deeper into each of the primary patterns for modeling domain logic, an overall look at all of them together is needed to enable you to make an informed choice.

Differences at a Glance

The primary factor that guides your choice between a Transaction Script, Table Module, and Domain Model is certainly the complexity of the domain logic you have to express. For the simple logic of a filing system (for example, archiving books or DVDs), it doesn't really matter which approach you choose. For an enterprise-class system, taking the wrong route might result in missed deadlines and dangerously move the project down the slope of failure.

Figure 4-2 captures the essential differences between the three patterns. It is never a matter of choosing the best approach; what really matters is picking the approach that works best in the project.

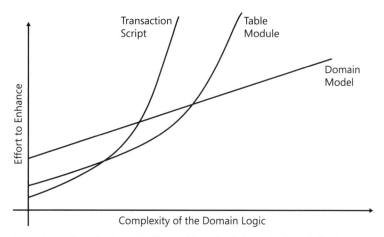

FIGURE 4-2 Complexity and efforts with each of the main domain logic patterns

The diagram in the figure doesn't come out of any scientific or even nonscientific polls of customers and fellow architects. Likewise, it doesn't deliver concrete information in terms of a measurement. *Complexity of the domain logic*, we say? Sure, but how much complexity? *Effort to enhance*? Sure, but how many days or months? So do not read Figure 4-2 as a scientific diagram. Instead, use it to grasp the sense of each pattern when compared to each other.

A similar diagram was first reproduced in Martin Fowler's superb book *Patterns of Enterprise Application Architecture* (P of EAA), from Addison-Wesley, 2002. (You can find it on page 29 of that book.) In our direct experience, we haven't found anything yet that casts doubt on the accuracy of this diagram. Because the diagram is totally unquantified, it doesn't make much sense to discuss the absolute starting position of each curve on the Y axis. Likewise, on the X axis we're mostly interested in the type of asymptotic curve rather than actual numbers.

In a nutshell, we find that Fowler's diagram captures at a glance the exact differences between the three patterns. So what are these differences?

Object-Based vs. Procedural Patterns

Object-based patterns have higher startup costs and a kind of linear growth with complexity. In other words, once you have grasped a good understanding of the Domain Model pattern, you are well positioned to design your system using that pattern whatever the complexity of the system is.

Designing the model to act as the foundation for a piece of software that faithfully represents the user requirements is a delicate art. Although metrics and practices exist, we found out that getting the model right is mostly a matter of experience. Experience sharpens your sight and mind and makes you think in a way that is not too little and not too big, but just right.

Objects provide abstraction, and abstraction inherently introduces a gap between requirements and the final software product. Your efforts include preventing mismatches and misinterpretation from sneaking in. A more complex system certainly takes more time and requires more work and attention, but it's manageable.

On the other hand, procedural patterns tend to reach a point of complexity beyond which adding new features has exponentially growing costs.

We used the word "complexity" quite a few times already. But how do you measure such a thing? When can you really call a domain's logic "complex," and when is it, instead, simple enough? How do you recognize complexity and simplicity in a domain's object model?

A Quick Measure of Complexity

Complexity is essentially a two-fold factor. In all cases, you have some amount of *inherent complexity*. This is the complexity deriving from an unavoidable amount of crisp and not contradictory requirements. This complexity can be managed more or less effectively, but you can't just make it go away. You have to work with it.

In addition, there's the whole challenge of *induced complexity*. This is the complexity triggered by any impedance mismatch that comes into existence among the various stakeholders of the system. A nasty effect of this mismatch is the misdirection it presents to the team. Misdirection typically leads to an abstract design that contains unnecessary or nonfunctional features, with the result of pushing the software to the limit. A common metric with which to measure the stakeholders' mismatch is *requirements churn*, which indicates the number of new or changed requirements the team gets per month.

You want some numbers to try to mark the boundary between object-based and procedural patterns, right? Complexity can't be quantified up front by counting classes in the object model or lines of code—you don't have code or design made yet. Requirements are therefore the only measurable information you can rely on up front.

The number of requirements can be used to form an idea about the class of complexity of the system. The order of magnitude for a moderately complex business application is certainly numbered in the thousands. It's unreasonable to expect to find less than a few thousand business rules in a real-world application. However, not all requirements have the same effect on the system or add significant complexity to the development or the final product. For example, in a Web portal where you just reuse the existing back office, requirements are mostly in the area of the graphical user interface. This system is inherently much simpler than a system (for example, a banking system) that involves building a back office to be shared by different applications (for example, online banking, trading, or customer care).

When you measure the complexity of a system, you expect to get numbers and quantities. However, in software systems it's easier to recognize complexity than it is to explain how to spot it.

> **Note** We expect some readers at this point to exclaim, "Hey, I'm new and you can't explain how to spot complexity in a software system. How would I ever know it when I saw it?" Seriously, recognizing complexity in a software system is not like conducting a litmus test to determine the acidity of a material. There's no paper that turns red or blue to give you a clear and observable response. It's a matter of experience, education and, yes, gut feeling.

Let's move on and get up close and personal with the four main patterns for modeling the domain logic. We start from the simplest of all—the Transaction Script pattern.

The Transaction Script Pattern

When it comes to organizing your business logic, there's just one key decision you have to make. Do you go with an object-oriented design or with a procedural approach? You are choosing a paradigm to design the business logic; it's about architecture, not about technology. However, the hardware and software platform of choice—the overall technology—can drive you toward a particular model of business logic.

The Transaction Script (TS) pattern is probably the simplest possible pattern for business logic; it is entirely procedural. Like all the other patterns we cover in this and the following chapters, TS owes its name and classification to Martin Fowler. For further reference, have a look at page 110 of his book [P of EAA], which we mentioned earlier in the chapter.

Generalities of the TS Pattern

TS encourages you to skip any object-oriented design and map your business components directly onto required user actions. You focus on the operations the user can accomplish through the presentation layer and write a method for each request. The method is referred to as a transaction script.

The word *transaction* here generically indicates a business transaction you want to carry out. The word *script* indicates that you logically associate a sequence of system-carried actions (namely, a script) with each user action.

When to Use TS

TS is extremely easy to understand and explain. Each required user action proceeds from start to finish within the boundaries of a physical transaction. Data access is usually encapsulated in a set of components distinct from those implementing the actual script.

TS doesn't have any flavors of object-oriented design. Any logic you model through a TS is expressed using language syntax elements such as IF, WHILE, and FOR. Adding a new feature to an existing user action mostly means adding a new branch or subroutine somewhere in the existing code.

TS is suited for simple scenarios where the business logic is straightforward and, better yet, not likely to change and evolve.

TS seems to be the perfect choice for a Web portal that relies on an existing back office. In this case, you end up with some pages with interactive elements that trigger a server action. Each server action is resolved by making some data validation, perhaps making some trivial calculations, and then forwarding data to the back-office system.

Honestly, with such simple requirements there's no need to spend much time planning a domain model.

Note Simplicity and complexity are concepts that are not easy to measure. More importantly, the perception of what's simple and what's complex depends on a person's attitude and skills. If you've been doing object-oriented design for years and know your stuff well, it might be easier and faster for you to arrange a simple domain model than to switch back to procedural coding. So TS doesn't have to be the choice every time you feel the complexity is below a given universally recognized threshold. More simply, TS is an option that you should seriously consider once you feel you know all about the system, and when it doesn't look overly complex in terms of requirements and business rules. Objects make code elegant, but elegance is a positive attribute only if code works and is done right. There's nothing to be ashamed of in using TS— and especially in using TS when it is appropriate.

What's Good About TS

TS is a simple procedural model that presents the application logic as a collection of logical transactions. Simplicity is the hallmark of TS. It has no startup costs for the team and works well with rapid application development (RAD) environments.

TS is ideal for projects with only a small amount of logic, tight deadlines, and access to rich integrated development environments (IDE) such as Visual Studio.

Using a procedural approach doesn't mean you need to have monolithic code. A high-level transaction can be broken down into simpler and reusable routines and layers. One of the most common layers is the persistence layer, where you find smaller components that handle data access and other chores. This is the layer that can deliver you some degree of reusability. Figure 4-3 shows the big picture of a TS-based system.

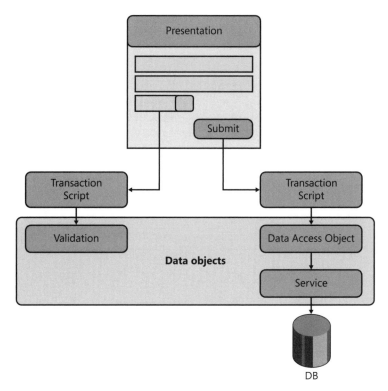

FIGURE 4-3 Relatively rich methods calling into underlying layers attending to data access and other chores

What's Bad About TS

Simplicity is the major strength and most critical weakness of TS. Setting up a TS is as easy as creating one or a few container classes that expose logically related methods. As shown in Figure 4-3, each method implements a particular transaction script and, optionally, interacts with helper data objects that perform a variety of tasks—from validation to data massaging, from calculation to physical data access.

Note that there's nothing but common sense to prevent you from placing all the code, including data access code, in a transaction script. Likewise, it's mostly common sense to suggest to you how to group scripts.

In general, TS has remarkable potential for code duplication. It is not unlikely that you'll end up with a number of transactions accomplishing very similar tasks. The resulting application might not look really different from a tangle of routines. If it's not spaghetti code, it might perhaps be some *bucatini code*. Your code will still look tangled, but at least it will be a more coarse-grained tangle.

> **Note** *Bucatini code* is not an officially registered term in software development. However, it has the same meaning as spaghetti code, except that it refers to richer building blocks of code— exactly the difference between spaghetti and bucatini. (Bucatini is a variation of spaghetti; it's just thicker and has a hole running through the center.)

Code duplication and spaghetti code can be avoided by extracting chunks of code and promoting them to the rank of a method. This is usually what the process of refactoring does. Refactoring certainly helps mitigate some issues inherent with TS. However, refactoring has a limited range.

As the volume and content of requirements grow, it usually gets harder to refactor, for at least two reasons. First, you run behind schedule and don't feel like spending more time to redo what you already did, even if it means better code. Second, even when you make a point of refactoring your code regularly, it will take longer and longer to adjust as the complexity of the domain logic grows. This concept is well captured by the curve that represents TS in Figure 4-2.

To add insult to injury, touching a tangle of routines can be risky from a testing perspective too. Don't forget software regression testing. You might find out that a newly added feature causes the software to stop working or perform poorly compared to previous versions. You have one more thing to fix and, more generally, you just can't make it work without a good battery of regression tests.

Fight Duplication: One Is Enough

More generally and beyond the context of TS, code duplication is a nasty beast to fight. In the case of changes to the code, it will cause you headaches because you have to find all the places where you have similar code. It also is confusing and unfriendly to new developers on the team and makes testing (regression tests, in particular) much harder to do.

However, your real enemy is *duplication*, not just code duplication. A well-designed system doesn't repeat the same feature in multiple places—be it code, documentation, unit tests, or perhaps use cases. What are your weapons to fight off duplication? One is the broad application of object-oriented principles such as encapsulation and inheritance. Another one is *cohesion*—that is, when classes carry out tightly related activities and have a small number of responsibilities.

The Pattern in Action

Overall, designing domain logic according to TS is not a hard task. You get the list of required transactions by looking at the actions available in the presentation layer or, more generally, you look at the use cases defined for the system.

After you have the list of transactions, you implement each transaction in a method housed in a component. In the Microsoft .NET Framework, a component is essentially a class compiled to an assembly.

Designing Business Components

The basic point is that each transaction has its own method in some component. What happens within the body of the method is entirely up to you. You can have all the code in one place; or you can delegate the execution of child steps to some shared helper objects. These helper objects collectively form specific layers, such as validation, formatting, and persistence. (See Figure 4-3.)

All classes that implement transaction scripts can be referred to as *business components*. You can derive all business components from a unique parent. In this way, you ensure that all classes have a common base behavior. What would be a typical behavior you might want to share among all business components? You might want to share the constructor to make sure that all business components receive the same information upon initialization. Another example is common error handling. Handling exceptions pretty much breaks nearly any nicely designed model and should be considered up front. Security is another example. A base class can offer a one-stop method to check for authorization.

In addition, you might want to use the base class to define members that import external objects within the boundaries of the business layer to address cross-cutting concerns such as logging. Generally, you can build the base class to support dependency injection (which is defined in Chapter 3) and thus receive and consume external objects that supply a service to the script.

Implementing Business Components

You can have one or more transaction scripts per business component. The most popular approach entails that you factor your transaction scripts into groups and then proceed with one business component per group. Each group will therefore feature logically related scripts. Methods on the business component class can be static or instance members. We'll return to the differences between static and instance members in a moment.

The following code snippet describes two sample processes: ordering a product, and booking a hotel room:

```
public class ApplicationAPI
{
    public int CreateOrder(OrderInfo order)
    {
        // Start the transaction
        // Retrieve and check product information
        // Check if the amount of goods being ordered is available
        // Check credit status
        // Calculate price, including tax, shipping, and freight
        // Add a new record to the Orders database
        // Add new records to the OrderDetails database
        // Commit the transaction
        // Return the order ID
    }

    public string BookHotelRoom(Customer guest, DateTime checkIn, DateTime checkOut)
    {
        // Start the transaction
        // Check room availability for requested stay
        // Check customer information (already guest, payment method, preferences)
        // Calculate room rate
        // Add a new record to the Bookings database
        // Generate the confirmation number
        // Commit the transaction
        // E-mail the customer
        // Return the confirmation number
    }
    ⋮
}
```

As you can see, both methods are grouped into a single business component and both methods involve several steps. Each step can be implemented through direct database calls (SQL commands, stored procedures, or perhaps ADO.NET code) or by placing calls to a specialized component or service.

The implementation of both methods is not particularly cohesive, which means that there's a lot of room for refactoring—and a significant exposure to problems if you don't refactor it properly.

Business Components as Command Objects

Alternatively, you can implement each transaction script in its own class. Each business component, therefore, features just one method. Put another way, in this case the business object is a sort of command object used to represent an action. This is exactly the definition of the *Command* pattern.

Note One of the most popular behavioral design patterns, the Command pattern uses objects to represent actions. The command object encapsulates an action and all of its parameters. Typically, the command object exposes a standard interface so that the caller can invoke any command, without getting the intimate knowledge of the command class that will actually do the job. Like many other design patterns, the Command pattern was originally defined in the book *Design Patterns: Elements of Reusable Object-Oriented Software* (Addison-Wesley, 1994). Authored by Erich Gamma, Richard Helm, Ralph Johnson, and John Vlissides—the Gang of Four (GoF)—the book is a landmark in software engineering.

When the TS business component is a command object, you extract an interface and encapsulate all required parameters as public properties of the class. Here's how to rewrite the preceding code to use the Command pattern:

```
public interface IApplicationCommand
{
    int Run();
}
public class CreateOrderCommand : IApplicationCommand
{
    OrderInfo _orderinfo;
    int _orderID;
    // other internal members

    public CreateOrderCommand(OrderInfo order)
    {
        _orderInfo = order;
    }

    public int OrderID
    {
        get { return _orderID; }
    }

    public int Run()
    {
        // Start the transaction
        // Retrieve and check product information
        // Check if the amount of goods being ordered is available
        // Check credit status
        // Calculate price, including tax, shipping, and freight
        // Add a new record to the Orders database
        // Add new records to the OrderDetails database
        // Commit the transaction
        // Get the order ID, and store it in the local member _orderID
    }
}

public class BookHotelRoom : IApplicationCommand
{
    Customer _guest;
    DateTime _checkIn, _checkOut;
```

```
    String _confirmationNumber;
    // other internal members

    public BookHotelRoom(Customer guest, DateTime checkIn, DateTime checkOut)
    {
        _guest = guest;
        _checkIn = checkIn;
        _checkOut = checkOut;
    }

    public String ConfirmationNumber
    {
        get { return _confirmationNumber; }
    }

    public int Run()
    {
        // Start the transaction
        // Check room availability for requested stay
        // Check customer information (already guest, payment method, preferences)
        // Calculate room rate
        // Add a new record to the Bookings database
        // Generate the confirmation number
        // Commit the transaction
        // E-mail the customer
        // Store the confirmation number to the local member _confirmationNumber
    }
    ⋮
}
```

The Command pattern allows the presentation layer to instantiate command objects indirectly through a factory, which makes the overall design inherently more extensible. When you opt for a common interface, though, you need to find out how to return values. A widely accepted solution is defining public read-only members where the *Run* method returns any values it wants to make publicly available through those fields or properties.

Considerations About the Command Pattern

Implementing the Command pattern in TS leads to a proliferation of little classes that can clutter up the application's namespace. However, the Command pattern has great potential, too. The ability to represent an action with an object also allows you to combine a series of activities into a larger transaction. Do you see the point?

Not only can you use the Command pattern to expose a transaction script to the presentation layer, you can also use it to bundle up smaller activities into the transaction script itself. In other words, all the steps outlined earlier for, say, *CreateOrderCommand* can be command objects as well. This means that you can, for example, also serialize commands to some medium and transfer them to a different process for handling. In addition, the list of commands in each transaction script can be read out of the configuration or modified dynamically. In the end, a command is just a class name, an assembly, and a bunch of parameters. And, of course, a common interface to make it run.

Static and Instance Methods

If you opt for multiple scripts in a single business object, a question arises with regard to the status of the methods. Should you use static methods or instance methods? Needless to say, if you opt for the Command pattern there's no option: methods are to be instance based.

In the .NET Framework, static and instance methods are nearly identical performance-wise. A static method is invoked without an instance of the host class being created. This means that static methods can directly use static variables and other static methods. Static methods can't talk to instance member variables unless they manage to get a reference to a particular instance.

For properties, the attribute *static* might, in some cases, bring benefits in terms of memory because only one copy of the property exists and it is shared by all instances of the type. For methods, though, the difference is very minor and limited to the need of creating or getting a fresh instance of the class every time you make a call to the method.

The bottom line is that any choice between static and instance methods is essentially a design choice. You can make this choice by applying a simple rule: any method that doesn't have contact with other members in the class should be implemented as a static method. This rule can be enforced by FxCop. Note, though, that this is a quick rule that applies to methods in the context of a TS. Generally, if a method or property is and should be tied to the class as a whole, it should be static. If the method or property is tied to a specific instance of the class, it's not static.

> **Note** FxCop is a free, static code-analysis tool from Microsoft. It analyzes managed assemblies and suggests possible design, performance, and security improvements. FxCop checks the compiled code for conformance to the Microsoft .NET Framework Design Guidelines. For more information, visit *http://msdn.microsoft.com/en-us/library/bb429476(VS.80).aspx*.

Passing Data to Transaction Scripts

How would you pass operational data to a transaction script? You generally use method parameters when scripts are exposed as public methods of a business component. You provide data through the constructor or public properties if you have a single class per transaction script.

Because you likely need to pass multiple values for each call, using lots of parameters on a method often turns out to be awkward. In this case, you store multiple scalar values in a new class. Such a class would clearly be a DTO. In the preceding code, both *Customer* and *OrderInfo* are DTOs. Here's another example:

```
public class Customer
{
    public string FirstName {get; set;}
    public string LastName {get; set;}
    public DateTime DateOfBirth {get; set;}
    public string PhotoID {get; set;}
    public Address Home {get; set;}
    public PaymentDetails MethodOfPayment {get; set;}
    :
    :
}
```

Obviously, DTOs can be nested and are plain containers of data with no behavior. If you're using DTOs to pass data among processes, the DTO class must be made serializable.

> **Note** The main point we want to make here about ways to provide data to transaction scripts clearly relates to DTOs, but it goes even beyond that. The TS pattern doesn't mandate any data types or formats. Providing data to scripts and retrieving data from scripts is up to you. So feel free to opt for the approach that best suits your preferences and design needs. We just listed the most common options that we have successfully employed in real projects. Don't feel limited to using only these.

The Table Module Pattern

The TS pattern envisions the domain logic as a series of transactions triggered by the presentation. Subsequently, modeling the domain logic means mapping transactions onto methods of one or more business components. Each business component then talks to the DAL either directly or through relatively dumb data objects. The logic is implemented in large chunks of code that can be difficult to understand, maintain, and reuse.

When you partition transaction scripts into business components, you often group methods by entity. For example, you create an *OrderAPI* business component to house all transaction scripts related to the "order" entity. Likewise, you create a *CustomerAPI* component to expose all methods related to action the system needs to perform on customers. And so forth.

Furthermore, in relatively simple scenarios the entity can also be mapped directly to a database table. In the end, you come up with one business component per significant database table.

In TS, you then create DTOs to provide and retrieve data. DTOs are custom data types, whose property set closely matches the columns in the underlying table.

The Table Module (TM) pattern simply formalizes this common practice in a new procedural approach.

Generalities of the TM Pattern

Compared to TS, TM is a more structured pattern because it provides more guidance on how to do things. The simple rule for this pattern can be summarized as follows: define a business component for each database table. The business component is known as the *table module class* and contains all the code that operates on the given table.

The table module class serves as a container and packages data and behavior together. The domain logic is broken into coarse-grained components that represent the entire table. The granularity of the table module class never reaches the level of a table row. Subsequently, the table module class can't get the identity of any individual rows it deals with. You always think in terms of a collection of table rows and need to specify a key or an index to reference a particular row.

How does the presentation layer exchange data with a TM business layer? Being strictly table-oriented, TM drives you toward record set–like data structures for passing data around. According to page 508 of [P of EAA], a record set (RS) is an in-memory representation of tabular data. An RS looks like the result set produced by some SQL query. However, you can make your implementation of an RS more valuable by providing a layer that disconnects it from the data source. In doing so, you make the RS behave like a DTO.

> **Note** Using RS-based data structures when you're modeling through TM is the most common and natural option. All that TM cares about is the subdivision of business methods by logical tables. With this done, you can happily use custom classes to carry data into and out of a table module class. The reason why you, in your own code, often end up using RS-based data structure is different. You often find record set data types packed in the software platform of your choice. In the .NET Framework, you have quite a few such helpful and ready-made classes, such as *DataSet* and *DataTable*.

When to Use TM

In general, an object-based pattern is the most versatile and powerful way of modeling the domain logic. An object model is a graph of objects that, in reality, you have to interface with a relational database. Filling the conceptual gap existing between the object-oriented and relational model might be a nightmare. Known as the *object-relational impedance mismatch*, this issue is addressed by ad hoc tools such as O/RMs.

The TM pattern sits somewhere in between TS and object-based patterns such AR and DM. It gives clear guidance on how to lay out your business components and make them interact with the rest of the system. It still works in terms of methods rather than objects, but it slowly takes you toward an object-oriented world.

In reality, if you organize your logic with one class per table, and encapsulate behavior in these classes, you're using an object model. Sure, the objects might not represent the domain of the problem; rather, the objects represent the underlying data model. However, in all cases where not much abstraction is required and a short gap exists between the object model and data model, TM is an excellent compromise. Compared to TS, it is based on a conceptual model—the data model—and is not a more or less loose collection of methods.

When in the system the presentation layer and DAL are based on tabular data structures, the TM model shines. In this case, the business layer can return ready-to-use data to the presentation layer, sometimes even via data binding. Likewise, the business layer can exchange data with the DAL without further data massaging. Figure 4-4 illustrates this scenario in the context of a .NET Framework application.

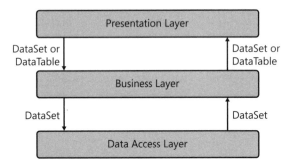

FIGURE 4-4 Presentation benefits from using business logic that handles *DataSet* objects and *DataTable* objects. Here, the business logic takes advantage of an ADO.NET-based DAL.

In .NET, you use *DataSets* most of the time. However, especially in the presentation layer, using a simpler *DataTable* can help minimize the amount of data transferred to and from the business layer. The DAL and business layer normally exchange *DataSets*, which provides greater flexibility that allows for batch updates and multitable read and write operations.

What's Good About TM

TM is not really more complex than TS. However, if you had to build it all by yourself, it probably would take more work than using a plain TS. More guidance from the pattern also means more rules to take into account—and, ultimately, more code to write. In particular, what would be your opinion of TM if you had to write your own *DataSet*-like class?

In the end, the best argument for using TM solutions is the support you get for table module classes from some IDEs, such as Microsoft Visual Studio.

In Visual Studio, including the latest version of Visual Studio 2008, you have wizards to create a data source. In Figure 4-5, you see the dialog box used to add a new *DataSet* item to your project.

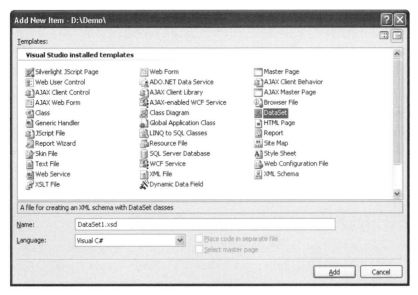

FIGURE 4-5 When you add a new *DataSet* item, Visual Studio creates a bunch of table module classes for you.

The wizards guide you through the steps necessary to pick up database items from a database connection and generate all necessary code for you. We'll have a quick look at this code in a moment. Figure 4-6 shows the final results of the wizard.

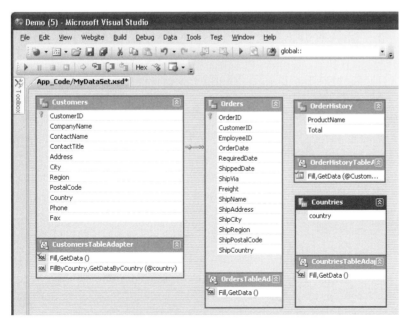

FIGURE 4-6 Visual Studio 2008 creates a visual representation of the table module classes and shows the data and methods of each.

Using the embedded *DataSet* designer, you can add tables from the database and define relationships and constraints. Each table module class is modeled after the table and exposes the collection of records, as well as the methods to work with on the table. At a minimum, you have *Fill* and *GetData* methods to run a query through the entire table.

Conceptually, another good point in favor of TM is that it leads you to having just one set of TM classes with a given set of functionalities, regardless of the underlying data sources—SQL Server, Oracle, and the like. If you build your TM model through Visual Studio, you have to replace the *Adapter* property of each table adapter object to make it use the right connection channel. If you do it all by yourself, consider that TM is a high-level interface that can easily encapsulate an additional and dynamically loaded gateway specific to a given data source.

What's Bad About TM

TM is object based but entirely database driven. It is not suitable for expressing a complex graph of entities, especially when the gap between the object model and data model is significant.

The major strength of TM is the support it finds in Visual Studio, which makes applying the pattern a piece of cake. This strength quickly turns into a relevant weakness when you consider that the code you get from wizards is a sort of black box.

Also, it's obvious that TM as an architectural model is *not* tightly coupled with Visual Studio and its wizards. You can have a system based on TM concepts with or without ADO.NET *DataSets* and with or without wizards. In summary, what's good and bad with TM is its integration with Visual Studio. The more you move away from the autogenerated TM-style code, the more you feel uncomfortable and tempted to either upgrade to an object-based pattern or downgrade to TS.

For this reason, TM is not all that popular for developers using the Java platform, even though some built-in RS-like data structure exists in JDBC. The *Rowset* object, in particular, is the counterpart of the ActiveX Data Objects (ADO) *RecordSet*—a component that can operate as a smart cursor and scroll through a result set connected in read and update mode, or just work disconnected on a cached set of rows.

Gimme a Quick Answer: TS or TM?

The answer here is limited to any scenarios where you just don't want or can't afford to use an object-based pattern. If you have to use a procedural approach, the quick-and-dirty answer would be the following.

On the .NET Framework, TM is mostly preferable because of the Visual Studio designers and code generators. Although they're not designed to be perfect (smile), code generators do a good job of getting you started in a matter of seconds. The code generated for a *DataSet* item is hidden from view, but it can be accessed, duplicated, edited, and reloaded into the project as a code file. In the worst case, you can just use the services of Visual Studio to grab some code and proceed from there with your own implementation.

Because of the Visual Studio facilities, in the .NET Framework it's often more convenient to stop there and avoid TS. It is different, of course, on another development platform. But, again, this is just the quick answer given to an architect who wants to take the procedural route.

The TM Pattern in Action

A TM business component is a class that represents the content of a table. However, in the real world you hardly ever need just that. In addition, you likely need to find represented in the component some of the relationships that exist between tables.

Internals of a Business Component

The table module class can have instance or static methods. With static methods, you tend to lose some of the benefits derived from encapsulation of data. A static method is simply the trigger of a query or a mapped stored procedure. Creating the business component as a collection of static methods makes it hard for you to implement more advanced capabilities, such as caching or lazy loading. With static methods, in fact, any buffer you define is globally shared. That's not too bad if you only read data; it's quite an issue if you intend to support in-memory updates, too.

In summary, members of a TM business component are essentially instance members. Let's delve deeper into the benefits of this approach.

First, you can initialize the class with the results of a query. Second, you can implement the Query Object pattern (see page 316 of [P of EAA]) and hold the results within the instance. With a static method, though, you are forced to use the query factory only as a way to get data to be processed elsewhere—for example, in the service or the presentation layer.

> **Note** The Query Object pattern refers to an object that represents the public interface to a database query. The *Query* object serves as an interpreter and accepts any information useful in preparing the SQL query through properties and methods. The Query Object pattern shields you from the details of the database and delivers a replaceable object, but it forces you to work with a relatively static schema for the query. In other words, you can't just run every query you like, only those whose syntax fits in the schema recognized by the interpreter.

Finally, if you opt for instance members, you can build your own hierarchy of objects, thus layering required functionalities. With static members, on the other hand, you have a flat collection of methods with only a global state.

Because the TM business component probably maintains relationships to data in other business components, do not expect in general to find a TM business component that merely lists methods to query and update a single table.

Typical Structure of a Business Component

In TM, a table module class has an internal data container that is initialized with the data to work with. The cached content is then filtered and manipulated by the various methods you define. Methods take as parameters any additional information they need.

Note that TM doesn't have the notion of an identity for child objects. This means that you'll have a table module class *Orders* representing a table or a view of orders, but not a class *Order* representing a row in the table or view. Put another way, the table module class refers internally to a collection of weakly typed data rows rather than to a collection of strongly typed *Order* objects.

As an example, let's have a look at a TM business component for managing orders:

```
public class OrdersManager
{
    private DataSet _data;
    public OrdersManager(DataSet data)
    {
        _data = data;
    }
    public DataTable Orders
    {
        return _ds;
    }

    public DataRow GetRow(int index)
    {
        return _ds.Tables[0].Rows[index];
    }

    public DataRow GetRowByID(int orderID)
    {
        return _ds.Tables[0].Select(...);
    }

    public int Update(DataRow row)
    {
        ⋮
    }

    public int Insert(int orderID, DateTime orderDate, ...)
    {
        ⋮
    }

    public int Delete(int orderID)
    {
        ⋮
    }
    ⋮
}
```

The class is initialized with some data, which could be the results of a query on a table or a view. In this case, any data set can be passed in, with no control over its real content. You might want to enforce a type control, by using typed *DataSets* or even your own strongly typed collections.

Alternatively, you might want to incorporate an ad hoc query interpreter to make sure you get a well-known schema of data. When you query for a particular order, or when you modify the data set, you can go directly to the database or decide to perform the operation in memory first and submit changes later.

Methods on a TM business component don't match one-to-one with actions on the presentation layer. In fact, the focus here is on the vision of data that the application has, not on the actions. This means that you likely need a sort of simplified service layer to script the tables of data exposed as the object model of the business layer.

Typed *DataSets*

In the .NET Framework, the ADO.NET subsystem introduces a new breed of object that looks and acts like the in-memory version of a modern powerful database—*DataSet*. At its core, *DataSet* is merely a data container specifically designed to manage tabular data, expressed in terms of tables, columns, and rows. *DataSet* has no notion of the provider that served its data, and it is a serializable object.

DataSet works in conjunction with other table-related objects such as *DataTable*, *DataRow*, and *DataRelation*. *DataSet* is a collection of tables and relations between tables. *DataTable* is a collection of rows and holds information about constraints and indexes.

All these objects are weakly typed. They are essentially containers of data, but any data in them is expressed as an *Object*. It turns out that a method that accepts a *DataSet* will be happy whether the DataSet it receives contains a collection of *Orders* and *Customers* or a collection of *Orders*, *OrderDetails*, and *Employees*.

Likewise, a *DataTable* is just an in-memory table, regardless of the schema. There's an application programming interface (API) for you to read and manipulate data columns, but it's just an API, and no differences in the underlying schema show up at compile time.

For this reason, Microsoft introduced typed *DataSets*. A typed *DataSet* is just a derived class that extends the set of members and forces compiler and callers to distinguish between a *DataTable* of orders and a *DataTable* of customers. The following code snippet captures the difference between a plain *DataTable* and *DataRow* and their typed variations for the "customer" entity:

```
public abstract class TypedTableBase<T> : DataTable, IEnumerable<T>, IEnumerable
                                 where T : DataRow;


[Serializable]
```

```
public partial class CustomersDataTable : TypedTableBase<CustomersRow>
{
    :
    :
    :
}
public partial class CustomersRow : DataRow
{
    private CustomersDataTable tableCustomers;
    internal CustomersRow(DataRowBuilder rb) : base(rb)
    {
        tableCustomers = (CustomersDataTable) this.Table;
    }

    public string CustomerID {
       get {
        return (string) this[tableCustomers.CustomerIDColumn];
    }
    set {
        this[tableCustomers.CustomerIDColumn] = value;
    }
    }
    :
    :

}
```

In a nutshell, the *CustomersDataTable* is just a *DataTable* that maintains a collection of *CustomersDataRow* objects. The *CustomerDataRow* class, in turn, is a specialized version of the *DataRow* that exposes as properties all the columns in the underlying row.

Note The notion of *typing* here refers more to giving ADO.NET general-purpose data containers a fixed schema and structure than to making their content strongly typed. A typed *OrderDataRow*, for instance, will expose an *OrderDate* property implemented as a *DateTime* value. However, the internal storage for the property is still an object. The object then is cast to the proper type—*DateTime*, in this case—only in the *get* accessor for the wrapper property. In other words, the typed attribute is there more for the compiler and Microsoft IntelliSense than to make your code faster. With custom collections and generics, on the other hand, you also get the benefits of an improved performance.

Table Adapters

Typed ADO.NET types add more control on types and schema over general-purpose containers such as the ADO.NET original types. But still, *DataSets* and *DataTables* have no behavior coded inside. Enter table adapters.

In ADO.NET, the data adapter acts as a two-way bridge between a data source and the *DataSet* or *DataTable* container. From an abstract point of view, a data adapter is similar to a command issued to a database. Internally, the data adapter uses an ADO.NET *Command* object to run the query and a *DataReader* object to walk its way through the records. The data adapter grabs all the data and packs it into an in-memory container—be it the *DataSet* or *DataTable*. Like commands and data readers, data adapters are specific to each ADO.NET data provider. So expect to find a data adapter class for Microsoft SQL Server, one for Oracle, and so on.

In the ADO.NET object model, the data adapter is a distinct component from *DataSet* and *DataTable* classes. You need to create it separately and instruct it to fill a *DataSet* or a *DataTable*:

```
SqlDataAdapter adapter = new SqlDataAdapter(connection, query);
DataSet ds = new DataSet();
adapter.Fill(ds);
```

Introduced with the .NET Framework 2.0, a table adapter is a data adapter designed to work with a specific typed *DataTable*. As an example, a customers table adapter knows how to fill *CustomersDataTable* and populate *CustomersDataRow*. It knows about the schema of the table and about the columns. It also exposes helper methods to callers so that callers can invoke specific queries and commands on the covered data set—the customers table.

Sound familiar? A table adapter is essentially a table module class for the table or view it is based upon. Here's an excerpt from the code of a table adapter:

```
public partial class CustomersTableAdapter : Component
{
    private SqlDataAdapter _adapter;
    private SqlConnection _connection;
    private SqlCommand[] _commandCollection;

    private SqlDataAdapter Adapter
    {
        get {
            if (_adapter == null)
                InitAdapter();
            return _adapter;
        }
    }

    // Other members here
    ⋮

    public int Fill(CustomersDataTable dataTable)
    {
        Adapter.SelectCommand = CommandCollection[0];
        int returnValue = Adapter.Fill(dataTable);
        return returnValue;
    }
    // Other methods here
    ⋮
}
```

There's no special base class or interface in the .NET Framework for a table adapter. And there's no stock table adapter class, either. Actually, a table adapter is a dynamically generated class that Visual Studio creates for you when you add a typed *DataSet* item to your project. Here's the code you need in your presentation layer to be able to use table adapters:

```
CustomersTableAdapter adapter = new CustomersTableAdapter();
CustomersDataTable tblCustomers = new CustomersDataTable();
tblCustomers = adapter.GetData();
```

You provide the Visual Studio wizard with a connection string and the list of tables and views you want in your TM model. The wizard figures out all the database details and creates all the typed containers and table-specific adapters for you. A TM model is thereby created for you in an assisted manner and, more importantly, in a fraction of the time it would take you to create it yourself.

The Table Data Gateway Pattern

The TM pattern for modeling the domain logic requires some helper classes to physically access the database. From a design perspective, these classes belong to the DAL, but they are obviously consumed by the table module classes.

In the .NET Framework, if you opt for table adapters and the power of the ADO.NET subsystem, everything you need for data access is there. You have typed *DataSets* and typed *DataTables* to act as your *RecordSet* type and table adapters to act as your table module classes. Which modules really care about physical data access? As mentioned, these modules are hidden in the table adapter implementation. They are based on a combination of ADO.NET objects, such as data adapters, commands, data readers, and connections. They work on a particular data store, either SQL Server, Oracle, or perhaps any store reachable through OLE DB and ODBC.

What if you use your own RS data structures? You need to fill these data structures with the results of one or more queries. You will probably create a relatively thin layer of code to take care of these chores. Essentially, you need a few methods out of a class to get a result set and assemble it into an RS data structure. This layer of code is referred to as the Table Data Gateway (TDG) pattern. Consider the following table module class:

```
public class OrdersManager
{
    private MyRecordSet _data;
    public OrdersManager(MyRecordSet data)
    {
        _data = data;
    }
    :
}
```

You call this code from the presentation as shown here:

```
MyRecordSet rs = OrdersGateway.LoadByCustomer(id, from, to);
OrdersManager tmc = new OrdersManager(rs);
```

Any update method you have in the table module class will fall into the TDG for physical data access. Figure 4-7 shows a possible interaction between the actors of a TM model when reading some data.

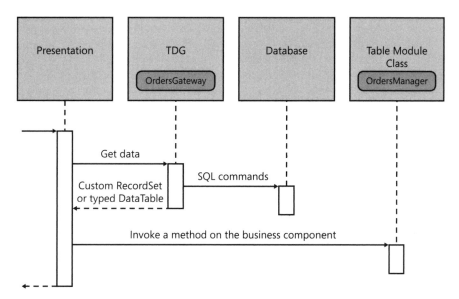

FIGURE 4-7 The presentation gets data via the gateway and then uses that data to initialize the table module class and work with it.

The data gateway and access to the database are buried in the implementation of the table adapters. In the end, Visual Studio 2008 wizards offer a free implementation of TM with a lot of details hidden from view. There's really no reason in .NET for not using table adapters and typed *DataSets* if you want to model your domain with a procedural approach.

The Active Record Pattern

When you look at an implementation of TM, you find quite a few objects attempting to represent a view of data, as the presentation layer perceives it. Even though TS and TM are both essentially procedural patterns, TM is based on the vision of data that the presentation layer has rather than on the list of use cases.

We could say that TM abstracts use cases and moves toward the data model behind them. It is an interesting step toward an object-based modeling pattern.

TM is based on objects, but it's not an object-based pattern for modeling the business logic. Why? Because it doesn't care much about the business and focuses instead on the tables. TM does have objects, but they are objects representing tables, not objects representing the domain of the problem.

The real shift toward an object-oriented design starts when you realize the target of the objects you're talking about. An object-oriented design is not when you just use objects to do your work. In this regard, TS also uses classes. Classes meant to be a mere syntax element of the programming language and classes meant to be the representation of an element in the data model do not have much to do with true object-oriented design.

The business or domain logic is the real point of a system. It is made of the allowed and required interactions between entities. Modeling the domain logic in terms of these recognized entities requires an object-oriented vision of the world rather than a procedural one. Your application is viewed as a set of interrelated objects—which is a different thing than using objects to perform data access and calculations.

The set of objects mapping to entities, plus special objects doing ad hoc calculations, form what is known as the domain's object model. This model has two main levels of complexity—simple and not-so-simple. A good measure of this complexity is the gap between the domain's object model and the relational data model you intend to create to store your data. A simple model is when your entities map closely to tables in the data model. A not-so-simple model is when some mapping is required to load and save domain objects to a relational database.

The Active Record (AR) pattern is your choice when you want an object-oriented design and have overall simple domain logic.

 Note In more practical terms, AR differs from TM because AR focuses on classes representing records in a table. That is, AR has a row-based view of the data, whereas TM focuses on entire tables.

Generalities of the AR Pattern

The AR pattern is described on page 160 of [P of EAA] as a data source design pattern rather than a domain logic pattern.

AR is any object that wraps a record in a database table or view. The object is expected to incorporate both data (column values) and behavior (methods for logic). The structure of an AR object should be as close as possible to the records of the associated table. For example, if you're building an AR object for the table Orders, you'll have a class *Order* with a set of properties that match the columns in the Orders table.

An AR object represents a row of data and typically embeds data access logic. Therefore, it requires some gateway to the matching record in the underlying table.

Typical methods on an AR object include find methods to grab results of common queries, CRUD operations, validation, and domain-specific calculations and cross-checks. For example, an *Invoice* object might need to validate individual scalar values (for example, number of items, date, progressive number, and customer ID), but it might also need to perform a more context-specific check with regard to the existence and validity of the PO number, check the payment terms, and calculate taxes.

Specifically, a typical AR class consists of instance properties representing the columns of the record in the database, instance methods acting on that specific record, plus optionally, a bunch of static methods working on all records in the table.

When to Use AR

Usually, AR does a good job in all scenarios where the domain logic isn't overly complex and, more importantly, doesn't require a thick layer of abstraction over the relational data model.

AR is an excellent choice for a large share of Web sites where, regardless of the number of tables involved, you often have an isomorphic correspondence between domain entities and relational tables.

In applications where you do not have a service layer (which is discussed in the next chapter), AR can be combined with TS. In this case, TS defines the code to respond to the user's actions and then uses AR to work on the data through an object-oriented interface. As you can see, TS replaces the service layer and script directly in the AR object model.

What's Good About AR

The success of AR depends on two factors: simplicity and frameworks. The two factors are closely related. AR is a conceptually simple model that is easy to grasp, but it still requires a good deal of work if you want to code your way through it.

Writing and maintaining one class for each table might be awkward, and this would be the least of your difficulties because you might have to consider using one or more DTOs per class or table. A friend of ours likes to reply to such statements with this observation: "Yes, it's boring, but we're developers at the end of the month, when we get our pay. So writing code is just our job."

We usually object to his statement with the fact that being productive is a must for everybody, including developers. And we're probably not alone in taking this position if a few companies out there have developed ad hoc frameworks for AR. This makes us think that a lot of developers find AR attractive in theory but boring in practice.

It is hard to deny that AR has a very good ratio between simplicity and the effectiveness of the resulting design. And it gets great support from vendors. Want a couple of illustrious examples? Try LINQ-to-SQL and Castle ActiveRecord.

What's Bad About AR

AR is good for relatively simple logic. This is good and bad news at the same time. If the application views data through a different perspective than the relational data model, it is up to you to organize data properly and fill in the gaps. Ideally, this extra abstraction layer lives between the object model and data model and is often referred to as the Data Mapper layer. With AR, you can incorporate this layer directly into the objects; but it gets harder and harder as the thickness grows.

Another issue with AR is the binding that exists between objects and the design of the database tables. If you happen to change the database, you have to update the AR object model and all of its related code. And, again, if you need to abstract from the database structure, all the mapping work is up to you.

In summary, with AR, as you move away from an isomorphic schema between the object model and data model, you get into trouble quickly. From this perspective, AR is the opposite of domain-driven design.

Finally, consider that long operations that involve loading or saving thousands of records might not find AR (or, in general, any object model) to be the ideal environment because of the additional workload involved with loading raw data into objects. With thousands of records, this can be a significant issue. In such cases, consider using ADO.NET directly, dressing it as a TS class.

The AR Pattern in Action

In an AR model, you have one class per database table. At first glance, this is not really different from the Table Module pattern. The devil is in the details, though. An AR class is a plain old .NET class whose properties match in name and type the corresponding table columns. To group multiple objects, you use arrays or collections. In other words, an *Order* class for an Orders table has an *integer* property for OrderID and a *DateTime* property for OrderDate, and so forth. A table of *Order* objects is represented by a collection of *Order* objects. How is this different from a table module class?

If you create TM entirely from scratch, there might be no significant difference. However, if you use ADO.NET types, the difference can be relevant. You use *DataRow* to represent an order record and *DataTable* to reference a collection of orders. The typed *DataTable* and *DataRow* are both generic containers of data. Data is stored as instances of the *System.Object* class and returned via a proper cast in a strongly typed manner. In TM, you don't have plain old .NET objects; this is just a key attribute of AR.

A Typical Active Record Class

Suppose you want to use the Active Record pattern to model the Orders table of a database. You create an *Order* class in the likeness of the columns in the table. Here's an example:

```
public class Order
{
    public Order()
    {
    }
    public Order(int orderID)
    {
        ⋮
    }

    public int OrderID {get; set;}
    public DateTime OrderDate {get; set;}
    public DateTime ShipDate {get; set;}
    public string ShipName {get; set;}
    public string ShipAddress {get; set;}
    public string ShipCity {get; set;}
    public string ShipCountry {get; set;}
    public string CustomerID {get; set;}
    public int EmployeeID {get; set;}
    ⋮

    public void Insert()
    {
        // Insert the record in the table
    }

    public void Delete()
    {
        // Delete the record from the table
    }

    public void Update()
    {
        // Update this record in the table
    }
    ⋮

    public static int GetOrdersCount()
    {
        // Return the number of orders in the table
    }

    public static List<Order> LoadAll()
    {
        // Load all orders in the table. If too
        // many records, consider exposing this
        // operation as a plain ADO.NET function.
    }
    ⋮
}
```

In addition, you find at least one method to load an order from the database and a constructor to build in memory an *Order* object to be inserted in the storage medium at a later time. Typically, the *Order* class has *Update*, *Insert*, and *Delete* methods to respectively update, add, and delete orders. Finally, a bunch of static methods might exist to implement common operations on orders—for example, a method to retrieve detailed information about the customer who placed the order or the employee who managed it.

Collections of Order types are plain arrays or a generic collection. You might or might not use a custom collection type to represent a set of *Order* objects. You create a custom collection type as shown here:

```
public class OrdersCollection : List<Order>
{
    ⋮
}
```

Alternatively, you can directly use the type *List<T>* to manage the collection of objects.

The Foreign-Key Mapping Pattern

Nearly all databases contain a bunch of tables that reference each other through foreign keys. When you track an order, you probably need to track the customer who placed it as well as the employee who managed it. When you track a book, you also need to relate the book to be tracked to its author and publisher.

A fundamental rule in the design of relational databases instructs you to keep this information in distinct tables and use foreign keys to build a logical relationship between tables. Specifically, a foreign key identifies a column in the referencing table that refers to a column in the referenced table. The column in the referencing table is normally the primary key in the referenced table.

As an example, consider tables named Orders and Customers. Among other columns, in the Orders table you would have the following:

```
CREATE TABLE Orders(
    OrderID int IDENTITY(1,1) NOT NULL,
    CustomerID nchar(5) NULL,
    EmployeeID int NULL,
    OrderDate datetime NULL,
        ⋮
    CONSTRAINT PK_Orders PRIMARY KEY(OrderID),
    CONSTRAINT FK_Orders_Customers FOREIGN KEY(CustomerID)
        REFERENCES Customers(CustomerID),
    CONSTRAINT FK_Orders_Employees FOREIGN KEY(EmployeeID)
        REFERENCES Employees(EmployeeID),
        ⋮
    CHECK CONSTRAINT FK_Orders_Customers,
    CHECK CONSTRAINT FK_Orders_Employees,
        ⋮
)
```

In the snippet, you recognize two foreign-key relationships: the relationship between *Orders* and *Customers*, and the one between *Orders* and *Employees*. *Orders* is clearly the referencing table. The *Orders-to-Customers* relation is based on the *CustomerID* column that exists on both tables. In this case, both tables have a column with the same name, but this is just arbitrary. What matters most is that both tables share the same value in some column. For example, the *CustomerID* column on *Orders* contains a value that is constrained to match the value on the referenced column *CustomerID* on *Customers*. How would you map this relationship in an AR model?

As you can imagine, there are essentially two ways: you map the raw value, or you expand the mapping to make the *Order* class point to a *Customer* object. On page 160 of [P of EAA], Fowler suggests you keep the AR model as simple as possible, where this mostly means as close as possible to the database structure. Put this way, it means you end up with the following:

```
public class Order
{
    :
    public int OrderID {get; set;}
    public DateTime OrderDate {get; set;}
    public string CustomerID {get; set;}
    :
}
```

The column *CustomerID* retains the raw value it has in the database table—namely, the ID of the customer.

Recently, popular AR frameworks such as LINQ-to-SQL and Castle ActiveRecord have been using the Foreign Key Mapping (FKM) pattern and deferred loading to expand the relationship. The FKM pattern is easy to figure out. It just tells you to drop the key column in the referencing object in favor of a property that points to a reference of the real object. Here's how it goes:

```
public class Order
{
    :
    public int OrderID {get; set;}
    public DateTime OrderDate {get; set;}
    public Customer Customer {get; set;}
    :
}
```

The entity reference is typically resolved when you instantiate the class so that the *Customer* property in the example holds a consistent value upon loading. AR frameworks typically provide facilities for this.

 Note On page 160 of [P of EAA], the FKM pattern is mentioned as a possibility to take into account and, in the end, the decision of whether to use it is left to the architect's discretion. As mentioned, lately most popular AR frameworks offer foreign key mapping by default.

Data Conversion

Another problem you should face when designing an AR model is data conversion. Should you bring into the class raw data as it appears in the database table? Or should you instead apply any type conversion that makes sense in the particular case?

As with foreign key mapping, this is mostly up to you. In general, type adaptation is fine, such as using *Nullable<int>* instead of *int* for nullable columns. Another possible adaptation regards transforming ticks into a *DateTime* object or perhaps XML strings to document object model.

What about, instead, grouping related properties into a new object? Is it recommended, for example, to use a custom *Address* type to package information such as address, city, region, postal code, and country?

You certainly don't commit a deadly sin if you use an *Address* type to group multiple properties. However, this would break the extreme simplicity of the model and start adding abstraction. If you are writing the AR model yourself, with no classes generated by frameworks, using abstracted types is doable at the price of writing more, and more complex, code. If you go with frameworks, you should check the availability of this feature before designing your object model.

Note Adding abstraction over an AR model is not a bad thing per se. However, the more you abstract, the more you move toward a Domain Model approach. (We'll discuss this in more detail in the next section.) If you choose to rely on frameworks, their built-in reverse-engineering features could be relatively rigid and stick to the structure of the database tables; if you need more flexibility, you should upgrade to richer modeling tools that push a domain-driven approach.

The Row Data Gateway Pattern

In TM, you group methods by tables and need a table gateway to implement physical data access. In AR, you end up having one class per table, but the class represents a single record in the table. The granularity is different—the record versus the table. To represent the whole table, you then use .NET generic collection objects closed on the type that represents the record in the table—for example, *List<Customer>*.

Subsequently, in AR you need a gateway to the record to grab all the stored data. Having a gateway adds yet another layer, which makes for more testable and simpler code. The Row Data Gateway (RDG) pattern delivers an object that acts as the direct interface between the wrapper AR class and the physical database. In other words, RDG will simply encapsulate all data access code for an Active Record, thus saving the Active Record class from knowing about database details.

If you use AR frameworks, the RDG implementation is buried in the folds of the provided infrastructure so that you don't have to worry about it. But an RDG is still there, and you should consider it if you happen to write an AR model yourself from scratch.

> **Note** Admittedly, RDG and Active Record have a lot in common and some people often have trouble seeing any key difference between the two. Our best answer is that they essentially do the same job, but an RDG class is expected to contain only database access logic, and no domain logic at all. This means that Active Record can embed an RDG class, but if an RDG class is extended with some domain logic methods, it should be automatically considered upgraded to the rank of an Active Record.

LINQ-to-SQL

The .NET Framework 3.5 comes with a new framework for mapping a SQL Server table to an object model. The resulting model can then be queried and updated programmatically in a way that doesn't require developers to deal with T-SQL commands and stored procedures.

Where does the LINQ-to-SQL name come from? The .NET Framework 3.5 supports the LINQ library, which is a unified query model and syntax that can address any class with a particular interface—either *IEnumerable* or *IQueryable*. By using LINQ, you can write SQL-like expressions (join, merge, group by, select) to operate on the properties of objects that are enumerable or queryable.

LINQ works natively on collections of in-memory data and is adapted to work on ad hoc object models through a queryable layer. This layer just takes care of mapping the syntax of the LINQ query expression to the underlying data structure and query engine.

LINQ-to-SQL maps the common LINQ query syntax over the SQL Server query engine. In addition, LINQ-to-SQL provides an object model that represents a selected group of tables and views. In the end, this object model is an implementation of the Active Record pattern.

Visual Studio 2008 comes with a designer through which you pick up a bunch of tables from a SQL Server connection. The tool then generates a C# or Visual Basic .NET class with all definitions. In Figure 4-8, you see the designer in action.

It is not much different from the designer in Figure 4-6 that builds a TM model. What it generates, though, is quite different. If you drop a reference to the Customers table, the designer creates an Active Record class named *Customer*.

The properties of the class correspond to the columns in the table, and foreign keys are mapped to referenced objects regardless of what the cardinality is. For example, the *Order* class will have a *Customer* property pointing to one instance of the *Customer* class and an *Order_Details* property pointing to a collection of *Order_Detail* objects. In LINQ-to-SQL, types used in foreign key mappings are not plain types, but framework types. Here's a code snippet that shows the implementation of the storage member for the properties:

```
private EntitySet<Order_Detail> _Order_Details;
private EntityRef<Customer> _Customer;
```

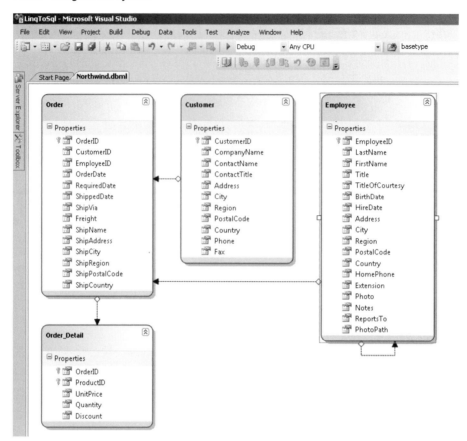

FIGURE 4-8 The Visual Studio 2008 designer for LINQ-to-SQL in action

In LINQ-to-SQL, you don't use the plain type to indicate a referenced object; instead, you resort to *EntityRef<T>*, where *T* is the type of the object. Likewise, for a one-to-many relationship you use the *EntitySet<T>* type instead of a plain collection type. The main benefit you get out of entity types is deferred loading. Through other features in the LINQ-to-SQL framework, you can enable deferred loading, meaning that values for referenced objects are loaded on demand. This service is free if you use entity types, but it has to be coded explicitly if you replace entity types with plain types.

Is LINQ-to-SQL an Active Record?

Some argue that LINQ-to-SQL is really an implementation of Active Record. The point is not far fetched, if you want to take the definition on page 160 of [P of EAA] literally.

In LINQ-to-SQL, classes primarily contain data; optionally, they can contain behavior. Behavior can be added through the mechanism of partial classes. More importantly, LINQ-to-SQL classes do not incorporate a row data gateway and are completely agnostic as far as data access is concerned.

How is a LINQ-to-SQL class loaded or updated? Data persistence is operated through the services of the *DataContext* class. This class represents the true gateway to data. Basically, it tracks all the changes to the object model and submits changes to the data layer. So is the LINQ-to-SQL object model an Active Record? All in all, we feel that it's kind of pointless to debate that.

In the end, LINQ-to-SQL can be viewed in two ways. It can be a mere tool for a data access layer—a sort of object-oriented ADO.NET engine—or it can be viewed as a simple O/RM tool that is limited to SQL Server, offers an Active Record-like object model, offers a smart query language, incorporates an RDG, and takes care of moving data between classes and tables. By default, the mapping in LINQ-to-SQL is defined through the designer and persisted via attributes. However, you can change the setting to use an XML file.

> **Note** All access to the LINQ-to-SQL object model occurs in the *DataContext* class. What kind of class is this? The data context is a container for all collections of records you put in the model—orders, customers, and the like. It tracks operations you do on objects and can expose mapped functions and stored procedures.

Castle ActiveRecord

As part of the Castle Project (*http://www.castleproject.org*), ActiveRecord (CAR) is a free and open-source implementation of the Active Record pattern available for the .NET platform. A typical class in a CAR solution is shown in the following code snippet:

```
[ActiveRecord]
public class Order : ActiveRecordBase<Order>
{
    [PrimaryKey]
    public int OrderID { get; set; }

    [Property]
    public DateTime OrderDate { get; set; }

    [HasMany]
    public IList<Order_Detail> OrderDetails
    {
        :
        :
    }
    :
    :
}
```

In the definition of the object model, you use attributes to inform the framework about the role of the properties and indicate whether they are mapped to columns, primary keys, or foreign keys. CAR must be initialized before you use any class. You typically do this when the application starts up. Mapping with the physical database occurs through an XML configuration file:

```
XmlConfigurationSource source = new XmlConfigurationSource("schema.xml");
ActiveRecordStarter.Initialize(source,
    typeof(Order), typeof(Customer), typeof(Order_Details));
```

CAR is built on top of NHibernate and the configuration file mostly serves the purpose of initializing the underlying NHibernate engine.

NHibernate is a rich O/RM framework that handles persisting plain .NET objects to and from an underlying relational database and not just to and from SQL Server. You provide an XML configuration file in which you essentially describe entities and relationships; based on that, NHibernate automatically generates ad hoc SQL code. (See *http://www.nhibernate.org* for more information.)

Note A good question is whether you should use Castle ActiveRecord, LINQ-to-SQL, or perhaps NHibernate. LINQ-to-SQL is a Microsoft technology—which makes a big difference in some cases and with some customers. The other options are open-source, albeit extremely popular, products.

NHibernate is a full-fledged O/RM that allows you to create a plain-old CLR object (POCO) domain model, where classes are not forced to implement any interface or inherit from a special base class. Castle ActiveRecord is a wrapper around NHibernate that infers a lot of things for you, thus reducing the learning curve. Castle ActiveRecord is preferable over NHibernate when you have simple domain logic and no legacy database around.

The Domain Model Pattern

In the design of the domain logic, when you opt for a procedural method or for an Active Record, you are essentially taking a data-centric approach. In this context, *data centric* means that you create the foundation of your system around your vision of the data model. The driving force of the business model design is not the business itself, but rather the data you use to make it happen.

In a data-centric approach, you typically start from the database and then model your business components around the required actions (that ultimately access the database) or codified tables. In .NET, the data-centric approach has met with a great deal of success because of the facilities built into Visual Studio and an array of made-to-measure classes that implement, free of charge, the TDG and RDG patterns.

As a matter of fact, Visual Studio allows you to build an average simple application, be it a Web site or a desktop application, in just a few hours without really requiring a lot of thinking up front. You work with the embedded designer, run through the wizard, maybe edit a bit of code, and here it is—the scaffolding of your application is ready to go. Everything is driven by data and happens to work just fine. Could you ask for anything more?

Note We're still young boys, but we've been working with Microsoft products and technologies for 15 years now. And we think we've learned one lesson in particular. Microsoft tends to supply a low-level framework and some higher-level tools such as controls, components, and designers. These tools are never designed to compete with analogous tools from third-party vendors. In addition, these tools target the average scenario and have the precise goal of doing a great job in most common situations.

We've experimented with the "First Law of Microsoft Technologies" several times and in a variety of contexts—from ASP.NET controls and components to business logic models, from workflows to AJAX libraries, and including unit testing, code editing, code refactoring and, of course, Windows-based user interfaces. Keep this consideration in mind when you evaluate higher-level Microsoft tools and facilities. They're excellent most of the time; they're likely unfit for some situations. But you have to be a good judge of your needs to decide which option is exactly right for you!

There might be situations in which a data-centric approach just doesn't work. Does it work at all, or does it just not work well enough? Most of the time, the second option is the accurate assessment. As the complexity of a system grows, focusing on data only is reductive; therefore, you need to focus on both data and behavior. Really, nothing prevents you from starting with a data-centric approach and then extending and enhancing components with methods to express any logic you need. However, in the long run, a data-centric approach doesn't scale well because the complexity of the system grows and, beyond a given point, adding new requirements might also be an issue.

The Domain Model (DM) pattern addresses these scenarios. DM focuses on the expected behavior of system and the data flows that makes it work. You focus on the real system, ideally with some good help from domain experts (mostly, the client), and try to render it in terms of classes. With DM, you consider the domain of the problem first and essentially fall into something called domain-driven design (DDD).

Note   When you opt for DDD, you are neither picking up a technology (something you can install and code), nor are you adopting a particular set of procedures to go through a problem. DDD is essentially a state of mind—a way of thinking that naturally puts the domain of the problem on top of everything else. You represent the system in terms of software entities, and you do so based on the behavior of real entities and the data they hold and manage.

DDD is an approach to software design that attempts to deal with complexity in a manageable, if not comfortable, way. When you opt for DDD, you are not necessarily choosing a DM pattern. But DM is the most natural choice. DDD is a discipline for software design introduced by Eric Evans in his book *Domain-Driven Design: Tackling Complexity in the Heart of Software* (Addison-Wesley, 2003). There's also a Web site you can check for information and discussions: *http://www.domaindrivendesign.org*.

Generalities of the DM Pattern

The DM pattern aims to get you an *object model* that is a conceptual model of the system. This object model is referred to as the *domain model*. The domain model describes the entities that participate in the system and captures any relationships and flow of data between them.

The domain model is a key deliverable in the project. By creating it and sharing it, the technical and business teams agree with one another's understanding of the problem. The domain model is not yet a piece of software and doesn't incorporate any concept or principle that is software or implementation specific. It has to be a formal model that bears witness that the technical and business teams understand each other and can fruitfully communicate.

From the abstract domain model, you proceed further toward *"a web of interconnected objects,"* to use the Fowler's words from page 116 of [P of EAA]. Entities in the domain model become classes with a proper set of methods and properties. Everything in the domain model has to be a class with a behavior, including customers, invoice items, and addresses. As a result, the sequence diagram of any method call might look like a sequence of object calls, as shown in Figure 4-9.

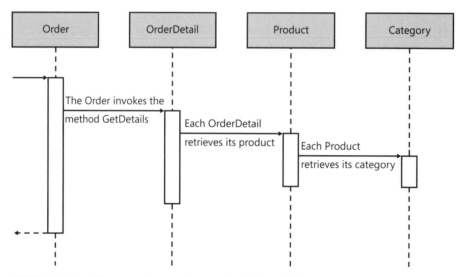

FIGURE 4-9 How things go when you have a web of related objects

DM is a sort of big brother to AR. DM is totally independent of the database and is a model that is, by design, as close as possible to real processes and not an idealized model of how an architect would have processes go.

 Important The software architect is an observer, so it isn't for him to say if the process to be modeled is a good one or is the best possible process for the company. The software architect's job is to model the process. Swarms of other professionals are there to help the company to improve processes, if ever needed.

Now we've reached the heart of the DM pattern and, in general, DDD. There are two points to consider.

First, collaboration between architects and domain experts is key to ensuring that enterprise processes are understood in any aspect and that requirements are outlined correctly and completely.

Second, because systems ultimately are based on software and databases, at some point someone has to take care of mapping the abstract model to an object model and a data model. This is precisely what makes DM expensive to adopt but also more powerful than other approaches.

> **Note** What's the (expected) role of the database administrator (DBA) in the design of the domain model? The DBA has to live within the business process as modeled and must create a database that supports the domain model. It isn't for the DBA to say if the domain model is a good one, in the same guise that it isn't for the architect to say if the business process is a good one. The entire differentiator is that the DM may or may not, and probably doesn't, make for a nice and pretty storage layer. In the end, we've found that modeling the process faithfully and living with a little database complexity is more successful than forcing a pretty database design only to build a slipshod middle tier over it.

When to Use DM

DM allows you to design a domain model for the system in total freedom, without feeling bound by platform and database constraints. The abstract domain model expresses some logic and describes a number of processes. This means that the domain model for an application should be the same for another application doing business in the same manner. Reusability of the business logic is a fundamental parameter to use in determining whether DM is a valuable investment.

If the customer needs to go right away with, say, online banking but also has concrete plans for other applications—such as back office, teller support, or perhaps trading applications—there's a clear advantage in reusing the same technological platform. The elements of the domain model are shared—account, customer, check, cash, withdrawal, deposit, loan, stock, and so forth.

The time it takes to design a domain model soon pays off. Costs can be amortized better in a long-term project, where reusing the business logic is essential.

If all that the customer needs is online banking functionality that requires you to use the existing back office, it doesn't make much sense to invest time and effort in a DM. In this case, you just architect a bit of the presentation layer (as discussed in Chapter 7, "The Presentation Layer"), create a small and local object model to carry out requests from the presentation, and go. What about future changes? Well, think it over. You're creating a Web site over an existing back office. Often the most complex feature the customer will ask you for is changes to the layout. If this is the case, there's nothing to be worried about and nothing that will make your design crumble.

Complexity is the driving force for the adoption of DM. Complexity should be measured in terms of the current requirements, but you should also look at possible enhancements or changes. As shown in Figure 4-2, DM has higher initialization costs than other approaches, but it goes linearly as the complexity grows. (See Figure 4-2.) Working with DM is more complex in simple scenarios, but it minimizes risks and the costs related to additional requirements and changes.

> **Note** Among other things, DDD is a state of mind. So skills and attitude also play key roles. A skilled team with significant experience with object-oriented design will probably find it easier to use DM also in relatively simple cases. The reverse is also true. The proper use of typed *DataSets* and a desire to work with a data-centric approach can still lead to creating a successful model. Even so, DM and DDD have greater potential than any other approach. But *potential* benefit doesn't necessarily mean *actual* benefit.

What's Good About DM

With DM, concepts are modeled as classes, and this approach harnesses the full power of object-oriented design. You can take advantage of all the features of object orientation, including encapsulation and inheritance, without being constrained by the database structure. This means that entities are in no way aware of the persistence mechanism used under the covers. Subsequently, at some point you can replace the data access layer without worrying about how this might affect the business layer.

The paradigm shift that objects created in the software industry 20 years ago was largely because of the need to work with complex business logic resulting from thousands of rules and sophisticated, or just tangled, processes. In this context, objects are in their natural environment and architects can use them to handle virtually any level of complexity.

DM is essentially driven by requirements, and it requires you to understand only the domain of the problem and to model it and its logic using classes. Pure design and few if any constraints. Hasn't this always been the life-long dream of architects and software designers?

What's Bad About DM

As you might have noticed already in this chapter, quite often the major strength of an approach, taken to the limit, becomes its most significant weakness. This fact also holds true for DM. First, it's not easy to envision a full system in terms of an abstract model where entities and relationships describe the processes and their mechanics. On the other hand, you need complexity to handle complexity. (See Figure 4-10.)

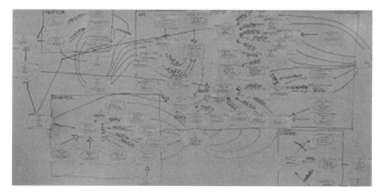

FIGURE 4-10 A sketch for a domain model. Can you believe you really often start from something similar?

The main hurdle on the way to DM is the O/R impedance mismatch. A domain model is an object model designed in a way that is totally independent of databases and other application-specific constraints, except the constraints of the business process that it models. This means that the same domain can be reused in any other scenario that requires the same logic. It's about the business, and only that.

How is this a bad attribute for a system? At some point, the system has to be implemented; and data has to be persisted. And you need to map the model to tables on one or more database systems. To the application's eyes, the domain model is the logical database (generally intended as the archive). This "database" is an object model and lacks a relational interface. Building this relational interface is both necessary and expensive.

It's really hard to build a DM without some help from an O/R mapper tool such as NHibernate or Microsoft's Entity Framework. The logical gap between the object model and the relational model is the critical point of a DM approach.

The DM Pattern in Action

When you adopt the DM pattern, you actually write a bunch of classes to represent entities in the abstract model. How is this different from, say, AR? The difference is all in the database independence. In DM, you have one class for each entity that crosses your way when you discuss the processes with domain experts. This certainly includes primary actors such as *Customer*, *Order*, *Invoice*, and *OrderDetail*, but it also includes auxiliary entities such as *Address*, *Payment*, *ShipMethod*, *ContactInformation*, and so forth.

Designing the Domain Model

A recurring scenario for domain objects is the one where they have common features you don't want to duplicate. If this is the case, you can define a base class containing all the desired plumbing and use it as the *layer supertype* of your domain model, as discussed on page 475 of [P of EAA]. Here's a possible schema for a *validation-enabled* layer supertype:

```
public interface ISupportsValidation
{
    bool IsValid  { get; }
    IList<ValidationError> Validate();
}

public class DomainObject : ISupportsValidation
{
    public virtual bool IsValid
    {
        get
        {
            try
            {
                return ConstraintValidator.IsValid(this);
            }
            catch
```

```
            {
                return false;
            }
        }
    }

    IList<ValidationError> ISupportsValidation.Validate()
    {
        IList<ValidationError> errors;
        errors = (IList<ValidationError>) ConstraintValidator.Validate(this);
        return errors;
    }
}
```

The custom *ISupportsValidation* interface defines the cross-cutting concern of object state validation. A Boolean property that indicates whether the object is in a valid state and a *Validate* method that returns details about reported validation errors are fine in most cases. What about *ConstraintValidator*? In this example, it symbolizes a custom validation block that uses attributes on class members to specify constraints. The *ConstraintValidator* object just checks whether all properties on a given domain object match the defined constraints. However, Microsoft Enterprise Library 4.0 provides a well-done validation application block that we are more and more frequently using in our projects. Enterprise Library comes with a *Validator* object that you instantiate and use as shown here:

```
Validator validator = ValidationFactory.CreateValidator(this.GetType());
ValidationResults results = new ValidationResults();
validator.Validate(this, results);
```

The *Validator* object checks all properties in a type being validated according to the validation attributes defined. Here are a couple of domain objects:

```
public class AddressInfo : DomainObject
{
    [StringLengthValidator (60)]
    public string Address { get; set; }

    [StringLengthValidator (15)]
    public string City { get; set; }

    [StringLengthValidator (15)]
    public string Region { get; set; }

    [StringLengthValidator (10)]
    public string PostalCode { get; set; }

    [StringLengthValidator (15)]
    public string Country { get; set; }

    public override string ToString()
    {
        string region = String.IsNullOrEmpty(Region) ? " " : " (" + Region + ") " ;
        return String.Format("{0}, {1}{2}{3}", Address, City, region, Country.ToUpper());
    }
}
```

```
public class Customer : DomainObject
{
    private AddressInfo _addressInfo = new AddressInfo();
    private ContactInfo _contactInfo = new ContactInfo();

    [NotNullValidator()]
    [StringLengthValidator (5, 5)]
    public virtual string ID { get; set; }

    [NotNullValidator()]
    [StringLengthValidator (40)]
    public virtual string CompanyName { get; set; }

    [StringLengthValidator (24)]
    public virtual string PhoneNumber { get; set; }

    [StringLengthValidator (24)]
    public virtual string FaxNumber { get; set; }

    public virtual AddressInfo AddressInfo
    {
        get { return _addressInfo; }
        set { _addressInfo = value; }
    }

    public virtual ContactInfo ContactInfo
    {
        get { return _contactInfo; }
        set { _contactInfo = value; }
    }
}
```

Here, *StringLengthValidator* and *NotNullValidator* are just two of the validation attributes that the Enterprise Library validation block supports.

How would you handle relationships in the domain model? The pattern we examined for the Active Record scenario works fine here, too. For example, for an *Order* you can have a foreign key mapping to a customer and a one-to-many relationship to order items. Here's an excerpt from the *Order* class:

```
public class Order : DomainObject
{
    private IList<OrderDetail> _details = new List<OrderDetail>();
    private Customer _customer;
    ⋮

    public virtual Nullable<DateTime> RequiredDate { get; set; }
    ⋮

    public virtual IList<OrderDetail> Details
    {
        get { return _details; }
        internal set { _details = value; }
    }
```

```
public virtual Customer Customer
{
    get { return _customer; }
    set { _customer = value; }
}
    :
public void AddDetail(OrderDetail item)
{
    _details.Add(item);
}

public void RemoveDetail(OrderDetail item)
{
    _details.Remove(item);
}
    :
}
```

In an Active Record pattern, the code that performs physical data access lives in the classes. This is *not* a feature of a domain model. A domain model is a full-fledged hierarchy of classes where you can take advantage of any skills you might have with regard to object-oriented design. But you don't care about which module will actually populate your objects or when it will do it. At the domain-model level, you must care about how you want to expose, say, order details—such as a list property, a find-all method, and more specific finder methods. You don't care about how order items are eventually loaded into an order. That's the responsibility of the persistence layer, which is concerned with data access.

The Logic in the Domain Objects

Domain objects do not contain any logic to load or save their state to a storage. All the code that creates transient (that is, in memory) or persistent (that is, loaded from a database record) domain objects lives outside the domain model in other classes of the business layer.

Domain objects feature methods only to implement pieces of business logic. Which methods you have depends on the role of the domain object in the overall model. Here's an example for the *Customer* class:

```
public virtual decimal GetOrdersTotal()
{
    decimal total = 0;
    foreach (Order order in this.Orders)
    {
        total += order.CalculatePrice();
    }
    return total;
}
```

The method goes through all the orders for a given customer and calculates the total amount. This is clearly a piece of business logic because it involves multiple objects in the domain and no external actor.

Persistence Ignorance

We just mentioned persistence and, at this point, we can't help but raise the point of *persistence ignorance* (PI) for domain classes. Before we go any further, we should clarify that PI is an important point for the design of a domain model only if you're using a framework (usually, an O/RM tool) to design your model and map classes to relational tables. The discussion is kind of pointless if you are building a domain model and data mappers yourself.

First and foremost, we should clarify the term *persistence ignorance*. It doesn't really mean that classes in a given domain model lack methods to perform database access. Classes in a domain model are always devoid of methods that explicitly perform data access. This is considered an antipattern.

Persistence ignorance (PI) is an application of the single responsibility principle we talked about in Chapter 3 and, in practice, states that a domain object should not contain code related to persistence because bearing responsibility for both persistence and domain logic would violate the principle. In LINQ-to-SQL, domain classes are tagged with attributes defining the mapping strategies and must use built-in types such as the *EntityRef* and *EntitySet* classes on their public interfaces. In Castle ActiveRecord, domain classes are derived from *ActiveRecordBase* and, as in LINQ-to-SQL, are tagged with mapping attributes. Therefore, both frameworks do not support a PI modeling style.

Finally, a highly debated point in Entity Framework (EF) v1.0 is persistence ignorance of the classes in the domain. In EF, classes are not persistent ignorant because you are forced to derive your classes from a framework-provided root class (or implement a bunch of interfaces). Persistence-ignorant classes are also referred to as plain-old CLR objects (POCO).

> **Note** Entity Framework is a Microsoft framework for providing data services. EF includes an O/R mapping tool but is not limited to that. EF, in fact, provides more services, such as query, view, and reporting services. Generally, EF is a platform aimed at solving the mismatch between object and relational models. Entity Framework is included in the .NET Framework 3.5 Service Pack 1, and designers come with Visual Studio 2008 Service Pack 1. From a persistence-ignorance perspective, EF domain classes are not entirely POCO in v1.0, but plans exist to make it pure POCO in v2.

What does it mean to a class to be (or not be) persistence ignorant? What are the benefits or drawbacks?

When you design a domain model using a framework, you might or might not be required to derive your classes from a given root class or to give each class a constructor of a given shape. The base class usually brings in some added value—typically, it brings in some scaffolding that helps map the content of the class to a physical table. Is this a bad thing? It depends. For sure, there are some circumstances under which this turns out to be a problem, such as the following ones:

- If a third-party library forces you to inherit from a given class, you can't derive your classes from any other class. (This is because multiple inheritance and mix-ins are not supported in the .NET Framework.)

- From a pure design perspective, deriving from a persistence-aware class adds new (and unnecessary) responsibilities to your domain classes.

- If you have to build the domain on top of other types defined in other, third-party assemblies, how do you persist any types created from a different root? If you can't release the constraint, you probably have to consider a different framework or do it all by yourself.

So let's assume that being persistence ignorant is a really good thing and being bound to the persistence engine of some framework limits your programming power. How can a general-purpose tool like an O/RM know how to persist a plain .NET class? Where should it look for direction about mapping? And, more importantly, how does it do it in a way that doesn't hurt performance?

A plain .NET class can't be persisted if some ad hoc code isn't dynamically emitted into the class. This is what O/RM tools that support POCO models actually do. So the whole point is not whether or not you need support for persistence—domain classes always need it. The real point is where you want this support to live: within the domain classes (persistence awareness like in EF and Castle ActiveRecord), or outside of the domain (persistence ignorance like in NHibernate).

Note Having persistence-related code living outside the domain requires some form of dynamic code injection. In other words, you avoid spoiling your domain objects with non-strictly business-related attributes and properties but, at the same time, those features are to be added to the objects when processed. A commonly used approach entails the creation of dynamic proxies. A dynamic proxy is a proxy class for a given type that adds missing capabilities on the fly. The CLR supports the dynamic creation of proxies for a given type only if the type inherits from *MarshalByRefObject* or *ContextBoundObject*. Castle DynamicProxy is a nice framework to try for this purpose. Find more information at *http://www.castleproject.org/dynamicproxy/index.html*.

Entities and Value Objects

When it comes to implementation, not all the classes in the Domain Model have the same attributes. Typically, you distinguish between entities and value objects. For both, you use classes, but with some slight differences.

The biggest difference is that classes for entities support the notion of an identity. Each instance of the class is unique and can be compared to others using just the object identity as the discriminating factor. For example, the entities in following code snippets are distinct:

```
Order o1 = new Order();
o1.OrderDate = 123;
Order o2 = new Order();
o2.ID = 123;
return o1 == o2; // returns false
```

In the .NET Framework, a plain class supports identity so that you don't have to take special care when building a class for an entity. You have to do something unusual only when you deal with *value objects*. What's a value object, and how does it differ from an entity class?

A value object class represents an entity in the domain that mostly contains data and lives for the data it contains. A value object is fully identified by a combination of values it contains. An entity object, on the other hand, has its own life and rich behavior regardless of the data it contains. Entity objects are usually objects with a longer lifetime. A value object represents an aspect of an entity and can live only in relation to an entity.

The *OrderDetail* class is the canonical example of value objects. The same order detail can be used with different orders because it is fully represented by the data it contains. What's different in the implementation of a value object? Two objects are equal if they have the same values in a given set of properties:

```
public class OrderDetail : DomainObject
{
    ⋮

    public override bool Equals(object other)
    {
        if (this == other)
            return true;

        OrderDetail obj = other as OrderDetail;
        if (obj == null)
            return false;

        return Order.ID == obj.order.ID &&
            Product.ID == obj.Product.ID;
    }

     public override int GetHashCode()
    {
        // If you override Equals, you must override GetHashCode too
        // so that two equal objects return the same hash code.
        // This is particularly important in domain models (see NHibernate)
        // to avoid duplicate objects in internal collections.

        // Get a unique, object-specific value or string and
        // return the hash code of that. Default implementation of the method
        // returns a unique but system-generated value that's not object-specific.

        // Get a number that combines order's ID and product's ID,
        // and get the hash code of that
        int hash = ID * 10000 + Product.ID;
        return hash.GetHashCode();
    }
}
```

Note In this context, value objects have nothing to share with value types as you might know them from the .NET Framework. Both entities and value objects are actually implemented through .NET classes, but the level of abstraction is totally different.

The Repository Pattern

As mentioned, generically speaking, the domain model contains classes with data and behavior, but the behavior refers only to the logic of the represented entity. It has nothing to do with how you load data into, say, an *Order* class or how you grab all orders issued in a given month. This code is generically said to belong to the data access layer. But how exactly do you arrive at this?

A good approach is to use the Repository pattern, which is described on page 322 of [P of EAA], to create a gateway through which code in the presentation or service layer can script the domain model and update the underlying data store or load from there data that is represented through the objects in the model.

Put another way, the Repository pattern adds yet another abstraction layer between the domain model and the data access code. The data access code is where you physically perform queries, run stored procedures, and deal with T-SQL and ADO.NET.

You typically have a repository object for each entity, such as customer, order, and product. The interface of the repository is up to you; but it will likely contain finder and update methods that work both on the single entity and on a collection of entities. Looking back at the Active Record pattern, we can say that the Repository pattern offers a way to group all the CRUD methods that in Active Record belong to the entity class.

By separating domain entities and persistence, you also gain another benefit. It won't take much effort to extract an interface for the repository and then use a factory pattern to encapsulate all database code in an object that implements the contracted interface. In this way, your domain can work with whatever data access layer and data provider you use. Here's a sample of the code you end up with:

```
// Ask the factory object to retrieve an instance of the
// repository for the Customer entity
CustomerRepository rep = Repository.GetFactoryFor<Customer>();

// Work with the repository
List<Customer> coll = rep.FindCustomersByCountry(country);
```

Internally, the repository factory can read the actual class to instantiate from a configuration file, thus making the overall solution completely extensible, database independent, and customizable.

Mapping Objects to Tables

What's inside the repository? You should think of the repository as a library of I/O functions available on a given entity. These functions work on the persistence layer, and possibly in an interface-based way that keeps them independent of details as much as possible. However, no matter how many layers of code you use, at some point you need to execute T-SQL commands via ADO.NET or similar frameworks.

When you use a DM pattern, the layer of code that does database stuff is the Data Mapper. The Data Mapper pattern, discussed on page 165 of [P of EAA], refers to a set of classes that map the logical entity (and all of its relationships) to a physical collection of tables and records, usually on a relational database.

For example, the Data Mapper does the dirty job of deleting an order. And it knows which records on which tables it has to touch to execute your command, preserve data integrity, and maintain a consistent state for the application.

In the worst case, the implementation of a Data Mapper for each entity is up to you. This is the major difficulty of a DM approach. Mapping domain objects to a database is hard and, obviously, time consuming. Using a tool for the job is often the only way out. O/RM tools exist specifically to assist you in this kind of job.

In summary, what's inside a repository for a given entity? Either you have a Data Mapper class or some corresponding code generated using the syntax of an O/RM tool such as NHibernate, Genome, and (why not?) Entity Framework. In Chapter 6, we'll say more about repositories, data mappers, and O/RM tools.

> **Note** One further comment is needed to explain the difference between entities and value objects. You don't need a repository or a data mapper for a value object. You need a repository only for an entity. The repository (or the mapper) for a given entity will certainly take care of all value objects that depend on a given entity.

The Special Case Pattern

When you design an object model (including a very special object model such as a domain model), you face the problem of handling failures in finder methods. For example, suppose that in the repository you have a method named *FindCustomerByID* that just returns a *Customer* object for the record in the database that matches the specified ID:

```
Customer FindCustomerByID(string id)
```

What if no such customer record is found? What should you return to the caller?

The Data Mapper will probably return an empty data reader or throw an ADO.NET exception. How would you bubble this up to the service layer or presentation layer? The first answer that springs to mind probably is to suggest returning NULL.

Ultimately, NULL is a valid answer where an object (of type *Customer*) is expected. But it is not a *precise* answer. For sure, NULL indicates that something went wrong. But what, exactly? The Special Case pattern can help. (See page 496 of [P of EAA].)

The pattern recommends that you create ad hoc types for each entity so that you return a valid object that contains implicitly more information about what happened. Here's an example:

```
public sealed class MissingCustomer : Customer
{
}
```

The *MissingCustomer* class can be employed wherever a Customer is accepted, signals a failure in the underlying code, and doesn't break polymorphism:

```
public Customer FindCustomerByID(string id)
{
    Customer c;
    :

    if (failed)
        return new MissingCustomer();
    return c;
}
```

If you designed the domain model to support validation, the caller only needs to invoke the *IsValid* property on the received object to see if something went wrong. If the caller needs more details, it calls other methods on the sample *ISupportsValidation* interface. If no validation is built into the model from the ground up, the caller has to implement a list of static checks against possible types. If this is what happens, though, we recommend that you stop for awhile and refactor the domain model to bring in validation support.

Workflows

Workflows and services are a fundamental part of a real-world business layer. Both are large topics that deserve a book of their own. We'll cover services in the next chapter, but we'd like to say a bit more on workflows and their connection to BLL design patterns.

For example, where would you stick workflows if you decide to use TS? Or TM? Frankly, both TS and TM are patterns that, when speaking in terms of complexity, are truly designed for low-workflow, high-data-retrieval systems. In TS, you could consider using a workflow to implement a transaction script and rely on designers to modify and code activities to improve reusability. However, to us, from a workflow standpoint, TS and TM look like somewhat special cases.

Instead, object-based BLL patterns such as Active Record and, especially, Domain Model allow for true workflow. You have workflow at different levels. The workflow in the BLL might occur between domain objects to implement a required behavior or in the service layer to orchestrate services, the persistence layer, and domain objects. If you stick the workflow in the objects, you accept the risk of reducing the likelihood of reusing domain objects for other applications and purposes. For this reason, workflow in the domain model is acceptable only if it is business workflow, innate in the domain, and not dependent on application logic.

For example, the service layer for ordering something would perhaps develop a coarse-grained workflow to check inventory, remove the item from inventory, issue the item to shipping, and place the call to bill the customer. The domain model would have a much finer-grained workflow. Looking just at shipping, domain objects would calculate a shipping cost based on the desired shipping option and product weight/destination, register the package with the shipper for pickup, record tracking information for later recall, print packing labels for the shipping department, and so forth.

Workflows are required, but how you develop them in the BLL relates to the level of complexity of the workflow and the problem's domain. In the end, it's a judgment call, and one that's often hard to make. The experience and knowledge of the architect are key. Again. And over and over again.

Summary

The design of an application is successful when it reproduces the customer's business structure and processes as faithfully as possible. It requires that architects grab a full understanding of the problem's domain, the processes, and data flows. This intimate knowledge of the business can hardly be gained only by interviewing customers and users or even by reading informally written requirements. Gaining this level of knowledge requires extensive collaboration between the stakeholders. The role of the architect is not that of forcing analysts and users to learn programming, but designing a programmable model out of the descriptions and jargon of domain experts.

From the requirements, you can proceed in essentially two ways: you can base your model on user actions or on the domain. If you opt for a procedural approach, you make your life easier, you proceed with a good pace, and you have limited overhead in whatever you do. To put it down in terms of patterns, you opt for either the Transaction Script or Table Module pattern.

Transaction Script is easy to understand and quick to develop. It doesn't scale well because the complexity of the domain tends to grow. This happens because code accumulates that has a variable level of cohesion and generally is difficult to refactor and rework as requirements change. Table Module has excellent support from Visual Studio and the .NET Framework, but it remains essentially a data-centric, table-oriented procedural model.

The shift toward a full object-oriented design leads you to consider an Active Record pattern or, better yet, a Domain Model pattern. The Domain Model pattern has the potential and flexibility necessary to let you deal with any sort of complexity in the domain. Because the Domain Model adds abstraction that separates you from the details of the underlying databases, you have to fill the gap in some way and map an otherwise abstract domain model onto tables and columns. This is challenging, as well as difficult and time consuming. And it requires a higher level of skill and the right attitude.

The business logic is the heart of the system, but it's not the whole system. However, the choice you make for the design of the business logic has an impact on other layers—in particular, the persistence layer or data access layer. These two layers together largely determine the success of your project.

Every approach has pros and cons. The right mix of patterns for the domain is not something that everybody can calculate out of a recipe or an algorithm. That's why you, the architect, get into the business.

Murphy's Laws of the Chapter

A successful business layer requires observation and modeling. It also requires an innate ability to do things in the simplest possible manner. "Do it simply but not simplistically," is one of our favorite mantras. And it gives a nod to the first Murphy's Law for this chapter:

- A complex system that works is invariably found to have evolved from a simple system that works.

- Investment in software reliability will increase until it exceeds the probable cost of errors.

- In theory, there is no difference between theory and practice, but in practice there is.

See *http://www.murphys-laws.com* for an extensive listing of other computer-related (and non-computer) laws and corollaries.

Chapter 5
The Service Layer

If you want service(s), serve yourself.

—Spanish proverb

In the previous chapter, we examined various approaches to the design and implementation of the business logic: Transaction Script (TS), Table Module (TM), and a couple of object-based approaches such as Active Record (AR) and Domain Model (DM). Of the four approaches, only TS—unquestionably the simplest—has a clear dependency on use cases that need to be supported by the presentation layer.

When you choose a TS procedural approach for the business logic, you define a list of methods starting from actions the user can trigger from the user interface. Each click or selection triggers a method on one of the TS objects. Although we could debate whether TS is an effective way of designing the business layer, we can't deny that TS makes the design of the system exceptionally simple.

What about all the other approaches? With all the other approaches, you have objects all the way around. You have table adapters in TM, objects representing a record in a table in AR, and an abstract object model in DM. The mere fact you have objects in your middle layers is not enough to make it all work from the UI perspective.

Think of a plain *Button1_Click* event handler in the world's simplest ASP.NET page. The handler is part of the presentation layer and represents the expected behavior of the system when the user clicks a given button. If you work with objects here, you end up implementing some logic in the presentation layer. On the other hand, a business component has to be instantiated and scripted to work, and some code is required for this. The code necessary to script the component might be as simple as calling the constructor and perhaps one method. More often, however, this code is fairly rich with *if-then-else* statements, needs to call into multiple objects, and waits for a service to return a response. This is definitely application logic folded into the presentation layer.

As we saw in Chapter 4, "The Business Layer," having some form and quantity of logic in the presentation layer might be acceptable sometimes. If you consciously decide to put some logic in the presentation layer and you're happy with that, it's fine. Otherwise, consider that with a different system design you can keep logic out of the presentation layer and keep the presentation layer free of business components.

How would you trigger system behavior from the presentation layer, then? You define an extra layer of code and place it in between the presentation layer and business layer. This extra layer is known as the *service layer*.

> **Note** Most of the time, the service layer is seen as part of the business layer in a Domain Model approach. Although this is probably a very common scenario, it is definitely not the only possible one. In general, a service layer defines an interface for the presentation layer to trigger predefined system actions. As the name itself suggests, the service layer is a sort of boundary that marks where the presentation layer ends and the business logic begins. The service layer is designed to keep coupling between the presentation layer and business logic to a minimum, regardless of how the business logic is organized within the business logic layer. So you can have a service layer regardless of what your choice of design patterns is for the business logic—be it Table Module, Active Record, or Domain Model.

What's the Service Layer, Anyway?

Conceptually, having a service layer in an application is nearly identical to having a TS. The difference—and it's a big difference, indeed—is in the implementation of the layer. In both cases, you end up with code that is invoked directly from the user interface. You have one method that takes some tailor-made data and returns some other data. Data is moved in to and out of the layer using data transfer objects (DTOs).

Within the service layer, though, a TS component just codes its way to the requested behavior without too much attention to abstraction and the organization of data and methods. It invokes anything it needs to do its job—including workflow, data access code, and serialization. In a service layer, things go quite differently.

A service layer doesn't really perform any task directly. All that it does is orchestrate the set of business objects you provide. The service layer has an intimate knowledge of the business logic (including components, workflows, and services), and likewise it knows the domain model, if any, very well. So, for example, if you have a business layer made with TM, the service layer talks to your table adapters through *DataSets*. Table 5-1 summarizes the options.

TABLE 5-1 Service Layer Actions Within the Business Logic Layer

Business Logic Pattern	Data Manipulation	Data Object
Table Module	Table adapters or, generally, objects representing a table in the data store	Typed *DataSets*
Active Record	Record objects—that is, objects that represent a record in a physical table	Record objects
Domain Model	Objects in the domain model	Objects in the domain model

Obviously, the service layer orchestrates business components, but it also orchestrates application-specific services, workflows, and any other special components you happen to have in the business logic.

Note As you can see, this layer that sits in between the presentation and business layers has the word *service* in the name and that word was chosen deliberately. As we'll see later in the chapter, this layer can be implemented using a Web service or a Windows Communication Foundation (WCF) service—you can code it with any service technology you prefer to use. But it also can be a plain .NET class running with or without marshal-by-reference capabilities. Most of the time, though, it is implemented as a collection of platform-specific services. This said, though, when we talk about the service layer you should interpret the word "service" as being a technology-agnostic term.

Responsibilities of the Service Layer

The idea of a service layer as described so far in this chapter springs from the Service Layer pattern defined on page 133 of Martin Fowler's book *Patterns of Enterprise Application Architecture* (Addison-Wesley, 2003), abbreviated as [P of EAA] in future references. According to Fowler's vision, a service layer (or SL) is an additional layer that sets a boundary between two interfacing layers. Today, this definition is generally and widely accepted. Let's discuss it for awhile and try to recognize the generalities of the pattern, as well as establish a number of practical guidelines for when to use it and learn its pros and cons.

What the Service Layer Is Intended For

A lot is being said in the industry about the importance of applying principles such as separation of concerns, low coupling, and high cohesion when designing software. When we discuss how to modify a given object model to make it expose a lower degree of coupling, the first approach we should consider is adding more abstraction. The schema in Figure 5-1 illustrates two tightly coupled classes. Essentially, class *Action* has a dependency on class *Strategy* because it uses methods of class *Strategy*.

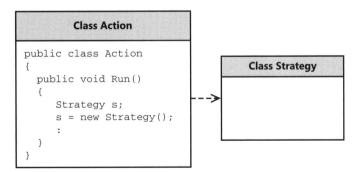

FIGURE 5-1 Two tightly coupled classes

To break this dependency, we can add an intermediate class that exposes to class *Action* only the set of operations that class *Action* needs to call. By sitting in the middle, the intermediate class breaks the dependency between *Action* and *Strategy*, as illustrated in Figure 5-2.

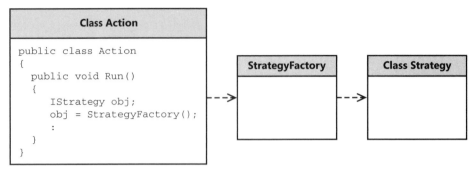

FIGURE 5-2 Breaking apart the dependency between two classes

With this design, you now hide class *Strategy* completely from class *Action*. At the same time, though, any functions that class *Strategy* was providing to class *Action* is preserved. The magic is all in the class in the middle. This intermediate factory class supplies a generic and common interface to its caller so that the caller keeps on invoking methods exposed by the interface regardless of what other changes are made in the architecture or the underlying class. Simple and effective.

How does this relate to the SL pattern?

The Service Layer pattern works in much the same way, except that it applies this factory pattern at a higher level of abstraction. The SL sits in between a pair of interfacing logical layers in a system and keeps them loosely coupled and neatly separated, but perfectly able to communicate with one another. Most of the time, we see the SL pattern used to define an application's boundary between the presentation layer and business layer. This is only the most common scenario. The principle, as inspiring as it might be in this context, has a broader application. Figure 5-3 shows the role of SL in a multilayer application.

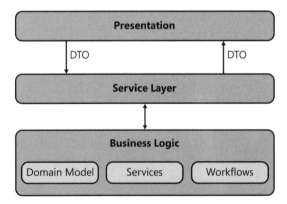

FIGURE 5-3 The service layer sets the boundary between the presentation and business layers.

Orchestrating the System's Behavior

As you can see in the figure, the service layer shields the presentation layer from all the details regarding the business logic. But it doesn't do just that. As will be clear in a moment, the content of Figure 5-3 is correct but not complete.

At its core, each user-driven interaction has two main actors: the user interface, as implemented by the presentation layer, and the module that responds to the user action, which is implemented by the service layer. It turns out that the service layer does more than just orchestrate the business logic. It also talks to the persistence layer, if there is any.

Any interaction originates on the presentation layer and finds a response in the service layer. Based on the received input, the service layer scripts the components of the business logic—including services, workflows, and objects in the domain model—and accesses the data access layer (DAL) as required.

Is the service layer the only part of the system directing database operations? Not really. The business logic can contain workflows and business services that are certainly not stopped from using the data access layer. The only part of the business logic that should be kept independent from any database details is the Domain Model, if any.

Factoring in this consideration, the schema in Figure 5-3 evolves into the schema depicted in Figure 5-4.

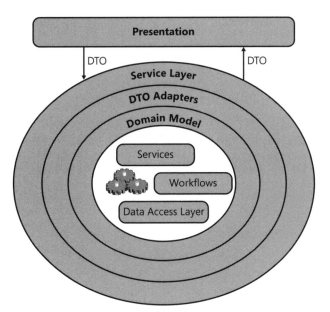

FIGURE 5-4 The service layer gets input from the presentation layer and orchestrates workflows, services, and data access components.

The service layer is the boundary between the presentation layer and other layers. It ideally gets and returns data transfer objects and internally converts data transfer objects into instances of the Domain Model classes wherever appropriate. Each of the methods exposed through the service layer orchestrates other services, invokes workflows, and performs database operations through data mappers or Object/Relational Mapper (O/RM)–supported languages.

> **Note** Using ad hoc data types, such as DTOs, to get data in to and out of the service layer is an ideal scenario, but it might not be applicable every time. Managing DTOs can be expensive when you have thousands (or even just hundreds) of domain objects and operations. In these cases, it is not uncommon to see such a prescription for good design abandoned in favor of a more practical technique. The most obvious alternatives to using operation-specific DTOs are using just one DTO per domain entity (essentially, a copy of the domain class without behavioral methods) or even the domain entity itself.

What's a Service, Anyway?

We already suggested that in this context the word *service* has a meaning that is free of any technology flavors and bias. In general, a service layer is a set of classes that expose logically related methods that another layer—typically, the presentation layer—can call. At this level of abstraction, a service layer is nearly the same as a Transaction Script library.

Devoid of any technology reference, the word *service* simply indicates a piece of software that services the requests that one layer sends to another. The expression *service layer*, instead, refers to a collection of services that collectively form an intermediate layer between two communicating layers.

What's Service Orientation?

Without beating around the bush, to many people today the word *service* means something more specific than just a piece of code that services incoming requests. This change of perspective has largely come about because of the advent of service orientation (SO) and service-oriented architectures (SOA).

Service orientation is a way of designing business processes as a set of interconnected services. Service orientation is not about technology itself, it is merely a different way of approaching the task of describing how a given business operates.

SOA, in turn, refers to IT architectures that view their resources as services and link and connect them both statically and on demand. In an SOA world, applications result from the composition and integration of independent services in a way that might be reminiscent of the design of forms in early rapid application development (RAD) systems. In an SOA application, the building block is the service rather than the components.

Our Definition of a Service

In a technology-agnostic scenario, we like to define a service as a business-related operation that all clients of the application can repeatedly execute. The list of clients includes users, other services in the application, and other parts of the business logic such as workflows.

For example, let's focus on a banking application and, in particular, on the task of converting amounts of money between foreign currencies. This operation is a good fit for a service. After you have defined the input and output data for the service, other parts of the application can repeatedly take advantage of the service. In addition, the code in the service is reused over and over again.

Here's a possible objection: if all the burden is with reusability, why not just use a plain class? Ultimately, when you implement the service, you actually use a class. So services and classes share a common substrate, but a service is something more specialized than a class that takes advantage of the surrounding environment and, thanks to that, gets its own autonomous life.

A service is a much better fit than a plain class in a service layer. We will even go further and say that there would probably be no emphasis at all on yet another layer if it weren't for services.

To see the bigger picture, let's have a quick look at the definition of *service* offered by the Organization for the Advancement of Structured Information Standards (OASIS):

> *A mechanism to enable access to one or more capabilities, where the access is provided using a prescribed interface and is exercised consistent with constraints and policies as specified by the service description.*

In a nutshell, a service is a class with something wrapped around it. We tried to capture this idea in Figure 5-5.

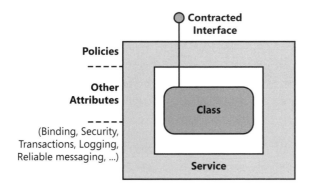

FIGURE 5-5 A service is a class within a nicely wrapped-up box.

The wrapped-up box is likely, *but not necessarily*, a run-time environment that provides additional functionalities well beyond the boundaries of the class. A class immersed in such a run-time environment will gain additional capabilities not coded in its own sources. And, more importantly, these extra features and policies can be configured without touching the source code of the class.

The run-time environment defines the difference between a service and a class. The run-time environment typically adds capabilities for searching, binding, security, logging, reliable messaging, and transactions and forwards messages to and from a service consumer. The run-time environment is usually controlled by declarative policies in a way that makes the overall system architecture fully configurable.

Service vs. Class

In the design of an application, service orientation allows you to use independent components with a fixed public interface. These components can be replaced at any time with no impact on the system as long as the contract with new components remains the same.

If the service is just "a class with something around it," what would stop us from creating a hierarchy of classes where the actual classes used in the application inherit any required extra behavior from parents? How is this different from the notion of a "service"?

That question is really more of a theoretical one. In practice, you don't want to write your own run-time environment for managing and servicing classes. In the real world, this possibility clearly stopped being worth the effort as much as 10 years ago, when Microsoft introduced Microsoft Transaction Server (MTS).

> **Note** From its inception, MTS was not dealing with services, public interfaces, and discoverability like SOA does today. But MTS was certainly promoting the idea that architects should focus only on the logic of business components—and their interaction and synchronization—leaving the burden of additional run-time features to a surrounding environment. A lot has happened since the MTS days, but in summary a class is still a plain piece of code, whereas a service is a class wrapped up in a nice and configurable box.

When it comes to implementing a system with services, you end up using some technology with a run-time environment that takes care of your classes. The run-time environment also publishes your classes as discoverable resources over some network.

In addition to being an autonomous, discoverable resource with a fixed interface, a service is also often a stateless component. In general, a stateless component scales better, has an overall simpler implementation, and can be employed in a larger number of scenarios.

Is Every Class a Service?

Admittedly, this is a question that expresses the difference between what you have and what you dream of having. Although the possibility of making every class a service sounds like a radical idea, it is probably less farfetched than one might think at first. So should every single class of an application be a service? Juval Lowy of IDesign has a nice chat on this topic on MSDN's Channel 9. If you are interested and want to hear more, here's the link: *http://channel9. msdn.com/ShowPost.aspx?PostID=349724*.

The key point is that after you have made your choice of a technology for the surrounding run-time environment, if this runtime is powerful enough, every class might get some benefit. Every class hosted as a service automatically benefits from provided system features, including security, transactions, tracing, logging, and so forth. (See Figure 5-5 earlier in the chapter.) And what about performance?

It's a debatable and also relative point. If the performance you can get is good enough, why should you care about the (obvious) overhead? Anyway, the concept of "every class as a service" is kind of a provocative and radical idea that we are likely to be faced with more often in the near future.

Services in the Service Layer

Architecturally speaking, the service layer applies a general and well-known principle of software design—low coupling—and possibly another principle, high cohesion, as well. It does that by defining an intermediate layer of code aimed at decoupling the user interface and the middle tier.

The advent of service orientation just made it more intriguing for architects to apply some of the tenets of service orientation to classes in the service layer. The result of this is that any service layer is made of services and only services. The fact that the service layer exists as a pattern at all is directly due to the concepts of services and service-orientation being applied to internal application logic versus external client operations. Let's take a brief look at the evolution of the service layer and how it has been applied within single-application architectures.

From Code-Behind to Services

Services in the service layer are invoked directly from the presentation layer. In a Web front end, this means the code-behind class of each page invokes the service layer. Similarly, in a Windows Presentation Foundation (WPF) or Windows Forms client, the code-behind class of the window or form hosts the logic for the invocation.

If you're using a Graphical User Interface (GUI) design pattern, such as the Model-View-Presenter (MVP) pattern, the service layer is invoked from the methods of the MVP presenter. (We'll cover GUI patterns in Chapter 7, "The Presentation Layer.")

It is common to see a canonical *Button1_Click* event handler in an ASP.NET code-behind class written as shown in the next code snippet. Needless to say, method names are totally arbitrary and only point to some action you might want to execute as the effect of the user action.

```
public void Button1_Click(object sender, EventArgs e)
{
    if ( ... )
    {
        // Primary route
        AccomplishFirstStep();
        if ( ... )
            TakeOneMoreStep();
    }
    else
```

```
    {
        // Secondary route
        PerformAnAction();
        IfHereTakeThisStep();
    }

    // Finalize the procedure
    CompleteAction();
}
```

The first level of abstraction you can build is a presenter. (See the discussions about MVP in Chapter 7.) A *presenter* simply offers a method in a separate class you call from within the code-behind class. The benefit of this is you encapsulate logic within the separate presenter class rather than sprinkle it throughout your ASP.NET code-behind classes. Maintenance is by far easier and the design is much less tightly-coupled. With a presenter class, the preceding code becomes code that looks like the following:

```
public void Button1_Click(object sender, EventArgs e)
{
    // The implementation of the MVP pattern ensures that the
    // window/form/Web page has a presenter object available
    // immediately after loading, typically using dependency
    // injection.
    this.presenter.PerformSomeAction();
}
```

The presenter's method then incorporates any logic you need to implement in the UI event handler. The service layer is even one step ahead of that, within the presenter class.

```
// From either the presenter, or directly in the code-behind class,
// you call a service method that orchestrates any required behavior.

public void PerformSomeAction()
{
    // This method belongs to the presenter class. It instantiates
    // the proxy of the "service" and places the call either synchronously
    // or asynchronously.

    // Prepares the DTO to pass data to the service
    PerformSomeActionRequest dto = new PerformSomeActionRequest();
    ⋮

    // Place the call.
    // NB: We're taking services literally as Web/WCF services here, but
    // performance reasons may suggest you opt for a serviced component if not
    // a plain class (especially in ASP.NET where service and code-behind
    // likely run on the same tier).
    SampleServiceClient proxy = new SampleServiceClient();
    PerformSomeActionResponse response = proxy.PerformSomeAction(dto);

    // Process results
    ⋮

}

[WebMethod]
```

```
public PerformSomeActionResponse PerformSomeAction(PerformSomeActionRequest dto)
{
    // The code you would otherwise run directly from the code-behind class
        .
        .
        .
}
```

If it sounds like it's just overhead added to the system, have a look at Figure 5-6, which offers a graphical view of the resulting model and its benefits.

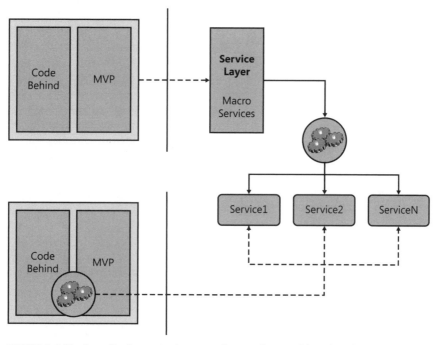

FIGURE 5-6 The benefit of a service layer: a unique and remotable point of contact between the UI and middle tier

 Important In the figure, the service layer is represented as a remote layer. This is not necessarily what you want or what happens in reality. Depending on the client you have (Web or Windows), the service layer might also be just another layer living on the presentation tier. In that case, your service layer wouldn't be Web services but might be serviced components or some vanilla class of your own design. The point is the abstraction the service layer provides, not necessarily the implementation of the layer itself.

A serviced component is the mechanism that enables COM+ services to be available to .NET Framework classes. When should you opt for a serviced component? The quick answer is whenever you need some of the additional services that COM+ provides: just-in-time activation, object pooling, declarative security, or distributed transactions. Are these plusses really beneficial today? You can get distributed transactions through the *TransactionScope* class. You can have declarative security through the features of the .NET Framework Code Access Security (CAS). You can have pooling and activation from some good dependency injection frameworks. In the end, we personally never use serviced components, but their use is not a bad thing per se. And, anyway, the list of COM+ plusses is not limited to what we've listed here.

When should you opt for a WCF service? Mostly when you need remotability. In other words, a WCF service is the recommended technology for a service layer when you need the ability of deploying the service layer on a dedicated application server. Likewise, it is an excellent choice when you need to make the service layer externally available in a service-oriented scenario. In this regard, the biggest benefit of WCF as a service technology is the configuration capabilities which, among other things, means a delicious pinch of aspect-orientation added to your solution.

Do we have any words of advice on Web services? WCF incorporates SOAP-based communication. With WCF you can easily switch to a different communication API of choice (sockets, remoting, or SOAP). Our advice is to use SOAP over HTTP—what Web services are all about—only if it is the only (or the best) option you have.

Benefits of a Service Layer

The service layer offers a unique point of contact between the user interface and the middle tier, where you concentrate the application logic. The application logic is that part of the business logic that springs directly from use cases. We'll return to the topics of application and business logic later in the chapter.

Services with their own surrounding run-time environment make it incredibly easier and more effective to remote pieces of the application logic. In Figure 5-6, the topmost schema shows a typical architecture that includes a service layer. You cross the boundary of the application UI with a *single* call toward a common programming interface—the service layer.

On the server side, the invoked method on the service layer orchestrates the required logic by making and coordinating calls to the Domain Model, specific application services, workflows, and whatever else your business layer is made of.

Without a service layer, you have direct calls to the application services issued from the presentation layer. The result is a fine-grained remote interface and a potentially chatty communication model. You take the risk of having to place multiple remote calls to accomplish the requested task. And this is not a good thing for performance.

Macro and Micro Services

The service layer is made of coarse-grained services, also referred to as *macro services*. Macro services just orchestrate operations that map to directly to use cases. Macro services do not contain any domain logic that relates to the core business. In other words, macro services don't know about invoices, products, or mortgages; instead, they know that to place an order they have to go through a well-known sequence of steps, such as checking the availability of the product and the amount of credit on the user account.

On the other hand, application services (also referred to as *micro services*) live on the server side and represent services specific to the application and functional to the domain logic. Examples of micro services are a service that performs currency conversions and a workflow-based service to calculate the quantity of goods that needs to be ordered to maintain appropriate inventory levels.

It is always preferable to have a service layer, as Figure 5-6 clearly shows. However, it is sometimes acceptable for the presentation layer to invoke an application service directly. This might be the case when the service method implements a simple, one-shot operation. In essence, the presentation layer should target an application service (thus bypassing the service layer) when it makes a direct call and there's no need to orchestrate multiple results and steps on the client.

The Service Layer Pattern in Action

As mentioned on page 133 of [P of EAA], the Service Layer pattern defines an additional layer that lives between two interfacing layers—typically, the presentation and business layers. In principle, this intermediate layer is just a collection of classes that implement the use cases of the application.

The advent of services and service orientation, though, made the whole solution even worthier and more successful. Services represent a loosely coupled counterpart to the presentation layer, and they offer an agreed-upon contract, reusability, and cross-platform deployment. And services, like plain classes, let you fine-tune the amount of abstraction you need.

Generalities of the Service Layer Pattern

The presentation layer of a real-world application is the primary user front end. Everything the user can do with an application passes through the presentation layer and the user interface.

Enterprise-class applications in particular, though, can have multiple application data presentation interfaces. One interface will certainly be a user interface—and perhaps there will be one for each supported platform, such as mobile, Web, WPF, Windows, Silverlight, and other software platforms. Another interface can be a back-office application that loads data into the system or extracts data and transforms it. Yet another interface is represented by a connector that attempts to use the application's –internal processing logic in a system-integration scenario.

In all these cases, a common application programming interface (API) is desirable. And it is even more desirable if it can be available through a number of transportation protocols and communicate via messages. (See Figure 5-7.)

The Service Layer pattern addresses the need of having a common layer of simple operations for any external interface the application is required to support.

The service layer contains operations that script the domain model and invoke application services in a sequence that is mostly determined by use cases. The service layer responds to input coming from the presentation layer. The presentation layer, in turn, doesn't care much about the module that operates at the other end. All that matters to it is that the module does what it claims to be able to do.

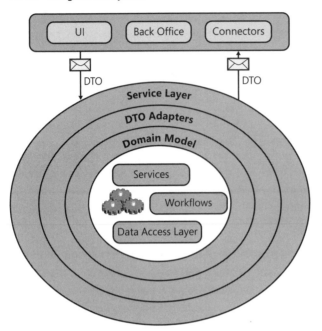

FIGURE 5-7 Multiple front ends for a common application's service-based back end

Neither the presentation layer nor the service layer contains (or should contain) business logic. The presentation layer knows only about the coarse-grained interface of the service layer; the service layer knows only about a contracted set of feasible interactions and takes care of the nitty-gritty details: transactions, resource management, coordination, and data massaging, as appropriate.

Real-World Examples of a Service Layer

The idea of a service layer has been around for at least five years now. The advent of SOA, which coincided with the appearance of service layers, reinforced the concept and made it even more attractive. Some would argue that it was SOA that actually inspired the idea of using service layers in multitier architecture. To debate the issue is pointless, just like debating whether the chicken or the egg came first.

Based on our experiences in the field, we would say that the purpose of the service layer, and the rationale behind it, is still something that some developers and architects fail to understand. So let us offer a real-world example.

Many of us have had the experience of being junior developers. And we all have had a dull and haughty boss at some time. It was not unusual in the early 1990s in a certain office in Rome, not too far from the Coliseum, to hear, *"Dino, we need to ship a customized version of product X to customer Y right now."*

Do you get the point? The boss is the *presentation layer*. All that he cares about is sending a simple command to his counterpart—say, a manager. To his eyes, the manager exposes a mere list of tasks and responsibilities. The boss doesn't care how the manager will actually accomplish the task, but he knows that the contract between the company and the manager says that he will do that. (The contract also implicitly says that if that manager doesn't fulfill tasks, he can be replaced.) The manager is the *service layer*. Finally, the manager coordinates other resources to get the job done.

If you look around, you find zillions of real-life scenarios where you can recognize an instance of the Service Layer pattern. Want some quick examples? Kids asking for money, editors demanding changes, you getting some cash at an ATM, and so on.

When to Use a Service Layer

The service layer should be used in nearly all applications of some complexity. There's probably no cost/benefit gain if a service layer is built into a simple filing system or used in a quick-and-dirty Web site such as temporary sites that stay posted for just a few weeks.

In multitier systems, there's almost no good reason for not having a service layer. One possible exception we can think of is when you end up with a single front end (for example, just the regular user interface) and a set of application services whose methods closely match the use cases of the system. In this case, the service layer will likely be just a dispatcher and no orchestration work will be required of it. Even a simple-minded service layer that merely forwards calls to a business layer is probably more than is needed.

Conversely, when you have multiple front ends with a significant amount of application logic, it is preferable to store the entire application logic in a single place rather than having it duplicated for each application interface.

> **Note** As we saw in the "Macro and Micro Services" section, you should include a service layer in an application if it makes sense for you to organize your services into macro and micro categories. Services in the macro category form the service layer.

What's Good About a Service Layer

The service layer adds abstraction and decouples two interfacing layers. Whenever this solution gets you a better system, you should build a service layer. A service layer favors the use of coarse-grained, remote interfaces that minimize traffic between the presentation and business layers.

When the service layer is implemented through services (for example, WCF services), you can realize additional benefits, such as the possibility of remoting the layer with extreme ease and changing binding settings through configuration.

What's Bad About a Service Layer

Because abstraction is the major strength of a service layer, for simple systems the service layer mostly represents overhead.

As we've mentioned a few times already, a service layer doesn't necessarily require a service technology such as WCF. In ASP.NET presentation layers, for example, you typically call the "service layer" from within the code-behind class—that is, in a local scenario. Having a WCF service here instead of a plain class would probably add overhead and likely degrade performance. Consider using WCF services in your service layer with a grain of salt and measure your performance numbers early and often. If performance suffers too greatly, choose another service layer technology.

> **Note** All in all, we think you need strong reasons to even consider Web or WCF services in the first place. For some ASP.NET pages, requiring cross-domain data, this is acceptable for sure. But most pages shouldn't be made to make several XML/HTTP network calls like that.

Where Does a Service Layer Fit?

The service layer is invoked from the presentation layer. But is it a local or remote call? As usual with architecture-related questions, the correct answer is, "It depends."

Fowler's first law of distributed object design recommends that you just don't distribute your objects. Our corollary to this law is, *"unless it's necessary or beneficial."* As you might know, necessity and benefits are extremely volatile concepts that are hard to measure, but they're easy to recognize in particular scenarios.

So where should you fit the service layer? In general, it is a good thing if you can have a service layer that can be moved across tiers quite easily. In this regard, a service technology such as WCF is just the right tool to use.

If the client is a Web page, the service layer is preferably local to the Web server that hosts the page. If the site is successful, you can relocate the service layer to a separate application server, thus increasing scalability.

If the client is a desktop application, the service layer is typically deployed to a different tier and then accessed remotely. The approach is the same in a Software+Services architecture, where the client contains little more than the GUI—that is, the entire application logic is remote. If the client is using Silverlight 2 and the service layer is published to the Internet, you have a perfect example of a Rich Internet Application (RIA).

The Service Layer Pattern in Action

The actual implementation of a service layer depends on two main technology-oriented choices. The first choice you have to make is what methods and calls to use as the basis for your service layer. Are they going to be plain classes or services? And if you opt for services, which service technology should you use? On the Windows and .NET platforms, you have quite a few options. You can opt for traditional WCF services, ASP.NET XML Web services, or perhaps REST-like services. (To learn more about REST services, see *http://en.wikipedia.org/wiki/Representational_State_Transfer.*)

If you're only a little bit familiar with the .NET Framework, you should know that creating a service—be it a WCF service or a Web service—is nearly as easy as creating a plain class decorated with a few attributes. Sure, there are a lot more details to take into account—such as the Web Services Description Language (WSDL) interface for Web services and configuration and data contracts for WCF services—but a service is ultimately a class with something around it.

Where does this take us? Well, upgrading a class in the service layer to the rank of a service is hardly a big deal. The level of complexity of the operation fits naturally into a standard refactoring process. It doesn't come for free, but it isn't a huge task either. Let's see how to design a class for the service layer.

Designing a Service Layer Class

Classes used in a service layer should expose a contract—either explicitly through a WCF service contract or implicitly by simply implementing an interface. Implementing an interface is always a good thing to do because it formalizes and clarifies what the class can and will do. The interface will probably use data transfer objects to accept and return data, and it will prefer chunky methods over chatty methods so that it can minimize roundtrips and maximize throughput.

How would you map required methods to interfaces and classes? Overall, you use the same principles that in Chapter 4 we applied to the Transaction Script pattern for the domain logic. Based on use cases, you prepare a list of required methods and then factor them into logical groups. Each group gets its own service or class. Where does this approach take you?

Most of the time, you probably end up having one service class per entity in the problem's domain—*CustomerService*, *OrderService*, and the like. It's all about the application requirements, however. If the number of required user actions is relatively small and the actions are somewhat closely related, a single service class is probably appropriate. Otherwise, a single service class can quickly become too large, as well as too difficult to maintain and change.

Generally, we don't think you should follow a strict rule stating that each entity gets its own service or that one service fits all user actions on entities. The service layer mediates between the presentation layer and the rest of the system. The service layer contains macro services (sometimes referred to as *use-case drivers*) that, in their programming interface, implement the real use cases.

The service layer typically evolves independently from the rest of the system and is the only interface for the presentation layer to call into internal application processes. If a use case changes, you modify the service layer but likely leave the business logic intact. In a relatively large application, the distinction between macro and micro services works quite nicely. For the programming interface of the service layer, you should look at your use cases first and then use common sense when it comes to organizing methods in classes. There's no general guideline that we can recommend as valid in all cases. The only guideline we will mention is this: "Look at your use cases and use common sense."

Implementing a Service Layer Class

A second and more practical rule is related to the implementation of a service layer class. We do recommend that each such class should expose an interface. This is a strict requirement if you opt for a collection of WCF services, but it is a good technique overall, regardless of the concrete technology you use for services. Here's a quick example:

```
public interface IOrderService
{
    void Create(Order o);
    List<Order> FindAll();
    Order FindByID(int orderID);
    ⋮
}
public class OrderService : IOrderService
{
    ⋮
}
```

There are a few things to point out in the code snippet. First, imagine the interface uses domain model objects directly. In this case, the *Order* class is exactly a representation of the Order entity we created in the domain model. If we're using an actual domain object, we are assuming a Domain Model pattern (which is described in Chapter 4) in the business logic. If you instead opted for a Table Module pattern, the *Order* class in the code snippet should be replaced with a typed *DataTable* or perhaps with a made-to-measure data container. We return to the topic of data transfer objects in a moment.

The *Create* method typically needs to orchestrate internal application services to check the credit status of the customer, check the availability of the ordered goods, and synchronize with the shipment company. The *Create* method is the perfect example of a service layer method—it offers a single point of contact to the presentation layer and is a multistep operation that interacts with various pieces of the domain model and business logic. The canonical implementation of a *Create* method will definitely *script* the domain model and business logic.

The *FindAll* method returns a list of orders, whereas *FindByID* returns a particular order. Again, assume we are using a Domain Model pattern (or an Active Record pattern) in the business layer and no ad hoc data transfer objects. As we'll see later, many architects recommend that Create, Read, Update, Delete (CRUD) methods should not appear in services. Finder methods such as *FindAll* and *FindByID* are essentially the R (read) in the CRUD acronym. Are these methods welcome?

Again, it depends on the use cases you have. You must have these finder methods if there's a use case that entails the user clicking somewhere to display a list of orders or the details of a single order. You should not have these methods in the service interface if you only have a use case that enables the user to escalate unprocessed orders to another department in the organization. In this case, you might still need to get a list of orders, or details of a single order, but this is an internal detail of the operation and shouldn't be visible at the presentation level.

Dealing with Roles and Security

Where would you handle roles and security? What if, say, a *FindAll* method must return only the orders that the current user can see?

If you take security seriously (and if you're even a bit paranoid about it), consider having each method in the service layer check the identity of the caller and refuse the call in the case of unauthorized users. Otherwise, the service layer can be designed to assume that the presentation layer has granted access to the sensitive portion of the user interface only to authorized users.

If you don't want to repeat authorization in each service method call, you might opt for declarative security and tag service methods with security attributes.

> **Note** Declarative security uses attributes to place security information into the metadata of assemblies, classes, and individual methods. The attribute indicates the type of demand you intend to use. Demands are typically used in libraries to protect resources from unauthorized callers.

What about roles? Checking roles and adjusting the response based on role inclusion is definitely a responsibility we assign to the application logic and, subsequently, to methods in the service layer. If roles are used, the service gets the identity of the call, figures out the role, and decides what to do.

How you handle roles and user authorization is an implementation detail. For example, in a WCF service you can leverage the *OperationContext* object. From the static *Current* property of the *OperationContext* class, you retrieve an instance of the *ServiceSecurityContext* and find out the identity of the caller.

> **Note** The service layer acts as the gatekeeper, and usually there's no need to push role checking into the BLL unless there is a good reason. However, if such a good reason exists and you have to send role information down to the BLL, that's fine. But a better design is to factor things such that the different roles the BLL methods would invoke are available at the service layer.

Service Layer and Transaction Script

Comparing the Service Layer (SL) pattern to the Transaction Script (TS) pattern is only natural at this point. In Chapter 4, we defined the Transaction Script pattern as a shell where you map each required user action to a method. The method proceeds from start to finish within the boundaries of a physical transaction. Data access is usually encapsulated and transferred using ad hoc containers.

What's the difference between the TS pattern and the Service Layer? Functionally speaking, they're nearly the same. However, if you look at the classification of patterns, you see some differences.

TS is a pattern for organizing the business logic; in this regard, TS is your business logic. SL, on the other hand, is a pattern to decouple two interfacing layers using services. SL works on top of an existing business logic layer. It scripts business components and accesses data components in order to implement a user action. SL is clearly for complex scenarios where you need to keep domain logic and application logic neatly separated.

Domain Logic and Application Logic

We already hinted at the two types of logic you have in most systems—domain logic and application logic. A generally agreed-upon definition exists for each. Let's explore.

Domain logic expresses business concepts, enforces business rules, and stores business information and the business state. Domain logic is commonly implemented in a domain model with objects that are ignorant about persistence, but data is stored and behavior is consistent with relevant business concepts and rules. Domain logic as a concept, though, also makes sense if you use typed *DataSets* for modeling the domain.

The domain logic is a sort of library that can be used by various applications interested in that functionality. In his book *Domain-Driven Design: Tackling Complexity in the Heart of Software* (Addison-Wesley, 2003), Eric Evans says the following:

> *State that reflects the business situation is controlled and used here, even though the technical details of storing it are delegated to the infrastructure. This layer is the heart of business software.*

Application logic is modeled after the various actions the software is designed to take. The application logic orchestrates domain objects and application services to serve presentation needs. Application logic is also referred to as the *application layer* Evans describes it as follows:

> *The tasks this layer is responsible for are meaningful to the business or necessary for interaction with the application layers of other systems. This layer is kept thin. It does not contain business rules or knowledge, but only coordinates tasks and delegates work to collaborations of domain objects in the next layer down.*

The application logic is about workflows that work out problems and is implemented in the service layer and kept separate from the business layer. The application logic implements use cases and, in doing so, it consumes the *library* represented by the *domain logic*. A good service layer is an extremely thin layer.

Note In this context, the term *workflow* just means a flow diagram that represents a required piece of work. It has nothing to do with technologies to code workflows, such as Windows Workflow Foundation.

Why have two types of logic in an application? Because the application logic has clear dependencies on application use cases and the user interface. Incorporating this logic in the domain model would make the classes in the domain inherently less reusable. This said, the separation between application and domain logic comes at a cost and mainly serves to deal with complexity. Including two types of logic in an application is not a prescription that is sane in all cases.

Note Entities in the domain logic are mostly standalone objects and have limited knowledge of other entities. Any interaction between entities (such as creating, deleting, or commanding entities to do something) is orchestrated by the service layer but is managed by domain logic. The only interaction between entities that is acceptable in the domain logic relates to logical dependencies between entities, such as Orders and Order Details.

Related Patterns

We presented the service layer as a collection of (service) classes that expose methods to the user interface. Most of the time, you will find it easy to match user actions to service layer methods. Like it or not, CRUD operations are common in the use cases of many enterprise applications. What the user really does is not much different than creating, reading, updating, and deleting some domain entities—sometimes multiple entities in a single operation.

The application logic that one expects from the service layer is essentially role management, data validation, notification, and adaptation of the data to the user interface or to the format that integrated systems might require.

When it comes to this, a few additional design patterns might help. Let's have a look at a few related patterns that help in the implementation of the service layer.

The Remote Façade Pattern

The Remote Façade (RF) pattern is formalized on page 388 of [P of EAA] as a set of methods that modify the granularity of existing operations already implemented elsewhere. An RF doesn't implement any new functionality. Rather, it places a different façade over an existing API. But why is an RF needed?

Motivation for Using the Remote Façade Pattern

RF exists to change the way in which an existing set of objects is accessed. It fits well in all scenarios where you like to call an existing API but don't like the API itself. An example might be when accessing a shipper's online services. Each shipper has a different API for registering packages for shipment, tracking packages, and other services, and all of them involve details your primary application logic can probably do without. By building a consistent API for your application, you can hide the details the shipper's API exhibits and allow your application to work with a cleaner interface.

In other words, if you want your code to deal with a simplified (or just different) interface, this necessity compels you to create an additional façade. In fact, this is precisely the definition of the classic Remote Façade pattern.

In particular, RF refers to a particular flavor of façade—a façade for remote objects. The benefit of this façade is that it allows you to create a coarse-grained interface over a set of fine-grained objects.

Object-orientation leads you toward the creation of small objects with neat and distinct responsibilities—fine-grained objects. These objects, though, are not suited for distribution. To effectively remote these objects, you need some adaptation. You don't want to change anything in the implementation of the fine-grained objects, but you want to be able to execute a batch of operations over a graph of these objects. In doing so, you need to create new methods that move around larger chunks of data. When you do so, you actually alter the granularity of the existing interface and create a remote façade. Turning again to shipping orders, you can ship multiple orders at once using your API, while mating the actual shipping requests to single packages using the shipper's API, assuming they don't support multiple shipments.

The Remote Façade Pattern and the Service Layer

By design, the service layer essentially has a coarse-grained interface because it tends to abstract a number of micro operations into a single endpoint that the application client will call. In this regard, the service layer is already a remote façade over the business layer and the objects in the domain layer—be it classes in the domain model or typed *DataSets*.

Where would you fit the service layer in a multitier application? We already raised this point earlier in the chapter. RF relates to the remotability of the service layer and how you move data to and from the application interface.

There's no need to run the service layer out of process when you have a Web presentation layer. And, in general, it is advisable that you always opt for a local approach unless something else is required. In doing so, you likely use plain domain model objects in the signature of service methods, as shown here:

```
public interface IOrderService
{
    void Create(Order o);
    List<Order> FindAll();
    Order FindByID(int orderID);
    ⋮
}
```

Later, if the need for a remote layer ever shows up, you might need to turn your service layer into a remote layer. If you use WCF, this can be as easy as adding a service contract attribute to the interface, as shown here:

```
[ServiceContract]
public interface IOrderService
{
    [OperationContract] void Create(Order o);
    [OperationContract] List<Order> FindAll();
    [OperationContract] Order FindByID(int orderID);
    ⋮
}
```

But what about data types? All nonprimitive types used in the signatures of WCF service methods require a *DataContract* attribute. Essentially, the attribute instructs the WCF runtime to automatically create data transfer objects for the specified types. Here's an example of the *DataContract* attribute:

```
[DataContract]
public class Order
{
    [DataMember] int OrderID {get; set;};
    [DataMember] DateTime OrderDate {get; set;};
    ⋮
}
```

An even less intrusive approach is possible if you use ASP.NET XML Web services. In this case, you don't even need to touch anything on the signature of the domain classes. You simply add a *WebMethod* attribute on remote methods in the service layer classes.

You need an RF when, at some point, you have to refactor the service layer to a more coarse-grained interface, when you need to use explicit DTOs in the signature, or both. The following interface is decoupled from domain objects and focuses more on the interactions taking place in the presentation layer:

```
public interface IOrderService
{
    void Create(OrderDto o);
    List<OrderDto> FindAll();
```

```
    OrderDto FindByID(int orderID);
    List<OrderDto> SearchOrder(QueryByExample query);
        :
        :
        :
}
```

The *OrderDto* class can be a superset or a subset of the domain's *Order* class (and its aggregate of dependent objects such as *OrderDetail*), and *QueryByExample* can be an ad hoc class carrying all the information the user interface requires and transmits into and out of a given form.

As a matter of fact, deep changes in the user interface might sometimes lead to changes in the service layer. It can even cause you to consider significantly refactoring the service layer or implementing an outermost wrapper, such as an RF.

The Data Transfer Object Pattern

The definition of the Data Transfer Object (DTO) pattern isn't that scary, is it? Based on page 401 of [P of EAA], a DTO is merely an object that carries data across an application's boundaries with the primary goal of minimizing roundtrips. Put this way, it seems to be a helpful pattern. The devil, though, is in the details.

> **Note** The DTO pattern described here is sometimes referred to as the Transfer Object pattern or the Value Object pattern. This is a little confusing because many who say "DTO" also use the expression "value object" to mean something different.
>
> In particular, in .NET, a *value object* (as opposed to a *reference object*) indicates a small object that uses its internal state instead of some unique identity value to compare itself to other value objects. Furthermore, in .NET, a value object is allocated on the stack and any reference to it points directly to its data. A reference object, conversely, is allocated on the heap and managed via a separate reference (yes, a sort of pointer). So be sure about the context when you use the term, or read about, *value objects*.

Motivation for Using the Pattern

There are two main scenarios for the DTO pattern. One is minimizing roundtrips when you call remote objects; another is maintaining a loose coupling between the front end and the classes of your domain model, if you have one.

In both cases, a DTO is nothing more than a container class that exposes properties but no methods. A DTO is helpful whenever you need to group data in ad hoc structures for passing data around. DTOs make clear sense when they are used in the context of a remote façade to send and receive data to accommodate multiple calls.

DTOs, though, also play a key role in a domain model scenario. You can't reasonably use native domain objects in the presentation layer in all situations. This is only possible if the presentation and service layers are both located in the same place, such as in a Web presentation layer. When the service layer lives on a different tier, you might not always use domain objects to exchange data. The primary practical reason that hinders this approach is that your domain objects might have dependencies on each other, even circular references, and this seriously affects their serialization capabilities.

As an example, consider that WCF doesn't handle circular references and neither does the XML serializer layer for ASP.NET XML Web services. At the same time, if you consider a domain model based on the content of the sample Northwind SQL Server database, you find out that each *Customer* object holds a reference to a list of *Order* objects; and each *Order* object refers to a *Customer* object. In complex domain models, circular references are a common thing.

Even when the web of domain objects can be serialized, you seriously risk having to move a lot of data around—perhaps as much as a significant share of the whole model. A collection of DTOs helps you avoid this risk and gets you a neater and niftier system. However, it introduces a new level of complexity. In Figure 5-7, we refer to this extra layer as the *DTO adapters layer*.

> **Note** If you're familiar with LINQ-to-SQL, you might know that the Microsoft Visual Studio 2008 designer allows you to automatically add a *DataContract* attribute to each class in the object model it creates. It doesn't even complain when you have a customer pointing to a list of orders and an order pointing back to a customer. How is that possible? Quite simply, the wizard ignores the *DataMember* attribute on *EntityRef<T>* types. As a result, during the serialization of an order, the reference to the customer is ignored.

Data Transfer Object and Service Layer

When we discuss DTOs in preliminary architecture meetings, we often hear objections raised regarding the use of DTOs. Data transfer objects can appear to be a waste of development time and resources. You know what? This makes perfect sense. The problem is that DTOs exist because they're necessary. They can be avoided at times, but they still play a key role in enterprise architectures.

In theory, we should advocate for the use of DTOs for whatever communication takes place between interfacing layers, including communications between the presentation layer and service layer. Additionally, we should advocate for the use of different DTOs for each distinct user-interface screen and even different DTOs for requests and responses.

In practice, things go differently. Having DTOs in the signature of service layer methods adds a whole new layer of code and, subsequently, complexity. This is acceptable as long as there's no better alternative. We like to emphasize that the costs of extensively using DTOs can be easily underestimated. When you end up having hundreds of domain objects, multiplying the number of classes by two or three can be a nightmare.

Our pearl of wisdom can be summarized in two points. Follow the DTO-only philosophy, but be pragmatic in your design. Stated another way, use DTOs only when there's a clear benefit, or a clear necessity, and use direct domain objects whenever you can. A task that possibly benefits from the use of DTOs is sending out only data that is strictly necessary or data in a format that better suits the user interface.

This point of limiting the use of DTOs is sometimes perceived as a typical complaint of lazy developers. There's much more behind this approach than just laziness. We estimate that the development cost of a full DTO implementation is comparable to the development cost of building an in-house, project-specific O/RM layer.

For O/RM layers, you have a number of helper tools—both commercial and open-source. For DTOs, on the other hand, you are left to your own devices and must build and manage them yourself. WCF and ASP.NET XML Web services generate implicit DTOs when they serialize data, but they offer limited control over the format of the data. By using attributes such as *DataMember* (in WCF) and *XmlIgnore* (in ASP.NET XML Web services), you can keep some properties out of the data transfer object. However, you have no automatic way to generate ad hoc DTOs for more advanced scenarios, such as when you need different classes for requests and responses or different DTOs for different UI screens. As far as we know, no wizards exist for this; all we need is a class designer with some awareness of the domain model. But there are none because the domain models between applications differ greatly. Our hope is that with the advent of Entity Framework, at least for its generated domain model, there will be soon a tool to create DTOs quickly.

The Adapter Pattern

When you use DTOs in multitier systems, you are likely adapting a domain object to a different interface. You are therefore implementing the Adapter pattern. One of the classic and most popular design patterns, Adapter essentially converts the interface of one class into another interface that a client expects.

As you can see, the usefulness of the Adapter pattern goes beyond the DTO scenario we're discussing here.

Motivation for Using the Adapter Pattern

The adapter is a class responsible for the logic necessary to lay out some data in a different format. For example, an adapter would extract bits from an integer read out of database table column and transform them into a sequence of Boolean values to suit the user interface.

In a multitier scenario, as you saw in Figure 5-7, the Adapter pattern is widely applied to render a domain object into a DTO and vice versa. You should not expect to find particularly complex logic in an adapter class, but you might need an explicit adapter class for some DTOs you have to produce.

The Adapter Pattern and the Service Layer

The need for an adapter class for each required DTO inevitably raises development costs. It also thickens the layer of code to traverse before a consumer can get data from the persistence tier.

When evaluating DTOs, you should continue to consider maintenance issues that would result from having a bunch of new classes. Keep in mind that for each of those classes, you likely need to have a duplex adapter—to adapt from a domain object to a DTO and to adapt from a DTO to a domain object. The following code snippet shows a very simple scenario: a DTO class that is a mere subset of the domain object. In this case, all the adapter logic belongs to the various getters and setters.

```
public class OrderDTO
{
    // Use [NonSerialized] if using this DTO through WCF methods
    private Order _order;

    public OrderDTO(Order order)
    {
        _order = order;
    }

    public int OrderID
    {
        get { return _order.OrderID; }
        set { _order.OrderID = value; }
    }

    public DateTime OrderDate
    {
        get { return _order.OrderDate.GetValueOrDefault(); }
        set { _order.OrderDate = value; }
    }

    public string EmployeeName
    {
        get { return _order.Employee.LastName; }
        set { }
    }
}
```

In other cases, you might need an ad hoc class that takes the starting object and fills the DTO. Here's a possible scheme for the class:

```
public class OrderDTO
{
    private OrderDTOAdapter _adapter;

    public OrderDTO(Order order)
    {
        _adapter = new OrderDTOAdapter(order);
        _adapter.Initialize(this);
    }
}

internal class OrderDTOAdapter
{
    private Order _order;

    public OrderDTOAdapter(Order order)
    {
        _order = order;
    }
```

```
public void Initialize(OrderDTO dto)
{
    dto.OrderID = _order.OrderID;
    dto.OrderDate = _order.OrderDate.GetValueOrDefault();
    dto.EmployeeName = _order.Employee.LastName;
    ⋮
}
}
```

The adapter layer can certainly be an extra layer of code to traverse but, all in all, we wouldn't give it more importance than it should have in terms of performance overhead. With an eye on Figure 5-7, we dare say that you experience the highest costs in the interaction with the domain model.

The service layer spends most of its time waiting to get the right collection of properly configured domain objects from the data access layer. The cost of adapting data to DTOs is certainly not null, but it's not of the same order of magnitude as creating and populating domain objects or DTOs. Read the sidebar titled "The Thickness of Layers Is Relative" if you would like to read about a live experience.

The Thickness of Layers Is Relative

More layers of code to traverse are not necessarily a symptom of worse-performing systems. Want an example? Read on.

When the user pages through a grid and places a request for a new page of data, you can likely afford to use, in the data access layer, the paging capabilities of the ADO.NET data adapter object to get paged data. Next, you adapt the retrieved content to a collection of domain objects (or DTOs) to return to the user interface. Let's look at the stacked layers.

In this case, you have raw data flowing first into the internal data reader used by the ADO. NET data adapter. Next, data is loaded into a *DataTable*, and from there it goes straight into DTOs or domain objects. Too many layers for you? What about an alternative?

You might implement paging over the database yourself. You get a data reader and then load the content into a collection of domain objects or DTOs. Doesn't this sound like a better solution? It is surely a neater solution, but we haven't mentioned the difficulties of testing, maintaining, and evolving the SQL code for effective paging.

With ADO.NET data adapters, you take what the ADO.NET framework provides and get working code faster. However, when you measure performance, you won't observe significant changes. Why is this so? Well, the major costs are in the instantiation of DTOs or domain objects. The extra adaptation layer only sped up coding without hurting performance.

Do not take this experience literally, but to the extent possible, learn from it. By the way, in that project we weren't allowed to use an industry-level O/RM tool. With NHibernate or another similar tool in place, we probably would have designed things differently.

DTO vs. Assembly

We probably need to make a strong statement about data transfer objects. Do we like or hate them? Well, it depends. DTOs are an excellent tool for explaining to kids the difference between theory and practice—that is, if kids can understand DTOs.

DTOs are a must-have in theory; in practice, they represent significant overhead. However, experience teaches that there's no overhead that can't be worked in if that is the only way to go.

In a service-oriented world, a DTO-only solution is close to perfection. In a developer-oriented world, a DTO-only solution sounds extreme and is sometimes impractical. As usual, it is a matter of finding the tradeoff that works for you in the project that you are engaged on. If you were to abandon the DTO-only principle to some extent, what else could you do? Essentially, you could use domain objects in a library (an assembly in .NET) and share that library across the layers.

Let's review some of the factors in this tradeoff.

Examining Some DTO Facts

In a multitier system, the service layer is responsible for decoupling the presentation layer from the rest of the system. To get this behavior, you need to keep in mind that the key guideline is to share data contracts rather than classes. A data contract is essentially a neutral representation of the data that interacting components exchange. The data contract describes the data a component receives, but it is not a system-specific class, such as a domain object. Ultimately, a data contract is a class, but it is an extra class specifically created for a particular service method.

This extra class is referred to as a data transfer object. Having a layer of DTOs isolates the domain model from the presentation layer, resulting in both loose coupling and optimized data transfer.

The adoption of data contracts adds flexibility to the schema of data. For example, with DTOs in place, a change in the user interface that forces you to move a different amount of data doesn't have any impact on the domain. Instead, the impact is limited to the DTO adapter layer. Likewise, you can enter changes to the domain without affecting the client.

With DTOs, you also work around the problem of circular references. When you create the domain model, you find it extremely useful to double-link entities, such as Customer-to-Orders and Order-to-Customer. As we've mentioned, classes with circular references aren't serializable. With method-specific DTOs, you brilliantly solve this issue also.

Note The real problem with circular references is not the lack of support from serializers. This is a false problem. On one hand, we welcome and love circular references between parents and children because this gives us unmatched power when it comes to querying and modeling real problem domains. On the other hand, a complex web of domain objects can't just be handed to an automatic tool for serialization. Even if you could rely on serializers that handle circular references, would you really use them? Would you really serialize a large share of a domain model? With doubly-linked parent and children, when you load an order, you likely also load all details of the order and product, category, customer, and employee information. In this regard, a DTO is a much safer and smarter approach. In a WCF world, the *NonSerializedAttribute* is your best friend because it lets you break the cycle of references at some precise point.

DTO in Action: Load an Order

Let's see how to address a couple of typical scenarios that involve actions on the service layer. Let's first consider a form where the user can pick up an ID to see the details of an order. As a result, the presentation layer invokes a method on the service layer with a similar prototype:

```
??? FindByID(int orderID);
```

The input is an integer, which should be good most of the time. What about the return type? Should it be a real representation of the Order entity you have in the system? This can be an *Order* domain model object, an *Order* class generated by LINQ-to-SQL, or even a typed *DataTable*. In any case, we return the entire graph of the order. Looking at the Northwind database, the graph could be as large as the one shown in Figure 5-8.

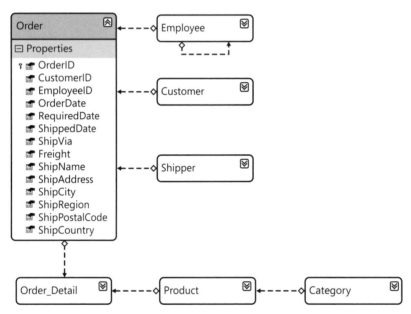

FIGURE 5-8 A possible graph for an Order entity

The user interface might need to show some data coming from linked objects, but there's probably no need to transfer the entire graph. An adapter layer can create a DTO that fulfills the data contract established between the service and presentation layers. Here's a better signature:

```
OrderServiceFindByIDResponse FindByID(OrderServiceFindByIDRequest request);
```

The naming convention is arbitrary; we opted for *<Service><Method><ContractType>*. Ideally, you have a different DTO for input data and output data. Here's a possible signature for the DTOs:

```
public class OrderServiceFindByIDRequest
{
    public int OrderID { get; set; };
}
```

```csharp
public class OrderServiceFindByIDResponse
{
    public int OrderID {get; set; };
    public DateTime OrderDate { get; set; };
    public DateTime RequiredDate { get; set; };
    public bool Shipped { get; set; };
    public DateTime ShippedDate { get; set; };
    public string FullAddress { get; set; };
    public string CompanyName { get; set; };
    public string ShipperCompany { get; set; };
    public List<OrderItem> Details { get; set; };
}
public class OrderItem
{
    public int OrderDetailID { get; set; };
    public int Quantity { get; set; };
    public string Description { get; set; };
    public decimal UnitPrice { get; set; };
    public decimal Discount { get; set; };
    public decimal TotalPrice { get; set; };
}
```

Internally, the service method queries the domain model and gets the graph of the order. The order is identified by its ID. Using a wrapper object for the order ID keeps you on the safe side in case there are additional parameters such as a range of dates.

Here's a possible implementation for the service method:

```csharp
public OrderServiceFindByIDResponse FindByID(OrderServiceFindByIDRequest request)
{
    // Load the graph for the order using the data access layer
    // (You can directly use an O/RM here or perhaps a repository or your data mappers)
    Order order = LoadOrderFromPersistence(request.OrderID);

    // Prepare the response using an adapter
    OrderServiceFindByIDAdapter adapter = new OrderServiceFindByIDAdapter(order);
    OrderServiceFindByIDResponse response = adapter.Fill();

    return response;
}

internal class OrderServiceFindByIDAdapter
{
    private Order _order;

    public OrderServiceFindByIDAdapter(Order order)
    {
        _order = order;
    }

    public OrderServiceFindByIDResponse Fill()
    {
        OrderServiceFindByIDResponse response = new OrderServiceFindByIDResponse();
```

```
        response.OrderID = order.OrderID;
        response.OrderDate = order.OrderDate;
        response.FullAddress = String.Format("{0}, {1}, {2}",
                                order.Address, order.City, order.Country);
        ⋮
        response.CompanyName = order.Customer.CompanyName;
        response.ShipperCompany = order.Shipper.CompanyName;
        foreach(OrderDetail detail in order.OrderDetails)
        {
            OrderItem item = new OrderItem();
            item.OrderDetailID = detail.OrderDetailID;
            item.Quantity = detail.Quantity;
            item.Discount = detail.Discount;
            item.Description = detail.Product.Description;
            item.UnitPrice = detail.UnitPrice;
            item.TotalPrice = detail.Quantity * detail.UnitPrice * detail.Discount;
            response .Details.Add(item);
        }

        return response;
    }
}
```

As you can see, the adapter flattens the Order's graph as appropriate to suit the presentation layer. The presentation layer, in turn, receives only the data it needs and in the format that it prefers. The presentation layer doesn't know anything about the Order object in the underlying domain model.

DTO in Action: Update an Order

Let's consider another example: the user navigates to a screen where she is allowed to enter changes to an existing order. How would you handle this in terms of data transfer between the presentation and service layers?

The response we get from the service method should contain a failure/success flag and additional information in case of errors. We clearly need an ad hoc class here. What about the input data for the service method? Ideally, we pass only the list of changes. Here's a possible signature for the method:

```
OrderServiceUpdateOrderResponse Update(OrderServiceUpdateOrderRequest request);
```

The response is simple. Possible errors reported to the user interface are caused by failures in the execution of the request.

```
public class OrderServiceUpdateOrderResponse
{
    public bool Success;
    public string[] Errors;
}
```

You can use a flag or perhaps an error code to indicate the success of the operation. You can also use another member to communicate additional information, such as a list of errors or suggestions for retrying.

> **Note** If the service is for internal use only and is not publicly exposed in an SOA manner (that is, it is a vanilla class), it might be acceptable for you to make it throw any exceptions directly to the caller—the presentation layer. If the service layer might not be local, and you want to reserve the possibility to move it to a different machine, you have to code the service to swallow exceptions and return ad hoc data structures. If you want an approach that works regardless of the service layer implementation, the only option is creating ad hoc structures.

We want to let the service know about what has changed in the order. How can we formalize this information? An order update is essentially a list of changes. Each change is characterized by a type (update, insertion, or deletion) and a list of values. To specify new order values, we can reuse the same *OrderItem* DTO we introduced for the previous load scenario:

```
public class OrderServiceUpdateOrderRequest
{
    public int OrderID;
    public List<OrderChange> Changes;
}
public class OrderChange
{
    public OrderChangeTypes TypeofChange;
    public OrderItem NewItem;
}
```

Internally, the service method loops through the requested changes, validates values, attempts updates, and tracks notifications and errors. Here's a general skeleton for the method:

```
public OrderServiceUpdateOrderResponse Update(OrderServiceUpdateOrderRequest request)
{
    // Count insertions (if only insertions are requested, avoid loading the graph)
    int insertCount = (from op in request.Changes
                        where op.TypeOfChange == OrderChangeTypes.Insert).Count();
    if (insertCount == request.Changes.Count)
    {
        foreach(OrderChange change in request.Changes)
        {
            Order newOrder = new Order();
            :

            InsertOrderIntoPersistence(newOrder);
        }
    }

    // Load the graph for the order using the data access layer
    // (You can directly use an O/RM here or perhaps a repository or your data mappers)
    Order order = LoadOrderFromPersistence(request.OrderID);
    foreach(OrderChange change in request.Changes)
```

```
    {
        switch(change.TypeOfChange)
        {
            .
            .
            .
        }
    }

    // Prepare the response    OrderServiceFindByIDAdapter adapter = new OrderServiceFindByI
DAdapter(order);
    OrderServiceUpdateOrderResponse response = new OrderServiceUpdateOrderResponse();
    .
    .
    return response;
}
```

There are some aspects of the method you can optimize. For example, you can avoid loading the order's graph from the data access layer if only insertions are requested. For deletions and updates, you likely need to have the graph available to check conditions and detect possible conflicts. However, you do not necessarily have to load the entire graph. Lazy loading could be used to minimize the quantity of data loaded.

Note It is not unusual that you have to dynamically adjust your fetch plan to be as lazy as possible. Most tools you might want to use in this context—from LINQ-to-SQL to NHibernate—allow you to dynamically configure the fetch plan. For example, in LINQ-to-SQL, you get this ability through the *LoadOptions* class in the data context.

When You Can Do Without DTOs

If we had to preserve the aesthetics and harmony of the solution and the purity of the architecture, we would opt for DTOs all the way through the system. However, we live in an imperfect world where pragmatism is the key to finding a happy medium between purity and reality.

We've learned from our experiences in the field that a DTO-only approach is impractical (even insane, we would say) in the context of large projects with hundreds of entities in the domain model. What can you use instead? There is only one alternative: using domain objects directly.

This solution, though, should not be applied with a light heart. In particular, be aware that some project conditions make it more favorable and worthwhile. Which conditions are those?

The ideal situation to partially or entirely remove the DTO constraint is when the presentation and service layers are located on the same layer and, ideally, in the same process. For example, this can be a .NET-to-.NET scenario where the same common language runtime (CLR) types can be understood on both sides. (See Figure 5-9.)

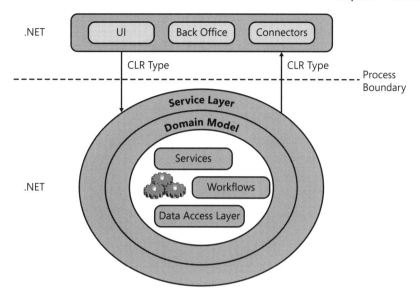

FIGURE 5-9 Avoiding DTOs in a .NET-to-.NET scenario

When the presentation layer is ASP.NET, services implemented as ASMX Web services or WCF services can live side by side in the same Internet Information Services (IIS) worker process. If the presentation and service layers are not hosted in the same process, you have an additional nontrivial problem to deal with: serializing CLR types over the process boundary.

As we've seen, in a domain model it's common and desirable to have circular references between objects. This is not an issue if objects are referenced in-process, but out-of-process references (and it doesn't matter whether it is the same layer or different tiers) are another story.

In a .NET-to-.NET scenario, you can opt for a .NET remoting bridge for the cross-process serialization. Unlike the XML serialization used for Web and WCF services, the binary formatter used by .NET remoting supports circular references. This is not the main point, though. Would you really want the entire graph to be serialized? If you did that, you would be back to square one. If DTOs are not a practical option, you can still use domain objects in the signature of service methods, but use smart and lazy strategies to pull data into these objects.

The presentation layer still expects to receive, say, an *Order*; however, the *Order* object it actually gets doesn't necessarily have all of its members set to a non-null value. To make it easier for the presentation layer to figure out which combination of data the domain object provides, you can implement in the domain object a number of alias interfaces. In this way, the presentation layer knows that if, say, interface *ILoadOrder* is found, only a contracted subset of properties is available. Note that when it comes to moving domain objects between tiers, there's no generally agreed-upon solution that works in all cases. Mostly, the solution is left to your creativity and to your specific knowledge of the project.

All in all, valid reasons for not using DTOs can be summarized as follows:

- There are hundreds of entities in the domain model.

- It is OK for the presentation layer to receive data in the format of domain objects (or, at least, an adapter layer on the presentation layer is not an issue).

- Presentation and service layers are co-located in the same process.

In many of our largest projects, we opt for a mixed approach. We tend to use mostly domain objects, thus saving our teams the burden of dealing with a lot of extra classes—which are a nightmare for maintenance. At the same time, when the distance between domain model and presentation layer is significant, we resort to made-to-measure and *handwritten*, DTOs.

Note The emphasis on the adjective *handwritten* is not accidental. The issue with DTOs is not the extra layer of code (whose benefits we largely recognize) that is needed, but with the need to write and maintain many more classes. With 400 classes in a domain model, this likely means managing more than 1000 classes. Avoid that situation if you can.

What we would really like to have is a tool that weds awareness of a domain model with the ability to generate the code for graphically designed DTO classes. We would gladly welcome a tool that was based on the Visual Studio 2008 class designer and that, for Entity Framework and LINQ-to-SQL, would provide the ability to add a DTO. Ideally, the wizard for doing this would let you select properties to import from an existing graph and add an autogenerated C# class to the project that you could further extend with custom properties.

A DTO, in fact, is *not necessarily* a mere a subset of a particular domain object, with some of its properties and none of its methods. A DTO can be significantly different from any domain objects. You don't need to have a one-to-one or one-to-*n* correlation between domain objects and DTOs. You can also have DTOs that are projections of a portion of the domain model. For this reason, we would welcome a designer tool for autogenerating code for DTOs.

What You Gain and What You Lose

If you have DTOs, your design of the system is loosely coupled and open to a variety of consumers—although they are not necessarily known at the time the system is architected. If you are at the same time the provider and consumer of the service layer and have control over the presentation, there are clear benefits in sharing the domain model via an assembly.

As usual, this is not a point that can be grossly generalized. You should realize that whatever options we propose here come with a "Well, it depends" clause.

A 100 percent DTO approach has its origins in SOA, which we'll say more about in just a few moments. The benefits of SOA go beyond the contract with and implementation of a service layer. SOA in a distributed application is all about ensuring a loose coupling between layers so that versioning, maintenance, and even evaluation of the threat model are simplified and made more effective.

As part of an SOA, an adapter layer placed in between the domain model and public data contracts isolates the domain model from the rest of the system. This arrangement costs you something, but it is an effort that pays off by allowing changes to be made without affecting consumers.

The problem is, will the payoff be enough for you? Will the subsequent cost/benefit ratio be positive? We all agree on the added value that an SOA brings to a distributed application. Can we afford it?

In large projects with hundreds of entities, DTOs add a remarkable level of (extra) complexity and work. Tightly coupled layers, though, might be a remedy that's worse than the disease.

An SOA is a great thing, but its benefits might not be evident when used with a single application. A strict adherence to SOA principles is especially beneficial for the information system as a whole, but that's not always so for a single application.

Service-Oriented Architecture

The interest in and need for a service layer in distributed systems has to do with *service orientation*. Service orientation is the paradigm according to which you envision the functionality of a software architecture as a collection of business processes that are, in turn, packaged and exposed as interoperable services. An architecture designed according to this service-oriented paradigm is said to be a service-oriented architecture (SOA).

This said, defining SOA is very difficult to do.

The principles associated with an SOA are nothing really new. Other computing paradigms (such as object orientation and CORBA) share some of the principles of SOA and actually inspired the definition of SOA. So what is really unique and valuable in an SOA?

The particularly valuable aspect of SOA is that it pushes a loosely coupled, service-based architecture to model business processes. SOA is also about interoperability and integration via open standards. With SOA, the solution is composed of services written using different programming languages, perhaps hosted on a variety of platforms, and likely supporting different binding models.

SOA is not a service; if you ask for a definition of an SOA service, you're off track. SOA is about principles for designing services—any flavor of services, including services in the service layer.

Note Many people talk about the benefits derived from the adoption of SOA principles. This book is no exception. However, we want to point out there's never been an ounce of measurable benefit for customers from architectural blueprints alone. It's always the successful implementation of a well-designed architecture, not the architecture itself, that generates benefits and added value for the customer.

Tenets of SOA

Once again, we're talking about services and faced with the same question: *what's a service?* In Figure 5-5, we essentially defined a service as a class with something around it. And earlier in this chapter, we said that in an SOA application, the building block is the service rather than the components. We can now expand on those basics and say that a service adheres to the common principles of object-oriented design, such as encapsulation and polymorphism, plus four more tenets:

- Boundaries are explicit.
- Services are autonomous.
- Use contracts, not classes.
- Compatibility is based on policy.

These tenets should inspire your design of services. But keep in mind that organizations might have different requirements and expectations. For companies, SOAs are like snowflakes or grains of sand: it's hard to find two alike.

Boundaries Are Explicit

An SOA service exposes a clear and explicit contract. Any interaction with the service takes place through this public interface. Methods on the interface represent entry points into the service machinery. Data in the methods' signatures represents the messages used and understood by the service.

When designing a service, as a developer you should manage to keep its interface (contract) as simple as possible, without hindering future enhancements. This means that service operations should accept a well-defined input message and respond with an equally well-defined output message. Input and output messages take the form of easy-to-serialize classes with no circular references and dependencies—just plain data containers.

Opting for message-based semantics also helps you avoid a remote procedure call (RPC) type of model of interaction. In an RPC-like model, consumers know something about the internal behavior of the service because this inevitably shines through the interface methods. It is desirable that consumers send a message and get a response—all in a single operation, with extreme simplicity and clear responsibilities.

Services Are Autonomous

For a service, autonomy means that each service is being deployed, managed, and versioned independent of the system in which it is deployed and consumed. This doesn't mean, though, that each service is an island and is totally isolated from the rest of the system.

An autonomous service is essentially a loosely-coupled service. It is designed and deployed independently from other services, but it is able to communicate with other services using contract-based messages and policies.

Service contracts are designed to be static and shouldn't be modified after the service is published. To fulfill this requirement, message-based semantics is the only way to go because of the flexibility it allows you to build into the contract.

Use Contracts, Not Classes

In Chapter 4, we suggested that developers define an object model to represent the various entities that populate a given problem domain. This means having classes such as *Customer*, *Order*, *Product*, or typed *DataTables* for analogous database tables.

The object model that represents the data within the system is made of classes that combine behavior and data into a single platform-specific and language-specific construct.

In SOA, one of the goals is interoperability; in light of this, no platform-specific detail can ever cross the service boundary. Subsequently, classes are not among a service's best friends. This is yet another reason for pushing message-based semantics in the definition of a service.

When we say *message-based semantics*, we essentially mean that at the SOA level, services communicate by exchanging XML strings (messages). As a developer, you embrace the idea of services exchanging data messages with a fixed schema, but you actually code services using ad hoc classes. The service technology you use (for example, WCF) recognizes your classes as platform-specific types (for example, CLR types) and converts them into XML messages. The XML serialization and deserialization is entirely transparent to you. So does it ultimately mean that developers should actually care about classes, not contracts? No, quite the reverse.

For a developer, a service contract is a collection of methods exposed by a service. A data contract, on the other hand, is a collection of typed values that the developer expresses through a data transfer object. A data transfer object is still a class, but it's a completely different object than a domain model class.

Regardless of the technology view, at a lower level services communicate using XML schema-based messages in a way that is agnostic to both programming languages and platforms. This ensures broad interoperability and flexibility. Abstractly speaking, defining a service entails defining for it a service contract and a bunch of data contracts.

Implementation is the next step.

Compatibility Is Based on Policy

The fact that a service is reachable and callable is not necessarily a good reason for a consumer to place a call. The key point about this tenet is that a service consumer must be able to determine whether a given service has the capabilities it expects.

Service and data contracts are important, but not enough. Service and data contracts refer to *structural compatibility* and merely describe what is communicated—what you can call and what you will get back.

This tenet is about the *semantic compatibility* between services—whether a given service does exactly what the consumer expects. The semantic compatibility should be exposed and discovered via a publicly accessible and standard policy.

To express service-level policies, and enable them to be discovered or enforced at runtime, you can use the WS-Policy specification.

A Summary of the Tenets

SOA is a design discipline aimed at achieving interoperability and composability in the building of complex information systems for organizations. The essence of an SOA is the service.

A service can be used to expose business processes in the form of an application. Services can be composed into workflows. Services can be consumed by end-users, systems, or other services. The overall SOA model is not layered; it looks more like a fractal.

The four main tenets we just described in this section apply to the design of services in the context of an SOA. These tenets are high-level concepts and express the philosophy behind SOA. When it comes to actually building services, you might want to look at some of the derived principles that we mentioned earlier in the chapter and that we'll be summarizing in a moment.

Building an SOA is an incremental process and doesn't require a full overhaul of the existing business processes. You don't need to build an SOA in an organization to add value. Keep in mind that an SOA is a means, not an end. You need to build applications that model existing business processes in a faithful and effective manner. SOA principles—but not necessarily all of them—do help in this task.

What SOA Is Not

As it should be clear by now, SOA is about services, but it is not a service technology. Using services in an application doesn't make the application an SOA. SOA is about principles that inspire good service-modeling techniques.

As disappointing as it might sound, SOA is a gray area. To many people in the IT industry, SOA is just a more generic name for a Web service. SOA and Web services are not unrelated. SOA is not a Web service, but a Web service might be the result of an SOA.

In some cases, the SOA philosophy is too extreme for an organization and requires an incremental approach. As a result, it is not uncommon in a system to find that some features are SOA and some not. As a matter of fact, a large share of today's production Web services systems are not SOAs. As a matter of fact, there's a bit of confusion about SOA and a number of false myths surrounding it.

SOA Is Not a Revolution

Companies need an IT infrastructure that covers all present and future system requirements and runs and supports the business. Subsequently, the need for SOA is the need to integrate existing systems in order to implement business processes in software.

This problem is nothing new. Electronic Data Interchange (EDI) defines a set of standards that organizations use to exchange documents and arrange business transactions electronically, in an application-to-application scenario. EDI was not defined yesterday; it dates back to at least 15 years ago. For years, companies have been able to make their IT systems talk to internal and external customers. And years of experience with older technologies taught that resulting systems and, more importantly, underlying models were not flexible enough to meet business demands.

As a result, EDI, CORBA, COM, and Distributed COM (DCOM) followed one another in the vain attempt to define a model for distributed systems that was effective, affordable, and in line with modern business necessities. SOA is just the latest step in the direction of enabling a company to run its business and publish its services for other companies to interact with and integrate with their own business processes.

SOA builds on past technologies and improves them by introducing a paradigm shift. Instead of remotely invoking methods on objects, you pass messages between services designed to fulfill a few key tenets. SOA is not a revolution; it is an evolutionary paradigm.

SOA Is Not a Technology

You should see SOA as a general design philosophy rather than a technology for writing concrete services. In this regard, SOA is entirely independent of any vendors and products.

The major benefits of SOA come from applying SOA design principles to a particular organization. SOA needs are never the same and vary from one company to another. You won't get SOA by choosing a product or a vendor; you get SOA by investing your time in understanding the principles and learning how to apply them to the whole IT infrastructure.

SOA Is Not a Web Service

Because SOA is a design philosophy and not a technology, it can't just be yet another fancy name for Web services. Having (Web) services in an application is far from being a clear and unequivocal symptom of an SOA.

In an SOA solution, you might likely find Web services. But not all Web services are SOA services. And not all SOA solutions have Web services. Equating Web services with SOA is a common mistake. Organizations that boast of moving to SOA but implement only a few Web services, betray a clear lack of understanding (or a misunderstanding) of the SOA world.

SOA Is Not a Goal

You should aim at building an SOA for your customers. And, ideally, customers should not ask you to build an SOA. SOA, in fact, is not a fashion trend.

You might remember, in the early 1990s, all the hype about object-oriented programming. And just OOP—a mere implementation detail—was often presented as a plus of a given product. The message was something like, "Buy product X, it will solve problem Y, and it is object oriented."

How can we forget that time when a customer approached us declaring his absolute need for an object-oriented new version of a certain application. "What's your problem?" was the question we asked. "We have a lot of problems, and we know we need an object-oriented application" was the amazing answer.

With SOA, perceptions are not very different.

As an architect, you should first focus on the problem and then fight to find and deliver an effective solution. For distributed systems, this might mean identifying coarse-grained services that model the business processes. Then you might leverage Web services as the implementation technology for an SOA solution. SOA, like OOP 20 years ago, should never be your goal. It is, instead, a means to build an effective solution.

SOA and the Service Layer

When it comes to building the service layer of a distributed system, you need to arrange a few services and make them interact with the presentation layer and the rest of the system. Is there any value in using SOA principles here?

SOA in Practice

Applying SOA means extracting some practical design rules from the SOA tenets and measuring them in the context of a real system. Applying SOA principles to a service layer means having coarse-grained services that act as a remote façade facing the business logic.

As a result, you have the following practical rules:

- Services in the service layer do not implement any business logic.
- Services in the service layer script and consume the business logic whatever that logic might entail, including workflows, domain objects, and application services.
- Application services—that is, services that implement pieces of the business—might or might not be SOAs themselves.
- Data exchange happens through DTOs (via data contracts) and not by using classes in the domain model.

- Services do not distribute and share objects, and service methods do not work on objects. Services are limited to getting and returning a collection of values formalized in a schema.

- Services in the service layer should aim at a UI-oriented interface.

- Application services should aim at a business-oriented interface.

- Any services with an entity-based interface tend to expose plain CRUD operations. These services are referred to as CRUDy and, for what it matters, are not SOAs.

- Services should be deployed and versioned independently of the system in which they are deployed and consumed.

- To the extent that it is possible, do not modify service and data contracts. When you absolutely need to do that, apply versioning.

What practical benefits does an application derive from following these rules?

What's Good About Using SOA in the Service Layer

The adoption of SOA principles in the design of services brings quite a few benefits. In addition to gaining reusability, you have simplified versioning and an analysis of the threat model.

However, if we confine ourselves to considering the benefits of SOA in the service layer of a distributed system, the key benefit is that you have loosely coupled services where the operations and data to be exchanged are contracted and well defined. This approach allows you to change the internal implementation of the service, and even replace or relocate the service, without affecting the clients.

In general, the service layer is a very special layer of services. We would even say that the service layer contains the most coupled grouping of services you can think of. In this regard, SOA is often overkill, and some of its practical rules can often be ignored without many worries.

SOA Antipatterns

This chapter is about the service layer; it is not about principles of service orientation, nor is it about a specific service technology such as WCF. We briefly covered the essence of SOA, ran through its tenets, and listed some practical rules for architecting better services.

Strict observance of SOA principles might not be necessary in a service layer because, most of the time, the same organization controls both the services and consumers. Services in the service layer are not as autonomous as they are in a pure SOA context because they exist just to sit in between and accommodate the presentation and business layers. The worst thing imaginable in SOA—the breakage of a contract—is not a tragedy in the realm of a service layer when you control both consumer and producer.

This said, we should note that some principles of SOA are still well received in a service layer, and some of the most classic antipatterns of SOA are still worth a look for future reference.

Two extremely popular antipatterns of SOA are *CRUDy* and *Chatty*. Both patterns refer to attributes of service contracts. Let's tackle CRUDy first.

CRUDy Interfaces

Guess what? Most of the typical operations requested of a service layer have to do with the creation, deletion, update, or query of domain objects—purely CRUD. What should we do? Should we quit the project because someone said that CRUD methods in a service contract are bad? It depends on what you mean exactly by the phrase "a CRUDy interface."

In our opinion, a service contract like the following one makes total sense, even though it implies CRUD operations:

```
FindOrderByIDResponse FindOrderByID(FindOrderByIdRequest request);
CreateOrderResponse CreateOrder(CreateOrderRequest request);
UpdateOrderResponse UpdateOrder(UpdateOrderRequest request);
DeleteOrderResponse DeleteOrder(DeleteOrderRequest request);
```

There are two aspects to consider. First, is there a use case that requires you to create, update, delete, or look up an order? If so, you need such methods no matter what. From a design perspective, you're OK as long as you publish service methods that map to business operations triggered by real-life business events. For example, if the shipper didn't find the consignee, he needs to update the state of the order. This triggers a business event such as "ConsigneeNotFound," and you must have an Update service method to modify the data store—even if it does look CRUDy.

Second, what happens within such a CRUDy service method? Creating or updating an order (or any other entity in a domain model) is hardly a one-shot database operation. It involves, instead, a unit of work. The whole unit is accomplished with a single call, ideally following a particular use case. This is just fine and entirely acceptable. Even one-shot database operations are acceptable from within a service layer if they match a use case.

What should be avoided then?

In a service, you should avoid having methods with a finer granularity than the business event that triggers them. Suppose that the processing of a new order requires three steps: checking the availability of the product, checking the credit status of the customer, and creating the order. You're fine if you expose one overall *CreateOrder* method that internally dictates the actions to be taken. Otherwise, you fall into the CRUDy antipattern if you expose the three internal actions as contracted methods.

By letting implementation details leak out of the service layer, you at least violate the third tenet of SOA—share only contracts—but more importantly, you encourage a stateful (and coupled) conversation between the presentation and service layers.

CRUDy interfaces are a fancy name; the real enemy is bad design.

Note Designing services is different from designing components for, say, Microsoft Visual Basic 6.0 applications. In a non-service world, it might make sense to design stateful components that represent objects that the user interface interacts with. This is no longer the case with services.

Chatty Interfaces

Related to the real sense of CRUDy is the *chatty interfaces* antipattern. This antipattern is characterized by a service contract that encourages an RPC-like behavior. In other words, the service exposes to the presentation layer a set of fine-grained methods that the presentation layer calls in a workflow to accomplish the desired action.

Let's recall the previous example of the creation of an order. A chatty interface is when the service exposes a similar contract:

```
bool CheckGoodAvailability(Order order);
bool CheckCreditStatus(Order order);
bool PlaceOrder(Order order);
```

The presentation layer then likely consumes the service through the following code:

```
Order o = new Order( … );
if (service.CheckGoodAvailability(o) &&
    service.CheckCreditStatus(o))
{
    service.PlaceOrder(o);
    ⋮
}
```

The opposite of a chatty interface is a *chunky interface*. A chunky interface is fully represented by the following code:

```
CreateOrderResponse CreateOrder(CreateOrderRequest request);
```

In a chunky interface, information for the service (as well as return values) is composed in a comprehensive document-like package. A badly designed CRUDy interface is also a chatty interface.

The Very Special Case of Rich Web Front Ends

The service layer is the topmost layer on the business layer. Depending on your system topology and deployment options, the service layer might live side by side with the presentation or be hosted remotely on a different tier. A special case occurs when the front end is a Web application.

In an ASP.NET Web application, the presentation is split into two tiers—the Web browser running some JavaScript code, and the Web server hosting code-behind files and presentation logic written in a managed language. Most of the time, the service layer is co-located in the same IIS worker process as the presentation logic. So far, so good.

The scenario significantly changes with the advent of AJAX, Silverlight and, in general, rich Web front ends. Why is this so?

In a rich Web scenario, the Web browser code is richer than ever and begins to contain much more than just user interface tricks, such as roll-over effects and a bit of drag-and-drop functionality.

The richer the Web browser, the more layered the presentation layer becomes. And the service layer faces the need to be redesigned to better address new challenges, especially in the area of security.

Refactoring the Service Layer

With the progressive consolidation of AJAX and the advent of Rich Internet Applications (RIA), we entered an age of client applications greedy for communication capabilities and rich with connectivity options. For example, a key feature of both ASP.NET AJAX and Silverlight 2 is the ability to connect to a given service and command operations.

The Web browser sends requests over HTTP and receives data back. The client logic then processes results and updates the user interface. The JavaScript Object Notation (JSON) is the preferred data-interchange format when a browser-based, JavaScript-powered user interface is used. XML and SOAP, on the other hand, are still the most favored option in Silverlight 2.

So with a rich Web front end, the presentation logic can be split between the browser and the code-behind class on the Web server. Any communication between clients and the Web server happens through public endpoints exposed by the Web server and called back from ASP.NET AJAX or Silverlight 2. Which endpoints should you expose out of the Web server for Web browsers to call? The real service layer? Or something running on top of it? The answer springs naturally from the diagram displayed in Figure 5-10.

Exposing the real service layer to just any Web-based client is definitely a security hazard. Therefore, a wrapper layer is needed. We like to call this the *AJAX Service Layer.*

Why Rich Web-Based Clients Are a Problem

The service layer is the gateway to the core of your system. As such, any access to it must be fully examined and authorized. On the other hand, client-to-server connectivity and related security is nothing new. It's just the way in which architects and developers planned distributed applications for years. In this context, effective security measures and threat models have been developed over years. Such a security experience is fully endorsed by the WCF platform because it supplies a number of powerful options to securely deploy and configure services in an organization. How can rich Web-based clients represent a problem?

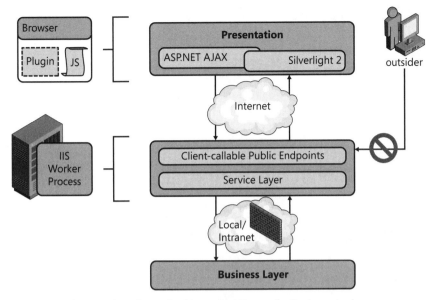

FIGURE 5-10 An extra layer is required to protect the application's service layer.

In a classic Web scenario where the presentation logic is isolated on the server, you typically use forms authentication to filter users at the gate. Unauthorized users never connect to pages that, posting back, would access the service layer. Security for the service layer is easily implemented using Code Access Security (CAS), roles, or perhaps WCF or Web services features.

When you plan to expose services to JavaScript-powered clients, will you really make the connection directly? In theory, you can do it. In practice, a service exposed to a JavaScript client is automatically exposed to any user on the Internet. Credentials cannot be sent as part of the message because this would require ad hoc JavaScript capabilities and, more importantly, these capabilities could easily be "borrowed" by attackers and incorporated into their platforms.

To send credentials, you should use encrypted cookies as in plain ASP.NET forms authentication. The service, in turn, will first check cookies and then proceed with its logic. You have to do this, but you don't want to place this burden right in the services forming the service layer. Here's why an extra layer of AJAX-specific services (the aforementioned AJAX Service Layer) is required. (See Figure 5-11.)

The AJAX Service Layer makes sense only for rich Web clients and, from a certain point of view, it replaces the code-behind layer of managed code that backs classic ASP.NET and Windows/ WPF user interfaces. The AJAX Service Layer lives on the Web server and can be co-located with the service and business layers. This is definitely a design choice that should be made by the architect, who knows all the details of the system and all the expectations set for it.

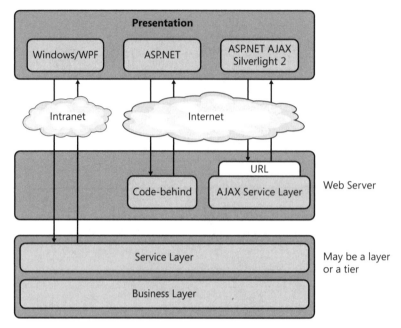

FIGURE 5-11 The application's service layer and the AJAX Service Layer

 Note A guiding principle in REST is cookie avoidance. If you avoid the encrypted cookies of ASP.NET authentication, you are stuck using HTTP Basic Authentication. Hence, to avoid sending credentials out as clear text, you are forced to use SSL/TLS. This is just how things are. That said, we recommend using a security cookie in RESTful scenarios if you have the infrastructure in place (as it is with ASP.NET). However, be aware that it also means some clients might not be able to deal with it.

Refactoring for Functionality

One of the most compelling features of presentation layers based on ASP.NET AJAX and Silverlight 2 is the ability to invoke services directly from the client—a Web-based client. This possibility introduces a new scenario and offers plenty of new development opportunities. At the same time, though, it also raises some new concerns.

A first factor to tackle is the identification of service endpoints and data exchange policies. A second factor to carefully review is, of course, security. Services are essentially a collection of HTTP endpoints that preferably receive and return HTTP packets with JSON content. The main reason for dropping XML and SOAP in favor of JSON is that JSON is much easier to handle from within a JavaScript-powered client than any XML-based format.

Commonly used technologies for implementing services didn't support JSON until a few months prior to the writing of this book. In the .NET platform, both the ASP.NET XML Web service and WCF platforms underwent some rework to enable JavaScript clients. The WCF platform, in particular, introduced in .NET 3.5 a new type of binding specifically aimed at JavaScript clients. In this way, the core service remains isolated from the binding details. Does this mean that you can call one of your application's core WCF services from JavaScript? You definitely can. And you definitely should if you don't have security concerns. Otherwise, you definitely should consider adding an intermediate layer of services.

Refactoring for Security

Rich Web-based clients are essentially simple connection tools that take advantage of the HTTP network protocol and its connectivity model. As disappointing as it might sound, HTTP wasn't designed with security in mind.

> **Note** If this last sentence leaves you a bit baffled and confused, consider the following. HTTP has no native security features in it. What about HTTPS, then? As commonly defined, HTTPS is a uniform resource identifier that combines HTTP with a cryptography engine, such as Secure Sockets Layer (SSL) or Transport Layer Security (TLS). HTTPS is like HTTP except that it uses a different port (port 443 instead of port 80) and adds a cryptography mechanism down the stack between TCP and HTTP. In this regard, HTTP even with the final *S* is not a technologically secure protocol if you're looking for authentication and authorization. You need HTTP authentication on top of it or something like ASP.NET support (cookies and such). Authorization is, of course, up to the individual application. If you still find this statement hard to buy, consider that when HTTP is used, WCF leverages its own infrastructure and bindings to ensure security and authentication.

Interaction with simple Web-based clients requires simplicity and necessarily forces you to take some protocol-level security measures. In other words, ASP.NET AJAX clients can talk to services but only over simplified security channels that do not account for credentials. (The underlying reason is that any work to insert credentials in the packet should be done in JavaScript, and then they can be easily copied, understood, and replayed.)

How can you then secure your services and ensure that only authorized users can gain access? You need to refactor your client pages and your service layer to enable services to grab credentials from authentication cookies. The services then will refuse the call if unauthorized access is attempted. Would you really refactor your service layer for security reasons, especially considering that other presentation implementations might not have the same security needs? No, it makes more sense to add an extra layer of services for rich Web-based clients to use. That handles the special security issues for you.

> **Note** We like to recall that in a pure REST approach, you should not rely on authentication cookies. A pure REST approach would recommend using HTTP Basic Authentication coupled with SSL/TLS, and that's for each call.

Designing an AJAX Service Layer

An AJAX Service Layer essentially exists to decouple rich Web presentation layers from the heart of the system and to suit the browser-based user interface. An AJAX Service Layer is extremely thin, and all that it does is secure the calls checking credentials and forwards the call into the service layer.

How would you write services for an AJAX Service Layer? In .NET, you typically write services either as ASP.NET XML Web services or WCF services. In both cases, services are to be script-enabled, meaning that you have to tweak their runtime so that they can accept calls coming from a JavaScript-powered client.

Note Although the Silverlight 2 platform is often mixed with the ASP.NET AJAX platform, some clear differences exist. In particular, Silverlight 2 runs managed code within the browser and thus it can support most of the features that simplify the service model for AJAX callers. As an example, Silverlight 2 clients can happily manage SOAP calls that AJAX clients do not recognize.

Script-Enabling ASP.NET XML Web Services

A scriptable ASP.NET XML Web service can be installed on .NET Framework 2.0 with ASP.NET AJAX Extensions 1.0 installed. You just don't need the latest .NET Framework 3.5 to expose ASP.NET XML Web services.

You write an ASP.NET XML Web service class in the same way you write a plain Web service for a .NET application. The model is exactly the same; the ASP.NET run-time environment, though, is a bit different. (See Figure 5-12.)

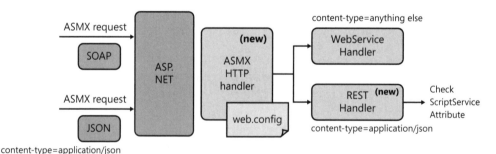

FIGURE 5-12 The run-time environment of ASP.NET XML Web services

The ASP.NET runtime still receives a request for an ASMX resource. In an ASP.NET AJAX application, though, a different HTTP handler is registered to handle such requests. The newly configured handler will act as a factory handler and looks at the *content-type* header of the incoming request.

Note The content-type header tells the server how to interpret the incoming request. If set to *application/json*, it tells the server to assume the content is JSON.

If the requested content type is application/json, the factory instantiates an AJAX-specific handler, known as the REST handler. Otherwise, the incoming request flows as usual and the request is serviced by the traditional ASP.NET 2.0 handler for Web services requests. What's the difference between the two handlers? Well, the standard ASMX handler understands and knows how to deal with SOAP requests. The AJAX-specific ASMX handler only understands JSON requests and, as an extra security measure, also checks that the Web service class behind the request is decorated with the *ScriptService* attribute.

The *ScriptService* attribute explicitly declares that the service is enabled to accept calls from a JavaScript-powered client. If the attribute is missing, the REST handler refuses the call.

In summary, a service implemented as an ASP.NET XML Web service is a class decorated with the *ScriptService* attribute and that exposes a few Web methods. The run-time system is also enabled to generate a JavaScript proxy for the service that packs input data for the call as a JSON string. Likewise, the REST handler also serializes to JSON any return value for the caller. No SOAP at all is involved in an ASMX Web service call in ASP.NET AJAX applications. The following code shows a simple service just to help you form an idea about what it looks like:

```
[ScriptService]
public class TimeService : ITimeService
{
    [WebMethod]
    public string GetTimeFormat(string format)
    {
        // Check credentials (see later)
        ⋮

        // Forward to the application's service or business layer
        ⋮
    }

    ⋮
}
```

The interface is not strictly required, but it is helpful to have. Each method on the service class can be further specialized using the optional *ScriptMethod* attribute. The attribute allows you to serialize data for the method using XML instead of JSON, and it enables the method to be invoked over an HTTP GET call.

Note, though, that 99 percent of the time, having default settings on the *ScriptMethod* attribute are just fine. Disabling the HTTP GET calls, as well as requiring an ad hoc content type, are security measures aimed at discouraging method calls via script injection. In fact, when a *<script>* tag is injected, it can refer only to the specified URL via a GET and cannot set a particular content type.

An AJAX Web service is referenced within the page with an *.asmx* extension—the same extension that is used for classic SOAP-based ASP.NET Web services. As you saw in Figure 5-12, the handler factory can distinguish between SOAP and non-SOAP calls. However, this just means that the same service is simultaneously exposed to SOAP and JSON callers. The following configuration script disables all forms of calls except JSON calls:

```
<system.web>
  <system.webservices>
    <protocols>
      <clear />
    </protocols>
  </system.webservices>
</system.web>
```

You add this script to the *web.config* file of the application that hosts the ASMX Web service.

Script-Enabling WCF Services

The first release of the ASP.NET AJAX Extensions created to support ASP.NET 2.0 didn't include any support for WCF services. Only with the .NET Framework 3.5, the WCF environment has been endowed with proper tools to enable integration with an AJAX presentation layer. This support goes under the name of the WCF Web programming model.

In a nutshell, the WCF Web programming model permits you to expose service methods through HTTP GET and POST requests. In this way, WCF is enabled to support plain-old XML (POX) style messaging instead of SOAP. To invoke a WCF service method from within a JavaScript client, you need to use a mandatory endpoint binding and a specific behavior.

The tailor-made binding that enables the WCF Web programming model is *webHttpbinding*—a sort of basic HTTP binding that precludes the use of SOAP. The ad hoc behavior is *webScriptBehavior*, which enables JSON data encoding and enables JavaScript callers.

Because WCF separates binding details from the service code, there's nothing special you have to do to create an AJAX-enabled WCF service:

```
[ServiceContract(Namespace="Samples.Services", Name="WcfTimeService")]
public interface ITimeService
{
    [OperationContract]
    string GetTime();
}

public class TimeService : ITimeService
{
    public DateTime GetTime()
    {
        return DateTime.Now;
    }
}
```

As in the preceding code snippet, you just create a regular service contract interface and then implement the interface in a service class. You then publish the service in an IIS host and reference it through a JavaScript proxy from within an ASP.NET AJAX page.

The generation of the JavaScript proxy happens care of the extended run-time environment for both ASP.NET XML Web and WCF services. We'll cover this aspect in just a moment.

> **Note** In Silverlight 2 client applications, you reference services (both ASP.NET XML Web services and WCF services) through a proxy generated by Visual Studio 2008 as you would do in a regular ASP.NET or Windows Forms application.

Generating JavaScript Proxies

You need a proxy class in order to invoke a Web or WCF service from within a browser-hosted page. The proxy class is a JavaScript class that is generated by the service runtime when a particular URL is invoked. For both ASP.NET XML Web services and WCF services, the URL takes the form of *<url>/js*.

The proxy class is based on the Microsoft AJAX Client Library and leverages the built-in AJAX stub for *XMLHttpRequest*. The call model is that of asynchronous calls. The proxy class saves you from the burden of knowing about URLs and serialization of parameters. A proxy is employed in both ASP.NET AJAX and Silverlight 2 clients. In the former case, though, they are JavaScript classes; in the latter case, they are managed classes.

JSON vs. XML

In a rich Web application, at some point, you need to call some server-based code. In doing so, you likely need to pass some input data and wait to receive some other data back. Clearly, a serialization format is required to transform platform-specific data (for example, a .NET object) into an HTTP network packet. For years, this field has been the reign of XML. To a large extent, this is still the reign of XML, but not when a Web browser is used as the client.

JSON is the emerging standard format for browsers and Web servers to exchange data over HTTP when a script-led request is made. The main reasons for preferring JSON over XML can be summarized by saying that overall JSON is simpler than full-blown XML and gets a free deserialization engine in virtually any browser that supports JavaScript.

JSON is not designed to reach the heights of complexity and portability of full XML, but it is just as sophisticated as a simple and lightweight XML limited to nodes and attributes. When used in a service-based context, JSON requires HTTP endpoints to understand the format and to be able to serialize to it and deserialize from it.

One of the creators of JSON loves to label his creation as the "X in AJAX," which is overall quite a correct statement. If you look at the official acronym, the *X* in AJAX stands for XML. However, this is not what happens in the real world. Why is that so?

The Web proposes a simplified model of interaction that might not need a rigid schema, validation, or both. Is a schema and a bit of type information useless or mandatory?

Having schema information available wouldn't be a bad thing per se, but not at the cost of creating an XML parser written in JavaScript. If we were using XML for browser-to-server AJAX-style interaction, any browser would receive XML from any invoked endpoint. Subsequently, the browser ought to be able to process any XML data. Is a JavaScript XML parser affordable?

Writing a full-blown XML parser in JavaScript is perhaps beyond the scope of the language. In any case, no browsers today provide this feature. At the same time, the success of AJAX is largely because today's browsers support all required technologies. A well-performing parser for the full XML syntax is not a trivial piece of code to write in JavaScript. And a simpler parser limited to just nodes and attributes would actually produce a language really similar to JSON. At that point, the big difference would be the style of the brackets: angle brackets or curly brackets.

Today's browsers, instead, provide native support for a JSON deserializer. Where is it? It's the plain old JavaScript *eval* function. Among other things, the *eval* function takes a JSON string and returns a corresponding JavaScript object. This is possible because JSON uses a notation that is nearly the same as the notation internally used by JavaScript to represent objects.

Put another way, it's not that *eval* was created to support JSON. It's JSON that has been set up so that the JavaScript's *eval* function can read it. Either way, as far as browser-to-server communication is concerned, JSON is a far better option than XML. That's why JSON is ultimately the *X* in AJAX.

Securing the AJAX Service Layer

Services in the AJAX Service Layer are called by two groups of users—legitimate users and outsiders. Legitimate users connect through a regular Web front end, be it ASP.NET AJAX or Silverlight 2. Outsiders reach the URL using any platform they can—usually a custom, full-trust application.

To welcome the former group of users and reject the latter group, you have to identify a piece of information that only the former group can easily provide. As Figure 5-13 shows, the key difference between legitimate users and outsiders is the authentication cookie that authorized users grab through a login page.

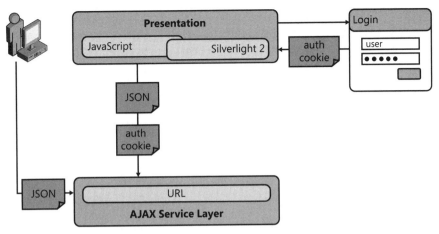

FIGURE 5-13 Legitimate users and outsiders around a service layer

Detecting Outsiders

As mentioned, when you have a rich Web presentation, you end up with a layer of client-callable application services not necessarily designed to be public services, but that happen to be public services. As a result, they are accessible to both legitimate users going through the interface of the application and outsiders who discover the right IP address or URL.

Any security barrier you place around services at the network level (for example, a firewall) would likely stop legitimate calls too. And how could you filter legitimate calls from outsider calls? When legitimate calls come from a plain Web browser and from the Internet place, this is really hard to do. Needless to say, this would be much easier in an intranet or extranet scenario.

What kind of logic should you expose through the server? Is it really possible for you to isolate critical resources from the Internet? Not really. If a given piece of logic is required, it's because some clients, at some point, have to invoke it. And when the client is a Web-based client, the (legitimate) request can only come over HTTP from the Internet. And if a legitimate caller can do it, an outsider can also do it. This is what happens in reality. Don't be optimistic; think defensively.

So in the end, how can you detect outsiders and keep them off the site? You have to identify a token of information that legal users can show and outsiders cannot. The simplest and most effective piece of information is an authentication cookie generated by ASP.NET forms authentication.

Login Pages Never Go Out of Style

To protect critical services, you isolate in a protected area of the site any ASP.NET pages that need to invoke a sensitive service method. After they are placed in a protected area of the site, these pages require that users go through a login step.

The login page gets credentials from the user and verifies whether the user is authorized to visit the page. If all is fine, the request is authorized and an authentication cookie is generated and attached to the response. From now on, any requests the user makes to the application, including service requests, will bring the cookie.

Services in the AJAX Service Layer must participate in the game, too. Essentially, a service should check the authentication cookie to ensure that it is being called by a legitimate user through an approved workflow and path. Only if the authorization is successful should the service proceed with the method execution.

> **Note** It is ultimately up to you to decide whether the sensitive code should be part of the AJAX Service Layer or be placed elsewhere in the business layer. We presented the AJAX Service Layer as a layer living on top of the application's service and business layer. However, it can also be just your service layer. This makes sense particularly in all those applications where you only have a rich Web presentation layer.

At the very minimum, a login page contains input controls to collect the user name and password plus a button to trigger the authentication process. In ASP.NET, login pages require that forms authentication is turned on. Furthermore, anonymous users should be denied access to any resources within the protected area. Here's a sample configuration script you can use:

```
<location path="ProtectedAreaOfTheSite">
    <system.web>
        <authorization>
            <deny users="?" />
        </authorization>
    </system.web>
</location>
```

If necessary, login pages can be placed on a different server and work over HTTPS. This solution, however, has no impact on the security of the AJAX Service Layer.

Checking Identity and Authorization in the Service

Methods in the AJAX Service Layer are extremely thin and limited to checking permissions for the logged-in user and passing the call down the stack. Here's the typical skeleton of a service method:

```
public DateTime GetTime()
{
    // Get the user name and check permissions.
    CheckIdentity();

    // Proceed with regular code-typically call a method
    // on the application's service layer
    :
    :
}
```

In the sample code, *CheckIdentity* is an internal function that gets the name of the currently logged-in user and verifies whether the user has been granted enough permissions to call the service method:

```
private void CheckIdentity()
{
    // Get the user name
    string user = HttpContext.Current.User.Identity.Name;

    // Check permissions
    if (AuthenticationHelper.VerifyUser(user))
        return;

    // Thrown an exception
    throw new InvalidOperationException("Invalid credentials");
}
```

How can the service method get to know about the currently logged user? It basically gets this information from the ASP.NET runtime via the *HttpContext.Current* object. This approach is natively supported for ASP.NET XML Web services. However, it requires some extra work if you employ WCF services.

By default, in ASP.NET AJAX applications WCF services run side by side with the ASP.NET runtime in the IIS worker process. ASP.NET captures the *.svc* request and begins processing it. Next, WCF kicks in and gets hold of the request. After this point, the request is never returned to ASP.NET. As you can see, there's no interaction between WCF and ASP.NET. The net effect is that *HttpContext.Current* is always *null* when invoked from within a WCF service.

To make WCF and ASP.NET recognize each other, you need to enable the ASP.NET compatibility mode in WCF. You turn it on in the configuration file, as shown here:

```
<system.serviceModel>
    <serviceHostingEnvironment aspNetCompatibilityEnabled="true" />
    ⋮
</system.serviceModel>
```

This setting only enables the compatibility mode for all services hosted by the ASP. NET application. Each service is required to express its explicit approval of the model. A service does this by decorating the service class—not the service contract—with the *AspNetCompatibilityRequirements* attribute, as shown here:

```
[AspNetCompatibilityRequirements(
        RequirementsMode = AspNetCompatibilityRequirementsMode.Allowed)]
public class TimeService : ITimeService
{
    ⋮
}
```

Note that, by default, a WCF service has the *RequirementsMode* property set to *NotAllowed*. If this value is not changed to either *Allowed* or *Required*, you get a run-time exception as you attempt to make a call to the service.

Summary

Modern distributed systems have an extra layer of code between the presentation and business layers. This layer is often referred to as the service layer. Another common name for this type of code is the *application layer*.

Essentially, the service layer implements the application logic. The application logic is the list of actions that, triggered from the user interface, end up scripting the objects and services in the business logic. In the service layer, you implement the use cases and expose each sequence of steps through a coarse-grained method for the user interface to call.

A service layer offers through a set of services a programming interface upon which multiple presentation layers can be built. In this context, presentation layers include the regular user interface as well as back-office applications and application interfaces for additional supported platforms. A service layer is almost always useful to have because it decouples the application interfaces from the middle tier. The only situation where you might want to consider doing without it is when you know in advance that you'll be having just one, and only one, presentation interface.

In the design of services, you might want to take into account a few principles and practices. In particular, you might want to embrace service orientation and share data contracts instead of rich domain classes. This principle is safe and sound, but it often clashes with the real world. In our experience, a mixed approach that uses data contracts only in a few situations and domain-specific classes in others is acceptable as long as you have a very large domain model containing large numbers of objects to justify it and as long as the presentation layer and middle tier share the same software platform.

Murphy's Laws of the Chapter

The quotation at the top of the chapter says it all. If you want services, serve yourself. And the first Murphy's Law of this chapter reflects that very well. It says, don't trust even the most documented interface: there's always an undocumented feature. We know how to work under pressure, and we often look with some envy at agile methodologies designed to address the development team's quality of life. We have no personal experiences with agile that demonstrate how "quality of life" co-exists with software development. In fact, we find it hard to believe things are really as relaxing and enjoyable as the books about agile claim they are. Perhaps in our case we live by a weird corollary to some Murphy's Law: "We're never as agile as we would like to be."

- The documented interfaces between standard software modules will have undocumented quirks.

- Good enough isn't good enough, unless there is a deadline.

- You can never tell which way the train went just by looking at the track.

See *http://www.murphys-laws.com* for an extensive listing of other computer-related (and non-computer-related) laws and corollaries.

Chapter 6
The Data Access Layer

High thoughts must have a high language.

—*Aristophanes*

The data access layer (DAL) is a library of code that provides access to data stored in a persistent container, such as a database. In a layered system, you delegate to this layer any task that relates to reading from, and writing to, the persistent storage of choice.

No matter how many abstraction layers you build in your model, at some point you need to open a connection to some database. That's where and when the DAL fits in. Over the years, a few patterns have been devised to design a DAL that is efficient and extensible. This chapter covers a number of these patterns.

It is key to note that the concept of a DAL is a bit nebulous. The idea of a DAL is extremely clear when you think of a classic layered system from a high level. From this perspective, a system has a presentation layer where you essentially define the user interface, a business layer where you define the object model and the behavior of the system, and finally the data access layer where you go down to the database and run queries and updates. The layers ideally live in clearly delineated compartments, and each talks only to the layer immediately on top and immediately below. So, for example, no communication whatsoever should be expected between the presentation and data access layers.

Put this way, what's really nebulous about the data access layer? If you attempt to detail a DAL a little bit more (as you should do, at some point, when you build a real system), a number of points arise. In this chapter, we identify and discuss the goals and responsibilities of a data access layer and delve deep into patterns and practices to meet expectations and requirements.

What's the Data Access Layer, Anyway?

A DAL has a precise set of responsibilities that are relatively easy to spot. The implementation of these responsibilities, though, depends on other functional and nonfunctional requirements you get from stakeholders. To address responsibilities, design patterns exist to guide you through the design and implementation stages.

Before we proceed any further, though, you should note that the data access layer exists as a separate software entity only if you have organized your business logic using the Domain Model pattern. As we saw in Chapter 4, "The Business Layer," using the Domain Model pattern has you define a particular object model. The object model describes data and behavior of any entities that participate in the problem's domain. A domain model created using the Domain Model pattern can be significantly different from any sort of relational data model, and this raises the need for a DAL to implement persistence. Relational data models, such as those employed within a Transaction Script or Table Module implementation, simply shuttle data to and from the persistence media. More complex applications have to deal with the complexity of adapting their in-memory object-based data model to the relational data model of persistence. The complexity associated with deciding what data is stored where is handled by the DAL.

Put another way, when you organize the business logic using patterns other than Domain Model, including even Active Record, persistence is built into the business logic and the DAL is in effect merged with the business layer. The DAL, in this case, is essentially a collection of stored procedures and embedded SQL statements.

You need a tailor-made DAL only if you have a full-fledged domain model created using the Domain Model pattern.

Functional Requirements of the Data Access Layer

The design of a DAL is influenced by a number of requirements that stakeholders can impose. Should the DAL persist an object model or simple collections ("tuples") of values? Should the DAL target one particular database or a few databases? Let's review in a more formal way the typical functional requirements of a DAL.

Database Independence

The DAL is the only place in the system where connection strings and table names are known and used. Based on this fact, you can conclude only that the DAL must be dependent on the features of a particular database management system (DBMS). So how can you really achieve database independence? And why is database independence so important? Let's start with the latter question.

Essentially, database independence means that your DAL is able to offer the same services—such as Create, Read, Update, Delete (CRUD), transactionality, and query—to the rest of the system, regardless of the capabilities of the final data storage media. After you come up with a model that includes, say, a *Customer* object, your DAL is able to work with that object whether it is ultimately persisted to a Microsoft SQL Server database or an Oracle database, or even to a table named *Customer* that maps directly to the *Customer* object or is less easily mapped. The DAL shields the business layer from this sort of detail.

To an external observer, the DAL should look like a black box that plugs into the existing system and encapsulates access for reading and writing to a particular DBMS. Database independence is a common requirement for a good deal of enterprise applications, especially back-office applications. How can you achieve that?

Configurable as a Plug-in

There are many possible ways to achieve database independence, and the final choice also depends on other requirements. In general, database independence requires that you use a common, cross-database application programming interface (API), such as OLE DB. But OLE DB is too generic and COM-based to survive in the .NET world.

In the .NET Framework, ADO.NET supplies a database-agnostic API to create connections, commands, and transactions regardless of the physical database. In this way, you have just one DAL written using an high-level API. Although this is definitely a possible approach, this is not what we mean when we refer to database independence.

In our opinion, you reach real database independence only when you devise your DAL as a black box with a contracted interface and read the details of the current DAL component dynamically from a configuration file.

For example, once it obtains a reference to the current DAL, the service layer communicates with the DAL in a polymorphic way using the methods on the public contract. If you store a reference to the actual component in a configuration file, you can switch from, say, Oracle to SQL Server in two simple moves: create a DBMS-specific component that implements the required interface, and adjust a given entry in the configuration file.

Finally, you can make your system independent of the database by using an O/R Mapper (O/RM) tool. In this case, the O/RM provides you with a common API and allows you to switch to different databases by simply changing a configuration parameter. Our experience has been that sometimes we're allowed to use O/RM tools and sometimes not (a nonfunctional requirement). When we're told not to use an O/RM tool, it's usually because the tool is open-source and the client questions its pedigree. To paraphrase, when this happens, "The client is always right."

Persisting the Application's Object Model

The DAL must be able to persist the application's data regardless of the format of the data. An application's data can be expressed as tuples of values or through an object model—be it an Active Record or a full-fledged Domain Model approach.

If having an object model is a requirement, the DAL must be able to persist the model down to a relational schema. Clearly, this creates the notorious object/relational impedance mismatch. A relational database, in fact, stores tuples of values, whereas your object model builds a graph of objects. As a result, a mapping between the two models is an absolute necessity and the primary goal of the DAL.

Persisting the application's object model refers to the ability of loading data into newly created instances of the object model and saving the content of an instance back to the database.

Persistence should happen regardless of the DBMS used and also in a way that is independent of the physical structure of the tables. As an example, consider a scenario where you have a *Customer* class in the application's object model. The DAL should be able to manage persistence of the class not only to a variety of databases, but also to tables with a different structure.

Figure 6-1 shows an overall model where the business layer persists the application's object model to the supported database.

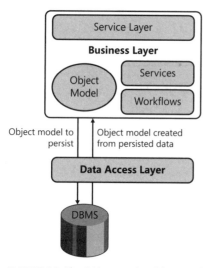

FIGURE 6-1 The DAL saves the object model down to the database and builds instances of the object model from data in the database.

> **Note** An object model designed with the Domain Model pattern doesn't know about the DAL. If the object model is an Active Record, on the other hand, the DAL is incorporated in the framework you use for implementing the model. In a pure Active Record implementation, such as Castle ActiveRecord (see *http://www.castleproject.org* for details), persistence methods are instance methods defined on the classes. Read methods, conversely, are commonly exposed as static methods on the classes of the model.

Both the business layer and the service layer don't know much about the underlying database. They just set up communication with the DAL to pass and receive data.

Which component of the business layer will physically invoke the DAL? This is a typical responsibility of the services in the service layer.

Responsibilities of the Data Access Layer

A DAL has four main responsibilities with regard to its consumers. In the first place, a DAL has to persist data to the physical storage and supply CRUD services to the outside world.

Second, the DAL is responsible for servicing any requests for data it receives. The DAL must be able to provide transactional semantics. And finally, the DAL must handle concurrency properly. Conceptually, the DAL is a sort of black box exposing four contracted services, as shown in Figure 6-2.

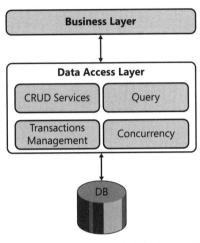

FIGURE 6-2 A conceptual view of the DAL's interior

If your team creates the DAL within the project, you take on these responsibilities yourself and write from scratch the code that addresses them. If you can use an O/RM tool, it will save you from worrying about a number of these concerns. In this case, all that you need from the business layer (more exactly, from the service layer) is for it to script the API of the O/RM to implement the use cases.

CRUD Services

The DAL is the only layer in a system that holds the keys to the database. There should be no other place in your system where information about the database is held and managed.

CRUD services are a set of methods that take care of writing objects down to relational tables and vice versa, and loading result sets into newly created instances of classes in the application's domain model. CRUD Services work with *persistent* and *transient* objects. A persistent object is an instance of a class in the domain model that represents some information extracted from the database. For example, if you load an *Order* from the database, you have a persistent object. If you, instead, create in memory a new *Order* for further insertion into the database, you have a transient object.

What kind of code do you write to implement CRUD services? For each type in the object model, you essentially create a specific mapper class that implements an interface. The interface lists all the database-specific tasks (well, CRUD tasks) you ever need to execute on the type. Internally, the mapper for the type uses ADO.NET or perhaps LINQ-to-SQL to do its own SQL stuff.

The implementation of CRUD services is usually guided by the Data Mapper pattern as defined on page 165 of Martin Fowler's book *Patterns of Enterprise Application Architecture* (Addison-Wesley, 2003), which is abbreviated as *[P of EAA]* for the remainder of the chapter. Figure 6-3 provides a graphical view of a sample mapper and illustrates the primary role of CRUD services for a given type.

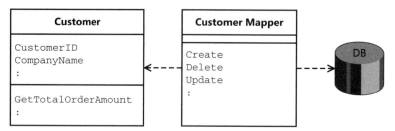

FIGURE 6-3 A data mapper implementing CRUD services for the type *Customer*

Query Services

The *R* in CRUD services stands for Read and, in some cases, this task requires quite advanced and rich capabilities. Most of the time, a DAL consumer needs to query for ad hoc data. But not all the queries are the same, nor do they require the same treatment.

In some situations, you can identify a few common queries that run from multiple places within the business and service layers. If the command is the same and the result set is the same, you then hard-code the query to some method of a repository object and reuse it at will. Let's consider a query such as *GetOrdersByCountry*. What do you expect from it exactly? For example, it can be a method that just runs the following command:

```
SELECT * FROM orders WHERE countryID=@countryID
```

In this case, you always receive a collection of *Order* objects with no information whatsoever about order items and products.

In other situations, the same conceptual *Get-Orders-By-Country* query might generate different data—for example, a collection of *Order* objects plus order items information. What should you do? Should you expose two slightly different *GetOrdersByCountry* methods out of your DAL? And what if, depending on the user interface, the user might ask the system to return orders, order items, *and* products by country? Will you define yet another look-alike method in the DAL?

A better approach consists of defining a repository class where you define all hard-coded queries you use and reuse throughout the business layer. In addition, you define a general-purpose query object that is configured programmatically and produces ad hoc SQL code when executed.

The main purpose of such a query object is to collect input data—essentially, criteria—through its set of properties and methods and then generate dynamic SQL for the database. Such a query object is the ideal tool to compose queries dynamically out of the content of a UI form.

The query object isn't a replacement for SQL; instead, it is a more object-oriented and flexible way of dynamically generating the SQL code for the database. Put another way, the query object we're discussing here is a replacement for a SQL-based string-builder object.

The query object is an instance of the Query Object pattern, as defined on page 316 of [P of EAA]. According to the pattern, the resulting query object is built as a class that owns a set of criteria. A set of criteria is a simple class with a property name, a value, and a logical operator that puts the property name and value into relation.

> **Note** Another pattern that is commonly associated with the implementation of query services in a DAL is the Repository pattern. (See page 322 of [P of EAA].) A repository is normally a type-specific class that groups common queries for a given object. So you might have a *CustomerRepository* and an *OrderRepository*. In addition to grouping common hard-coded queries, a repository can be designed to accept query criteria and return matching objects. Internally, the repository uses a query object to run the SQL query as expected, but to the application's eyes it hides the database query phase.

Transactions Management

In the DAL of an enterprise-class application, you don't want to go down to the database for each and every change to the application's data and related domain or object model. Quite obviously, this approach would generate a lot of traffic toward the database and multiply the noise around each database call—such as open connection, prepare packets, close connection, and so on. On the other hand, "minimize roundtrips to the database" is a golden rule of every application architect and developer and one of the favorite mantras of database administrators (DBAs).

In a well-built DAL, you should provide a model to keep track of all significant changes to the application's data that occur in a unit of work. In this way, you can persist those changes back to the data source in a single step and at a later time. A unit of work is a logical (business) transaction that groups a number of database calls.

By introducing the notion of a unit of work in a DAL, you essentially create a class that maintains a list of domain objects that have been affected by changes. This class also exposes transactional semantics (such as begin, commit, and roll back) to persist changes down to the database within a physical database transaction. Internally, the unit of work ends up calling the data mapper to perform any CRUD activity on the database. If you triggered the unit of work class via its transactional interface, access to the database occurs transactionally.

Figure 6-4 gives you an idea of the role of the unit of work class and its interaction with entities in the domain or object model, the DAL consumer, and the database.

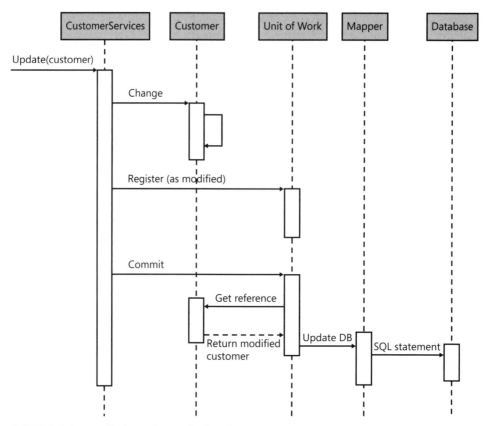

FIGURE 6-4 An overall schema for a unit of work

In particular, when the DAL consumer issues an order to update a customer, the customer is registered with the unit of work as a modified object. Later on, when the consumer decides that the business transaction is complete, it tells the unit of work class to commit. Next, the unit of work class loops through the list of modified objects and performs a scheduled action (insert, delete, or update) against the database.

The unit of work class described here refers to the Unit of Work pattern (UoW), as described on page 184 of [P of EAA].

Note There are quite a few examples of the UoW pattern in popular database-related APIs that you know and probably have used frequently. One is certainly the *DataSet*'s batch update feature. You load data into *DataSets* and then use a data adapter to submit changes to a database. In addition, LINQ-to-SQL also provides a sample UoW implementation via the *SubmitChanges* method of the base *DataContext* class. In LINQ-to-SQL, you can make changes to a bunch of objects and have those changes tracked by an instance of the *DataContext* class.

Handling Concurrency

As mentioned, going down to the database for each change you enter during a business transaction is simply impractical. In fact, avoiding this behavior is a no-brainer in any average complex system. That's why the UoW pattern emerged—it provides a common solution to a recurring problem. When users work offline from the database, two main issues arise. One is transactionality, which is properly addressed by UoW. Another one is concurrency.

In a multiuser environment, working offline from the database poses a data-integrity issue. User A loads its own copy of product 1234 and updates the description. Because the operation is part of a longer business transaction, let's assume that changes are not committed immediately. At the same time, user B loads another copy of the same product 1234 and updates the URL that links to the product's picture. Suppose also that user B commits the changes immediately. What happens when user A attempts to commit changes to the description?

You might say, "Well, nothing" because the users actually updated distinct fields. OK, so what if both users entered different descriptions for the product? There's a concrete risk that product description changes introduced by the first user get lost. This is often called "last writer wins."

A policy is required to handle concurrent user access to the same database records. The chance of conflicts in data access is not the same in all systems; likewise, the cost of handling a conflict is not the same in all systems. This said, an optimistic approach to concurrency is recognized as the best starting point for all systems.

An optimistic approach to concurrency means that your users in their sessions can freely *try to* update any records in the database. The result, though, is not guaranteed. In particular, the DAL fails if it detects that a record being modified has already been updated in the meantime.

Handling concurrency in an optimistic fashion requires an ad hoc data mapper that builds a special proxy version of a given entity—such as *CustomerProxy* instead of *Customer*. What's the difference between *CustomerProxy* and *Customer*? The former contains original values from the record read at creation time, whereas the latter does not. When the data mapper is then about to persist the instance of the customer, it will add a WHERE clause to the SQL statement to ensure at least that the columns being modified have not been modified lately.

The idea behind optimistic concurrency is in the Optimistic Offline Lock (OOL) pattern, defined on page 416 of [P of EAA]. There are various ways of implementing OOL and various policies regarding the resolution of conflicts. This pattern describes the problem in the most general terms.

Note Optimistic concurrency is the opposite of pessimistic concurrency. Pessimistic concurrency, especially when a user is working offline, is a much worse beast. Personally, we have never seen an implementation of a pessimistic offline lock. We have serious doubts also about using a pessimistic online lock via the locking manager built into the DBMS. So when might you want to consider alternatives to optimistic locking?

You stop thinking optimistically when you realize that the cost of resolving a conflict is dramatically high, because the conflict itself has a heavy impact on the system or because, given the characteristics of your system, you will have too many conflicts within a unit of time. However, pessimistic concurrency means essentially creating a lock manager—that is, a component external to the database that maintains a list of locked records and supports a compensation mechanism for locks that time out. Even if it works, it would be a curse for scalability. So what? In the real world, you always use an optimistic approach to offline concurrency and use policies for handling conflicts to mitigate unpleasant effects.

Putting It All Together: The Data Context

All the conceptual responsibilities that a DAL should face turn into a relatively standard set of programming features when you move up to design and implementation. How would you tie all these features together in an organic set of classes and methods?

In short, you need a sort of super class that represents and conducts a session of work with the underlying storage. The DAL consumer uses such a super class as its gateway to the storage. O/RM tools have their own super class; so should your personal DAL.

The super class that provides access to the DAL and its CRUD, transaction, and concurrency services is often referred to as the *data context*.

The Data Access Layer and Other Layers

Figure 6-5 shows a bird's-eye view of a layered system, as we presented it in Chapter 4 and Chapter 5, "The Service Layer." As you can see, typically the presentation layer talks to an application layer mostly made of macro services—in Chapter 5, we called it the service layer. In turn, the service layer consumes the other components of the business layer, such as the domain model and other micro services.

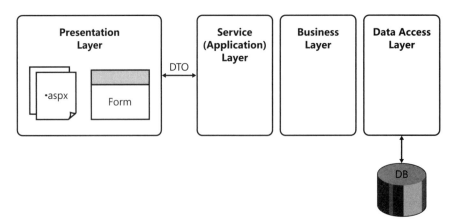

FIGURE 6-5 A high-level view of a layered system

Which parts of the system have access to the DAL? Should the DAL be isolated within the business layer? Or should it be a reusable layer accessible to the service layer? And what about the presentation layer?

The DAL and the Business Layer

In Chapter 4, we explored four main patterns for the domain logic in the business layer: Transaction Script (TS), Table Module (TM), Active Record (AR), and Domain Model (DM).

If you lean toward a relatively simple organization of the domain logic (for example, based on a Table Module pattern), the DAL is merely a set of table adapters that pick up data from the DBMS through queries and save data back using stored procedures or SQL commands. In this case, the DAL is logically merged with the business layer and might even be part of the same assembly. What if you move toward a more object-oriented scenario, such as an Active Record pattern? The DAL serves the purpose of reading and writing data on behalf of the classes in the AR object model. Patternwise, the situation is similar to using a Table Module pattern, except that you use an object model instead of table-based containers. The DAL is logically incorporated in the business layer and is not really visible outside of it.

With a Transaction Script pattern, to render the business logic, all that you expect from a DAL is the ability of doing plain CRUD stuff. In TS, the focus is on the user action rather than on some object that models a business entity or a database table. The DAL is therefore responsible for retrieving any data, and for performing any data action, within the boundaries of a single TS transaction. Also, in this case, distinguishing two layers for business and data access is useful mostly from a design perspective. In practice, the business layer is logically fused to the data access code.

If you lean toward a domain-driven design and opt for a DM pattern, the DAL you need is essentially a tool in the hands of the service layer to pump data within the domain model classes. At the same time, the service layer needs to talk to the DAL to order updates to the persistence storage. In a DM world, the DAL is complementary to the business layer and it is mostly consumed by the service layer.

The DAL and the Service Layer

When you have domain-driven business logic, the DAL is a tool through which the object model is persisted, as illustrated in Figure 6-1. The service (or application) layer gets input from the presentation through data transfer objects (or any other alternate approach you opt for). The service layer implements all use cases by scripting any objects in the business layer. The business layer includes the domain model as well as application services and workflows.

At the same time, the service layer scripts the DAL to get any data it needs to initialize the domain model, track changes, identify objects, and perform command updates to the underlying storage. (See Figure 6-6.)

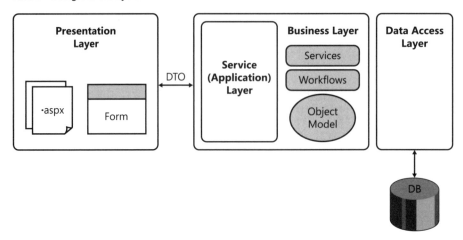

FIGURE 6-6 A high-level view of the layered system when you have a domain model

The DAL and domain model are not in contact directly. The service layer, instead, scripts both. This is the whole architectural point here.

The DAL and the Presentation Layer

Is this section really necessary? Can the DAL ever be extended so that it can see and touch the presentation layer? This doesn't happen in an ideal design. Period.

However, we all have a family, we all live in the real world, and we all have bills to pay. And we all need to be pragmatic in some cases. So, in the real world, it might happen that the presentation layer calls into a few methods of the DAL.

The key point here is not so much the fact that you can take a shortcut to gain a quick solution to a specific problem. It is more important that you recognize you are ultimately taking a shortcut. The shortcut of invoking a piece of the DAL from the presentation layer is acceptable as long as you are fully aware of what you are doing. The *only* reason to ever consider using a presentation-to-DAL shortcut is to save valuable development time. From a team perspective, it is perhaps just as important that you pass the message around clearly— you should try to avoid presentation-to-DAL shortcuts. We realize that pragmatically those shortcuts, if controlled, are definitely possible and helpful, but they represent inappropriate tight coupling between disjoint layers—use the quick solution when you need it, but definitely refactor things at the earliest possible moment.

For example, you might invoke the DAL directly from the presentation layer to grab a chunk of data that the presentation layer needs. Consider a simple Get-Order use case. The presentation layer provides an ID and receives order information for display. In an ideal service-oriented architecture (SOA) design, you create a service with a *GetByID* method and use data-transfer objects to move data. For a single method call, and in a lazier scenario, this is probably too much of an effort. Hence, you might consider a direct binding between the presentation layer and the DAL.

> **Note** The shape of the DAL mostly depends on the architect's vision of the business layer. But, to some extent, things also work the other way around: the DAL might influence the business layer. It's like the old story of which came first, the egg or the chicken. Your known constraints and your attitude determine where you start from and, subsequently, what influences what. As a matter of fact, there's a limited set of reasonable combinations between the set of patterns you use to design the business layer and those you consider for creating a DAL.

Designing Your Own Data Access Layer

We started this chapter by saying that no matter how many abstraction layers you place in your model of the system, at some point you need to open a connection to some database. The layer where this happens is referred to as the DAL. After recognizing this core fact, though, we discussed the overall responsibilities of the DAL. Now it's about time we delve deeper into the topic and say more about implementing your own DAL.

All in all, we don't expect architects and developers to write a DAL from scratch on a regular basis. Many applications, even within an enterprise, run happily on typed *DataSets* and Active Record object models. As we said earlier, in these cases the DAL is available out of the box. You need a separate DAL with certain advanced capabilities only if you have a domain model. And also in that case, choosing a companion O/RM tool will make your life easier and ensure you can take a more relaxed approach to the project's deadline. If you can employ an O/RM tool, a large share of the topics we're going to discuss—essentially more detailed implementations of the patterns we listed earlier—are of limited interest. The O/RM, in fact, provides all of them off the shelf. In the end, the primary purpose of this section of the book is illustrative.

> **Note** Thankfully, it doesn't happen every day and on every project, but sometimes it might happen: imagine your best customer delivering a requirement that forces you to design a system that runs on two distinct DBMS and doesn't make use of any O/RM. If you can imagine that happening to you, this chapter will be helpful.

The Contract of the DAL

We recommend that you design the DAL in a way that separates the interface from the implementation. After you have abstracted the capabilities of the DAL to a contract, consumers can get a particular implementation of it and work in peace.

You start by defining the general interface for the DAL—the data context. Next, you implement this interface in any modules you need that perform data access tasks against a particular DBMS, or even a particular O/RM. The layer that consumes the DAL—whether it's the business, service, or even presentation layer—receives a reference to the currently selected DAL. You provide a factory to build the current DAL. To ensure full independence from the database structure, the

DAL and its consumer will communicate using business entities (domain model objects, objects in an Active Record model, typed *DataSets*, or plain data transfer objects).

This approach has a number of benefits.

In particular, the application can easily support a variety of data sources and have a specialized DAL for each supported DBMS. With this architecture in place, to make your application support, say, Oracle, all you have to do is create an Oracle-specific DAL and make it visible to the application. In addition, impersonating the DAL for testing purposes is a piece of cake.

The Separated Interface pattern (which is described on page 476 of [P of EAA]) formalizes the design rule of keeping the DAL interface neatly separated from the component that actually implements it.

The Separated Interface Pattern

In general terms, the Separated Interface pattern addresses the problem of separating the interface that describes a certain functionality from its implementation. The pattern prescribes that you use different packages (for example, assemblies in the .NET Framework) for the interface and any of its implementations. Only the definition of the interface is known to any packages that need to consume the functionality. Let's turn this general pattern to the world of data access.

Applied to the design of a DAL, *Separated Interface* means that you define a contract for all the functionality you expose through the DAL. The contract is ultimately an interface compiled to its own assembly. Which part of the system is going to consume the DAL? As mentioned, it largely depends on the pattern you selected for the domain logic. Without loss of generality, let's assume the consumer is the service layer. Figure 6-7 provides a graphical overview of distinct packages implementing the service layer, the DAL contract, and specific DALs.

The assembly with the service layer holds a reference to the assembly that defines the DAL interface. Each DAL implementation does the same. The service layer consumes a concrete implementation of the DAL without knowing it directly. For this to happen, an additional component is needed to find the right implementation and to instantiate it.

Note Should you really employ a Separated Interface pattern for the DAL even when the application is not expected to support multiple DBMSs? Any DAL requires a super class to provide the operational context—a sort of bridgehead to plan actions against the database. So the correct question is another. Should you extract an interface from the data context even though you have no requirement saying that both Oracle and SQL Server should be supported? Well, simplified testing is a good reason to opt for such a pattern. And generally, the Separated Interface pattern pushes a more layered design with loose coupling between the DAL and its consumers, which is never a bad thing per se.

The assembly where you define the DAL interface is also a fine place to keep all the DTOs, if you have them. The DTOs are DAL agnostic as well, and you'd need them to define the interfaces, anyway.

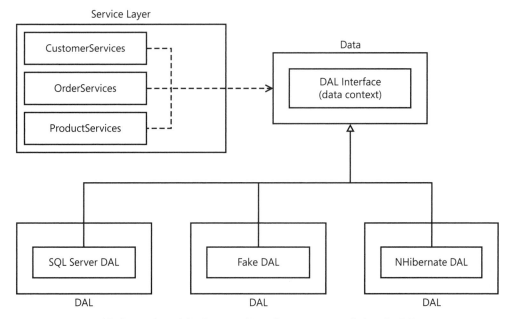

FIGURE 6-7 A graphical overview of the Separated Interface pattern applied to the DAL

Program to a (DAL) Interface

The Separated Interface pattern is useful in any scenario where a given functionality of the application might be implemented through a different behavior based on runtime conditions. The DAL is just one of these cases.

As you might have noticed yourself, there's a much more general principle of object-oriented design at work here. It is precisely the principle that the Gang of Four (Erich Gamma, Richard Helm, Ralph Johnson, and John Vlissides), in their excellent *Design Patterns: Elements of Reusable Object-Oriented Software* (Addison-Wesley, 1995), describe as "Program to an interface; not to an implementation."

When you apply this principle, clients are unaware of the concrete types they end up using. And clients just don't care about concrete types, as long as the objects they receive expose an agreed-upon interface. Clients and concrete types are decoupled because clients know only about the interface.

Based on this principle, you place the interface and implementation of the DAL in separate packages (for example, assemblies), and you put a factory in the middle so that any clients, such as a class in the service layer, can get a reference to the current DAL. (See Figure 6-8.)

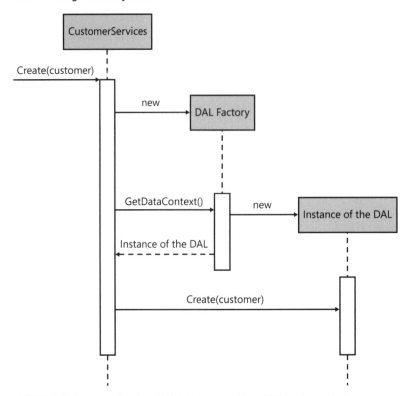

FIGURE 6-8 Programming to a DAL interface, not to a DAL implementation

In the figure, when the service layer gets to add a new customer to the storage, it first instantiates the DAL factory and invokes a method to get a reference to the current DAL, whether the current DAL stores information using SQL Server, Oracle, or perhaps a fake DAL for testing purposes. Internally, the factory figures out the currently registered class mapped to the DAL interface. It then instantiates the concrete class and returns the reference.

The DAL client doesn't know about the concrete DAL type, but it does know about the interface. So it uses the methods on the interface to instruct the actual DAL to add a new customer. Abstractly speaking, the DAL factory finds and returns an instance of a component with certain capabilities. We could rephrase this concept by using more evocative terms, such as the factory *locates* an instance of the right DAL service on behalf of the client and *injects* it in the client's space.

There are essentially two patterns for the scheme in Figure 6-8. One is based on the Plugin pattern as described on page 499 of [P of EAA]. One is based on the emerging Inversion Of Control pattern. Before we tackle both approaches, let's have a quick and preliminary look at some code showing how to abstract the capabilities of a DAL.

Abstracting the Capabilities of a DAL

The following code snippet shows a sample interface for the data context—the entry point in a data access layer. The code is an adaptation of the companion source code.

```
using ManagedDesign.Northwind.Data.QueryModel;
namespace ManagedDesign.App.DAL
{
    public interface IDataContext : IDisposable
    {
        // Query services
        IList<T> GetAll<T>() where T : class, new();
        IList<T> GetAll<T>(int pageIndex, int pageSize) where T : class, new();
        IList<T> GetByCriteria<T>(Query query) where T : class, new();
        IList<T> GetByCriteria<T>(Query query, int index, int size) where T : class, new();
        T GetByID<T>(object id) where T : class, new();
        int GetCount<T>();
        int GetCount<T>(Query query);

        // CRUD services (well, mostly CUD)
        void Add(object item);
        void Delete(object item);
        void Save(object item);

        // Transaction management
        bool IsInTransaction { get; }
        bool IsDirty { get; }
        void BeginTransaction();
        void Commit();
        void Rollback();
    }
}
```

Later in the chapter, we'll return to the *IDataContext* interface and delve a bit deeper into each member. For now, our goal is just to give some substance to an otherwise abstract concept. The previous code snippet shows you a sample data context and demonstrates how the responsibilities are distributed. You won't see any member explicitly referring to concurrency. The concurrency is managed within the implementation of persistence.

The Plugin Pattern

What do you expect from a DAL factory? A *factory* is an object concerned with the creation of instances of a class exposing a given interface. Usually, there's no additional logic involved in a factory. A factory is a class with one method: the method gets a new instance of a hard-coded type and returns.

When you add to the factory some additional logic to determine at run time which concrete type the factory has to return, you actually move toward a more sophisticated Plugin model.

Generalities of the Plugin Pattern

On page 499 of [P of EAA], the Plugin pattern is described as a basic factory pattern with some special features. In particular, the Plugin pattern suggests that you read the information about the type to create from an external configuration point.

In the .NET Framework, this configuration point is likely to be the *web.config* file of a Web application or the *app.config* file of a Microsoft Windows presentation layer. However, for ease of deployment and management, the configuration point is any storage that is external to the application. It can also be a database or a custom text file expressing any syntax you feel comfortable with. All that's important is the type information, no matter how you obtain it.

Another key point of the Plugin pattern is that the client that consumes the interface doesn't link the actual implementation. With regard to the DAL scenario, this means that the assembly that implements the service layer doesn't include a reference to the assembly that contains the actual DAL component. The DAL assembly, instead, is loaded in memory dynamically on demand. In the .NET Framework, this means using a pinch of reflection.

Figure 6-9 updates Figure 6-8 to show the sequence of a sample DAL operation when the Plugin pattern is employed.

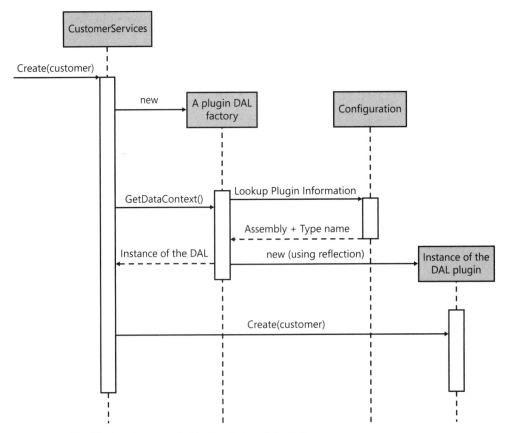

FIGURE 6-9 The Plugin pattern applied to the design of the DAL

The DAL Factory in Action

Imagine a factory class like the one shown in the following code snippet. As you can see, the class is trivial and is merely an implementation of the Factory Method pattern:

```
public class DalFactory
{
    public IDataContext GetDataContext()
    {
        // Instantiate the concrete type of DAL
        return new SqlServerDataContext();
    }
}
```

Put this way, the factory is not really useful. The *DalFactory* class simply isolates in a class the logic that creates an instance of a fixed type with certain capabilities—the *IDataContext* interface in the example. We need some more logic to read from a configuration file which type should be instantiated and returned.

We can then move to the following implementation:

```
// This class will be called by any clients interested in getting
// actual implementations of IDataContext. As you can see, callers
// are not required to specify which interface they want. Callers just
// invoke a method (GetDataContext), get an implicitly created object,
// and plug that object into the application's mainstream.
public class DalFactory
{
    private static IDataContext _instance = null;

    static DalFactory()
    {
        // Read assembly and type information from a standard
        // section of the .NET config file
        string asm = ConfigurationManager.AppSettings["DAL-Assembly"];
        string cls = ConfigurationManager.AppSettings["DAL-Type"];

        // Dynamically load the assembly and instantiate the type
        Assembly a = Assembly.Load(asm);
        _instance = (IDataContext) a.CreateInstance(cls);
    }

    public IDataContext GetDataContext()
    {
        // Return the DAL plugin currently selected in the configuration file
        return _instance;
    }
}
```

This is definitely an implementation of the Plugin pattern that works and fulfills expectations. Any consumers of the DAL don't know about the concrete type, and they don't link it to their own assembly. In addition, the configuration point is placed outside the application and changing configuration details doesn't require a rebuild. In other words, to switch to a different DAL (for example, for testing purposes) all that you need to do is edit the related entries in the configuration file.

We'll refer to the class that represents the entry point in the Plugin implementation as the *plugin factory*—the *DalFactory* class in the example. We'll refer to the actual classes instantiated by the plugin factory as *plugins*. Therefore, a plugin is any class that implements the interface hard-coded in the implementation plugin factory. With regard to the example, a plugin is any class that implements *IDataContext*.

Building a DAL Plugin

The Plugin pattern is built around the principle that the client of the plugin factory (that is, the service layer) doesn't know the concrete type it instantiates through the plugin factory. The plugin factory class will read from the configuration layer any information that can lead to identifying and loading the concrete type. As mentioned, the *web.config* file can be an ideal location to place this information, as shown here:

```
<configuration>
  <appSettings>
    <add key="DAL-Assembly" value="ManagedDesign.App.SqlServerDAL" />
    <add key="DAL-Type" value="ManagedDesign.App.SqlServerDalFactory" />
  </appSettings>
    ⋮
</configuration>
```

A typical plugin that contains a DAL implementation may take the following form:

```
namespace ManagedDesign.App
{
    public sealed class SqlServerDalFactory : IDalFactory
    {
        public IDataContext GetDataContext()
        {
            return new SqlServerDataContext();
        }
    }
}
```

In the example, *SqlServerDataContext* implements the aforementioned *IDataContext* interface targeting a SQL Server database. This means that methods such as *Add* or *GetAll* will be implemented using ADO.NET with the SQL Server data provider or, perhaps, LINQ-to-SQL.

Finally, how can a client (say, an application service) consume a DAL? Let's see an example:

```
public class CustomerServices
{
    private IDataContext _context = null;

    public CustomerServices()
    {
        // Figure 6-9 details the work flow occurring when you run this code.
        IDalFactory factory = new DalFactory();
        this._context = factory.GetDataContext();
    }
```

```
public void Create(Customer item)
{
    if (item == null)
    {
        throw new ArgumentNullException("The specified customer cannot be null");
    }
    else if (!item.IsValid)
    {
        throw new ArgumentException("The specified customer is not valid");
    }
    else if (Exists(item.ID))
    {
        throw new ArgumentException("The specified customer already exists.");
    }
    else
    {
        this._context.Add(item);
    }
}
    .
    .
    .
}
```

We'll return later in the chapter to the implementation of typical DAL responsibilities in a sample class such as the aforementioned *SqlServerDataContext* class.

Service Locator vs. Plugin

In literature, there's another pattern with a very similar goal as Plugin: the Service Locator pattern. A service locator is an object that knows how to retrieve all the services that an application might need. Is there any significant difference between the Service Locator and Plugin patterns? In both cases, you have an object that a client calls to get objects that provide some known interfaces. Actually, the boundary between the two is very blurred. They are functionally equivalent, and you can use both and be equally happy. At the end of the day, what matters is that the resulting code can load external components and work with them effectively. This is much more important than the subtlety of the approach.

The Plugin pattern exists to inject a concrete implementation where the client expects a given interface. The main purpose of the Plugin pattern is making the code extensible and flexible. As a nice side effect, with a Plugin implementation you also loosen up dependency between components.

The main Service Locator focus, instead, is achieving the lowest possible coupling between components. It represents a centralized console that an application uses to obtain all the external dependencies it needs. In doing so, you also incur the pleasant side effect of making your code more flexible and extensible.

Both patterns hide the complexity of component lookup, handle caching or pooling of instances, and offer a common façade for component lookup and creation.

Service Locator is a pattern originally defined by Sun for Java development—the full formulation can be found at the following URL: *http://java.sun.com/blueprints/corej2eepatterns/Patterns/ServiceLocator.html*. Here's a common implementation for the pattern:

```
// A possible (type-checked) implementation of the Service Locator pattern
public class ServiceLocator
{
    private static const int CONST_IDATACONTEXT = ...;

    public object GetService(Type t)
    {
        if (t == typeof(IDataContext))
        {
            return new SqlServerDalFactory();
        }
        :
        :
    }

    public object GetService(int serviceID)
    {
        switch(serviceID)
        {
            case CONST_IDATACONTEXT:
                return new SqlServerDalFactory();
            :
            :
        }
    }
    :
    :
}
```

Quite obviously, you can modify the preceding reference implementation of the Service Locator to add support for configuration (an aspect also covered by the original pattern specification) and to add specific methods that return classes implementing specific interfaces. When you do this, Plugin and Service Locator tend to be the same thing.

Note Often patterns originate from different people and different contexts; quite reasonably, they might express the same idea with different verbiage. In this case, the applied code produces the same effect. For example, this is the case for the Service Locator pattern and the Registry pattern. Both patterns present themselves as *finders*. A registry, as described on page 480 of [P of EAA], is a centralized object that other objects use to find common objects and services. They are essentially the same thing. So why do they have different names, then?

The idea of a "service locator" arose in the context of solutions aimed at reducing dependency between components. The "registry" originates as a helper component that objects in an application use to retrieve common objects and services they need. In other words, in the "registry" there's no explicit idea of loosening dependency between components. Likewise, in a "service locator" the focus is on dependencies. But whether you implement a registry or a service locator, you obtain the same effect. An interesting article on this subject can be found at *http://martinfowler.com/articles/injection.html*.

The Inversion of Control Pattern

Let's briefly recap the design of the DAL we came up with. First, we separated the DAL interface from its implementation and created distinct assemblies. Next, we set up a Plugin model so that any DAL consumer calls into a factory and gets an instance of the currently selected DAL. By changing the configuration, we can switch from one DBMS to another (and even to a fake DBMS for testing purposes) without rebuilding the application.

The Plugin model works great and is extremely easy to implement for our purpose of handling the dependencies on any given specific DAL implementation. Generally, using the Plugin pattern throughout an application as a way to reduce dependencies can be a debatable choice. This is not because it is an incorrect model per se, but because a possibly better option exists. Enter the Inversion of Control (IoC) pattern.

Injecting a Reference to the DAL

We already covered IoC in detail Chapter 3, "Design Principles and Patterns," and deeply explored its goals and the inspiring principle. Here we are basically discussing the applicability of inversion of control to a DAL scenario, as an alternative to the Plugin model.

> **Note** For the purpose of this discussion, IoC and Dependency Injection (DI) are synonyms. They are not always considered synonyms in literature, as sometimes you find IoC to be the principle and DI the application of the principle—namely, the pattern. In reality, IoC is historically a pattern based on the Dependency Inversion Principle (DIP) by Robert Martin. The term *dependency injection* was coined by Martin Fowler later, as a way to further specialize the concept of inversion of control.

The basic idea behind IoC is that the consumer of some functionality doesn't bother managing dependencies itself but delegates this burden to a specialized component. Let's apply this principle to the DAL.

As shown in Figure 6-10, the DAL consumer logically depends on the DAL interface and its implementation. However, we don't want the service layer (or any other consumer of the DAL) to be directly involved with tasks such as locating the DAL implementation and instantiating the proper type. Ideally, we want an intermediate object to inject into the DAL consumer all required references to external objects.

The dependency injector finds the DAL implementation and makes it available to the consumer. Typically, the consumer class exposes a constructor or a setter property through which the dependency injector can *inject* all the references it finds.

What kind of class is the dependency injector, and who writes it? Today, a number of frameworks exist to help you with IoC. So, in the end, you never write your dependency injector. As we'll see in more detail later in the "Inversion of Control vs. Plugin" section, the availability of terrific frameworks is what makes IoC so affordable and increasingly popular.

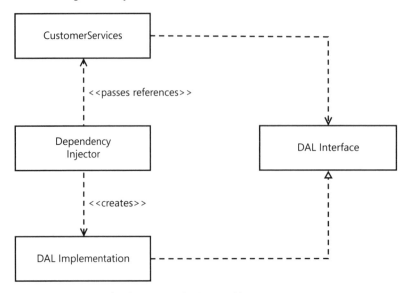

FIGURE 6-10 Dependencies among the DAL and its consumers

The structure of a dependency injector depends on the framework you use, but we won't stray too far from the truth if we say that a dependency injector uses its own configuration layer to register mappings between the interface and corresponding implementations.

Is this really different from an implementation of the Plugin pattern? We'll get back to that question in just a moment.

Inversion of Control in Action Through Unity

To see IoC in action, you need to pick up an IoC framework first. In particular, Microsoft's Unity Application Block (Unity, for short) is a lightweight IoC container with support for constructor, property, and method call injection. It comes as part of the Enterprise Library 4.0. Let's use that for our demonstrations.

Virtually any IoC framework is built around a container class. You bind the container to some configuration information so that application code can obtain references to instances of specific concrete objects, based on requests for an interface. Let's see how to proceed with Unity:

```
// Instantiate the container class
IUnityContainer container;
container = new UnityContainer();

// Bind to working information saved to the <unity> section of the configuration file
UnityConfigurationSection section;
section = (UnityConfigurationSection) ConfigurationManager.GetSection("unity");
section.Containers.Default.Configure(container);

// Now you have a fully configured container
:
```

The *<unity>* section in the .NET configuration file looks like the following:

```
<configuration>
    <configSections>
        <section name="unity"
                 type="Microsoft.Practices.Unity.Configuration.UnityConfigurationSection,
                       Microsoft.Practices.Unity.Configuration" />
    </configSections>
    ⋮
    <unity>
        <containers>
            <container>
                <types>
                    <type type="ManagedDesign.App.DAL.IDataContext,
                                 ManagedDesign.App.DALCore"
                          mapTo="ManagedDesign.App.DAL.SqlServerDataContext,
                                 ManagedDesign.App.SQLServerDAL">
                    </type>
                </types>
            </container>
        </containers>
    </unity>
    ⋮
</configuration>
```

The *<types>* section lists mappings between interfaces and corresponding implementations. Whenever the container is requested to resolve a dependency on a given interface type, it promptly replies by serving an instance of the corresponding implementation class.

How can you programmatically get the implementation class? You use the *Resolve* method, as shown here:

```
IDataContext impl = container.Resolve<IDataContext>();
```

Our final step consists of sketching a possible new organization for the code so that classes in the service layer can be injected with their due dependencies.

Dependency Injection Mechanisms

There are three ways to inject dependencies into a class—using the constructor, a setter property, or an interface. In this case, we need to inject the DAL implementation into a service layer class. The three aforementioned options become the following:

- Add a new constructor to each service layer class that consumes the DAL.

- Add a new setter property (or method) to each service layer class that consumes the DAL.

- Define a new interface, and implement it within each service layer class that consumes the DAL.

All techniques are valid, and the choice is up to you. We would opt for injecting through the constructor because this way you make it clear from the beginning what the dependencies of a class are. The *CustomerServices* class will look like the following:

```
public class CustomerServices
{
    private IDataContext _context = null;

    // Inject the dependency via the ctor
    public CustomerServices(IDataContext context)
    {
        this._context = context;
    }
    :

}
```

The class now features one constructor that receives everything it needs from the outside world.

> **Note** Where is the *Unity* container class physically created and managed? The IoC container is created outside of the *CustomerServices* class care of any layer of code that actually consumes an instance of *CustomerServices*—regardless of whether it is code in the presentation layer or a WCF custom factory. Before calling *CustomerServices*, this layer of code gets hold of the Unity container, resolves all dependencies, and passes required objects down to the constructor.

Inversion of Control vs. Plugin

Both the IoC and Plugin patterns provide your application with the fundamental decoupling between the DAL implementation and DAL consumers. Both are good solutions from a design perspective.

So what's better, IoC or Plugin?

Some people argue that IoC is preferable because you can spot dependencies right from the constructor (or, in general, from the injection mechanism) of the consumer class. If you use a Plugin, instead, you need to inspect the source code of the consumer class to spot dependencies. We agree with this point.

Some people argue that IoC is preferable because it makes for an application that's easier to test. Honestly, we don't agree with this point. If IoC and Plugin are implemented as discussed here, testing is not an issue in any case.

Some people argue, in general, that IoC is preferable because it works better in scenarios where you're writing code that will be incorporated in other applications. It's clear that a *CustomerServices* class is inherently more reusable across applications if it is designed to accept the DAL interface reference via the constructor instances of all the components it uses. If such a *CustomerServices* class instantiates any needed components via a factory, it creates a dependency between the host application and the factory. And this might be a problem.

In general, therefore, the emerging approach is IoC, but using a Plugin is not necessarily a bad idea and, additionally, it is an approach that works great in a number of situations.

In our opinion, the biggest benefit of using IoC is the support you get from frameworks. IoC frameworks perform a lot of magic and provide a number of services and facilities (for example, aspect-oriented capabilities) that you have to code manually in a Plugin scenario. Many of these features are so sophisticated that to implement them in a Plugin scenario, you have to, well, shape your own Plugin framework as an IoC framework.

Laying the Groundwork for a Data Context

We recognized the importance of separating the interface of the DAL from its implementation and agreed that a DAL consumer needs, first of all, to get a reference to the DAL implementation, either by using a Plugin approach or perhaps through dependency injection.

The consumer doesn't know any details of the actual implementation. In particular, it doesn't know about the target DBMS and doesn't care about the language being used to run queries and stored procedures. All that the consumer knows about is an interface that summarizes all the possible functions that the DAL provides. We refer to such an interface as the *data context*, and typically plan to have one distinct data context for testing purposes and one for each low-level data access API we intend to support.

The *IDataContext* Interface

For the sake of discussion, let's briefly recall the definition of the *IDataContext* interface we gave earlier in the chapter:

```
public interface IDataContext : IDisposable
{
    // Query services
    IList<T> GetAll<T>() where T : class, new();
    IList<T> GetAll<T>(int pageIndex, int pageSize) where T : class, new();
    IList<T> GetByCriteria<T>(Query query) where T : class, new();
    IList<T> GetByCriteria<T>(Query query, int index, int size) where T : class, new();
    T GetByID<T>(object id) where T : class, new();
    int GetCount<T>();
    int GetCount<T>(Query query);

    // CRUD services (well, mostly CUD)
    void Add(object item);
    void Delete(object item);
    void Save(object item);

    // Transaction management
    bool IsInTransaction { get; }
    bool IsDirty { get; }
    void BeginTransaction();
    void Commit();
    void Rollback();
}
```

In the interface, you recognize a bunch of methods for CRUD services, some methods for specialized query services, and methods to provide transactional semantics. Table 6-1 details the various members.

TABLE 6-1 Members of a Typical Data Context

Member	Description
Add	If the DAL is working transactionally, this method adds an object to the in-memory repository. Otherwise, it adds objects directly to the storage.
BeginTransaction	Turns on the transactional mode.
Commit	Commits all pending changes in the in-memory repository to the physical storage.
Delete	If the DAL is working transactionally, this method deletes the specified object from the in-memory repository. Otherwise, it deletes the specified object directly from the storage.
GetAll<T>	Retrieves all instances of the specified type (Customer, Order) in the underlying database.
GetByCriteria<T>	Executes a query. The query is expressed using a custom type that models a query through a set of operators and clauses.
GetByID<T>	Retrieves the instance of the given type (Customer, Order) whose identifier matches the passed value.
GetCount<T>	Returns the number of objects of the specified type that the given query would select.
IsDirty	Boolean property, indicates whether this instance of the DAL contains any pending changes not yet saved to the storage.
IsInTransaction	Boolean property, indicates whether this instance of the DAL works transactionally.
Rollback	Discards all pending changes, and resets the transactional mode.
Save	If the DAL is working transactionally, this method updates the specified object in the in-memory repository. Otherwise, it directly updates the storage.

The methods in the interface reflect many of the responsibilities of the data context we identified at the beginning of the chapter. You find methods to add, delete, and update objects to database tables. You find methods to track changes occurring in a unit of work. You find methods to query for objects as simple as *GetAll* and *GetByID*, plus a more sophisticated *GetByCriteria* method to arrange for dynamically built queries.

In our companion source code, we have a hierarchy of classes like those shown in Figure 6-11.

As you can see, in the companion code we have a data context for SQL Server, a testing data context, plus a data context specific to an O/RM tool such as NHibernate. In many real projects, though, the use of an O/RM tool is complementary to crafting your own DAL. Put another way, you craft your own DAL when requirements stop you from using any commercial or free O/RM tools.

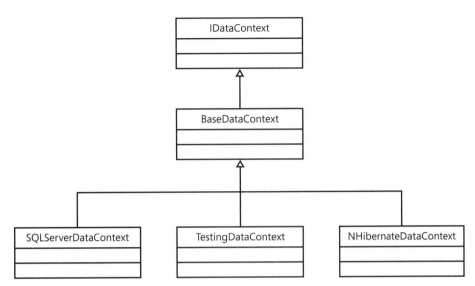

FIGURE 6-11 Hierarchy of data-context classes

In a real project, you first determine whether it is appropriate to use an O/RM tool for the DAL. If it is, your data context comes from the O/RM API. As far as NHibernate is concerned, the data context is the *Session* class and the counterpart to our *IDataContext* interface is the *ISession* interface. It is coincidental that our sample contract for *IDataContext* is nearly identical to the NHibernate's *ISession* interface. We'll tackle the implementation of a DAL using an O/RM later in the chapter.

A Common Class for the Data Context

The interface for the DAL can optionally be partially implemented in a base class. All concrete implementations of the DAL will then derive from this base class. Figure 6-12 shows a possible diagram for the *BaseDataContext* class.

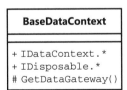

FIGURE 6-12 Class diagram for *BaseDataContext*

In addition to providing support for all members of *IDataContext*, the base class also takes care of the disposal interface. The following code snippet demonstrates a sample implementation of *IDisposable* for a class that implements the *IDataContext* interface we presented earlier:

```
public abstract class BaseDataContext : IDataContext, IDisposable
{
    // Internal members
    protected bool _isInTransaction = false;
    protected bool _isDirty = false;

    // IDataContext implementation
    public virtual bool IsDirty
    {
        get {return _isDirty;}
        private set {_isDirty = value;}
    }

    public virtual bool IsInTransaction
    {
        get {return _isInTransaction;}
        private set {_isInTransaction = value;}
    }

        ⋮

    // IDisposable implementation
    public virtual void Dispose()
    {
        if (this.IsInTransaction)
        {
            this.Rollback();
        }
    }
}
```

The preceding code contains a bit more than just a sample implementation of *IDisposable*. In particular, we incorporated in the listing a couple of *IDataContext* members—the *IsDirty* and *IsInTransaction* properties.

The implementation of the Boolean properties is provided for pure reference. There's nothing really remarkable there, except perhaps for the private setter. The implementation of other methods, such as *GetAll* and *Add*, is left to your imagination at the moment.

The key thing that is going on here is that we finally reached a point where some code that interacts with a database is required. The next point to address is how you would provide a gateway to the storage.

Crafting Your Own Data Access Layer

Under the covers of the data context class, a number of interesting things happen that represent the body and soul of the DAL. A DAL is about persistence, management of business transactions, concurrency, lazy loading, maybe caching, and more. In this section, we'll basically go through the typical responsibilities we've already identified for a DAL.

Implementing the Persistence Layer

The main purpose of the persistence layer is to provide a mapping between the types in the domain logic and physical tables in the DBMS. You resort to data context methods such as *Add*, *Delete*, or *Update* when you just want to make persistent any changes (insertions, deletions, or updates) to objects in the domain model.

So with an eye on the *IDataContext* interface, let's focus on the *Add*, *Delete*, and *Update* methods.

The Gateway to Storage

To persist in-memory changes, you need some mapping logic and a gateway to a DBMS-specific context. As mentioned, the Data Mapper pattern helps a lot here. The pattern is defined on page 165 of [P of EAA]. In brief, a data mapper is the class that takes care of persistence on behalf of a given type.

You usually define a data mapper for each type in the domain model. For example, you have a *CustomerDataMapper* class for the type *Customer*, an *OrderDataMapper* class for the type *Order*, and so on.

How do you create and manage data mappers within the data context class? You typically define an *IDataMapper<T>* interface and add a method to the data context class that returns a type-specific implementation of the interface. Next, you yield to the data mapper for each persistence operation. Here's the edited code for the *BaseDataContext* class:

```
public abstract class BaseDataContext : IDataContext, IDisposable
{
    // Define a placeholder for methods that return a data mapper
    protected abstract IDataMapper<T> GetDataMapper<T>();
    protected abstract IDataMapper<T> GetDataMapper(Type t);

    public void Add(object item)
    {
        Type t = item.GetType();
        GetDataMapper(t).Create(item);
    }

    public void Delete(object item)
    {
        Type t = item.GetType();
        GetDataMapper(t).Delete(item);
    }

    public void Save(object item)
    {
        Type t = item.GetType();
        GetDataMapper(t).Update(item);
    }
    :
}
```

Note The implementation we provide here for persistence methods in *BaseDataContext* is temporary and mostly provided for illustrative purposes. It will soon get to its final shape as we move on to consider transactions, in just a few sections.

What methods should appear in the *IDataMapper* interface? At a minimum, you find the following:

```
public interface IDataMapper<T>
{
    void Create(T item);
    void Update(T item);
    void Delete(T item);
}
```

The parameter *item* of type *T* indicates the object to add, remove, or update in the data storage. Details of the mapping between the specified object and the tables in the database are known by each class that implements *IDataMapper<T>*.

As you might have noticed, the *GetDataMapper* method is declared *protected* and *abstract* in the base data context class. This means that each derived class—that is, each concrete and DBMS-specific implementation of the data context—*must* implement *GetDataMapper*. In this way, we let subclasses define what a data mapper actually is and how it behaves. This approach is based on the Template Method pattern, as originally defined by the Gang of Four.

Note The Template Method pattern is designed to let subclasses redefine given steps of an algorithm implemented in the parent class. Admittedly, the Template Method pattern is somewhat similar to the Strategy pattern. Well, some differences exist if you want to be picky. The Strategy pattern allows callers to redefine an entire algorithm; the Template Method pattern allows you to redefine single steps without changing the overall algorithm. Subsequently, you end up using inheritance with the Template Method pattern, and delegation with Strategy.

Should we have more methods in the *IDataMapper* interface? And if so, which methods? When, at the beginning of the chapter, we presented the typical responsibilities of a DAL, we mentioned CRUD services. As is widely known, CRUD is an acronym that stands for *Create, Read, Update, Delete*. Now that we are discussing the implementation of a DAL, we suddenly switched from saying "CRUD services" to saying "persistence layer." What's the point with the name change? The persistence layer is a subset of CRUD services, as it might not include Read services. So the persistence layer is more CUD services than CRUD services. We'll treat Read features in the next section when we discuss query services.

A Factory for Data Mappers

The *BaseDataContext* class features an abstract method named *GetDataMapper* that is responsible for providing a type-specific data mapper. The method is abstract and must be defined in any class derived from *BaseDataContext*—that is, in any implementation of the system's DAL. Let's see how it works for a DAL based on SQL Server:

```
namespace ManagedDesign.App.DAL
{
    public class SqlServerDataContext : BaseDataContext
    {
        protected override IDataMapper<T> GetDataMapper<T>()
        {
            // Customer
            if (typeof(T) == typeof(Customer))
            {
                return (IDataMapper<T>) new CustomerDataMapper();
            }

            // Order
            else if (typeof(T) == typeof(Order))
            {
                return (IDataMapper<T>) new OrderDataMapper();
            }

            // Product
            else if (typeof(T) == typeof(Product))
            {
                return (IDataMapper<T>) new ProductDataMapper();
            }

            // Unsupported type
            else
            {
                throw new MissingDataMapperException("Unsupported type");
            }
        }
    }
}
```

All data mapper classes belong to the same assembly as the data context class, and all together, they form the SQL Server–specific DAL.

Although simple and effective, the implementation provided here for the data mapper factory is very basic. But is it simplistic, too? Let's see.

It certainly fulfills the "Do the simplest thing that could possibly work" principle—a pillar in the agile methodology field. But what are possible alternatives? One is certainly using inversion of control. In this case, you just create an instance of the IoC container in the *GetDataMapper* method and use it to resolve any dependency. Here's how to do that using Microsoft's Unity:

```
protected override IDataMapper<T> GetDataMapper<T>()
{
    // Save type information
    Type t = typeof(T);

    // Instantiate the container class
    UnityContainer container = new UnityContainer();
```

```
        // Bind to working information saved to the <unity> section of the configuration file
        UnityConfigurationSection section;
        section = (UnityConfigurationSection) ConfigurationManager.GetSection("unity");
        section.Containers.Default.Configure(container);

        // Resolve the data mapper
        IDataMapper<T> mapper = (IDataMapper<T>) container.Resolve(t);
        return mapper;
    }
```

Needless to say, the management of the unity container can be moved up to the base data context class and exposed as a private member.

It is key to note that IoC containers have a long list of positive features, but there's a drawback too: you can't catch errors at compile time. Compared to using a list of *IF* statements, the preceding code is inherently more elegant and doesn't require you to edit source code when you add a new entity to the domain model. On the other hand, if you at some point add a new entity to the domain model, you are probably in the context of a large refactoring and updating the source code of *BaseDataContext* is really a minor issue.

Inside Data Mappers

Here's a possible implementation of the data mapper class that manages the persistence of the *Customer* type:

```
namespace ManagedDesign.App.DAL
{
    internal class CustomerDataMapper : IDataMapper<Customer>
    {
        // NOTE: plain SQL statements embedded in the class
        private static readonly string _cmdInsertCustomer = "...";
        private static readonly string _cmdDeleteCustomer = "...";
        private static readonly string _cmdUpdateCustomer = "...";
        :

        public virtual void Create(Customer item)
        {
            SqlHelper.ExecuteNonQuery(ProviderHelper.ConnectionString,
                        CommandType.Text,
                        this._cmdInsertCustomer,
                        this.BuildParamsFromEntity(item));
        }
        public virtual void Delete(Customer item)
        {
            SqlParameter prmID = new SqlParameter("@ID", SqlDbType.NChar, 5);
            prmID.Value = item.CustomerID;
            SqlHelper.ExecuteNonQuery(ProviderHelper.ConnectionString,
                        CommandType.Text,
                        this._cmdDeleteCustomer,
                        new SqlParameter[] { prmID });
        }
```

```
        public virtual void Update(Customer item)
        {
            SqlHelper.ExecuteNonQuery(ProviderHelper.ConnectionString,
                        CommandType.Text,
                        this._cmdupdateCustomer,
                        this.BuildParamsFromEntity(item));
        }
        ⋮
    }
}
```

The mapper class does know about connection strings, stored procedures, SQL commands, cursors, data readers, and the like. When writing this code, you need to unleash any ADO. NET and T-SQL skills you might have.

In particular, the connection string is obtained through a helper class that reads it from the configuration layer. Parameters are used to ensure typed values and fight off SQL injection. Plain T-SQL statements are used, but stored procedures can be employed as well. Finally, the *SqlHelper* class from the Microsoft Data Access Application Block is used instead of plain vanilla ADO.NET classes, such as *SqlConnection* and *SqlCommand*. You could also use LINQ-to-SQL. The point is, the data is accessed and you can switch implementations without hurting higher-order layers.

You might need a few helper methods to perform some chores such as building an array of *SqlParameter* objects from a *Customer* object. This particular task is accomplished by the *BuildParamsFromEntity* method:

```
protected virtual SqlParameter[] BuildParamsFromEntity(Customer item)
{
    SqlParameter prmID = new SqlParameter("@CustomerID", SqlDbType.NChar, 5);
    prmID.Value = item.ID;
    SqlParameter prmName = new SqlParameter("@CompanyName", SqlDbType.NVarChar, 40);
    prmName.Value = item.CompanyName;
    SqlParameter prmPhone = new SqlParameter("@Phone", SqlDbType.NVarChar, 24);
    prmPhone.Value = item.PhoneNumber;
    ⋮

    return new SqlParameter[] { prmID, prmName, prmPhone, ... };
}
```

As you can see, the SQL code for the various operations is embedded in the class. It can either be plain T-SQL statements or stored procedures. In any case, what we need here is plain data access code with nothing more than simple table-oriented statements: no loops, no conditions, no logic. We'll return later in the chapter to the role that stored procedures ideally have in the design of a DAL, according to our way of looking at things.

Bridging Types and Tables

Data mappers are essentially developer-created classes that fill the logical gap between the object model (or domain model) and the physical structure of databases.

The code snippet we just presented assumes a substantial one-to-one correspondence between the in-memory model and the physical data model. So each method on the data mapper is resolved in a single call to a single table. Each instance of a class in the object (or domain) model maps to a row in a table. The more the logical model is distant from the physical organization of tables, the more sophisticated a data mapper needs to be.

Put another way, the data mapper is a class that takes an entity from the in-memory object (or domain) model and persists it to the selected storage—whatever this means in practice. As an example, consider a *Customer* class with a property *Address* of type *AddressInfo*, as shown here:

```
public class Customer
{
    public Customer()
    {
        this._addressInfo = new AddressInfo();

        ⋮

    }

    protected AddressInfo _addressinfo;
    public virtual AddressInfo Address
    {
        get { return this._addressInfo;
    }

    ⋮

}
```

The type *AddressInfo* groups properties such as *Street*, *City*, *PostalCode*, *Region*, and *Country*, as shown here:

```
public class AddressInfo
{
    public string Street {get; set;}
    public string City {get; set;}
    public string PostalCode {get; set;}
    public string Region {get; set;}
    public string Country {get; set;}
}
```

In this case, there's no direct correspondence between the entity *Customer* and a table in the database. It's more likely, in fact, that the table has a distinct column for each of the properties in the *AddressInfo* than a single property for the whole address. Properly mapping properties to columns (and tables) is the primary responsibility of the data mapper. The aforementioned method *BuildParamsFromEntity* does just this, as shown here:

```
protected virtual SqlParameter[] BuildParamsFromEntity(Customer item)
{
    // Create the return array
    List<SqlParameter> parms = new List<SqlParameter>();
```

```
// @CustomerID from property ID
SqlParameter prmID = new SqlParameter("@CustomerID", SqlDbType.NChar, 5);
prmID.Value = item.ID;
parms.Add(prmID);

// @CompanyName from property CompanyName
SqlParameter prmName = new SqlParameter("@CompanyName", SqlDbType.NVarChar, 40);
prmName.Value = item.CompanyName;
parms.Add(prmName);

// @Address from property AddressInfo.Street
SqlParameter prmAddress = new SqlParameter("@Address", SqlDbType.NVarChar, 60);
prmAddress.Value = item.AddressInfo.Street;
parms.Add(prmAddress);

// @City from property AddressInfo.City
SqlParameter prmCity = new SqlParameter("@City", SqlDbType.NVarChar, 15);
prmCity.Value = item.AddressInfo.City;
parms.Add(prmCity);

// @Region from property AddressInfo.Region
SqlParameter prmRegion = new SqlParameter("@Region", SqlDbType.NVarChar, 15);
prmRegion.Value = item.AddressInfo.Region;
parms.Add(prmRegion);

// @PostalCode from property AddressInfo.ZipCode
SqlParameter prmZip = new SqlParameter("@PostalCode", SqlDbType.NVarChar, 10);
prmZip.Value = item.AddressInfo.ZipCode;
parms.Add(prmZio);

// @Country from property AddressInfo.Country
SqParameter prmCountry = new SqlParameter("@Country", SqlDbType.NVarChar, 15);
pmCountry.Value = item.AddressInfo.Country;
parms.Add(prmCountry);

    :
    :

return parms.ToArray();
}
```

Members of the *Customer* type are mapped to parameters for the SQL statement or stored procedure. In other words, the state of an object has been serialized to a tuple of values. The same happens the other way around when you run a query: from a tuple of values the data mapper builds an object.

Want to see a more real-world scenario of type-to-table bridging? Read on.

> **Note** How well designed is your database? The preceding code assumed we were using a database like Northwind, which certainly doesn't represent a best practice for its lack of normalization at various points. In Northwind, address information is stored in the Customers table. A well-designed database might present a more normalized form where customer's name information is stored in one table while the address information is stored in another. The domain model might feature an *AddressInfo* structure, regardless of the details of the physical database tables. If you change the structure of tables, you don't update the domain model; instead, you focus your changes in the data mapper. In any other scenario for the BLL, you have to enter changes to the business components.

Cross-Table Operations

What if the user triggers an action that results in the insertion of an order? An *Order* class is likely to contain a bunch of order items, which likely requires you to operate on multiple tables. Another realistic scenario for operating on multiple tables is when the same entity is fragmented on a variety of tables—for example, because the (legacy) database has a limited page size and/or because tables have grown over the years beyond the page size and you've been forced to add new related tables.

In any case, in a data mapper method you might need to run multiple operations. Here's an example:

```
public virtual void Create(Order order)
{
    // Insert order in the Orders table
    SqlHelper.ExecuteNonQuery(ProviderHelper.ConnectionString,
                CommandType.Text,
                this._cmdinsertOrder,
                this.BuildParamsFromEntity(order));

    // Insert individual order items in the OrderItems table
    foreach(OrderItem item in order.OrderItems)
    {
        SqlHelper.ExecuteNonQuery(ProviderHelper.ConnectionString,
                CommandType.Text,
                this._cmdinsertOrderItem,
                this.BuildParamsFromEntity(order));
    }
}
```

Note SQL Server 2008 comes with a nice feature that can help optimize the preceding code—Table Value Parameters (TVPs). TVPs allow you to pass user-defined tables of data as an argument to a query or a stored procedure. Instead of having the query take a long list of parameters, you simply pass just one parameter–a TVP. In a stored procedure, you still query the TVP for data and then operate as usual with scalar data. So a TVP is not going to transform SQL Server—neither in an object-oriented DBMS, nor in an O/RM. Using a TVP is an excellent way to write simpler and more effective ADO.NET code that targets SQL Server 2008. Note that to use a TVP, you should indicate a special parameter type—precisely, *SqlDbType.Structured*—and have it defined in the database. A TVP is a temporary table saved to Tempdb.

There a few points to consider here—first, roundtrips to the database. For *N* order items, you get *N+1* roundtrips to the database. Can you make it a single batch of SQL statements? That's really hard to do with a stored procedure or embedded SQL. It's definitely a possibility if you generate the SQL code dynamically. (By the way, using dynamic SQL is just what O/RM tools do. See later text for more details.)

Another point relates to the (re)use of connections. If you use *SqlHelper*, as we did earlier, you pick up a new connection from the pool (or create a new connection if no pooling is enabled) every time you run a command. You can optimize this by creating a connection object at the beginning of the method and using that for all subsequent calls within the method. This is not an option, however, if your fragmented entity spans different databases. In this case, the best you can do is try to minimize the number of connections to the extent that it is possible.

Finally, you need the operation to occur within the boundaries of a transaction. In this case, where should you put the transaction boundaries? Certainly not in the SQL code. A better possibility is placing the transaction scope in the *Create* method:

```
public virtual void Create(Order order)
{
    using (TransactionScope tx = new TransactionScope())
    {
        // Your data access code here
        ⋮

        // Commit the transaction
        tx.Complete();
    }
}
```

However, the whole topic of transactionality requires a broader approach in the context of a DAL. We'll get to that in the upcoming "Implementing Transactional Semantics" section.

Implementing Query Services

So far, we focused on going down to the database for writing. Let's see how to read and map result sets to a graph of objects. In particular, we'll focus on the creation of a query model that abstracts away SQL and gains you complete independence from a particular relational DBMS. Through the model, you design your queries as objects and then pass them on to a specific object that translates it to SQL.

> **Note** If the expression "query model" sounds a bit too abstract, consider that LINQ is nothing more than an "idiomatic" query model supplied by the latest C# and Visual Basic .NET compilers. As we saw in Chapter 3, an *idiom* is the technological counterpart of a design pattern. Put another way, an idiom is a design pattern hard-coded in a language and exposed through ad hoc syntax elements.

A Repository of Objects

In a world where data is managed via tuples, a query is essentially the act of processing a string of SQL against a set of database tables. If successful, the query gets you some tabular result sets back.

In a world where data is managed via objects, a query is the act of invoking a method on an object. The query gets back a collection of other objects. Returned objects can be built directly from a result set or picked up from some sort of intermediate cache, depending on the internal strategy of the repository. In an object-oriented world, you query using objects and get objects back. (See Figure 6-13.)

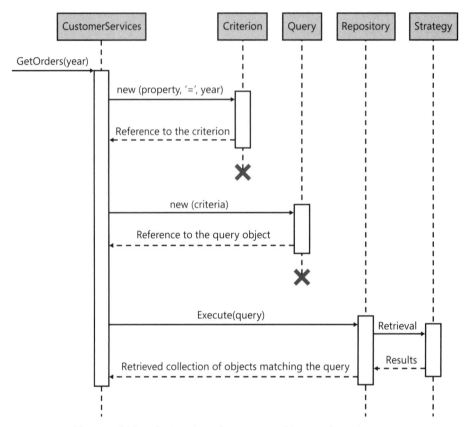

FIGURE 6-13 The overall idea of a repository for common objects and queries

The consumer of a DAL doesn't directly run a SQL query via ADO.NET or LINQ-to-SQL. (Nothing but the DAL should be touching any form of SQL or directly hitting a persistence repository.) The consumer of a DAL accesses a repository and specifies its search criteria. If the search is successful, it gets back a collection of objects that match the criteria. What happens inside of the repository is an implementation detail—it can be that a SQL command runs or the object is picked up from an internal cache.

Hold on, though! By saying "implementation detail" we *don't* mean that SQL is unimportant or not relevant. We basically mean that any access to the database—still executed through good SQL code—is not your primary concern, at least not at this stage. You have a model to represent the application's domain, and you need to have a query model to interrogate it.

If the domain model is mapped to a set of tables, you need to map your query model to a set of SQL statements (or stored procedures) that retrieve proper result sets and map them to proper objects.

If you're building the DAL yourself, as we're trying to do in this section, you write your repository class. If you're writing the DAL through an O/RM tool, you find a readymade repository in the programming model of the tool.

Implementing a Repository

The idea of a repository in the DAL is formalized in the Repository pattern, as defined on page 322 of [P of EAA]. In a nutshell, a repository is a class that exposes a bunch of query methods. Which methods? Methods as generic as *GetAll*, *GetByID*, and *GetCount*? Or methods as specific as *GetCustomersByCountry*, *GetOrdersByYear*, and *GetDiscontinuedProducts*?

Guess what? It depends.

In general, you might want to have general-purpose query methods in the repository, plus any specific query method that is *really* reused across the DAL. This is a point that deserves a bit of attention. Reusing a method is *not* like reusing a stored procedure. It makes sense to have a stored procedure like this in the database:

```
CREATE PROCEDURE [dbo].[getCustomersByCountry]
    @CountryID smallint
AS
BEGIN
    SET NOCOUNT ON;

    -- OK let us use * only for the sake of readability :)
    SELECT * FROM customers WHERE countryID=@CountryID
    ⋮

END
GO
```

It might not make the same sense to have a method in the repository that wraps the stored procedure. Why? Because of the returned values and, incidentally, because of the different abstraction level where methods and stored procedures live.

> **Note** By the way, the different abstraction level where methods and stored procedures live is, in our humble opinion, one of the reasons that ultimately arouses the debate around using O/RM tools for building a data access layer. Database guys seem to be unable to look outside the fence of stored procedures. Developers, on the other hand, seem to forget that there's still SQL running at the bottom of it.

Because methods encapsulate calls to SQL, the same stored procedure (or SQL statement) can be called from within two methods expecting significantly different outcomes. The stored procedure is reused, but the method is not. If you are unable to look beyond stored procedures, there's the concrete risk of flooding the repository with tons of methods doing essentially the same thing—calling a piece of SQL and then building the proper object graph to return.

This approach can be taken one step further: represent the query as an object, configure the query, and pass the query to the repository. And let the repository figure out how to serve you—either through direct database access or through cached results.

A query is, then, an instance of a generic *Query* class you add to the DAL assembly along with a class that represents a *Criterion* in a formal way. What about specific queries you know you'll be running frequently? Add a *GetCustomersByCountry* method that reuses an ad hoc query object and returns the expected results.

You can implement a repository class in various ways. It can be a unique *Repository* class, or it can be a type-specific *Repository<T>* class or even a *CustomerRepository* class. To keep it simple (and keeping it simple is always a good thing, unless proven otherwise), we opted for adding a bunch of methods to the *IDataMapper* interface. Here's the new version of the *IDataMapper* interface:

```
public interface IDataMapper<T>
{
    // Persistence
    void Create(T item);
    void Update(T item);
    void Delete(T item);

    // Repository
    IList<T> GetAll();
    IList<T> GetAll(int index, int size);
    int GetCount();
    int GetCount(Query query);
    T GetByKey(object key);
    IList<T> GetByCriteria(Query query);
    IList<T> GetByCriteria(Query query, int index, int size);
    string TranslateQuery(Query query);
}
```

The few methods listed here represent the low-level tools we leverage to build the entire set of query services in the DAL.

 Note Is there anything important missing here? Well, for a real-world DAL, you should also consider adding a *GetByPropertyValue* to quickly filter by a property value. The method will take a property name, an operator, and a value and arrange a quick query based on a relatively simple and single *WHERE* clause. This is a fairly common requirement.

Basic Query Capabilities

If you look back at the definition of the *IDataContext* interface, you see that we have a set of query methods nearly identical to the methods we have in a type-specific mapper. This is not coincidental. The implementation of type-specific query methods in the upper level data context just falls down to the data mapper implementation, as shown here:

```
public abstract class BaseDataContext : IDataContext, IDisposable
{
    // Placeholder for a method that returns the actual data mapper
    protected abstract IDataMapper<T> GetDataMapper<T>();
    ⋮

    public IList<T> GetAll<T>() where T : class, new()
    {
        return GetDataMapper<T>().GetAll();
    }

    public IList<T> GetAll<T>(int index, int size) where T : class, new()
    {
        return GetDataMapper<T>().GetAll(index, size);
    }

    public IList<T> GetByCriteria<T>(Query query) where T : class, new()
    {
        return GetDataMapper<T>().GetByCriteria(query);
    }

    public IList<T> GetByCriteria<T>(Query query, int index, int size)
            where T : class, new()
    {
        return GetDataMapper<T>().GetByCriteria(query, index, size);
    }

    public int GetCount<T>() where T : class, new()
    {
        return GetDataMapper<T>().GetCount();
    }

    public int GetCount<T>(Query query) where T : class, new()
    {
        return GetDataMapper<T>().GetCount(query);
    }

    public T GetByID(object id) where T : class, new()
    {
        return GetDataMapper<T>().GetByKey(id);
    }
    ⋮
}
```

So the real magic happens within the data mapper implementation. Let's take a look at a possible data mapper implementation for basic queries for the *Customer* type in the realm of a SQL Server database:

```
namespace ManagedDesign.App.DAL
{
    internal class CustomerDataMapper : IDataMapper<Customer>
```

```csharp
{
    // NOTE: plain SQL statements in the class
    private static readonly string _cmdSelectAll = "...";
    private static readonly string _cmdSelectByID = "...";
    private static readonly string _cmdSelectCount = "...";
    ⋮

    public virtual Customer GetByKey(object id)
    {
        // BTW, this is an instance of the Special Case pattern
        Customer customer = new UnknownCustomer();

        // Prepare parameters
        SqlParameter prmID = new SqlParameter("@ID", SqlDbType.NChar, 5);
        prmID.Value = id;
        SqlDataReader reader = SqlHelper.ExecuteReader(
                    ProviderHelper.ConnectionString,
                    CommandType.Text,
                    this._cmdSelectByID,
                    new SqlParameter[] { prmID });

        if (reader.Read())
                customer = BuildEntityFromRawData(reader);
        reader.Close();
        return customer;
    }

    public virtual int GetCount()
    {
        int count = (int) SqlHelper.ExecuteScalar(
                    ProviderHelper.ConnectionString,
                    CommandType.Text,
                    this._cmdSelectCount);
        return count;
    }

    public virtual IList<Customer> GetAll()
    {
        List<Customer> customers = new List<Customer>();
        SqlDataReader reader = SqlHelper.ExecuteReader(
                    ProviderHelper.ConnectionString,
                    CommandType.Text,
                    this._cmdSelectAll);
        while (reader.Read())
        {
            customers.Add(BuildEntityFromRawData(reader));
        }
        reader.Close();
        return customers;
    }

    public virtual IList<Customer> GetAll(int index, int size)
    {
        List<Customer> customers = new List<Customer>();
        SqlDataAdapter adapter = new SqlDataAdapter(this._cmdSelectAll,
```

```
                    ProviderHelper.ConnectionString);
    DataSet ds = new DataSet();
    adapter.Fill(ds, index, size, "Customers");
    DbDataReader reader = ds.Tables["Customers"].CreateDataReader();

    while (reader.Read())
    {
        customers.Add(BuildEntityFromRawData(reader));
    }

    reader.Close();
    return customers;
}
    ⋮
}
}
```

As you can see, implementing a set of query methods is mostly a matter of writing some ADO.NET code that works on top of some good SQL statements and stored procedures. The object-oriented layer we have in our context requires that you load tuples of data received through result sets as transformed into more manageable objects. This is the main purpose of the helper method *BuildEntityFromRawData*:

```
protected virtual Customer BuildEntityFromRawData(DbDataReader reader)
{
    Customer customer = new Customer();
    customer.ID = (string) reader["CustomerID"];
    customer.CompanyName = (string) reader["CompanyName"];
    customer.AddressInfo.Street = reader["Address"] is DBNull
                            ? string.Empty : (string) reader["Address"];
    customer.AddressInfo.City = reader["City"] is DBNull
                            ? string.Empty : (string) reader["City"];

    ⋮

    return customer;
}
```

In your implementation of the DAL, you are welcome to use plain ADO.NET, but you can also use some higher level libraries such as Microsoft's Data Access Application Block, which is where the *SqlHelper* class comes from. (See *http://msdn.microsoft.com/en-us/library/cc309504.aspx* for more information.)

What about paging?

Without beating around the bush, we'll say that paging is a hard thing to do without compromises. In a DBMS-specific scenario, you typically write ad hoc SQL statements or stored procedures that use DBMS-specific features, such the *ROWNUM* clause in SQL Server 2005 and newer versions. (Although this clause was only recently introduced in SQL Server, a similar feature has existed in Oracle for a much longer time.) You can then use the *SqlHelper*'s *ExecuteReader* method to get a data reader and load data into in-memory objects.

In the sample code, we opted for a different approach in order to make a different point. In the paged version of *GetAll*, we used a special overload of the data adapter's *Fill* method. The method takes a nonpaging statement, loads it all, and then discards what doesn't fit in the specified range of records. In the abstract, it is not certainly an optimal approach. However, it is much easier to write and maintain.

This point takes us to an age-old debate in the ADO.NET community—*DataSets* vs. data readers.

The bottom line is that, to fill a *DataSet*, an adapter uses a data reader, loads the result set into a *DataSet*, and returns the *DataSet* to the caller. Next, the caller takes data out of the *DataSet* and copies it into another object. So a direct use of the data reader is always faster. Period. Using a *DataSet* generates code that is easier to read, write, and maintain. Period.

Is this a definitive and absolute statement in favor of using data readers? Not necessarily. Not all applications are so sensitive to performance that they feel sick if a few milliseconds are lost. In most cases, using a *DataSet* instead of a data reader doesn't make any difference to users. Sure, you might have heard that data readers give you, say, a 300 percent performance boost over *DataSets*. OK, but what is the advantage in absolute terms of milliseconds? In our experience, most of the time you can afford a solution that is slightly slower but more maintainable. But this is also not a definitive and absolute statement.

As usual, it depends.

 Note If you're using a TS or TM model, you're probably stuck with *DataSets* and *DataTables*. Now consider memory thrashing. If you're on a loaded system and using *DataTables* as intermediate throw-away objects, you're thrashing memory. And this is bad. Now consider a repository that does some caching. The *DataTable* isn't such a bad idea considering its ability to record changes and upload only those changes to the database when asked. This is a good thing. This said, it always depends.

Query by Criteria

A query system based only on *GetAll*, *GetCount*, and *GetByID* is not realistic, although these are exceptionally handy shortcuts. Let's add a structured and flexible mechanism to generate queries dynamically. Enter the *Query* class.

A query is essentially a collection of criteria, members, and order clauses. Here's an excerpt of the class *Query* from the companion source code:

```
public sealed class Query
{
    private List<Criterion> _criteria = new List<Criterion>();
    private List<Members> _members = new List<Member>;
    private IList<OrderClause> _orderClauses = new List<OrderClause>();
```

```
    public List<Criterion> Criteria
    {
        get { return _criteria; }
    }

    public List<OrderClause> OrderClauses
    {
        get { return _orderClauses; }
    }

    public List<Members> Members
    {
        get { return _members; }
    }

}
```

The collection *Members* contains all the members in the class being queried to be added to the result set. The collection *Criteria* lists the conditions for the WHERE clause. Finally, the collection *OrderClauses* indicates how to sort the content. You are pretty much free with respect to the definition of the query model. As an example, here's a possible implementation for the *Criterion* class.

A criterion is essentially an aggregation of three pieces of information: a property name, a value, and an operator to relate both.

```
public class Criterion
{
    public string PropertyName {get; set;}
    public object Value {get; set;}
    public CriteriaOperator Operator {get; set;}
}
public enum CriteriaOperator
{
    Equal, NotEqual, GreaterThan, LessThan, Like, ...
}
```

Note that the query is entirely declarative and completely independent from any SQL dialect. To execute the query, you certainly need to translate it to a particular DBMS. However, this responsibility doesn't logically belong to the *Query* class itself. It is rather the task of a data mapper–specific method—for example, *TranslateQuery*.

```
public string TranslateQuery(Query query)
{
    // Generate some DBMS-specific SQL code that represents
    // the logical content of the given query object

    :

}
```

Here's how to put it all together in the *GetByCriteria* method that callers invoke through the repository:

```
public IList<Customer> GetByCriteria(Query query, int index, int size)
{
    // Generate the SQL command based on the query object
    string command = TranslateQuery(query);

    // Execute the query and return a collection of Customer objects
    return GetSelectedCustomers(command, index, size);
}

private IList GetSelectedCustomers(string command, int index, int size)
{
    List<Customer> customers = new List<Customer>();
    SqlDataAdapter adapter = new SqlDataAdapter(command,
            ProviderHelper.ConnectionString);
    DataSet ds = new DataSet();
    adapter.Fill(ds, index, size, "Customers");
    DbDataReader reader = ds.Tables["Customers"].CreateDataReader();

    while (reader.Read())
    {
        customers.Add(BuildEntityFromRawData(reader));
    }

    reader.Close();
    return customers;
}
```

The beauty of *GetByCriteria* is that you generate SQL dynamically and in a way that is optimized for the underlying DBMS. However, the majority of developers don't have to deal with SQL. Only a small team of SQL gurus can work on it. They receive input coded in the members of a class and write the best-ever SQL code for the scenario.

Being generated dynamically, the SQL code is something that can be adapted to any run-time condition and, as such, is on average more effective than any possible hard-coded stored procedure. (We'll return to this point soon.)

> **Note** Obviously, the query model can't address all possible query scenarios. Based on your mapping logic, it can perhaps include JOINs, but not GROUP BY and other more sophisticated statements. Quite simply, when you have a scenario that your handmade DAL (or even an O/RM) can't handle properly, you just fall back to the old-faithful SQL. In this case, you typically write a stored procedure and create in the repository a wrapper method for the hard-coded SQL. Nobody will blame you for doing this.

Implementing Transactional Semantics

A business transaction is any sequence of operations that involve the domain model and the business logic. Most of the time, a business transaction is coordinated by classes in the service layer. If you have domain logic organized according to the Transaction Script pattern (which is discussed in Chapter 4), you match a business transaction to a method on some class that provides a physical transactional boundary, if any is required.

With domain logic organized according to the Table Module or Active Record pattern, you reason in terms of tables—although the data (and therefore the model itself) is represented using different data containers. A business transaction, therefore, is a sequence of operations on your objects. You need to track changes to these objects and decide when it is time for those changes to be saved to the storage. There are a number of reasons for grouping operations together. One is certainly performance—handling numerous small changes to the database can be problematic in a production scenario. Another reason is the functional requirement of having an application that works when occasionally connected to the rest of the system.

In a DAL based on typed *DataSets* or an Active Record framework (for example, LINQ-to-SQL), the framework itself provides you with the ability to make changes in memory and then persist them back to the storage at a later time. This is the purpose of ADO.NET Batch Update, for example. But it is also one of the key capabilities of the LINQ-to-SQL's *DataContext* class.

What if you have a handmade DAL and a completely customized domain model? Unless you use an O/RM tool, you have to create your own framework for handling business transactions. Another fancy name for this concept is *unit of work (UoW)*, and there's a pattern associated with it. (See page 184 of [P of EAA].) Figure 6-14 shows a diagram for a unit of work.

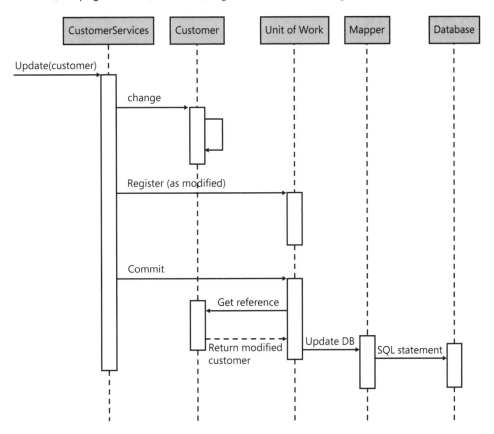

FIGURE 6-14 The unit of work in action

Defining a Unit of Work

In our initial definition of the *IDataContext* interface, we reserved a section for the transactional semantics:

```
public interface IDataContext : IDisposable
{
    // Transaction management
    bool IsInTransaction { get; }
    bool IsDirty { get; }
    void BeginTransaction();
    void Commit();
    void Rollback();
    ⋮
}
```

The preceding members of the interface endow the data context object with the capabilities for creating transactions around individual persistence operations, as well as creating sequences of persistence operations. Here's how to extend the data context class to support units of work:

```
public abstract class BaseDataContext : IDataContext, IDisposable
{
    // Template method implemented by derived classes
    protected abstract void ExecuteScheduledAction(ScheduledAction action);

    // Stores the actions that form the unit of work
    List<ScheduledAction> _uow = new List<ScheduledAction>();

    // State of the unit of work
    protected bool _isInTransaction = false;
    protected bool _isDirty = false;

    public virtual bool IsDirty
    {
        get {return _isDirty;}
        private set {_isDirty = value;}
    }

    public virtual bool IsInTransaction
    {
        get {return _isInTransaction;}
        private set {_isInTransaction = value;}
    }

    ⋮

    public void Add(object item)
    {
        if (item == null)
        {
            throw new ArgumentNullException();
        }

        ScheduledAction action = new ScheduledAction(item, ActionType.Create);
        ProcessAction(action);
    }
```

```
    public void Save(object item)
    {
        if (item == null)
        {
            throw new ArgumentNullException();
        }

        ScheduledAction action = new ScheduledAction(item, ActionType.Update);
        ProcessAction(action);
    }

    public void Delete(object item)
    {
        if (item == null)
        {
            throw new ArgumentNullException();
        }

        ScheduledAction action = new ScheduledAction(item, ActionType.Delete);
        ProcessAction(action);
    }
    :
}
```

Even from an incomplete code snippet, you should be able to see the point. All persistence operations are now executed by a scheduler. Each action is wrapped by an instance of the *ScheduledAction* class and passed on to the DAL scheduler. In turn, the DAL scheduler will figure out whether the DAL is working transactionally and either add the action for a later commit or execute it immediately against the database.

Scheduled Actions

The *ScheduledAction* class is a class that represents an action to take on an entity object:

```
public class ScheduledAction
{
    private object _target;
    private ActionType _type;

    public enum ActionType
    {
        Create,
        Delete,
        Update
    }

    public ScheduledAction(object target, ActionType type)
    {
        this._target = target;
        this._type = type;
    }
```

```
    public object Target
    {
        get { return _target; }
    }

    public ActionType Type
    {
        get { return _type; }
    }
}
```

Each persistence method calls into an internal method of the data context class named *ProcessAction*. This is the place where the data context determines whether the DAL is operating transactionally or not.

```
private void ProcessAction(ScheduledAction action)
{
    // If we're within a business transaction, schedule the action for later
    if (this._isInTransaction)
    {
        _uow.Add(action);
    }
    else  // If we're not in a business transaction, schedule the action for now
    {
        using (TransactionScope tx = new TransactionScope())
        {
            this.ExecuteScheduledAction(action);
            tx.Complete();
        }
    }
}
```

If the data context is within a transaction, any persistence action is scheduled for later execution. If the data context is not working transactionally, any actions execute immediately. Even when executed immediately, the action goes within a database transaction to group together possible cross-table operations.

All the code shown so far belongs to the base data context class, except the method *ExecuteScheduledAction*. Declared protected and abstract, this method is actually implemented by a DBMS-specific data context class. Here's a SQL Server example:

```
protected override void ExecuteScheduledAction(ScheduledAction action)
{
    // Execute the action on type Customer
    if (action.Target.GetType() == typeof(Customer))
    {
        Customer target = (Customer) action.Target;
        IDataMapper<Customer> mapper = new CustomerDataMapper();
        switch (action.Type)
        {
            case ScheduledAction.ActionType.Create:
                mapper.Create(target);
                break;
```

```
            case ScheduledAction.ActionType.Delete:
                mapper.Delete(target);
                break;
            case ScheduledAction.ActionType.Update:
                mapper.Update(target);
                break;
        }
    }

    // Execute the action on type Order
    else if (action.Target.GetType() == typeof(Order))
    {
        Order target = (Order) action.Target;
        IDataMapper<Order> mapper = new OrderDataMapper();
        switch (action.Type)
        {
            case ScheduledAction.ActionType.Create:
                mapper.Create(target);
                break;
            case ScheduledAction.ActionType.Delete:
                mapper.Delete(target);
                break;
            case ScheduledAction.ActionType.Update:
                mapper.Update(target);
                break;
        }
    }
    ⋮
}
```

When the DAL works in transaction mode—that is, the *IsInTransaction* property returns true—any persistence action is scheduled for later execution. More pragmatically, this means that a reference to the action is stored in an internal collection of *ScheduledAction* objects. Let's see how to start and commit business transactions.

Managing DAL Transactions

The consumer of the DAL decides whether it wants to execute some operations transactionally. When this is the case, it merely informs the data context of the intention. The method *BeginTransaction* exists precisely for this purpose:

```
// This class is "typically" invoked by the presentation
public class CustomerServices
{
    private IDataContext _context = null;

    public CustomerServices()
    {
        IDalFactory factory = new DalFactory();
        this._context = factory.GetDataContext();
    }
```

```
// Execution of this method is typically bound to a UI event
public void AddOrder(Order order)
{
    _context.BeginTransaction();
    _context.Add(order);

       ⋮

    _context.Commit();
}
}
```

Any call to data context methods—such as *Add, Delete,* and *Save*—are tracked through the list of *ScheduledAction* objects and eventually processed when the consumer invokes *Commit*:

```
public void BeginTransaction()
{
    if (this._isInTransaction)
        throw new InvalidOperationException();
    else
    {
        this._isInTransaction = true;
        _uow.Clear();
    }
}

public void Commit()
{
    if (!this.IsInTransaction)
    {
        throw new InvalidOperationException();
    }
    else
    {
        foreach (ScheduledAction action in actions)
        {
            Object target = action.Target;
            if (target == null)
            {
                throw new InvalidOperationException();
            }
        }

        using (TransactionScope tx = new TransactionScope())
        {
            _uow.ForEach(
                delegate(ScheduledAction action) {
                    this.ExecuteScheduledAction(action); }
            );
            tx.Complete();
        }

        this._isInTransaction = false;
        _uow.Clear();
    }
}
```

```
public void Rollback()
{
    if (!this._isInTransaction)
        throw new InvalidOperationException();
    else
    {
        this._isInTransaction = false;
        _uow.Clear();
    }
}
```

The Unit of Work pattern is hard to avoid in the real world, and the primary reason is simply that often more than one database action needs to be included in the same transaction. The UoW pattern makes this necessity easier to code for. After you set up the DAL to support UoW, you have all the information you need in a single place. In addition, the overall design of your code, far from becoming too abstract—as the use of such a pattern might suggest at first—gets surprisingly clear and easy to maintain and evolve.

Implementing Uniquing and Identity Maps

Tightly related to the concept of a unit of work is the idea of *uniquing*, which is typically obtained by implementing the Identity Map (IM) pattern as discussed on page 195 of [P of EAA]. During a unit of work, you typically want to avoid duplicates of the same object—for example, you don't want to have two *Customer* objects referencing the data from the same database record. For this reason, your DAL maintains a list of objects you have retrieved, and it consults this list whenever a domain object is requested of it.

Getting Unique Objects

The IM pattern is defined as a map that keeps track of all objects read from the database. The purpose is to return to callers an existing instance instead of running a new query. The identity map is hidden in the finder object that exposes query services—a repository, the data context class, or both. A schema for an identity map is shown in Figure 6-15.

If the finder can get the requested object directly from the map, that's fine. Otherwise, it gets a reference to the object from the database and then it saves the reference into the map for further requests. Here's a revised implementation of the *GetByID* method in the base data context class that uses an identity map:

```
public abstract class BaseDataContext : IDataContext, IDisposable
{
    private IdentityMap _identityMap = new IdentityMap();
    ⋮

    public T GetByID<T>(object key) where T : class, new()
    {
        // Attempt to retrieve the object from the map
        T item = (T) _identityMap.GetObject(typeof(T), key);
```

```
        // If the object is not available, obtain it and store
        // the new reference in the map
        if (item == null)
        {
            item = GetDataMapper<T>().GetByKey(key);
            _identityMap.PutObject(item, key);
        }

        // Return the object
        return item;
    }
}
```

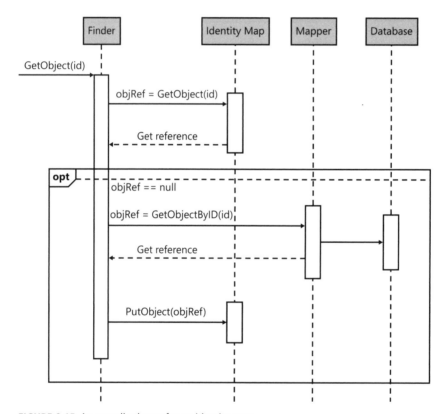

FIGURE 6-15 An overall schema for an identity map

The identity map should be used everywhere in the DAL where you have a piece of code that gains access to an object. All *GetXxx* methods should first check the identity map if you have one.

Implementing an Identity Map

In terms of implementation, an identity map is often implemented using a pair of nested dictionaries. The outermost dictionary uses the type of the object as its key. The value is another (child) dictionary, which represents the identity map for the given type. The child dictionary uses the primary key of the object as its key, whereas the value is the actual object reference.

An identity map is often implemented using a hash table. The reason is that a hash table is the data container with the fastest access time to a contained object. A hash table, in fact, is based on a hash algorithm according to which, once you know the key of an object, you can access the stored object in a constant time, $O^{(1)}$, regardless of the size of the table. (In this regard, a hash table is a much better choice than an array or a classic collection.)

The following code snippet shows a sample implementation for an identity map:

```
public class IdentityMap
{
    private Hashtable _mappedTypes = new Hashtable();

    public IdentityMap()
    {
    }

    public object GetObject(Type t, object key)
    {
        // Get the map for the specified type
        Hashtable map = GetMapForType(t);

        // Return the content for the specified key
        return map[key];
    }

    public void PutObject(object item, object key)
    {
        // Get the type for the object
        Type t = item.GetType();

        // Get the map for the specified type
        Hashtable map = GetMapForType(t);

        // Add the object to the hash table
        map[key] = item;
    }

    private Hashtable GetMapForType(Type t)
    {
        // Try to find the map from the current list
        Hashtable map = (Hashtable) _mappedTypes[t];

        // If no map is found, create a new one
        if (map == null)
        {
            // Add a new entry to the hash table for the specified type
            Hashtable newMap = new Hashtable();
            _mappedTypes[t] = newMap;
            map = newMap;
        }

        return map;
    }
}
```

The identity map is *not* related to smart forms of data loading (for example, lazy loading) and is *not* necessarily related to caching and the use of a cache as a form of optimization.

Uniquing Is Not Like Caching

To understand the role (and importance) of an identity map, let's set the clock back to ten years ago and consider how, at that time, a business object (BO) would have implemented a unit of work against a database. We have the following steps:

1. The BO begins a transaction.

2. The BO gets the record from the Customers table where the ID column matches a value of 1234.

3. The BO proceeds and executes a long list of essential operations.

4. The BO updates the record on the Customers table with an ID of 1234.

5. The BO proceeds and executes another long list of essential operations.

6. The BO commits the transaction.

The following facts come as no surprise:

- A second, concurrent unit of work that fetches record 1234 before the first unit of work reaches step 6 would get the original, unmodified values from the database.

- Within the same transaction, if the BO fetches record 1234 beyond step 4, it would get modified values that have not been committed to the database yet.

Let's see how the unit of work would execute in a Domain Model scenario:

1. The consumer orders the DAL to begin a new transaction.

2. The consumer instructs the DAL to retrieve an instance of the *Customer* class for an ID of 1234. The DAL looks up the identity map and finds it empty. Next, the DAL queries the database, builds a *Customer* object for record 1234, and adds a reference to the object to a private list known as the identity map.

3. The consumer proceeds and executes a long list of essential operations.

4. The consumer orders the DAL to update the *Customer* object with an ID of 1234.

5. The consumer proceeds and executes a long list of essential operations.

6. The consumer orders the DAL to commit.

What happens if a concurrent unit of work attempts to read Customer 1234 before the first unit of work has reached step 6?

This concurrent unit of work would ask its own instance of the DAL to retrieve Customer 1234. This instance of the DAL has its own (probably empty) identity map, at which time the second DAL instance will likely go to the database for the query. The consumer would then receive original, unmodified values from the database.

What if, within the same business transaction, the consumer once again needs to fetch Customer 1234? If an identity map is in place, the existing reference to the *Customer* object is returned. If the request comes beyond step 4, the consumer receives the updated *Customer* object.

As the name suggests, the primary purpose of an identity map is to ensure that unique in-stances of domain objects are managed within a single business transaction. And a business transaction is implemented through the unit of work DAL interface.

If you want, you can still say that IM gives you a sort of cache. But it is a cache with a very short duration—the business transaction—and with limited performance benefits. How many times will you fetch the same *Customer* in the same business transaction? It is extremely un-likely that you need to fetch the same object more than once.

> **Note** The certainty of having just one domain object to reference the same physical chunk of data in a business transaction makes your DAL neater and inherently more consistent. It also might add some benefits in terms of performance but, as mentioned, that is a secondary point.
>
> When using the Identity Map pattern, you should ensure that two objects are considered to be equal by using an algorithm based on their content. For this reason, it is recommended that you override in your domain classes the *Equals* and *GetHashCode* methods that all .NET Framework classes expose.
>
> *Equals* is used for explicit comparisons through the == operator. *GetHashCode* is used to ensure that objects with the same logical content are given the same hash code, which makes them the same when they are added to a hash table, as they are in the most common implementations of an identity map. To generate new content-based code, you normally use the primary key of the record to generate a hash.

An Identity Map Looks, Walks, and Quacks Like a Cache

Ultimately, an identity map is often perceived as a cache. The popular slogan of *duck typing* can be applied here, too. An identity map looks like a cache, walks like a cache, and quacks like a cache. But is it really a cache?

Again, the rigorous answer is no, but let's talk about it.

What is your definition of a cache? We think we could agree on the following definition. A cache is a collection of objects that have been computed earlier. The cache makes these objects available to code in a way that is faster than starting a new computation.

Admittedly, this definition applies perfectly to an identity map; so an identity map really looks, walks, and quacks like a cache.

The point is that the benefits you get in terms of performance from a real cache are significantly different from the performance benefits you get from an identity map. The main difference between a real cache (for example, the ASP.NET *Cache* object or even the ASP.NET page output cache) and an identity map is the duration.

An identity map should live for the time it takes to complete a business transaction. In many real-world implementations—such as LLBLGen Pro, Entity Framework, NHibernate, and LINQ-to-SQL—the identity map is not bound to a single business transaction. Put another way, the identity map is not released when the consumer commits the unit of work. It is, instead, bound to the data context and, as such, it lasts a little longer. An identity map is a short-lived object that just doesn't remove objects from memory like a canonical cache would do.

The data context object has different names in different frameworks, but the purpose is the same—and so it is with the internal implementation of the identity map. So *Context* (LLBLGen Pro), *ObjectContext* (Entity Framework), *Session* (NHibernate), and *DataContext* (LINQ-to-SQL) free the identity map when their instance is disposed of.

Different instances of the data context have their own identity map for their own uniquing purposes. If this looks like a cache to you, then OK—an identity map is a cache!

> **Note** Regarding application-level caches, an interesting platform developed by Microsoft is Velocity. Velocity is a distributed in-memory application cache platform for developing high-performance applications. Velocity can be used to cache any serializable Common Language Runtime (CLR) objects and provides an ad hoc API for access. Velocity can be configured to run as a service accessed over the network, or it can be run embedded within the application. If you think you need a serious platform for object caching within a DAL, Velocity is more than a custom implementation of an identity map, so it is perhaps the right way to go. For more information, read *http://msdn.microsoft.com/en-us/data/cc655792.aspx*.

Caching and Queries: A Not So Powerful Duo

Let's assume for a moment that you have set up a true and long-lasting cache in your DAL to avoid going back to the database over and over again. This is not an absolute guarantee of stunning performance.

With a cache in the middle, you first have to go through the cache to see whether the object, and often whether *all* the objects, you need are there. If any object is missing, you arrange a database query and then sync up the cache. And even when you find objects in the cache, you have to figure out whether or not they are stale (or assume they are not).

As you can see, there's a lot of extra work to do with a cache. This amount of work grows with the complexity of objects from a domain model and the ramifications of using them. And we are *not* considering here the possibility that the cache is located out of process.

There might be tricks, like versions or timestamps, to speed up the process of determining whether a given set of objects is already in the cache. In the end, you get real benefits from caching domain objects only when you cache simple objects (that is, those with no relationships like simple lookups) and when you can figure out quickly whether they work for you (or when you can safely assume they do). Using a timed cache, for example, might help because you can assume that if the object is in the cache, it is not stale.

Implementing Concurrency

When a lot of operations are performed in memory that could possibly end up updating the database, you have a potential problem—the consistency of the data for the application is at risk. Imagine that one user selects a chunk of data and modifies it in memory, but she's following a flow within the UI that retains changes for a longer time. At the same time, another user selects the same chunk of data but modifies it instantly. What *should* happen when the first user attempts to save her own copy of the same data to the same table?

As usual, the answer is, "It depends." And, in particular, it depends on your implementation of concurrency. First, it depends on whether or not you have support for concurrency. Moreover, this is *not* an unusual scenario, so consider concurrency early in your design.

Don't Worry, Be Optimistic

With the DAL we have outlined so far, no conflict would be raised. Both users will successfully update the database. However, because both are writing to the same record (or set of records, in general), the last set of changes overwrites the first set of changes. It is nothing more than the *last-win* policy. And it is the approach to concurrency that you get for free in any multiuser system.

If you're OK with this policy, you can jump to the next topic.

Ad hoc policies for concurrency and data conflicts are *not* a must in any application. Some entities might need concurrency protection, while others might not. Even within entities, some properties might need to deal with concurrency while others might not. Simply updating a product date or description might not affect other properties, such as quantity on hand or stocking location.

What's the solution? Quite simply, instead of just executing the SQL command to persist changes, you try to execute it under stricter conditions. In other words, you do not use the following code to update a product description:

```
UPDATE products SET description=@desc WHERE productID=@id
```

You use, instead, the following:

```
UPDATE products SET description=@desc
            WHERE productID=@id AND
                  description=@originalDescription
```

What's the difference? In the latter example, you also ensure that the content for the field you're going to update hasn't changed since your last read.

ADO.NET with DataSets, LINQ-to-SQL, and O/RM tools provide a built-in implementation for a pattern to handle data conflicts (much like they implement the Unit of Work pattern for you). This pattern is known as Optimistic Offline Lock (OOL), which is fully described on page 416 of [P of EAA]. How can you apply OOL to a custom domain model?

You need a specialized data mapper and an enhanced version of the entity class.

Specializing the Data Mapper

To handle optimistic concurrency, you need a data mapper that incorporates SQL commands with a longer WHERE clause so that it can check whether the record you're updating is still the same as the record you read earlier:

```
public class OolCustomerDataMapper : CustomerDataMapper
{
    private static readonly string _cmdUpdateCustomerOOL = " ... ";

    public override void Update(Customer item)
    {
        int rows = SqlHelper.ExecuteNonQuery(
                    ProviderHelper.ConnectionString,
                    CommandType.Text,
                    this._cmdUpdateCustomerOOL,
                    this.BuildParamsFromEntity(item));

        // Your failure policy here ...
        if (rows == 0)
            throw new ConcurrencyException();
    }
    :
    :
}
```

Needless to say, the UPDATE statement has a fairly long WHERE clause:

```
UPDATE Customers SET
    CompanyName=@CompanyName,
    ContactName=@ContactName,
    ContactTitle=@ContactTitle,
    :

    Fax=@Fax
WHERE
    CustomerID=@CustomerID AND
    CompanyName=@OriginalCompanyName AND
    ContactName=@OriginalContactName AND
    ContactTitle=@OriginalContactTitle AND
    :

    Fax=@OriginalFax
```

If the underlying record has been modified since it was initially read, the command fails and the number of affected rows returned by *ExecuteNonQuery* is zero. It is the only sign that something went wrong. It is up to the data mapper to degrade gracefully or, better, just throw an exception to outer layers of code.

Creating a Proxy for the Entity

As you can see from the source code of the optimistic SQL command, you need to know updated values to store in the table, as well as the original values upon which the code operated to make the changes in memory. Put another way, your entity class—say, *Customer*—must track original values side by side with current values.

Adding new properties to the *Customer* class in the domain model is a very bad idea. The domain model is a *model* for the *domain* and shouldn't be cluttered with implementation details like extra properties for OOL. How else would you handle concurrency issues, then?

You might want to create a proxy class for the entity, as shown here:

```
public CustomerProxy : Customer
{
    // Add extra properties
    public string OriginalID {get; set;}
    public string OriginalCompanyName {get; set;}
    public string OriginalAddressInfo {get; set;}
      ⋮
}
```

The proxy will be consumed by methods in the data mapper that deal with data serialization to and from the entity:

```
protected virtual Customer BuildEntityFromRawData(DbDataReader reader)
{
    CustomerProxy customer = new CustomerProxy();

    // Fill "standard" properties
    customer.ID = (string) reader["CustomerID"];
    customer.CompanyName = (string) reader["CompanyName"];
    customer.AddressInfo.Street = reader["Address"] is DBNull
                           ? string.Empty : (string) reader["Address"];
    customer.AddressInfo.City = reader["City"] is DBNull
                           ? string.Empty : (string) reader["City"];

      ⋮

    // Fill "original" properties
    customer.OriginalID = customer.ID;
    customer.OriginalCompanyName = customer.CompanyName;
    customer.OriginalAddressInfo.Street = customer.AddressInfo.Street;
    customer.OriginalAddressInfo.City = customer.AddressInfo.City;

      ⋮

    return customer;
}
```

```
protected virtual SqlParameter[] BuildParamsFromEntity(Customer customer)
{
    CustomerProxy item = (CustomerProxy) customer;

    List<SqlParameter> params = new List<SqlParameter>()

    // @CustomerID from property ID
    SqlParameter prmID = new SqlParameter("@CustomerID", SqlDbType.NChar, 5);
    prmID.Value = item.ID;
    params,Add(prmID);

    // @CompanyName from property CompanyName
    SqlParameter prmName = new SqlParameter("@CompanyName", SqlDbType.NVarChar, 40);
    prmName.Value = item.CompanyName;
    params,Add(prmName);

    // @Address from property AddressInfo.Street
    SqlParameter prmAddress = new SqlParameter("@Address", SqlDbType.NVarChar, 60);
    prmAddress.Value = item.AddressInfo.Street;
    params,Add(prmAddress);

    :

    // @CustomerID from property ID
    SqlParameter pOrigID = new SqlParameter("@OriginalCustomerID",
                                        SqlDbType.NChar, 5);
    prmOrigID.Value = item.OriginalID;
    params,Add(prmOrigID);

    // @CompanyName from property CompanyName
    SqlParameter prmOrigName = new SqlParameter("@OriginalCompanyName",
                                        SqlDbType.NVarChar, 40);
    prmOrigName.Value = item.OriginalCompanyName;
    params,Add(prmOrigName);

    // @Address from property AddressInfo.Street
    SqlParameter prmOrigAddress = new SqlParameter("@OriginalAddress",
                                        SqlDbType.NVarChar, 60);
    prmOrigAddress.Value = item.OriginalAddressInfo.Street;
    params,Add(prmOrigAddress);

    :

    return params.ToArray();
}
```

As you can see, the data mapper and the proxy include all columns in the table. What if you need to update only one column? Is checking the current content of only that column a form of optimization?

No. It is, rather, a conceptual mistake.

The idea behind OOL is that the DAL returns data to be presented to an end-user. That data represents a state of the application. The user makes some choices based on what she's presented. Those choices are then saved as changes to the database. When you apply these changes, you realize that something is different now in the database. This means that *potentially* the user would have made different choices, if only she had known about a different set of values.

Conceptually, therefore, the DAL should check the entire record and fail if a difference is found. Pragmatically, if you know that in a given situation a limited check is acceptable, code your way to that. But, keep in mind, that it is your deliberate choice.

Using a Timestamp Column

There's an alternative to using a long WHERE clause to ensure that the row you're editing is the same row you've loaded into the current object. You can add a new column to each table of the database and store there either a timestamp or a version number. At that point, the WHERE clause of an UPDATE statement will simply check the value of that column. Likewise, the value of the column will be updated during any writing operation.

Using an additional column for programming purposes requires a certain degree of access and freedom on the database. And for this reason, it might not be a practical solution every time. It is the most efficient approach if you can afford it.

Implementing Lazy Loading

When you ask your object model to return a *Customer* instance with a certain ID, what data would you expect it to contain?

For sure, the returned object will store personal information about the customer, but what about its relationships to, say, orders? And what about relationships between orders and order items, and so on? The more complex the object model, the more you risk pulling up a very large graph of objects.

Lazy loading indicates the DAL's ability to load only a portion of the object graph based on some rules. When you add this capability to your DAL, you have implemented the Lazy Load pattern (LL).

On-Demand Data Loading

Defined on page 200 of [P of EAA], the LL pattern refers to an object that doesn't hold all the data it needs, but knows how to retrieve it on demand. Applied to a domain model object such as *Customer*, this pattern enables you to enhance the original class with the ability to prioritize data. When you load an instance of a *Customer*, only essential data is loaded—for example, only personal information. Later, when some piece of code needs to go through orders associated with the customer, that information is located and loaded.

Lazy loading, though, expresses an idea that, when applied, provides a form of optimization. It simply says, "Hey, load the smallest amount of data that you're pretty much sure to use." Who defines what "smallest amount" means? And, more importantly, are we sure that the meaning of "smallest amount" is constant over time? The answers to these questions are dictated by the needs of your application. However, lazy loading as a pattern is a good one. Like all patterns, it should be tailored to your specific requirements. Figure 6-16 shows the typical behavior of a *Customer* class that supports lazy loading.

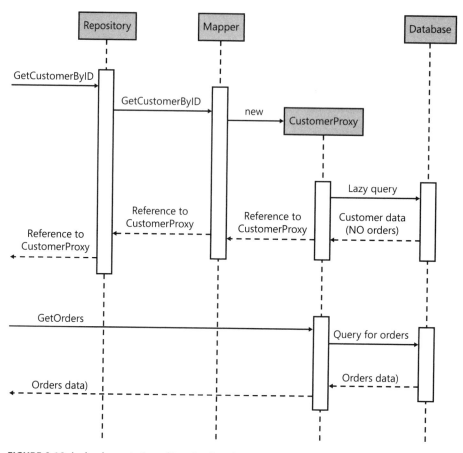

FIGURE 6-16 An implementation of lazy loading for the *Customer* class

The DAL consumer first makes a request for a *Customer* object. Through the repository and the data mapper, a SQL query is run to retrieve all the data the class should contain in accordance to the LL policy. This policy is hard-coded in a proxy class (more on this in a moment.) In other words, the requestor doesn't receive the "real" *Customer* class but a proxy to it, generated by an LL-enabled data mapper.

Let's say that the *Customer* proxy lacks any information on orders. When, later, the requestor asks for orders, the proxy takes care of invoking the mapper and runs an ad hoc query. Now the *Customer* proxy *also* contains order information.

Note Using proxy classes might give rise to an issue that you should be able to spot and deal with. The data mapper returns an instance of *CustomerProxy*, whereas the caller expects a *Customer*. Because *CustomerProxy* inherits from *Customer*, the compiler has nothing to complain about and the code works perfectly at run time. Why bring this up, then?

Here's why. The objects will not be the same. In particular, the issue can be raised by tests for equality between *Customer* objects you might have in the code. Logically, a *Customer* and a *CustomerProxy* that contain data from the same database record are the same. The CLR, though, recognizes two objects as equal only if they reference the same memory address. However, by overriding the *Equals* and *GetHashCode* methods on *Customer*, you can implement a new equality policy that looks at content rather than memory address. In this way, *Customer* and *CustomerProxy* instances will be the same if they reference the same database record.

Hard-Coded Fetch Plans

Lazy loading is tightly connected with the idea of a *fetch plan*. A fetch plan indicates your strategy to retrieve data within a class. If you hard-code the lazy-loading policy within a class, you have a static fetch plan. This is the most common idea associated with the expressions *lazy loading* or, in Microsoft's jargon, *deferred loading*.

A common way to implement lazy loading with a static fetch plan entails creating a proxy class for each entity intended to support LL. A static fetch plan indicates that the proxy class implements some rules to determine what is eagerly loaded and what is loaded in a deferred manner.

The proxy class is DBMS specific and definitely belongs to the DAL. A proxy class extends a domain model class, but it is not part of the domain model. It lives in the DAL assembly. Here's a sample proxy class for the *Employee* entity. The *Employee* entity includes a couple of properties that are little used and take up a lot of space—photos and personal notes. The idea, therefore, is to load these properties only on demand. Here's a sample proxy class:

```
internal public sealed class EmployeeProxy : Employee
{
    private bool _notesLoaded = false;
    private bool _photoLoaded = false;

    public override string Notes
    {
        get
        {
            string notes;
            if (!_notesLoaded)
            {
                EmployeeDataMapper mapper = new EmployeeDataMapper();
                notes = mapper.GetNotesByID(this.ID);
                _notesLoaded = true;

                // Caches notes for later use of the instance
                base.Notes = notes;
            }
```

```
            else
            {
                // If cached, just returns
                notes = base.Notes;
            }

            return notes;
        }

        set
        {
            base.Notes = value;
            _notesLoaded = true;
        }
    }

    public override Bitmap Photo
    {
        get
        {
            Bitmap photo;
            if (!_photoLoaded)
            {
                EmployeeDataMapper mapper = new EmployeeDataMapper();
                photo = mapper.GetPhotoByID(this.ID);
                _photoLoaded = true;

                // Caches photo for later use of the instance
                base.Photo = photo;
            }
            else
            {
                // If cached, just returns
                photo = base.Photo;
            }

            return photo;
        }

        set
        {
            base.Photo = value;
            _photoLoaded = true;
        }
    }
}
```

The *EmployeeProxy* class is marked *internal* because it is essentially an internal class. Shouldn't this be public instead, as at some point we are probably handing out an instance of it to the BLL? The *EmployeeProxy* class is never exposed to the outside world because the data mapper always casts it to *Employee*.

The proxy inherits from the domain model class and overrides a few properties to implement lazy loading. When any of these properties are requested, if data is not in memory, it is loaded through direct access to the database and cached for later use.

The data mapper has an active role in the implementation of LL, as it is the data mapper that returns an instance of the proxy instead of the original domain class, as shown here:

```
protected virtual Employee BuildEntityFromRawData(DbDataReader reader)
{
    // Create an instance of the object to return
    Employee employee = new EmployeeProxy();

    // Populate the object with eager-loading properties only
    employee.ID = (int) reader["EmployeeID"];
    employee.FirstName = (string) reader["FirstName"];
    employee.LastName = (string) reader["LastName"];
    ⋮

    // Lazy-loading properties are skipped

    return employee;
}
```

In general, you have one proxy class for each entity that supports lazy loading. This means that the proxy class determines in a static and fixed manner what is loaded eagerly and what goes into the lazy category. In a real-world DAL, this might be a limitation. Lazy loading is an important feature to have but, at the same time, you also need a mechanism to bypass it. A unique and static proxy class is not the ideal answer—it does lazy loading *always* and *always* on the same properties.

Having multiple proxies is not an attractive option either, as it leads straight to a proliferation of classes and sets up your worst maintenance nightmare.

In a perfect world, you would be able to specify on a per-query basis which properties you want to have available right away and which properties should be pulled up on demand. And always in this perfect world, you would be able to generate ad hoc proxy classes on the fly. This would be the configuration for a *dynamic fetch plan*.

Specifying a Dynamic Fetch Plan

We could even say that a serious implementation of lazy loading is not possible without support for a dynamically configurable fetch plan. So even though static proxies are effective, they probably address only a small number of scenarios.

The setup of a dynamic fetch plan is not exactly a walk in the park. It assumes a query model where you dynamically indicate which properties you want to load and under which conditions this should happen. The query model we presented earlier allows you to shape the query as an object, and it gives you the required level of flexibility. But this is only the first step.

Once you have successfully translated the query into SQL and run it, you get a data reader or a *DataTable*. The next step consists of loading the content of the data reader into a graph of objects. If you use objects from the domain model, the best you can do is fill only the properties for which the query can retrieve values. However, any access to empty (lazy) properties is destined to fail. And this is exactly where proxies fit in.

But how can you write a proxy class if the list of members to lazy-load is known only at runtime? This is the essence of a dynamic fetch plan.

In the perfect world we mentioned a moment ago, proxies are generated on the fly using *Reflection.Emit* to wed great performance and greatest flexibility. But using this rather advanced form of reflection is not trivial and, honestly, it is beyond the standard skills of the vast majority of developers.

The bottom line is that implementing by hand serious lazy loading with dynamic fetch plans requires a significant effort, which leads to a major point we'll develop further in a moment—a serious and well-built DAL looks and acts very much like an O/RM tool.

Note *Reflection.Emit* allows you to dynamically generate new types, methods, and even code at runtime. It is not a feature you would use every day, but it is a key ingredient for lazy loading (O/RM tools use it), mocking types, method interception to produce code metrics, proxying services, and implementing aspect-oriented programming (AOP) aspects.

In the .NET Framework, *Reflection.Emit* competes with CodeDOM generation. With CodeDOM, you have total control over the code and work at a higher level of abstraction, as you use classes to generate classes and code. However, you need to explicitly start a compile process either to disk or memory. And, more importantly, the generated assembly is closed and can't be further extended. With *Emit*, instead, you need to know Microsoft intermediate language (MSIL) because you are required to use it to specify the code. It is much faster, there's no need to compile, and the assembly you create can be extended with new types at any time.

Lazy Loading in Data Access APIs

Lazy loading with fetch plans exists in a number of data access APIs, but it comes in quite different forms. Let's briefly review them.

In ADO.NET, you find a very rudimentary form of lazy loading with no fetch plan support. The functionality all comes out of the data adapter's ability to sync up a given *DataSet* to reflect the current state of the database.

In NHibernate—one of the most popular O/RM tools—the support for lazy loading and fetch plans is total and top quality. You can change the fetch plan at runtime and for each query. For each query, all fields are eagerly loaded unless you mark them as lazy in the mapping file. Therefore, you can have, say, a *Customer* object with lazy loading enabled for its orders. In this case, any access to the *Orders* collection of the *Customer* object is resolved with a dynamic database query on demand.

In LINQ-to-SQL, lazy loading (referred to as *deferred loading*) can be enabled and disabled programmatically through a Boolean property—*DeferredLoadingEnabled*. When lazy loading is enabled, only the first level of the graph is processed by the query. For example, only customer information is loaded, not any orders for the customer and not any details for the orders. However, any subsequent access to orders is resolved correctly through a new database roundtrip. This happens automatically, and the developer doesn't even realize it. When you disable lazy loading, though, all the data you can access is data that has been loaded eagerly. You can control this amount of data using the *LoadWith* method on the *DataContext* class. Note that once you have disabled lazy loading, no attempt is ever made at a later time to grab any data not currently in memory. In other words, with *DeferredLoadingEnabled* set to *false*, you won't be able to retrieve *Orders* from an instance of the *Customer* class unless you specified a fetch plan through *LoadWith* that preloaded orders.

In ADO.NET Entity Framework 1.0 (EF), the situation is slightly different from LINQ-to-SQL. The main difference is that EF doesn't offer a Boolean *DeferredLoadingEnabled* property. Another difference with LINQ-to-SQL is that EF *never* loads for you any associated entities (say, orders for a customer) that haven't been explicitly subjected to eager loading. EF, in fact, offers a query builder that plays a role analogous to *LoadWith* in LINQ-to-SQL. EF allows you to load data as you go, but only through a specific method you have to invoke, say, every time you need to access orders for a customer. In a certain way, EF defers loading of missing data *ad infinitum* and never runs a query implicitly. The development team made this choice in EF version 1.0 in observance of the "No hidden network roundtrips" principle. EF provides you with a *Load* method on entity classes through which you can programmatically load any external data associated with a domain object. In this way, you can specify a fetch plan dynamically.

Power to the DAL with an O/RM Tool

Why should you write a DAL yourself? Is it because you have a strict nonfunctional requirement that explicitly prohibits the use of an O/RM? Or is it because you think you would craft *your* DAL better than any commercial O/RM tools?

In a domain-based world, a well-built DAL is nearly the same as a well-built O/RM tool. And an O/RM tool has a team of people (usually, very smart people) entirely devoted to that. They spend their working hours thinking about new features, experimenting, and receiving and processing feedback. Very few outside developers can compete with them.

In this book, we went through a handmade DAL for essentially two reasons. One reason was to give you a concrete idea of how it works and how to design it. As you saw, it's a nontrivial exercise. Another reason was to make it clear—in practice—that O/RM tools are an instrument naturally suited to building layered systems with a domain-driven approach.

Object/Relational Mappers

We identified four main responsibilities for a DAL: persistence, querying, managing transactions, and maintaining concurrency. At least the latter two responsibilities are general enough to be delegated to an ad hoc tool that has the appropriate capabilities. In our sample implementation of query services, we also came up with a rather generic interface—the Query Object pattern—the same pattern that an ad hoc tool can supply out of the box. The only area where handcrafted code might make some sense is in the area of data persistence. But the inherent power of O/RM tools helps to generalize persistence, too.

In the end, when opting for an O/RM tool, it is not like you are handing your house keys to a stranger. You are simply using a more advanced, automated tool.

Do I Really Need an O/RM Tool?

How do you start up your car? You probably turn the key or press a button. And under the hood, you release some power that activates the engine. Turning the key to release power is definitely a very simple and easy approach. It delivers you the expected results with minimum effort—you have, in the end, a high-level tool to leverage.

To release the power that starts the engine, you can also make some wires contact one another. This is a low-level approach that requires different skills and is within the reach of fewer drivers of automobiles. A low-level approach, however, is appropriate in particular scenarios. You play with wires if you're stealing a car or if, for whatever reason, the higher-level mechanism (key, button) is not working.

When it comes to building a DAL, the O/RM is your key (or button). It is a high-level tool for achieving your goal. If, for whatever reason, it doesn't work effectively, you can still look under the hood and "play with the wires."

So why shouldn't you just turn the key to start up your car? Why should you care about wires? Or, worse yet, would you really consider designing and crafting your own automobile ignition system?

If Only We Could Have an Object-Oriented DBMS

The primary purpose of an O/RM tool is for fighting off any object-relational impedance mismatch between your object model and its storage layer. Object-oriented databases (ODBMS) never captured the heart of the IT community; relational databases (RDBMS) are, therefore, the sole alternative. But an RDBMS stores its data as tuples of values.

Until a few years ago, layered systems primarily represented their own data using containers mirrored from RDBMS tables. In the .NET world, this is well described by *DataSets* and typed *DataSets*. From there, the evolution of layered systems quickly brought people—at different speeds depending on their skills and background—to consider a more conceptual approach to data representation. And this is where object models such as the Active Record pattern entered the picture.

From table-based models such as Active Record to domain-driven design (DDD), it was—to paraphrase Neil Armstrong descending the Apollo 11 lunar lander's platform—only a small, conceptual step, but a huge step in the design of a proper architecture. In DDD, you design a model for the domain first. And you do that in a way that is totally independent from storage and implementation considerations.

After you have the model, you have to persist it, though. And here's the mismatch between the object-oriented representation of data and the tuple-based, relational model of most commonly used DBMSs.

If you could use an ODBMS, things would be much easier. An ODBMS would provide built-in persistence, rich query services, transactions and concurrency, lazy loading, and identity maps. And maybe more. You would create the domain model and that would be it. There would be no friction between the domain model and data model. Figure 6-17 captures the point.

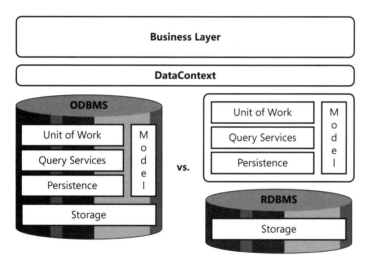

FIGURE 6-17 Object/relational impedance mismatch

In absence of impedance mismatch, you don't have to go through a formal Object/Relational mapping layer to persist a query of your objects. But either of the following two things happens:

- You do not use objects to express your domain, and you use an RDBMS for storage.
- You use objects to express your domain, but you use an ODBMS for storage.

The former approach delivers architectures in which the middle tier is based on (typed) *DataSets* and large portions of the business logic are isolated in business objects, when they are not buried for pseudo-performance reasons in stored procedures.

The need for a domain-based approach originates from the need to deal with the complexity of real-world scenarios. To tackle complexity, you need a domain-driven approach. And when you use such an approach, either you opt for an ODBMS or you introduce an O/R mapping layer.

Although some ODBMSs exist, we have never been fortunate enough to see one in any of our customers' sites. And we guess that many of you have had a similar experience. Ultimately, an ODBMS is a storage system that provides transparent persistence and transaction and query services for objects. Put another way, it is a high-performance O/RM tool built into the database platform. (See Figure 6-17.)

In an imperfect world where you have to deal with an RDBMS, an O/R mapping layer is a necessity, and certainly not a quirk. Where you need to make your decision is, if ever, on how you represent the domain logic. Once you have opted for an object-based representation, especially if it's a domain model, an O/R mapping layer is the natural offspring.

Creating an O/R Mapping Layer

In a scenario where you have to deal with O/R impedance mismatch, you have to create an O/R mapping layer. But how?

You can craft your own DAL and build into it the ability to persist objects, query objects, and access objects transactionally. This is doable, but it is definitely a lot of work. And, more importantly, of that huge amount of work, only a relatively small part of the effort is devoted to core business functionality. Most of the effort required is for general-purpose stuff such as managing transactions and writing to storage. You can call it a DAL, but it is in the end a more or less sophisticated O/R mapping layer.

To speed up development and provide a richer set of features, you can build the O/R mapping layer using a commercial or open-source O/RM tool.

An O/RM tool translates your object model into a form that can be stored to a relational database. At the same time, an O/RM tool offers an API to retrieve the same data from the database as a graph of objects. Relationships between objects and constraints are preserved in memory and in the database.

Sample O/RM Tools

What is the main benefit you get out of an O/RM tool? Essentially, productivity. Quite a few O/RM tools, both free and commercial, exist in the marketplace. Vendors have been working on such tools for years, and the level of sophistication of an average O/RM tool is currently far beyond the capabilities of a single team. (Not to mention that, for the team, persistence normally is more of a widespread concern than the primary focus.)

Table 6-2 lists a few popular O/RM tools currently available.

TABLE 6-2 Main O/RM Tools

O/RM	More Information
Entity Framework	*http://msdn.microsoft.com/en-us/library/bb399572.aspx*
EntitySpaces	*http://www.entityspaces.net*
Genome	*http://www.genom-e.com*
LINQ-to-SQL	*http://msdn.microsoft.com/en-us/library/bb386976.aspx*
LLBLGen Pro	*http://www.llblgen.com*
NHibernate	*http://www.nhibernate.org*

Using an O/RM tool will not necessarily give you extra days off. And an O/RM tool is *not exactly* a wizard or a rapid application development (RAD) instrument. It is still a programming tool, however, and a sophisticated one too. Using an O/RM tool can enhance your productivity as long as you know the tool and supply a well-built domain model.

> **Note** We've been using O/RM tools for years in larger projects. In particular, we used NHibernate for quite some time. Using an O/RM tool brought us a lot of benefits. However, we haven't been able to really quantify (and appreciate) it until, in a recent project, the customer had a requirement that we either use a Microsoft O/RM or build our own O/RM. At the time, Entity Framework was still a Beta product, so we had to create a custom O/RM. We shipped the project more or less on deadline, but it was a nightmare. Long live O/RM tools!

Using an O/RM Tool to Build a DAL

After you bring an O/RM tool into the project, you have a data context object out of the box. So you typically start using the API of the O/RM directly in the service layer. The O/RM, therefore, is your DAL. An O/RM tool is made of three main elements:

- An API for CRUD operations
- A query model plus an ad hoc query language to speed up the definition of most queries
- An API for mapping metadata (such as classes to tables or properties to columns)

CRUD operations and the query model are typically exposed out of a root object, which plays the role of the data context class (such as the *SqlServerDataContext* class) we created earlier in the chapter.

Each O/RM product has its own data context object, and each product gives this data context object a different name and nearly the same capabilities. For example, the data context object is named *Session* in NHibernate and *ObjectContext* in ADO.NET Entity Framework (EF). In the remainder of the section, we'll go through the main points of using an O/RM to build a DAL, mostly focusing on NHibernate, but also touching on EF.

> **Note** NHibernate is an open-source product that can be considered to be the current *de facto* standard for O/RM tools. A number of other great commercial products are available—for example, LLBLGen Pro—but NHibernate, maybe because it is free and because of its overall feature set, has many users and a lot of credibility in the industry.
>
> What about EF? We bet that EF has a bright future, but it probably does not rank with the best in its current form (because it is version 1.0). There are some good things in EF, but currently EF does not cover what developers have come to expect from other O/RMs. If some features are improved in later versions, EF (likely EF v2.0 *and* in the context of the .NET Framework 4.0) will probably be the only way to go. And it will likely be much more than just an O/RM tool.

The O/RM Is Your Data Context

As we've seen, you start using the DAL in the service layer. As pointed out in Chapter 5, the service layer is not necessarily a set of *WCF services*. Additionally, we tend to use WCF services when we need to remote services or when we need specific policies such as *WS-Security*. In general, for our discussion here a service is a piece of code that services any requests from the presentation layer.

If you choose an O/RM, you leave the O/RM the burden of mapping to a particular database or to a family of databases (in the case of fragmented entities). In practical terms, this means that you directly use the data context object provided by the O/RM tool and have no need to employ plugins or inversion of control. You pick up an O/RM and that's it.

Here's how you typically get hold of a data context in NHibernate. To start out, you typically create a helper class to act as a factory for the data context:

```
public class SessionHelper
{
    // Configuration and ISessionXxx interfaces are defined in the NHibernate assembly
    private static Configuration _cfg;
    private static ISessionFactory _sessionFactory;

    static SessionHelper()
    {
        _cfg = new Configuration();
        _cfg.Configure();
        _sessionFactory = cfg.BuildSessionFactory();
    }

    public static ISession GetNewSession()
    {
        return _sessionFactory.OpenSession();
    }
}
```

The *Configure* method reads information from the application's configuration file and determines, among other things, which database driver should be used. In your service layer, you create a new NHibernate session and start coding your queries and updates:

```
ISession dal = SessionHelper.GetNewSession();
```

The *ISession* interface has a list of members that is nearly identical to our *IDataContext* interface. And, by the way, this is not a mere coincidence!

In EF, the data context is the *ObjectContext* object. However, you don't use this object directly. You take advantage of a Visual Studio 2008 integrated tool to visually generate a domain model. The tool also delivers a class derived from *ObjectContext* where collections of domain objects and ad hoc CRUD methods are bound together. (If you know LINQ-to-SQL, it is not really a different model.)

```
// AdventureWorksEntities is created by the Visual Studio 2008 EF wizard.
// AdventureWorksEntities inherits from ObjectContext and is your data context object
AdventureWorksEntities context = new AdventureWorksEntities();
```

From here onward, in the service layer you start coding against the API of the O/RM of choice.

Object Services with an O/RM

In NHibernate, to add a new object to the underlying storage you first create an instance of the domain class and get a transient object. Next, you call the method *Save* on the data context:

```
// Create a new customer object
Customer customer = new Customer();
customer.ID = "MD";
customer.CompanyName = "Managed Design";
⋮

// Add customer to the storage
session.Save(customer);
```

When you call *Save*, you are actually instructing the O/RM to provide for persistence. However, in NHibernate persistence happens asynchronously and leverages an internal layer of caching. So in the end, when you call *Save* you have no certainty of when the object will be actually written down to the database. If you need to, you call *Flush* to commit the change instantaneously:

```
// Add a newly created customer to the storage
session.Save(customer);
session.Flush();
```

Of course, *Flush* commits the entire set of pending changes in the session.

To delete the records that correspond to a given domain object, you use the method *Delete*. The method *Update* serves the purpose of updating a record in the database. Also in this case, you should use *Flush* to commit changes in a synchronous manner.

In EF, you have analogous generic methods named *AddObject* and *DeleteObject* to add and delete database records corresponding to domain objects. You have no explicit method to update. In addition, you also have in your domain-specific data context class a bunch of domain-specific CRUD methods, such as *AddToCustomer* or *DeleteCustomer*. Here's a code snippet that adds a new customer:

```
Customer customer = new Customer();
customer.ID = "MD";
customer.CompanyName = "Managed Design";
:

// Add customer to the storage
context.AddObject("Customers", customer);
```

To update a customer object, there are two possible ways to go. If the object is a persistent object you created through the data context, you simply edit the properties in the object and then call *SaveChanges*:

```
// Get a persistent object through the context (using LINQ-to-Entities)
Customer customer = (from c in context.Customers
                     where c.ID == "MD"
                     select c).First();

// Update the object
customer.ContactInfo.Name = "Andrea Saltarello";
:

// Persist changes
context.SaveChanges();
```

Another scenario is when the object matches a stored record but has not been obtained directly through the same instance of the context that will be used to persist it. In this case, you have to first attach it to the object context for persistence and mark all of its properties as *modified*:

```
// The customer object come from outside the scope of this code:
// it can be a cached object or an object built from the content of a DTO
context.Attach(customer);

// Mark properties as "modified"
ObjectStateEntry entry = context.ObjectStateManager.GetObjectStateEntry(customer);
entry.SetModified();

// Further update the object explicitly
customer.ContactInfo.Name = "Andrea Saltarello";
:

// Persist changes
context.SaveChanges();
```

As you can see, the model in EF offers more facilities but also pops up two different ways of doing essentially the same thing. We find the NHibernate model of updating not so trivially "easy" to use as in EF when the object context is the same. At the same time, a slightly less simple approach (but still "very easy" for the average, non-RAD-dependent developer) avoids in NHibernate the need to use two update models and attach/detach semantics.

Transactions with an O/RM

In NHibernate, you can see the Unit of Work pattern showing off the *ISession* interface. You find methods such as those we listed in our own DAL—*BeginTransaction*, *Commit*, and *Rollback*. Although familiar, it is an O/RM specific API. Let's see how to implement a business transaction with NHibernate:

```
// All types here are defined in the NHibernate assembly
ITransaction tx = Session.BeginTransaction();

// Get the customer object that matches the given ID
Customer customer = (Customer) session.Load<Customer>("MD");
customer.ContactInfo.Name = "Dino Esposito";

// Do other work here
// So far all changes occurred in memory
  :
  :

// Commit the transaction (and flush the session)
tx.Commit();
tx.Dispose();
```

As long as you update domain objects within a transaction, all changes happen in memory and are committed only when you invoke *Commit*. Also, the session is flushed when you commit.

In EF, the *SaveChanges* method offers an implicit implementation of the Unit of Work pattern. All the tracked changes are committed within the boundaries of an implicit transaction when you call *SaveChanges*. So the *ObjectContext* object in EF doesn't offer methods such as *BeginTransaction* and *Commit*; however, this doesn't mean that you can't explicitly manage transactions in EF. Nicely enough, you do that using the familiar *TransactionScope* class. Here's an example:

```
MyEntities context = new MyEntities();
  :
  :

using (TransactionScope tx = new TransactionScope())
{
    // Do some work updating domain objects
      :
      :

    // Save changes (but do not reset change tracking)
    context.SaveChanges(false);

    // Do some other non-database-related but still
    // transactional work.
    using (MessageQueue q = new MessageQueue("SomeQueue"))
    {
        // Define a message
        Message msg = new Message( ... );
        q.Send(msg);
    }

    // Commit the transaction
    tx.Complete();
```

```
    // Accept (finally) changes to the object context
    context.AcceptAllChanges();
}
```

In EF, you typically resort to *SaveChanges* for business transactions that involve only the domain model and a single context. Otherwise, you escalate to full transactional semantics and use *TransactionScope*—which is not a new API, but a (familiar) part of the .NET Framework.

Note the *false* argument passed to *SaveChanges* in the case of a possibly distributed transaction. By passing *false*, you reserve the possibility of retrying the same set of changes to the EF context later if the overall transaction fails. If you call *SaveChanges* with no arguments (or pass *true*), you lose your changes if the surrounding transaction fails. This is because *SaveChanges(true)* resets change tracking on all objects before it exits.

With a value of *false* passed to *SaveChanges*, you reserve the chance to retry your context changes later, if needed. However, a simple call to *SaveChanges(false)* isn't enough to save the context. You also have to explicitly mark all changes as accepted after calling *SaveChanges*. You do this by calling *AcceptAllChanges*.

Querying with an O/RM

NHibernate supplies a query model based on query criteria you provide and a few simple methods to get references to persistent objects. The *Load* method provides a quick way to retrieve an object if you know its key:

```
// Retrieves the object from the database (if not cached)
Customer customer = session.Load<Customer>("MD");
```

If you don't know the key to retrieve an object, you need a proper query. NHibernate offers a tailor-made query language named the Hibernate Query Language (HQL). The syntax of HQL has several points in common with SQL, but it uses objects instead of sets.

```
// Create and execute query object from an HQL command
Query q = session.CreateQuery(
    "from Customer c where c.CountryID=:countryID order by c.CompanyName");
q.SetInt("countryID", 1234);
List<Customer> customers = q.List<Customer>();
```

For programmatic query creation, you use some specific criteria, as shown here:

```
// Define criteria
ICriteria criteria = session.CreateCriteria(typeof(Customer));
  :
  :
// Translate the query
QueryTranslator queryTranslator = new QueryTranslator(criteria, query);
queryTranslator.Execute();
```

```
// Set first and last record to access (for pagination)
criteria.SetFirstResult(pageIndex * pageSize);
criteria.SetMaxResults(pageSize);

// Grab results
List<Customer> customers = criteria.List<Customer>();
```

Note that the power of the HQL language might not be matched by the *Query* object. And both HQL and *Query* objects might not be able to express the database query you need, especially when advanced SQL capabilities are required. In this case, you just use the O/RM to run a query in the native SQL of the underlying DBMS. In NHibernate, the method to use is *CreateSqlQuery*.

In EF, the set of capabilities is similar. The object-oriented query language is Entity SQL (ESQL), which is mapped to the LINQ-to-Entities syntax. Here's a sample code snippet:

```
var q = from c in context.Customers
        where c.CompanyName.StartsWith("M")
        select c;
List<Customer> customers = q.ToList();
```

LINQ-to-Entities is an idiomatic query language; you can use the ESQL syntax through a query builder:

```
string cmd = @"SELECT VALUE Contact FROM MyEntities.Contact AS Contact
                WHERE Contact.LastName = @ln AND Contact.FirstName = @fn";
ObjectQuery<Contact> query = new ObjectQuery<Contact>(cmd, context);

// Add parameters
query.Parameters.Add(new ObjectParameter("ln", "Smith"));
query.Parameters.Add(new ObjectParameter("fn", "John"));
```

In EF, you can also use ad hoc ADO.NET-like objects to control all aspects of the query. You can open an *EntityConnection* to connect to the EF domain model and execute an ESQL query using an *EntityCommand*. You access results using a data reader, however. Loading data into objects remains your responsibility. But because there's no syntax around, this technique is also the fastest. But performance is not entirely dictated by the architecture.

The Domain Model and Persistence Ignorance

There's an important consideration to be made regarding O/R mapping tools. An O/RM is primarily an instrument to persist objects to relational tables. Any O/RM, therefore, consumes a domain model. Should the O/RM impose requirements over the domain model?

In NHibernate, there's no hidden link between the internal workings of the O/RM and the domain model you use. You write your hierarchy of classes in total freedom, compile them to an assembly, and then map classes to tables using the XML-based NHibernate mapping files. When an object model has no dependency on anything outside of it—and especially no dependencies on the layer that will actually persist it to a database—it is said to be a

Persistence Ignorant (PI) model or a Plain Old CLR Object (POCO) model. As an example, a POCO object is not forced to derive from a base class, implement a given interface, or provide a specific constructor.

NHibernate fully supports POCO objects. LINQ-to-SQL and EF do not support POCO objects. This means that when you create a domain model for EF—referenced as an Entity Data Model (EDM)—you end up with a set of classes deriving from a common, and system-provided, parent class.

It is probably safe to assume that version 2.0 of Entity Framework will have full support for PI. But why is PI so important?

Why Is Persistence Ignorance So Desirable?

Forcing domain classes to implement an interface, or derive from a given base class (as in EF v1.0), makes it really hard to integrate external, legacy classes into the domain model. In addition, and maybe more importantly, not supporting POCO means creating hidden dependencies between the domain model and the rest of the world. In a domain-driven world, you want no marker interfaces, no base classes, and no partially implemented classes with some autogenerated code. You want classes to express a behavior and manage some data. You just want plain .NET classes. With EF v1.0, this is not the case.

At the same time, Microsoft envisions EF as more than a plain O/R mapping tool. In the near future, the EDM will become currency for services—any services—to exchange. This idea is brilliant and envisions a better world for software. But to be able to achieve this goal, the EDM must be totally free of dependencies on consumers, whether it is the O/R mapper or any other service.

Although PI is definitely the emerging approach, it would be interesting to review the reasons that led Microsoft to design the Entity Framework's EDM with a non-PI approach. In a nutshell, it was the need to ensure that each object in the domain model could supply a certain behavior when persisted or manipulated by the framework.

This need is real.

So how are other O/RM tools addressing it? If the domain model is made of POCO objects, at some point some code should be added to provide a specific behavior. How do you add extra, dynamic code to the plain .NET classes you have in the domain model?

We see two main approaches: aspect-oriented programming (AOP) and dynamic proxies.

AOP essentially allows you to add cross-cutting *aspects* to a class. An aspect is a piece of software that applies to an object. With AOP, you add behavior on the fly to an object. The problem is that for performance reasons this should happen at the CLR level. And currently, there's no AOP flavor in the CLR.

Dynamic proxies are the approach used by NHibernate and most other current O/RM tools. It consists of using *Reflection.Emit* to dynamically inject code in the current assembly to decorate an object with a new behavior, one that is not hard-coded in its sources.

As usual, time will tell. The .NET Framework 4.0, however, is going to be fun to use. This is exactly what you would call a major release.

To SP or Not to SP

We spent a lot of time discussing how to build a custom DAL, and then we concluded that for a Domain Model pattern, using a O/R mapping layer is the only way to go. We also concluded that a well-built DAL is like a simple O/R mapper. Ten years ago, the scenario was radically different.

The best and fastest computers in a company used to be those equipped with a DBMS. Object-orientation was still in its infancy as far as the Microsoft platform was concerned. (C# was the first easy-to-use, object-oriented language we had from Microsoft, and it came along in 2002.) Envisioning a system as "a database with some business code around" was an excellent approach. And we built quite a few systems that way. Stored procedures were by far the way to go rather than using plain SQL statements. Storing simple logic in stored procedures seemed safe and sound. And having aspects such as security moved up to the business layer looked like a misplacement and a sure loss of performance.

Today, we live in a different IT world.

About Myths and Stored Procedures

It is probably safe enough to assume that everybody who made it this far knows exactly what a stored procedure (SP) is. An SP is essentially a *subroutine* defined within a database in a relational DBMS, such as SQL Server. An SP is then available to any code that connects to the database and presents proper credentials.

We feel that the word *subroutine* is key here to understanding the scope and benefits of stored procedures. And we mean the scope and benefits of stored procedures as perceived *today*. We recognize that, for example, ten years ago the general feeling about SPs was different, and overall more favorable. But ten years in software is like a geological era.

According to Wikipedia, a subroutine is a portion of code within a larger program, which performs a specific task and can be relatively independent of the remaining code. Applied to database programming, the notion of a subroutine leads to grouping several SQL statements, forming a single complex processing statement—in other words, a stored procedure. In this way, the caller code has a single point of contact with the database that is easier to secure, test, optimize, and maintain—and it even runs faster.

These statements capture the strength and weakness of stored procedures. Whether each characteristic mentioned in the previous paragraph is a strength or a weakness depends on the context. In particular, it depends on the application you are building, the requirements and constraints you get from the client, and ultimately the complexity of the logic and how you organize that complexity. Also, the methodology you use might put stored procedures in a bad or good light.

Trying to be as balanced and neutral as possible, we would say that SPs are not an absolute evil. But, at the same time, for applications of some complexity that are designed and implemented with today's vision, patterns, tools, and techniques, SPs are probably an obsolete instrument. Our bottom-line judgment is that the usage of SPs should not be patently avoided, but they should be avoided until proven necessary or helpful.

Note In past code snippets, for brevity, we frequently placed SQL strings in classes. Those strings can be plain SQL statements as well as references to stored procedures. There's a crucial point here that is easy to overlook: who writes that code? The assumption we make is that everyone writing SQL knows what they are doing. C# developers are not necessarily good at set-based programming and typically do not write optimized SQL. It is more often the case that hand-written SQL is inelegant and inefficient. Moreover, it's a maintenance nightmare.

SQL code—whether it's a hard-coded string or a stored procedure—should be written by people who live and breathe SQL, not left to C# middleware developers. As an architect, you should use your development resources appropriately. Of course, we're referring to the SQL code you hand-write in the application. In terms of something LINQ-to-SQL creates, or dynamic queries NHibernate or EF produce, that's a different story. That SQL code is highly optimized and the benefits of OR/M tools are significant.

Over the past 10 to 15 years, the tendency has been to build systems according to tried and true design patterns, but there is one area that for some reason people seem to overlook. People still all too often mix business logic in stored procedures, which clouds the distinct nature of layers and their prescribed function. It's very easy to sneak a little business logic into a stored procedure, but is this the right thing to do? Here are some traditional arguments we hear for building complex stored procedures, and while some of them might have been more true 10 years ago, today things have changed significantly. So let's go through some of those stored procedure myths and legends and take a reasoned look at each, with an eye toward today's technology versus yesterday's.

Myth: Stored Procedures Are Faster Than SQL Code

SQL is a language through which you declare your intentions about the operations (query, update, or management operations) to execute on the database. All that the database engine gets is text. Much like a C# source file processed by a compiler, the SQL source code must be compiled in some way to produce a sequence of lower-level database operations—this output goes under the name of *execution plan*. Conceptually, the generation of the execution plan can be seen as the database counterpart of compiling a program.

The alleged gain in performance that stored procedures guarantee over plain SQL code lies in the reuse of the execution plan. In other words, the first time you execute an SP, the DBMS generates the execution plan and *then* executes the code. The next time it will just reuse the previously generated plan, thus executing the command faster. All SQL commands need an execution plan.

The (false) myth is that a DBMS reuses the execution plan only for stored procedures. As far as SQL Server and Oracle DBMS are concerned (admittedly, we don't know much about other products), the benefit of reusing execution plans applies to any SQL statements. Quoting from the SQL Server 2005 online documentation:

> *When any SQL statement is executed in SQL Server 2005, the relational engine first looks through the procedure cache to verify that an existing execution plan for the same SQL statement exists. SQL Server 2005 reuses any existing plan it finds, saving the overhead of recompiling the SQL statement. If no existing execution plan exists, SQL Server 2005 generates a new execution plan for the query.*

The debate around SPs performing better than plain SQL code is pointless. Performancewise, any SQL code that hits the database is treated the same way. Performance is equivalent once compiled. Period.

Myth: Stored Procedures Are More Secure Than SQL Code

Before executing any SQL statement, the database engine matches the credentials presented by the caller to the rights granted to that login for the involved resources. Based on the results, the engine decides whether or not to execute the statement.

Put this way, stored procedures are obviously a better option than plain SQL code from a security standpoint. Why is that so? A stored procedure is a recognized entity within the database and can be secured explicitly and declaratively by the database administrator (DBA). You take advantage of the DBMS security infrastructure to protect the stored procedure because the stored procedure is a database resource.

A plain SQL statement is a string that is dynamically sent down for execution; the database engine doesn't know it as an internal resource and can't associate privileges to it. It can do this only for tables or views it invokes—which is clearly a different level of granularity. As a result, security over the operation as a whole should be enforced programmatically by the caller layer.

We feel that everybody agrees with this big picture. The point is that two opposite . conclusions can be drawn from this. And they largely depend on people's attitudes, skills, and vision.

If you've grown up with a database mindset, you usually stop here and conclude that stored procedures are a must-have in the design of the DAL.

But ask yourself these questions: What kind of operations should you perform in a stored procedure, and what kind of signature can you design for them? And how many stored procedures do you actually need in a large system?

In our view, if you consider SPs as a must-have item, you dangerously move down the slope of considering the SP layer the repository of (at least some) business logic. And this is something we *strongly* advise you not to do. We'll return to this point in a moment. First let's finish the discussion on security.

Security is a cross-cutting concern and should be tackled from the presentation layer down to the database. Role-based security is the most flexible and effective approach today. With role-based security all the way through, you build a double barrier: a programmatic barrier through middle tier, role-based security, and a declarative database barrier through the DBMS engine. And this is unrelated to using dynamic SQL code or stored procedures.

If you focus on stored procedures to implement security in a system, you tend to have database people and development people working separately. Security, as stated earlier, is rather more a team sport. So we basically revert to a common point raised by SP advocates who say, "Use SPs if you want good security." If you want good security, this is precisely why you should stop considering SPs as a must-have item. We don't say this because there's something bad about SPs; we say it because having SPs at the center of the universe leads you to making poor design decisions—in terms of security. You can still have SPs, but do not include them for security reasons. And do not include them for implementing logic. Why would you have them, then? Mostly for taking care of table access.

 Note To write good stored procedure and table access code, you must have inner knowledge of the implementation of the database. This is perhaps something you might want to leave to LINQ-to-SQL or some O/RM tool. This is not something you want to leave to C# middleware developers.

Myth: Stored Procedures Can Be Used to Fend Off SQL Injection

This argument is similar to the previous one about performance. It is definitely correct to state that with stored procedures you reduce the surface for SQL injection attacks. This is because stored procedures use typed parameters. For attackers, it is then harder to send, say, a string where a number is expected and vice versa.

However, the same capabilities are offered by parameterized queries. ADO.NET, for example, provides a great deal of support for building parameterized queries. And ADO.NET is used everywhere in the .NET platform for data access. ADO.NET is also used by Entity Framework, NHibernate, and other O/RM tools. A plain SQL statement built using parameters exposes the same surface-to-SQL injection as do stored procedures.

Myth: Stored Procedures Can Be Used to Reduce Brittleness of SQL Code

There are many versions of the Holy Grail in software. One is the quest for a coding model that happily survives changes in the database model. What if I change something in one of my tables? Will this affect my surrounding code? This is a common concern. But the correct answer, again, is not found in stored procedures.

If you store SQL commands in the data access layer (as we did in the discussion of a handmade DAL earlier), you create a dependency between your code and the physical data model. If the data model changes, your code might need updates. We like to argue that, ultimately, such a dependency is isolated in a standalone data mapper class and that SQL statements are defined as private members of the class. So a dependency clearly exists, but it has a very limited scope. If any changes occur to any tables, the data mapper class *must* be updated. But it is the only class that you need to update, and attention is limited to the DAL's assembly.

Do you really make your code independent from changes in the data model by using stored procedures? When the data model changes, you have two types of updates to implement: changes to the SQL code, and changes to the caller code. Honestly, we don't see the difference between stored procedures and plain SQL statements isolated in a data mapper class.

That stored procedures reduce the brittleness of data access code is, in our humble opinion, a myth. And that myth is the child of an old-fashioned way of looking at the design of systems—where essentially database people and the development team have little communication.

If you really want to achieve independence from the physical data model, you should opt for a domain-driven design of the system and consider the database as a simple persistence layer. The data access code will be left to the O/R mapping layer, generated dynamically, and made of parameterized queries (or, why not, even stored procedures).

What Stored Procedures Are For

We tackled this point already in Chapter 4 when we pointed out the gray areas in the design of the business logic. Let's briefly summarize.

What's a database for your purposes? Is it a plain persistence layer, or is it more? And if it is more, what exactly is it? In as unbiased a manner as possible, we dare say that a database is the following:

- It is the repository of a collection of data.

- It enforces data rules.

- It ensures data integrity.

- It shares data resources with a number of applications.

We obviously agree that a database is a really rich tool with more than tables to hold data. But all the extra features we might recognize have nothing to do with the design of a software architecture for applications.

So what's a software application in your own mind? Is it a plain wrapper around a database, or is it more? And if it is more, what exactly is it? In as unbiased a manner as possible, we dare say that a software application is the following:

- It is made of a presentation layer to talk to end-users.
- It is made of a business logic to process user requests.
- It is made of a data access layer to manage its data in a persistent manner.

The answer to the question, "What are stored procedures for," is tightly related to your vision of a software application. If your attitude is, "There's no application without a database," it is essential for you to live on and thrive on stored procedures. It's an attitude and a lifestyle; but not the only one.

Our definition of a software application is different.

The business layer lives outside of the database, and the database is a rich tool that provides persistence under the control of the data access layer. This vision still leads us to using stored procedures, optimizing indexes, and defining constraints and relationships. But we do this with the sole purpose of optimizing the performance of the persistence layer.

A stored procedure is like a subroutine in plain SQL code. So using stored procedures is not a bad thing. It's what is placed in the stored procedure that really matters to us. What do we recommend that you have in a stored procedure? Just CRUD stuff and possibly CRUD stuff on a per-table basis. CRUD stuff concerns basic I/O operations plus integrity, nullability, type checking, and indexing. Conditions and loops might be acceptable as long as they are functional to an optimal execution of CRUD operations and are not, instead, a sign that the stored procedure has an intimate knowledge of entities and logical elements. Stored procedures live in the data access layer to return and update data, not to interpret data in any way.

Note If you put CRUD stuff in the stored procedures, you actually write code using the DBMS-specific variation of SQL. And SQL is tailored for the tasks. If you add more logic, you end up implementing logic using a *set*-based language, which is another concept from a classic procedural programming language perspective. Some programming constructs, such as loops, are exceptionally poorly performing and difficult to do when implemented using set-based languages, yet loops are often required in the business logic layer. Why use the wrong programming idiom for the job?

Should You Use Stored Procedures?

Let's put it this way. Stored procedures are a tool. As such, they might or might not be helpful. The statement, "Never use stored procedures," is inaccurate and not valid all the time. But the statement, "Always use stored procedures," is really not the answer either. The truth is somewhere in the middle—stored procedures have their place, but use them wisely and appropriately.

Consider also that using stored procedures requires the intervention of a DBA. In general, in large companies, changing SPs is never easy, and during development you might need to do that quite often.

The idea often associated with stored procedures that we want to fight is that stored procedures should be used to express, all or in part, the business logic. Never put more than data rules in a stored procedure, if you ever happen to use them. And consider using stored procedures if there's a measurable benefit—typically, in terms of performance or perhaps in the ease of coding a certain task.

What About Dynamic SQL?

As we've seen, a number of myths have arisen over the years from contrasting SQL code and stored procedures. In our opinion, the debate over the difference between stored procedures and plain SQL code is no longer topical. Given the evolution of software design, and in light of current design principles for layered systems, the real debate is whether to use handcrafted, static SQL or autogenerated dynamic SQL.

Embedding SQL Statically

By static SQL, we mean SQL code that is statically embedded in the application—either in the form of plain SQL statements or stored procedures. These days, we don't see any significant difference between stored procedures and plain SQL code. In both cases, the DAL knows about the signature (for example, parameters) of the SQL code that creates a dependency and presents issues in terms of testing and debugging.

Stored procedures are a possible approach only if you envision the application as a database with some code around it. This is not our vision, though. In our opinion, it is a very limited and shortsighted view, indeed.

Statically created SQL has a number of issues—quality of code, maintenance and testing, for example. If you embed SQL code, you have to write and maintain it. Embedded static SQL is a less than optimal approach, and it is not mitigated by the use of stored procedures. Furthermore, with stored procedures you have to involve the DBA.

The Turning Point Created by O/R Mappers

Dynamically generated SQL is a more modern approach that goes hand in hand with the evolution of software architectures. Dynamic SQL is associated with O/R mapping tools. In an O/RM-based world, you reason in terms of objects and express your queries and updates using the metalanguage supported by the tool.

As we've seen, NHibernate features HQL, where you use properties from domain objects instead of columns from tables. Similarly, in ADO.NET Entity Framework you use LINQ-to-Entities for the same purposes. In addition, most O/RM tools offer criteria-based queries, where you build the query using a more object-oriented approach, basically composing the query as an object.

An O/RM tool shields you entirely from the details of the DBMS query language. If you want to change the target DBMS, you just change some details in the configuration file. If you modify your data model, you change only the mapping between the domain model and data model.

> **Note** If at some time you enter changes to the structure of tables in your database, you have to change something somewhere else. Trusting that there might be an approach to software that saves you from the burden of at least checking the DAL for regression is disingenuous, if not silly. Changes to the data model *never* go unnoticed, but O/RM tools can only minimize the impact of these changes, as they represent an intermediate layer between the domain model and data model.

Do You Still Need a DBA?

Yes, we do in fact need DBAs, but we need them to do the things that are central to managing the database. That in itself is a huge undertaking. Quite simply, they should do the things they are trained to do. DBAs aren't trained to be architects any more than any other developer. If a DBA wants to be an architect, that's fine, but when he's an architect, he's an architect. When (or if) he has to again be a DBA, at that point he's a DBA. After all, the *A* in DBA does **not** stand for *architect*. And a good architect knows that mixing layers is a bad thing. Business logic in the database is as bad, or worse (because it's harder to maintain), than business logic in the presentation layer.

Summary

A strong wind of progress and evolution has been blowing in the IT industry for at least the past ten years. Recently, this wind freshened, especially with regard to software architectures.

The possibility of pursuing domain-driven design for applications was once only the unconfessed dreams of the geekiest geeks just a few years ago. Today, in this book (which certainly is not the first on the subject), we are discussing the importance of a domain model and its repercussion on the other layers of the architecture. And, amazingly, we find powerful tools to support us in the effort of building better systems for our clients.

The data access layer is a critical part of each application—just like the presentation and business layers.

The data access layer, however, lives on the border of the database and always has been tightly coupled with the database. Gaining independence from the physical structure of the database is another, often unconfessed, dream of many IT professionals.

In the end, you currently have two options for the middle tier of a layered system. You can render your application's data through tabular containers such as typed *DataSets*, or you can opt for a more or less abstract object model. In both cases, you end up persisting data down to a relational database, which creates an impedance mismatch. The former approach worked quite nicely for several years—the first years of the .NET revolution.

At some point, many companies along the entire spectrum of the industry realized the benefits of the .NET platform. And their information systems were old enough to justify a rebuild. Suddenly, the community of software professionals was expected to deal with an unprecedented level of complexity.

From here, the need for a domain-driven design arose and, subsequently, the need for working with data at a more conceptual level. Inevitably, the role of the database has been downgraded to that of a mere persistence layer. The data access layer that we created for years as a wrapper around stored procedures is now obsolete and out of place. The data access layer has evolved toward becoming an O/R mapping layer.

In this chapter, we first identified in an abstract way the responsibilities of a DAL. Next, we discussed patterns and principles to implement a DAL manually. Finally, we jumped to the conclusion that an O/R mapper tool is a necessity when you pursue a domain-driven design. As the final step, we introduced NHibernate and ADO.NET Entity Framework and outlined the future direction of Entity Framework, which confirms the aforementioned trend.

With the advent of the O/RM, the age of stored procedures as the primary repository of data access logic is definitely gone.

Murphy's Laws of the Chapter

Something is going on in the data access field—maybe even a true paradigm shift. We're moving away from stored procedures and classic SQL programming. We're embracing new tools that provide (or support) an object model and offer to dynamically generate SQL code for us. This consideration introduces the Murphy's laws of this chapter. Who knows if embracing O/RM is really the right thing? Only hindsight can tell us for sure. And just because we're delegating work to tools and their run-time environment, let's just hope the tools have good memory.

- The only perfect science is hindsight.

- When putting something into memory, always remember where you put it.

- There is never time to do it right, but always time to do it over.

See *http://www.murphys-laws.com* for an extensive listing of other computer-related (and non-computer) laws and corollaries.

Chapter 7
The Presentation Layer

And the users exclaimed with a laugh and a taunt: "Cool! It's just what we asked for, but not what we want now."

—Anonymous

No applications would be usable without a user interface. No matter what kind of smart code you lovingly crafted in the middle tier, it couldn't be consumed by any users if it didn't have a way to present it to the users.

Many architects, however, tend to consider presentation as the less noble part of the system—almost a detail to tackle after the business and data access layers have been fully and successfully completed. The truth is that the user interface (UI), business logic, and data access code are equally necessary in a system of any complexity. Your attitude, your preferences, and even your skills determine the "priority" you assign to each layer and, subsequently, the order in which you focus on the various layers. But the effort you put in, and results, must be the same for each layer—that is, they must be great.

As a matter of fact, the presentation layer is often the last part of a system to be developed, and it is too often highly dependent on the capabilities offered by development tools such as Microsoft Visual Studio 2008.

The other approach (not treating all these layers equally) is not bad per se and doesn't necessarily lead you to failure. At the end of the day, the presentation layer is really a layer that can be bolted onto an existing middle tier. And precisely the ability to unplug an existing UI to replace it with a different one is a key requirement for a presentation layer, as we'll see later in the chapter. So what's the reality of the presentation layer? Is it really the simplest part of a system? Well, it depends.

For sure, a significant part of the presentation layer can be created using powerful, high-level tools. The availability of such smart tools, however, might cause architects and developers to overlook the importance of using a good design for the presentation layer. The implementation of a presentation layer can be a really simple matter (as in a data-entry ASP .NET page), but it can also become quite a complex mess of views, subviews, and navigation flow in enterprise scenarios.

In the end, our point is this: feel free to use rapid application development (RAD) facilities, wizards, widgets, and direct database data binding as long as you know what you're doing. If the presentation layer is complex enough—that is, it is a graphical presentation plus a large dose of application logic—you should look around for guidance and patterns in much the same way you do for the business layer and the data access layer.

User Interface and Presentation Logic

The presentation layer is made of two main components: the user interface and the presentation logic (also often referred to as the UI logic). The user interface provides users with the tools to use the program. Any behavior that the program can carry out is exposed to the users through graphical or textual elements in the user interface. These elements—mostly graphical elements nowadays—provide information, suggest actions, and capture the user's activity with input devices such as a keyboard and mouse.

Any actions a user takes within the user interface become input for the other component of the presentation layer—the presentation logic (PL). The presentation logic refers to all the processing required to display data and to transform user input into a command for the back-end system. In other words, PL has to do with the flow of data from the middle tier to the UI and from the UI back to the middle tier.

The presentation logic is strictly related to the display of data to the screen. It is a distinct type of logic compared to the application logic—the organization of a response for a given user request—and the business logic—the services and workflows that provide a response for a given business task. (See Figure 7-1.)

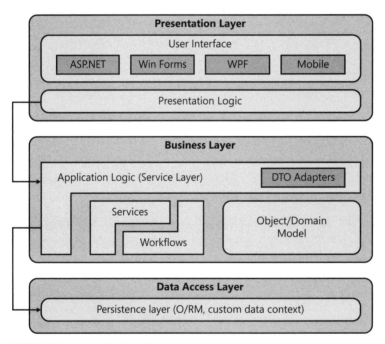

FIGURE 7-1 An overall view of a layered system

As you can see clearly in the figure, the presentation layer is the interface between the user and the system. On one end, it provides the (mostly graphical) tools for users to work with. On the other end, it contains the logic required to coordinate any user and system actions with the purpose of displaying and submitting data.

Responsibilities of the Presentation Layer

In our experience, if you ask software engineers to list some of the responsibilities of a presentation layer, you invariably hear some of the following words: validation, formatting, styling, usability. We would say that usability is an attribute rather than a responsibility and that features such as validation, styling, and formatting belong more to the UI components rather than to the presentation layer as a whole.

As an architect engaged in the design of a presentation layer, you have to fly higher—at least initially. Input validation, input masking, formatting, and visual styles are important aspects of the user interface, but they relate to the particular UI technology and platform you choose.

A different and higher level set of responsibilities exist for the presentation layer: independence from the physical UI, testability, and independence from the model of data.

Independence from Graphics

Graphical elements (typically, controls and widgets) make up the user interface of the application. Users see these components and interact with them, thus imparting commands and information to the back-end system.

The same logical content—for example, a list of orders—can be rendered in a variety of ways. In ASP .NET, for instance, you can use a *DataGrid* control as well as a *Repeater* control. In the former case, you get a tabular, multicolumn list; in the latter case, you might get a fancier representation of the same data. Where would you place a given button in the user interface? Should it be a push button or a link button? And what about colors, borders, styles, and fonts?

The presentation layer must be able to survive any changes in the graphical user interface that do not require a change in the data flow and in the presentation logic. As long as the change involves purely graphical stuff, the presentation layer must support it in a transparent way.

As a real-world example, consider what happens with blogs today. You open the configuration page, select a new theme or skin, apply your changes, and refresh the page. The same content is now displayed in a totally different way. The blog engine, though, doesn't have to be recompiled on the fly for the new theme/skin to apply.

Hold on! We're not saying that all presentation layers must necessarily offer users the ability to change themes and skins dynamically. Rather, a well-designed presentation layer makes it easy for developers to switch to a different UI during the development life cycle and, more importantly, it enables you to create a scenario in which the UI is loaded or generated dynamically to comply with run-time conditions.

Independence from UI Technology

The presentation layer must also be independent from the UI technology and platform. This requirement is much harder to meet, and sometimes it is just impossible to obtain total independence. So we should probably rephrase the responsibility as "independence from the UI technology and platform to the extent that it is possible (or desirable)."

More often than not, enterprise systems need to have multiple presentations—Web, Windows, mobile, and perhaps Silverlight. When this happens, it is desirable that, under the hood of obviously different user-interface components, the same presentation logic can be reused. Have a look at Figure 7-2.

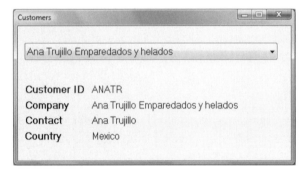

FIGURE 7-2 A Windows Forms user interface to show customer details

The figure shows a very simple Windows Forms application that presents some details about a selected customer. The form in the picture belongs to the Windows presentation layer of a system with multiple presentation layers. It retrieves data using a common application layer; the same application layer used by the Web page in Figure 7-3.

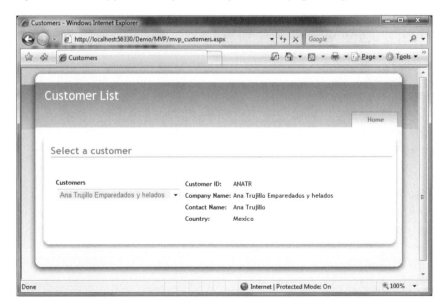

FIGURE 7-3 A Web user interface to show customer details

A well-designed presentation layer makes it easy for developers to reuse as much code as possible when it comes to supporting different UI technologies and platforms for the same logical user interface.

Note that the applications in Figure 7-2 and Figure 7-3 require different projects and different skills. However, they use the same presentation logic. In this particular case, the presentation layer can be architected to reuse the same assemblies, not just the same source code.

> **Note** Code reuse in the presentation layer is hardly total. Most of the time, all you can do is maximize the amount of reused code or binaries. You are targeting a different section of the .NET Framework, anyway, so you should not expect to achieve 100 percent code and binary reuse. For Silverlight, for example, you can't just reuse binaries. Even if the presentation logic addresses functionalities that both a Windows Presentation Foundation (WPF) and a Silverlight presentation can support, you have to compile classes for Silverlight and WPF separately because a different version of the CLR is involved. In this regard, expressing the goal as "maximizing code reuse" is more realistic than shooting for "total code reuse."

Support for Testing

The presentation layer should be tested to some (good) extent, just like any other part of the application. Testing the presentation layer, though, is trickier than you might imagine. You should test that when the user performs a particular action, the user interface is modified accordingly. For example, data should flow correctly in to and out of the user interface. In addition, the state of the user interface should be updated—some buttons might be disabled, some panels might be expanded or collapsed, and so on.

User-interface components work by triggering events that the run-time environment catches and maps to your own handlers. It's not easy (to say the least) to simulate a Click action from within a test environment. So you typically should let things go as usual but move testable code out of your event handlers. In this way, any event is handled by a method on a distinct and reusable class. This class is individually testable.

How would you then verify that a given action has generated exactly the expected results? You can't assert in a unit testing tool whether a given method has produced a certain visual result. However, you can come to an abstract description of the view (a form, an ASP .NET page, a window, or a Silverlight user control) and just test that the correct information has been delivered to the object that represents the view.

Abstraction is the key tool for adding testability to a presentation layer. And abstraction is obtained by separating concerns—in particular, by separating the view from the presentation logic. (We'll return to this point in a moment, as it is central to this chapter.)

> **Note** After you have an abstraction of a given form (for example, an interface that represents its contract to the outside world), you still have to map the content in the abstraction to the physical set of UI components. How would you test this?
>
> In practice, you don't use automated testing here. Automated testing is helpful for parts of the code that are subject to changes during development. Mapping data on UI components requires a trivial piece of code. You have to write it correctly, but after you've done it right nothing in the system can break it. The real point for which automated testing is important is ensuring that correct data flows into the view. This is a key point that forms the basis of passive and humble views; we'll return to this topic later.

Independence from a Model of the Data

An enterprise system has its own representation of data. In Chapter 4, "The Business Layer," we examined various options to organize the model of the data according to various patterns. Whatever model you choose for the data in the middle tier, the presentation layer should be unaffected. Or, at least, the presentation layer should be unaffected to the extent that it is possible.

In Chapter 5, "The Service Layer," we discussed data transfer objects (DTOs) and using them to carry data in to and out of the presentation layer. Using DTOs keeps the presentation layer completely independent of whatever model of the data you employ in the lower application layers. On the other hand, using DTOs everywhere adds significant overhead to the development phase—in theory, a pair of input and output DTOs is required for each call placed from the presentation layer down to the application logic. Of course, the expression "each call" means each call from whatever form or page you have in the presentation layer. It turns out to be, definitely, a large number of classes to write and maintain.

For this reason, DTOs are often used sparingly and just in the areas of a system where changes are more likely to occur. Making domain objects flow into the presentation layer creates a dependency. A dependency is neither a bad thing nor a good thing. It is just a feature of the system. A dependency added deliberately with due forethought might be a blessing for the system; failing to spot an implicit dependency between modules in a timely manner, however, is definitely a bad thing.

As far as the presentation layer is concerned, introducing a dependency on the model of the data might be acceptable. However, the guideline is to introduce such dependencies only when you have a clear benefit (or conversely, little or no risk) in terms of performance, maintenance, or both.

Responsibilities of the User Interface

Most of the time, the architect is not directly involved in the definition of graphical details regarding the user interface. It is a precise responsibility of the architect, instead, to ensure that quality characteristics (especially, usability and accessibility) are properly addressed.

The toughest part of the presentation logic is designing an abstraction of the view—for each view in the presentation layer. The abstraction of the view defines what data is exposed in input to and output from the view. The goal of the presentation logic is to ensure that the data flows correctly in to and out of the view.

After all the stakeholders have signed off on the public contract of each view, two distinct teams can work on the project. The development team can proceed with the implementation and testing of the presentation logic and the middle tier. The design team can come up with one or more graphical layouts for any of the supported user-interface designs. The resulting UI and presentation logic can be tied together at any time with minimal work.

Each view that makes up the user interface has its own set of responsibilities, mostly related to keeping the overall presentation metaphor as easy to use as possible.

Useful Data Display

Among other things, the user interface is responsible for presenting data to the user. Data includes general information, hints, and, most importantly, responses obtained from application-specific operations.

A good user interface always supplies users properly formatted data and displays it in useful visual styles. The user interface also encapsulates the effect of globalization and localization and uses proper settings wherever required.

Depending on the actual patterns you employ in the design of the presentation layer, the exact place where data is adapted for display might change. Most of the time, it happens in the presentation logic, but it is not unusual that some formatting and display logic is implemented through the properties of rich controls you have in the user interface. In this case, you also have the benefit that you can change it in a rather declarative way without writing or editing a single line of C# code.

Comfortable Data Entry

The user interface is the place where users enter data into the system. A usable presentation layer makes data entry comfortable for users to do by providing input masks and using appropriate controls for data input.

In this regard, rich controls and drag-and-drop are key features. Tabs also help to partition complex user interfaces while keeping the various parts at hand.

Whatever the underlying platform (Windows, Web, or mobile) is, data entry is a critical moment for the application. Of course, it is an especially critical moment for Web applications. Why is that so? Remember that security mantra? *All user input is evil.* So providing quick validation is another fundamental responsibility of the user interface. UI-level validation is not enough, but it is a good first step.

General Appearance

The look and feel of an application refers to the experience that a user has while using the application and the main features of its general appearance. Finding the right combination of controls, visual layouts, and styles is a process that can take time. And it is the aspect of the system that customers usually have the most questions about.

Typically, applications intended for public use, such as Web portals or productivity suites, have fancy user interfaces because one of their goals is just to grab the user's attention and leave a favorable impression. On the other hand, applications intended for internal corporate use lean toward a user interface that is more functional than visually pleasing.

In the end, it is a matter of following the customer's requirements. The UI architecture should be chosen according to the actual requirements.

Common Pitfalls of a Presentation Layer

To successfully meet all expectations users have regarding the presentation layer, an architect should simply treat the presentation layer like any other layer—and apply specific and proven design patterns. In a moment, we'll be delving deep into the mother of all contemporary UI design patterns—the Model-View-Controller (MVC) pattern.

Before we get to that, though, we'd like to make a few observations about the presentation layer with the purpose of hinting at common pitfalls to avoid.

RADness in the Presentation

Writing the user interface of a Microsoft Windows application is way too easy. Any new version of Visual Studio comes with a full bag of goodies for developers and seems to tell developers not to waste any time with design and separation of concerns. This is just the offspring of RAD.

A plain, old T-SQL query correctly attached to the handler of a *Click* event does the job. And it's quick and effective—and it just works. That's the beauty and the power of RAD. You point the mouse, click, select the properties of an element, and double-click and a stub of code is ready for you to fill. Wizards are also there to help you declare what you want (provided that the wizard understands you correctly and that you give it the right instructions).

RADness is not the ideal companion for the presentation layer of a large, enterprise-class system. Visual Studio 2008, of course, is still essential, but the more you care about the aforementioned responsibilities of a presentation layer, the more you should downgrade Visual Studio to the rank of a simple UI designer.

We suggest you use Visual Studio 2008 as a rapid UI designer rather than as a rapid application development tool. Visual Studio 2008 and all of its RAD features are tempting to use in many situations. But you should resist using it in some cases, abandon the point-and-click metaphor, and—guess what?—write more code on your own. From a mouse-based *point-and-click* metaphor, you should move to a keyboard-based *tap-and-tab* metaphor.

> **Note** Using RADness *a go-go* might cause you to build *autonomous views*. An autonomous view consists of a class that holds the state of the user interface and implements any behavior therein. Difficulty of testing is the primary reason why autonomous views are not so popular these days. An autonomous view contains in the same class both the presentation logic and user interface, which makes for difficult, if not impossible, testing. RADness certainly doesn't prevent proper separation of concerns between the user interface and presentation logic, but the temptation to put everything in a single place is so strong that only few can resist it.

Boundaries of the Presentation Layer

As it turns out, in a well-built and effective presentation layer, the UI is a thin layer and the presentation logic tends to take on all the client-side processing that is required to have data correctly flow into and out of the presentation layer. How thick should the presentation logic be?

In Chapter 4, we pointed out that it might be acceptable to have some business logic that is run on the client merged with the presentation layer, if not just duplicated in the presentation logic. As we've said repeatedly in this book, we live in an imperfect world, meaning that we have to make compromises more than we ideally would like to. The thickness of the presentation layer is limited only by scalability and performance requirements, if any. At the same time, though, the presentation layer should contain only its own presentation logic, plus any extra piece of business you deliberately, and in full awareness, decide to merge or duplicate.

The real danger is in another area, however.

We're not far from the truth if we say that user-interface facilities encourage developers to put more stuff and code in the presentation layer than it should reasonably contain. As a result, the presentation layer operates as a catch-all for the logic of other layers—mostly the middle tier, but often also the data access layer. Is this really bad? And if so, why is it all that bad?

Again, let's be pragmatic. It isn't all that bad if you're developing a temporary Web site that is destined to stay up only for a short time—for example, the three months around a user-group meeting. In such a case, you probably just shouldn't bother to write complex application layers and instead simply place an ADO.NET query in the *Button1_Click* event handler of a code-behind class.

So for Web sites that you use copy-cat designing for—to do the same few and well-known things—an approach that leverages simplicity and quick time to market isn't a bad thing per se. For these types of sites, you should feel free to make use of ASP .NET data source controls and all the canned code that Visual Studio 2008 wizards normally create for you.

Although such an approach is OK for simple applications, for large, durable, enterprise-class systems it is another story. When it comes to such types of applications, stuffing code in the presentation layer that logically belongs to other tiers is a tremendous sin. The UI must be isolated from code, and code must be layered, showing high regard for the separation of concerns (SoC) principle. Not only do properly factored layers have their concerns separated, but proper layering also allows for better testing, and therefore higher quality applications, because you can weed out the early bugs while enjoying a higher percentage of test coverage. That is, your test cases test more of your code. Moreover, keeping the logic in the appropriate layer also allows for easier presentation layer refactoring, application layer refactoring, and code re-use, all of which are real-world requirements.

What Users Get Is What You Want

WYSIWYG is a popular acronym for *What-You-See-Is-What-You-Get*. When this term is applied to RAD, it refers to the ability of some development tools to offer a live preview of what you will see after you have run the application. WYSIWYG in that case is mostly related to the user interface and declarative programming.

Whenever you take a declarative approach to coding rather than an imperative approach, you are delegating some responsibilities to some other layer of code—a layer that you don't control entirely. So you're ultimately hoping that the intermediate tool will understand you correctly and won't encounter any trouble of its own along the way. In software development, delegating to a third party makes development faster, but you should guarantee that users get exactly what you want them to.

This doesn't mean that you shouldn't trust Visual Studio 2008 or similar wizard-based products. The point is something else entirely. In a large system, likely being developed by several teams, classic declarative programming just doesn't work. You need to have in your presentation a layer of code that decides what to display, where to read settings, and how to apply them. Declarative programming is still a great option, but only if you write the engine and the wizards.

For enterprise-class applications, the slogan should rather be WUGISYW—*What-Users-Get-Is-What-You-Want*.

Evolution of the Presentation Patterns

When it comes to the presentation layer of a system, there is one fundamental principle to adhere to—keep the presentation layer separated from anything else, including business and data access layers. This principle is captured in Martin Fowler's Separated Presentation pattern, whose complete definition is available at *http://www.martinfowler.com/eaaDev/SeparatedPresentation.html*. Here is an excerpt:

> *Ensure that any code that manipulates presentation only manipulates presentation, pushing all domain and data source logic into clearly separated areas of the program.*

Separating presentation logic from business logic is only the first step toward creating a well-designed presentation layer. Separating the user interface from the presentation logic is another important characteristic of a presentation layer designed to meet the requirements mentioned in Fowler's definition. The internal organization of the presentation logic depends on a variety of UI patterns.

Ultimately, we recognize three main families of patterns: Model-View-Controller (MVC), Model-View-Presenter (MVP), and Presentation Model (PM). You should think of these patterns as base classes that are then specialized by a number of actual patterns, such as Model2 for MVC, Passive View and Supervising Controller for MVP, Model-View-ViewModel for PM.

Before we describe each pattern, we should note that these patterns span 30 years of computer design and programming. And many, many things have changed in the past 30 years. So, for example, the definition of MVC that worked in the 1980s and even the 1990s might not work today. As a result, probably nobody uses MVC today as its authors originally devised it. At the same time, a number of variations and refinements have been made to MVC to make it work in disguise. What we call MVC today doesn't match exactly the definition of MVC you find in the original paper. The same can be said for MVP. Two flavors of MVP exist and, in many applications, you actually use a personal mix of both. MVP just doesn't exist anymore—it is either Passive View (PV) or Supervising Controller (SVC). But in literature and in everyday technical conversation, *MVP* is still the most frequently used term.

Another huge point to consider is the impact that UI frameworks might have on the presentation layer. We're not talking about RAD tools to create forms and Web pages in a snap; we're talking, in particular, about platform-specific frameworks that offer an MVC idiom, such as Castle MonoRail (see *http://www.castleproject.org/monorail*) and ASP .NET MVC Framework (see *http://www.asp.net/mvc*). Developers using these frameworks enjoy nifty and highly usable facilities that cut down development time. And who cares about the purity of the approach compared to the original paper? If you have a framework that gives you testability and separation of concerns (and whatever else you ask for), by all means use it and don't get bothered by possible patterns it does or does not implement.

The purpose of this chapter is to discuss a set of guidelines for an effective design of the presentation layer, with a particular focus on enterprise-class applications. Let's start from what we had in the beginning of the software era and examine the requirements that brought us to today's patterns.

The Model-View-Controller Pattern

In the earliest software, the presentation layer was made of monolithic, autonomous views displayed to the user. The user interacted with the view and generated some input. The view captured the input, processed it internally, and updated itself or moved to another view. At a minimum, this model made it really hard to test the presentation pieces properly. A search for a better model ensued. Enter the Model-View-Controller pattern.

Moving Away from Autonomous Views

An autonomous view (AV) is similar to a Web or Windows form you obtain by using the RAD facilities of Visual Studio 2008 to their fullest. If you do so, in fact, you might end up having a form with a code-behind class that contains almost everything you need—presentation logic, business logic, and even data access logic.

> **Note** Visual Studio 2008 is a stunningly powerful tool with great facilities for developers. You must be able to master those facilities, though, and use them properly. However, we certainly don't believe that Visual Studio 2008 is a tool that promotes autonomous views without exercising a due separation of concerns. If you use Visual Studio 2008 properly, you can certainly create well-designed applications and user interfaces. What does *properly* mean in this context? You should use Visual Studio 2008 mostly as a plain IDE. Something still needs to handle the odd button click or list selection, and that is the code in the code-behind file. Having a wizard generate that isn't necessarily bad. It's what you do in the method skeleton that's generated that causes the grief. So is the problem with actually using the wizard, or rather with using what the wizard produces without thought? The latter.

An AV is a class that contains display and state information for the view, as well as the full logic to handle any user actions from start to finish. With such monolithic components, you can hardly fulfill the requirements for the presentation layer outlined earlier in this section. In particular, you have a presentation layer that is hard (if not impossible) to test and that has no separation of concerns between the user interface and presentation logic.

Separation of concerns (SoC) is important in the presentation layer for a number of reasons. First, as we saw in Chapter 3, "Design Principles and Patterns," it is a fundamental design principle that contributes to creating the right combination of coupling and cohesion for a component. Second, SoC makes it easier for the presentation layer to implement a navigational workflow to decide which view comes next.

To achieve testability and separation of concerns in the user interface, the MVC pattern was introduced back in 1979. The original paper can be found here: *http://st-www.cs.uiuc.edu/users/smarch/st-docs/mvc.html.*

MVC: Pattern or Paradigm?

It is not coincidental that the aforementioned paper refers to MVC as a paradigm. Let's look at an excerpt from the paper:

> In the MVC paradigm the user input, the modeling of the external world, and the visual feedback to the user are explicitly separated and handled by three types of objects, each specialized for its task.

Today, instead, we refer to MVC as a pattern. Pattern or paradigm? Is this question only the offspring of the attention to subtle differences that is typical of architects? Maybe. The Oxford English Dictionary indicates three synonyms for *paradigm*: pattern, model, and exemplar. In software terms, though, a pattern is a particular concrete and proven solution, whereas a paradigm indicates a family of similar patterns. Or, put another way, a paradigm indicates the base class from which a variety of concrete design patterns derive.

In our vision, the original use of the word "paradigm" means that MVC is a (deliberately?) loosely defined pattern. MVC shows the way to go, but it leaves the architect a lot of freedom when it comes to implementation details. This is probably the reason why so many variations of MVC exist. This is probably also the reason why different implementations are all referred to as *MVC*. Let's go through the original formulation of MVC and discuss its pros and cons.

Generalities of the MVC Pattern

The primary goal of MVC is to split the application into distinct pieces—the model, the view, and the controller. The *model* refers to state of the application, wraps the application's functionalities, and notifies the view of state changes. The *view* refers to the generation of any graphical elements displayed to the user, and it captures and handles any user gestures. The controller maps user gestures to actions on the model and selects the next view. These three actors are often referred to as the *MVC triad*.

In our opinion, the model is the trickiest part of the triad to understand because of changes to its role that have occurred over the years. Before going any further with details about the role of each actor in the triad, we'll briefly recap why the introduction of MVC was a milestone in software design.

In the 1980s, applications of any complexity were essentially based on a monolithic block of code that structured programming was just trying to break down into more usable and reusable pieces. The user interface was therefore a collection of autonomous views, each managing the screen real estate, capturing user-generated events, and deciding what to do after. Before MVC, the code was basically developed by nesting calls from the user interface down to the core of the system. As illustrated in Figure 7-4, with MVC three distinct actors come into play, each with a precise role. The interaction of these actors on stage is what makes the show.

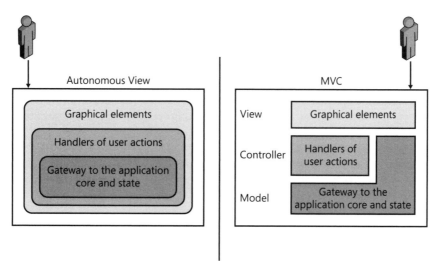

FIGURE 7-4 Autonomous view vs. MVC

MVC originated in a full object-oriented environment such as SmallTalk, where—we should say that—breaking down applications in terms of objects was quite natural.

What are the benefits of MVC?

There are several benefits. In the first place, you have simplified testing of the user interface. Taking code out of the view makes it easier to change the graphics without altering the behavior of the user interface. Yes, this is exactly the principle that supports code-behind classes that Visual Studio 2008 tools use profusely. Taking as much code as possible out of the view also encourages code structuring and logical layers. Separation of concerns, at whatever level, is helpful and viable when you want to achieve low coupling and high cohesion. Last but not least, splitting the presentation layer into distinct objects lays the groundwork for various teams to work on different parts of the application simultaneously—for example, designers taking care of the view and developers coding actual actions.

The Model in MVC

In the original formulation of MVC, the model is the object that represents the application's gateway to the business logic. In the model, you find the state of the application as well as data to expose through the view and actions to be invoked in response to user actions. The model is an object designed to hold state and reply to requests for state changes coming from the view. The model is also designed to execute actions requested by the controller that typically result in state changes.

This vision of the model made a lot of sense in the 1980s for all applications. Today things are a bit different.

Originally, MVC was conceived to be a pattern for building the *whole* application and not just the presentation layer. If you take a look at the many tutorials about the ASP .NET MVC Framework, you see that the model is created using the LINQ-to-SQL designer in Visual Studio 2008 in the context of an MVC application. It might seem, therefore, that you need to use the MVC pattern to have a distinct business layer. The truth, instead, is that MVC does most of its work with the view and controller and just requires a model for the data being worked on in the view. The model then can be your existing business layer (object model and services) or a new set of classes aptly created for the purpose of applying the pattern.

For simple applications, applying the MVC pattern means creating a view, controller, and business layer. In enterprise-class applications, you use the MVC pattern for getting separation of concerns and testability in the presentation layer. Subsequently, MVC is mostly a pattern for the presentation layer, and all that you focus on is the interaction between the view and the controller.

Figure 7-5 illustrates the interaction in MVC between the various elements of the triad.

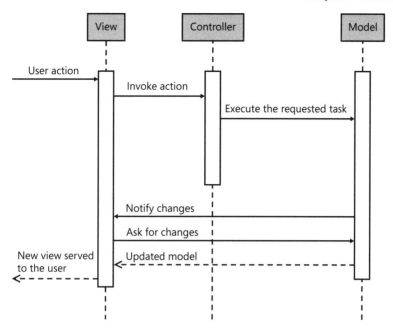

FIGURE 7-5 The MVC triad in action

From the diagram, can you spot any problems that would seriously affect large, multitiered applications? The model has some relationship to the view and gets invoked by the controller. It has multiple points of contact with the upper layer. This is the main point that, as we'll see in a moment, led the transition to a slightly different pattern—the Model-View-Presenter (MVP) pattern—more specifically designed for large and complex applications.

> **Important** We should say again that in this discussion we are considering the original formulation of MVC and that our main purpose is illustrating the evolution of presentation patterns. If your knowledge of MVC mostly comes from the implementation of it provided by some popular frameworks such as the ASP .NET MVC framework, you might spot a sort of misalignment between what Figure 7-5 shows and your understanding of how things go today. These differences exist because of some key changes that were made to the original MVC pattern that the ASP .NET MVC framework acknowledges.
>
> As mentioned earlier, the MVC pattern is loosely formulated and was not devised for the Web. So a variation of MVC was defined a few years ago that is all that Web MVC frameworks implement. Nicely enough. Among other things, this variation of MVC (known as Model2) also addresses the interaction between the model and the rest of the system. We'll return to the topic of Web variations of MVC in great detail later in the chapter.

Let's now delve a bit deeper into the role played by the view and controller actors in an MVC scenario.

The View in MVC

In MVC, the view is as *dumb, humble*, and *passive* as possible. (Dumb, humble, and passive are terms commonly used to describe the role of the view in an MVC scenario.) Translated as instructions for developing code, it means that the view should care only about painting the interface to display to users.

Ideally, the view is so simple and logic-free as to need virtually no testing. Users (and developers before users) can reasonably test the view by simply looking at the pixels on the screen. Anything else beyond pure graphical rendering should *ideally* be taken out of the view and placed in the controller and model. This includes, for example, the logic that determines whether a certain button should be enabled or grayed out at some point.

What are the responsibilities of the view in MVC?

A view is made of interactive controls (such as input fields, buttons, and lists), and it waits for any user actions. When the user, say, clicks a button, the view simply forwards the call to the controller. How this happens has changed quite a bit over the years and is definitely an aspect that largely depends on platform, languages, and development tools. In a .NET application, the view handles its events in the code-behind class and all it does is invoke a particular action method on the controller class. Here's some sample code:

```
void Button1_Click(object sender, EventArgs e)
{
    ViewController controller = new ViewController();
    controller.ActionForButton1Clicked();
}
```

The *ViewController* class in the example represents the controller for a particular view—be it a Windows form, Web form, or Silverlight user control. The controller features one method for each possible user action supported by the user interface. Each supported user action corresponds to an action on the controller.

Another key responsibility of the view is rendering.

In an MVC implementation, the controller updates the model by executing the triggered action. The model then notifies the view about pending changes on its state that the view might want to reflect in the user interface. The view reads the model and provides an updated interface.

The view and the model are bound according to the rules of the Observer pattern. In Observer, the subject (in this case, the model) notifies the observer (in this case, the view) about changes that have occurred. As a result, the view requests the current state from the model and works with it.

Note The forward of the user action to the controller can also happen automatically, by means of some machinery in the MVC framework of choice. This is exactly what happens in the ASP .NET MVC framework, where the view basically posts to a URL. A server-side module captures the requests, examines the URL, and figures out which action to execute.

The Controller in MVC

The controller is triggered by the view and executes an action that ultimately induces changes into the model. If the model is the business logic layer (BLL), the controller ends up invoking a method or a service on the BLL. If the model is a component that abstracts the BLL, the controller just invokes a public method on the model.

More precisely, the controller interacts with the model in a way that is coherent with the user action. The controller scripts the model to achieve the results expected from the given user action. The interaction can be as simple as invoking just one method, or it can require a series of calls and some flow logic. If the model is a comprehensive object that wraps the BLL, the interaction between the controller and model is much flatter and resembles a *fire-and-forget* call.

The controller has no idea of the changes inferred on the view by its interaction with the model. In MVC, the controller is just not responsible for updating the view. The controller doesn't exist in MVC to separate the view and model. In MVC, the view knows the model directly and the model knows the view through the Observer relationship. The controller gets input from the view and operates on the model in a unidirectional flow. The controller is not a mediator between the view and the model; it is rather the mediator between the user and the application.

The controller, however, has some responsibilities with regard to the view. In particular, the controller is responsible for selecting the next view to display to the user. If the user action doesn't require a switch to a different view, the controller simply proceeds with any interaction with the model that is required. Otherwise, it just creates a new triad for the new user interface—new view, new model, and new controller. (See Figure 7-6.)

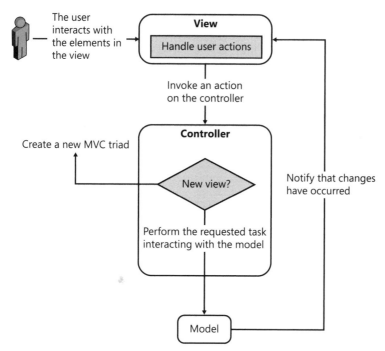

FIGURE 7-6 The MVC controller in action

In Figure 7-6, we used a flowchart decision block to symbolize the work the controller does to decide which view to display next. Deciding about the next view can be a not-so-simple task.

The MVC controller is concerned with the current view and is able to process only user actions that affect its own view. In theory, the MVC controller might delegate the user action to an additional view-controller class that decides whether the action belongs to the current view or a redirect is required. It turns out, though, that most of the time the MVC controller also acts as the view-controller. The controller (or the view-controller) is responsible for handling any user-generated event that has to be resolved within the same view or through subviews.

What if a different view is requested? How complex is the logic required to decide about the new view? If the next view can be selected through a simple *switch* statement, you might still be able to keep all the navigation logic in the MVC controller for a particular view. In this way, each controller holds the logic to navigate to all views you can reach from a particular one. If swarms of conditions show up, you're better off introducing a new class—the *application controller*.

The application controller is a centralized class that holds the logic for navigating around the application. Whenever a controller feels the need to display a different view, it does that by yielding to the application controller.

The application controller is created upon startup and is a global object. Here's an example for ASP .NET:

```
protected void Application_Start(object sender, EventArgs e)
{
    // Create an instance of the specific navigation service to use
    SiteNavigationWorkflow nav = new SiteNavigationWorkflow();

    // Register the navigator with an application-wide service
    NavigationController.Register(nav);
}
```

From within an ASP .NET page, you use code such as in the following snippet to navigate to a different view:

```
// Navigate to the view (URL in ASP .NET) referenced by the "customers" moniker
NavigationController.NavigateTo("customers");
```

The logic that figures out the new URL (or the new form, if it is a Windows application) is contained in the *SiteNavigationWorkflow* class. Here's an excerpt:

```
class SiteNavigationWorkflow : INavigationWorkflow
{
    public void NavigateTo(string url)
    {
        switch (url)
        {
            case "main":
                HttpContext.Current.Response.Redirect("~/default.aspx");
                break;
```

```
        case "customers":
          HttpContext.Current.Response.Redirect("~/CustomersPage.aspx");
          break;

          ⋮

     }
   }
}
```

Clearly, the navigation service can be implemented using a workflow if you have a particularly sophisticated logic to implement and frequently changing requirements to deal with.

To top off the discussion on the classic MVC pattern, we feel we must show the classic diagram that is used nearly anywhere to illustrate the mechanics of the pattern. It's well known that a picture is worth a thousand words. However, having trained developers and architects for years about how to use MVC, we find that a clear explanation is much better than a somewhat abstract diagram. Placed at the end of an MVC section, a diagram such as the one shown in Figure 7-7 can produce either of two effects: confirm your understanding or reopen the whole matter. In any case, you know you understand it or you know you do not!

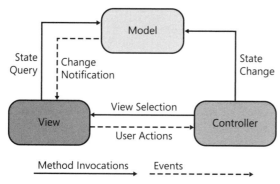

FIGURE 7-7 The classic MVC diagram

> **Important** Who really does update the view? Is it the controller that orders the view to refresh? Is it a notification from the model that triggers the view to refresh? Or is it perhaps the controller that informs the view that changes to the model have occurred? These questions are a good example of the implementation details architects must decide upon that make MVC a loosely formulated pattern.
>
> In the original MVC paper, two approaches are presented—one with a passive model, and one with an active model. A passive model is massaged by the controller which, in turn, operates under the solicitation of the view. The controller knows, or assumes, that some user actions can update the model; so it's up to the controller to notify the view about changes. This approach is too simplistic for the average complexity of today's software. We presented a more realistic scenario in this chapter, where an active model notifies the view of its changes and the controller is unaware of the effects that user actions might produce on the view. Obviously, two different implementations of a piece of code can both correctly raise the flag of MVC. But there's more.

A popular variation of MVC, the aforementioned Model2, takes yet another route. In classic MVC with an active model and a passive model, the view receives notification of the changes and grabs fresh data from the model. With Model2, on the other hand, the controller orders the view to refresh and passes all the information the view needs to update the interface. In Model2, there's no observer-like communication between the view and the model. As you can see, these are quite significant changes, but they all happen under the umbrella of MVC.

Model2: A Web Variation of MVC

Until recently with the ASP .NET MVC framework, on the Windows platform the MVC pattern has never been particularly popular. This reminds us of Microsoft Foundation Classes (MFC), which offered more than a decade ago an architecture with some points in common with MVC—particularly, the Document/View (DV) model. DV can be seen as a version of MVC where the view and controller are fused together.

We really don't know whether the MFC team intentionally discarded MVC to embrace DV; our feeling, however, is that DV blossomed autonomously during the design by simply applying correctly and diffusely the SoC principle. Principles and fundamentals never go out of style! And patterns are only a shortcut to a solution.

MVC was devised at a time when the Web had not yet come into existence. MVC can certainly be adapted to Web applications, but its original formulation targets desktop applications. On the other hand, the loose definition of MVC leaves room for frameworks to customize MVC to particular areas. This is exactly the case for Model2—an extremely popular Web variation of MVC. (You can find detailed information on the pattern at *http://java.sun.com/blueprints/ guidelines/designing_enterprise_applications_2e/web-tier/web-tier5.html.*)

Model2 is a pattern that was originally created for developing with Java Server Pages (JSP). It owes a lot of its popularity to the Struts framework. (See *http://struts.apache.org.*)

In a Model2 application, requests flow from the browser directly to a front controller implemented as an HTTP interceptor—in ASP .NET jargon, we would call it *an HTTP module*. In other words, the user interface of a Model2 application offers HTML input elements and all of them cause a link to be followed and an HTTP post to occur.

The front controller on the Web server captures the request and looks at it—in particular, it looks at the structure of the URL. Based on the URL, the front controller figures out which (MVC) controller should be instantiated to service the request. After the controller has been identified, a method is invoked that can affect the model. As the controller's method returns, the controller orders the view to render out to HTML. The view receives fresh data for its response directly from the controller. The output of the view is delivered to the front controller and sent back to the browser. (See Figure 7-8.)

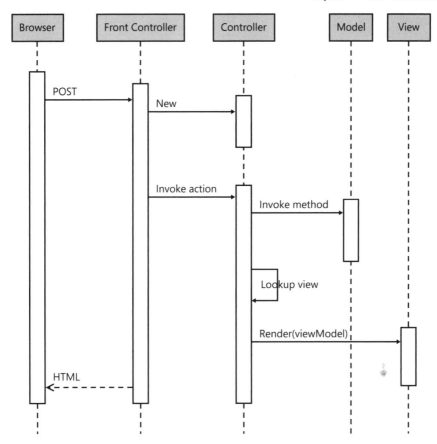

FIGURE 7-8 The Model2 diagram

 Note The front controller in the figure is not technically part of the Model2 implementation. The Model2 pattern exists because it is hard-coded into some specific frameworks. When you install such a framework, it extends the Web server by registering some helper runtime components such as the front controller.

There are a few differences between classic MVC and Model2. First and foremost, there's no direct contact, let alone an Observer relationship, between the view and the model. Second, the controller renders the view and explicitly passes display data to it. The user action is not captured and handled by the view. A system component in the Web server—the front controller—intercepts HTTP requests and figures out from the URL and headers which controller will be in charge of the request.

Model2 is just MVC adapted to a new medium—the Web—that just wasn't around at the time MVC was first devised. Today, people often people speak of MVC with regard to the Web, but what they actually mean (consciously or unconsciously) is Model2. Model2 is exactly the pattern behind the Microsoft ASP .NET MVC framework.

Note We said that classic MVC can be adapted to the Web, but hinted that Model2 is a better option. Why is this so?

Think of how the Web works. Any user action originates an HTTP post. The Web server captures these requests and maps them to a page class. The page class goes through its own life cycle, inside of which it figures out which action the user actually meant to be executed. In a classic MVC scenario, the page class figures out the right controller and invokes a method. The execution of the method modifies the model.

What about the refresh of the view? It is left up to you whether to push a refresh from the controller or use data binding to sync up the view and the model. As you can see, this route can be shortened quite a bit by using a front controller. By using properly formatted URLs, the front controller—for example, an HTTP module—can figure out from the URL (in a REST-like manner) the controller to use and invoke an action on it. You save the page life cycle and come up with an extremely passive view that needs virtually no testing. You pour your testing effort into the controller instead. What we have described as a general approach here applies literally to the ASP .NET MVC framework.

What object really plays the role of the model in a Model2 approach? Is the actor "model" actually your business layer? This is debatable, and we don't believe there's an answer that serves as an absolute truth. It is all about perspective. Here is our own.

As you see in Figure 7-8, the model can certainly match the BLL. However, in Model2 the view is completely detached from the model. At the same time, another, still unnamed, data holder object is around that the view knows intimately. It is precisely what we called the *viewModel* entity in Figure 7-8. This element contains all the data the view needs to do its job of creating HTML for the browser. The view knows the *viewModel* rather than BLL. The *viewModel* corresponds to the *ViewData* container (and all of its typed variations) in the ASP .NET MVC framework. Similar containers also exist in MonoRail (another .NET Model2 framework) and Struts. It certainly doesn't change the way you write your Web applications, but it's an interesting exercise to think about and is, in our opinion, the real *M* in the Model2 implementation of the MVC pattern.

Important It is a sharp and bold statement, but we feel we have to make it: today classic MVC is gone. However, some of its variations are healthy and thrive. They are Model2 for the Web and MVP for both the Web and Windows. In turn, and only more recently, MVP has undergone a facelift. In July 2006, Martin Fowler proposed to retire MVP entirely and replace it with two variations—Passive View (PV) and Supervising Controller (SVC). We'll return to this point later in the chapter.

The Model-View-Presenter Pattern

The advent of MVC is a key milestone because it made it clear that applications should be designed with separation of concerns in mind. SoC was already a known principle, but MVC put it into practice. MVC is not perfect, though.

Classic MVC has two big drawbacks. One is that the model needs to communicate to the view changes of state—typically through an Observer relationship. The other is that the view has intimate knowledge of the model. The view is refreshed when it gets a notification of changes in the model. How does it refresh?

The view basically reads from the model any information it needs and displays it through its UI elements. There's no explicit contract that states which data the view needs precisely. As a result, the view needs to have its own logic to select data from the big model and massage it into UI elements. This code can hardly be taken out of the view—the view is not as passive as it should be. And also, the view depends to some extent on the underlying platform or UI toolkit being used.

The controller is merely a mediator between the user and the application. By giving the controller the power to render the view while interacting with the model, you put it at the center of the universe. In this way, most of the presentation logic passes through the controller, and the controller is a plain class with no UI. The controller is an inherently more testable class.

By defining a contract for the view, you automatically make the presentation layer even more testable, as the view is now mockable. For the same reason, the view can be replaced with another view class implementing the same contract. This enables at least two interesting scenarios.

First, the presentation logic gains independence from the UI platform. As a result, the same controller can be reused in Windows and Web presentation layers. Why is this so? Well, the controller knows the view by interface; all that it needs is an object to work with that supports a contracted interface.

 Note The same presenter is easier to share between views operating on similar platforms. It's much easier to share a presenter between a Windows Forms view and WPF view than it might be when Windows Forms and ASP .NET are involved.

Second, the same controller can work with different views of the same application. This is an important characteristic with regard to the Software as a Service (SaaS) deployment model. In an SaaS scenario, an application is hosted on a Web server and offered as a service to customers. Think, for example, of an Enterprise Resource Planning (ERP) application. It is installed on a public server but made accessible to multiple customers, and each customer can have its own personalized edition with a different UI and also different business logic.

As you can see, there are a number of reasons to go beyond MVC. The next step is MVP.

Generalities of the MVP Pattern

MVP is a derivative of MVC aimed at providing a cleaner separation between the view, the model, and the controller. The pattern was originally developed at Taligent in the 1990s.

The paper you find at *http://www.wildcrest.com/Potel/Portfolio/mvp.pdf* offers an introduction to MVP that describes how and why the pattern has been devised.

Starting from the MVC triad, creators of MVP neatly separated the model from the view/controller pair, which they called *presentation*. The core of MVP is the strictly regulated interaction taking place between the view and the controller. In MVP, the controller is renamed to *presenter*. Figure 7-9 offers an overview of the MVP pattern and contrasts it to MVC.

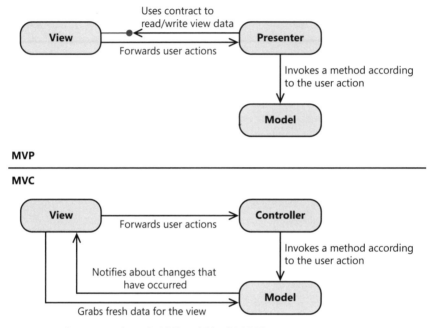

FIGURE 7-9 Actors at a glance in MVP and (classic) MVC

> **Note** For simplicity, the MVC diagram in the figure does not include any relationships deriving from the view selection process. For completeness, you should add an arrow moving from the controller to the view; however, this relationship would merely indicate the ability of the controller to hide or display subviews on the current view or switch to a different view. In no way does it refer to the controller's ability to write to the current view, as in MVP.

In the figure, two fundamental differences between MVP and classic MVC stare you in the face.

In MVP, the view and the model are neatly separated and the view exposes a contract through which the presenter accesses the portion of the view that is dependent on the rest of the system. Summarizing the situation further, we can say that MVP is a refinement of MVC based on three facts:

- The view doesn't know the model.

- The presenter ignores any UI technology behind the view.

- The view is mockable for testing purposes.

In addition, by extracting an interface out of the model, you enable a Presenter-First scenario, where both the view and the model are mockable for testing purposes. Having the presenter linked to the model only through an interface makes the aforementioned SaaS scenarios even easier to support. Figure 7-10 shows the diagram for the Presenter-First development methodology, which basically combines MVP with a strong testing orientation.

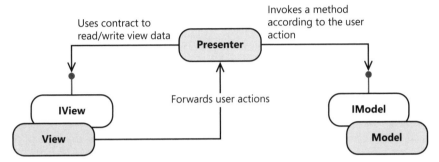

FIGURE 7-10 An MVP variation that enables a Presenter-First approach

> **Note** Presenter-First is a slight MVP variation that goes hand in hand with a test-driven development methodology. The presenter is mapped directly to user stories, and development focuses on the presenter component until all unit tests pass. Next, the focus moves on to the model. The view is virtually devoid of logic so as to need no automated testing whatsoever. For more information, have a look at *http://www.atomicobject.com/files/PresenterFirstAgile2006.pdf*.

Let's briefly go through the various elements of the MVP triad.

The Model in MVP

Let's face it—from the UI perspective, in modern multilayered systems the model actor now plays a secondary role. In the beginning, the focus on the model was primarily a way to draw people's attention to the separation of concerns. Today, SoC is an absolute necessity in large applications. So in a multilayered system, you already have a business layer with a domain model, a table module, or any sort of object model that suits you. And that is the model from an MVP perspective; it exists regardless of the pattern you employ for the presentation layer. As mentioned, the core of MVP is the interaction between the view and the presenter.

The View in MVP

In MVP, the view is devised to be as thin and passive as possible. This is the theory, anyway. In the real-world, a really passive view can be quite cumbersome to write and maintain and can add a lot of complexity to the presenter.

If you are familiar with physics—in particular, the Law of Conservation of Energy (LCE)—you know that the total amount of energy in any isolated system remains constant. It can't be re-created, although it can change forms. By paraphrasing LCE, we came up with a semi-serious *Law of Conservation of Software Complexity* (LCSC).

LCSC states that the total amount of complexity in a software system is always constant and can be moved across layers. This is to say that the amount of presentation logic does not vary. Where you place it is an architectural choice.

> **Note** A hilarious (but true) corollary to this law reminds us that complexity is constant in a production system but variable (mostly growing) during development. And, anyway, software complexity is never less than the complexity initially determined by functional requirements. In other words, unlike energy, software complexity can be created artificially. In our experience, this usually is done by zealous (and hyperpurist) developers and architects. Theory is good, but theory inappropriately applied is often a disaster waiting to happen.

If you opt for a passive view, you have an inherently more testable system because the logic in the view is reduced to an absolute minimum. Subsequently, you run no serious risk at all by not testing the view. Any piece of code can contain mistakes, but in the case of a passive view the extreme simplicity of the code only allows for gross and patently obvious mistakes that can be easily caught without any automated procedure.

In accordance with LCSC, the complexity taken out of the view moves to another layer—in this case, the presenter. A passive view is inevitably coupled with a more complex presenter. Opting for a passive view is a tradeoff between high testability and complexity in the presenter classes. This approach goes under the name of Passive View. (For more information, see *http://martinfowler.com/eaaDev/PassiveScreen.html*.)

> **Note** Although the driving force for PV remains maximum testability, there's another benefit in it that you might want to consider. In a Passive View approach, the view is a raw sequence of UI elements with no additional data binding or formatting. The presenter acts directly on the UI elements and works simply by loading data into them. There's nothing that happens in the UI that you can't spot easily. If there's something wrong in the UI, it's right before your eyes. Your eyes are your test harness.

You can also opt for a more active view that contains some logic as far as data binding and data formatting is concerned. Developing a richer view is easier and basically distributes the required complexity between the view and the presenter. The view needs to take care of some synchronization and adaptation work to make input data usable by user-interface elements. This approach goes by the name Supervising Controller. (For more information, see *http://martinfowler.com/eaaDev/SupervisingPresenter.html*.) In the next section, we'll return to Passive View and Supervising Controller with a practical example.

Because an SVC view is inherently more complex, it is more risky for you not to test the view at all. Opting for an SVC view entails making a tradeoff between testability and ease (and speed) of development. Testing an SVC view means testing a piece of user interface with logic and graphics—not exactly a walk in the park. How would you test a UI? For a

Web presentation layer, you can mock the view, send it a fixed model, and then check the resulting HTML. For a Windows or WPF user interface, our preferred approach is adding the view to the acceptance test checklist for end users to verify. During development, we test views by simply poking around. Every developer is the first tester of any piece of code he writes. No sane developer would check in his code if he's not quite sure and confident about it. This nonautomated test is not recommended for the entire application (in fact, in Chapter 3 we refer to Testing-By-Poking-Around as an antipattern), but this approach makes sense for a relatively simple piece of UI.

Note Is there any general approach to test-driving a graphical UI? The general idea is to force the view to generate nonvisual output that can be asserted in the unit test to verify the soundness of the UI. Some tools exist to help with this. For ASP .NET, an interesting tool is WatiN (available at *http://www.watin.sourceforge.net*), which you might want to consider along with the toolkit unit testing in the Visual Studio 2008 Team Tester edition. Another non-ASP .NET-specific automatic test tool for applications is IBM's Rational Robot. For more information, visit *http://www.306.ibm.com/software/awdtools/tester/robot*.

Using SVC doesn't mean you have to renounce testing. It still allows for a good deal of testability and it speeds up development. Passive View and Supervising Controller are both reasonable approaches to building the view in an MVP scenario. According to Fowler, you never use MVP; rather, you use either Passive View or Supervising Controller. Or you use a mix of the two.

The Presenter in MVP

A common question is, why this change in the name? Why is it a *presenter* and not a *controller*? The name *presenter* better conveys the sense of a component that is responsible for handling user actions; the presenter presents user requests to the back-end system; after that, it presents a response to the user.

The presenter sits in between the view and the model; it receives input from the view and passes commands down to the model. It then gets results and updates the view through the contracted view interface. Figure 7-11 illustrates the sequence.

If the user action requires navigating to a different view, the presenter is responsible for jumping to the new user interface. Usually, the presenter works in conjunction with an application controller such as the navigation service we examined earlier for the MVC controller.

MVP and Enterprise-Class Applications

MVP is not a pattern that can be implemented quickly. As we'll see in a moment, it requires you to define an interface and a presenter for nearly every view in the application—each Web form in ASP .NET and each form in Windows.

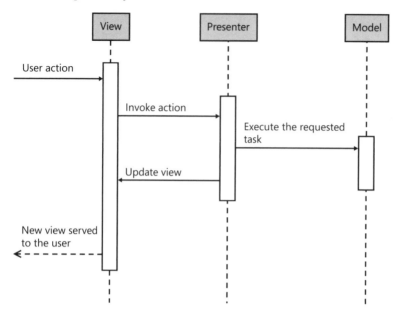

FIGURE 7-11 The MVP diagram

MVP provides guidance on how to manage heaps of views and, quite obviously, comes at a cost—the cost of increased complexity in the application code. As you can imagine, these costs are easier to absorb in large applications than in simple programs. MVP, therefore, is not just for any application.

In MVP, the view is defined through an interface and this interface is the only point of contact between the system and the view. As an architect, after you've abstracted a view with an interface, you can give developers the green light to start developing presentation logic without waiting for designers to produce the graphics. After developers have interfaces, they can start coding and interfaces can be extracted from user stories, if not from full specifications.

MVP is an important presentation pattern that can be a bit expensive to implement in relatively simple applications. On the other hand, MVP shines in enterprise-class applications, where you really need to reuse as much presentation logic as possible, across multiple platforms and in SaaS scenarios.

The Presentation Model Pattern

Another interesting pattern for the presentation layer is Presentation Model (PM). Developed by Martin Fowler, PM is also known as Application Model. Here's the link where you can find all the details: *http://martinfowler.com/eaaDev/PresentationModel.html*.

How does PM differ from MVP? Ultimately, it's not an entirely different type of animal. We like to consider it yet another variation of MVP that is particularly suited to a rich and complex user interface. On the Windows platforms, PM works well with user interfaces built with Windows Presentation Foundation and Silverlight. (Microsoft recommends it here: *http://msdn.microsoft.com/en-us/library/cc707885.aspx.*)

PM, like MVP, is based on three actors: the view, the model, and the presenter.

In MVP, the view exposes a contract to the presenter and the presenter talks back to the view through that interface. Binding of the data occurs through the implementation of the interface in the view class—the *Page* class in ASP .NET, the *Form* class in Windows Forms, and the *Window* class in WPF. The code that does the binding belongs to the view and can be as simple as a property assignment or as sophisticated as rich data binding.

In PM, the view doesn't expose any interface, but a data model for the view is incorporated in the model. The model is not the business logic, but simply a class that represents the state of the view. The view elements are directly bound to properties on the model. In summary, in PM the view is passive and doesn't implement any interface. The interface is transformed into a model class and incorporated in the presenter. See Figure 7-12.

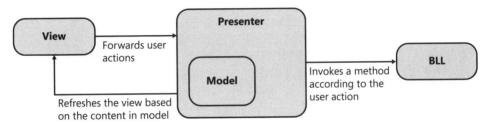

FIGURE 7-12 The triad in the Presentation Model pattern

The Model in PM

In PM, the model is *no longer* the business layer; rather, it is an ad hoc view's model that fully represents the state of the user interface. The model is a class with properties for each settable UI element in the view. For example, you have a collection property for the items to show in a grid, a property for the content of a text box, and even a Boolean property for the state (enabled or disabled) of a button. After you have fully initialized the model, the view is ready for rendering.

The model is updated by the presenter after an interaction occurs with the system's application logic. The model is usually encapsulated in the presenter. This class is referred to as the *PresentationModel* class.

The View in PM

The view is utterly simple. It is nothing more than a bunch of UI elements bound to properties in the model. Any events raised by the user are transmitted to the *PresentationModel* and end up updating the model. This happens for both selecting a check box and clicking a button.

When the user action requires an interaction with the BLL, the *PresentationModel* updates the model with the results it gets. The view is generally owned by the presenter so that the *PresentationModel*, after updating the model, just orders the view to render.

No information is passed to the view. The view holds a reference to the *PresentationModel*, and the model is exposed out of the *PresentationModel* class. The most boring part of the PM pattern is writing the synchronization code that keeps the view and model in sync. Thankfully, in the .NET Framework data binding helps a lot.

It should be noted, that view/model synchronization is bidirectional. When the user selects an item in a list, the model should be updated; when an action occurs that modifies the selection, the model is updated. For this reason, PM is a popular pattern. It is especially popular in combination with WPF because of the great support the WPF platform offers for two-way data binding.

The Presenter in PM

The presenter in the PM pattern accomplishes nearly the same tasks as in MVP and MVC. It receives events from the view and processes them against the presentation layer, business logic, or both. In PM, though, the presenter holds a model object and is responsible for filling it up with any state changes resulting from back-end operations. Finally, the presenter calls the view to refresh. Figure 7-13 illustrates the sequence.

As mentioned, the presenter class goes by the name *PresentationModel* and exposes public methods as well as all the public properties that form the data model for the view.

Choosing a Pattern for the User Interface

In this section, we started with autonomous views and went through 30 years of software evolution, discussing main patterns that emerged for designing applications and the presentation layer of multitier applications. We saw how MVC was a key step because it introduced the concept of SoC; then we moved on to consider two further refinements: MVP and PM. But let's briefly look for the bottom line as far as the presentation layer is concerned.

My Focus Is the Web

For an ASP .NET application, you have two main options in terms of patterns. You can go with the traditional ASP .NET pattern. (It's ultimately an implementation of the PageController pattern as described on page 133 of [P of EAA].) Or you can move toward MVC. In the latter case, you opt for the ASP .NET MVC framework.

The traditional ASP .NET pattern requires you to use page classes as controllers. The page receives events from the view and processes them against the application logic. The page is also responsible for navigation. This traditional model can be improved with a deeper separation of concerns by using a manual implementation of MVC or MVP.

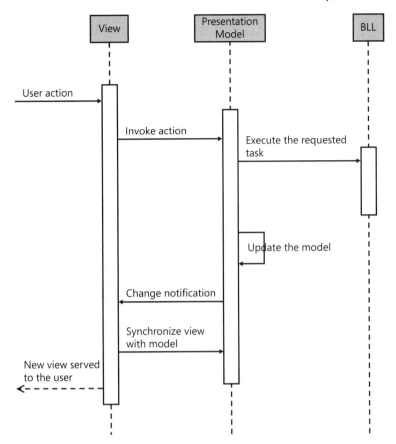

FIGURE 7-13 The Presentation Model diagram

However, the ASP .NET MVC framework offers an excellent implementation of Model2—the Web-specific variation of MVC. Microsoft's Web Client Software Factory (WCSF) library provides a basic library for speeding up the implementation of the MVP pattern.

If your primary focus is the Web, we recommend that you either stick to Web forms and improve them with a bit of separation of concerns or move to a different model of ASP .NET MVC.

My Focus Is Windows

All in all, MVP is the way to go if you're looking for a presentation pattern that goes beyond the basic capabilities offered by the .NET UI toolkit of choice—be it Windows Forms, Windows Presentation Foundation, or Silverlight.

If you're making extensive use of two-way data binding in WPF, Silverlight, or both, you might want to consider the PM pattern, which is often referred to as Model-View-ViewModel (MVVM) in WPF.

I Need to Support Multiple GUIs

A scenario in which you need to support multiple GUIs probably is the easiest to address: go for MVP. MVP is the pattern that provides the best combination of testability, separation of concerns, maintenance, and code reuse. It is possible to write a presenter and reuse it all, or in large part, in Windows and ASP .NET. It is possible to reduce the view to an interface that naturally leads to increased testability and independence from the graphics skins and UI toolkits.

To see a summary of the content of this section devoted to the evolution of patterns for the presentation layer, have a look at Figure 7-14. The leaves of the tree are, in our humble opinion, the presentation pattern you should actually consider today.

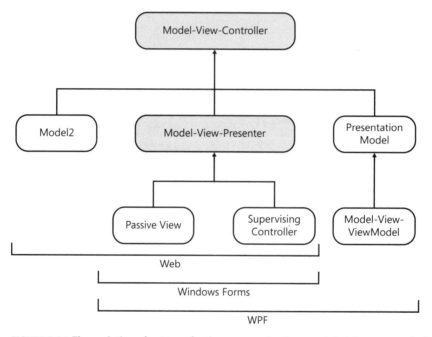

FIGURE 7-14 The evolution of patterns for the presentation layer and their impact on platforms.

UI and Behavior-Driven Development

Behavior-driven development (BDD) is a methodology for application development that was introduced by Ken North in 2003. BDD puts the presentation layer—specifically, the UI—at the center of the universe. It is not a pattern for designing software like MVC or MVP; it is, rather, an approach to developing a system starting from the UI.

The driving force of BDD is delivering high value to customers. This is realized through a method that has the ultimate goal of preventing scenarios like the one in the satirical quotation at the beginning of this chapter: users politely smile, congratulate the team for the effort, agree that the application meets acceptance tests, but...it's not what the company really needs and wants.

The key point of BDD is coming to a full understanding of the system's expected behavior and, next, to an effective implementation. According to the BDD methodology, the first piece of code that the team focuses on is the UI. The UI is then shared with stakeholders quite soon in the project life cycle.

Stakeholders, including end users, can therefore provide early feedback and drive the team to effectively build a UI that looks and behaves in the most appropriate way. Taken to the limit, BDD means that any features in the system are there because there's a piece of user interface that directly or indirectly requires them.

BDD embraces the principle of YAGNI (You Aren't Going to Need It) and is an excellent antidote to the typical fatal attraction that developers and architects have for complexity—especially unnecessary complexity. This fatal attraction is well expressed by Michael A. Jackson in his book *Principles of Program Design* (Academic Press, 1975):

> *[Programmers] often take refuge in an understandable, but disastrous, inclination towards complexity and ingenuity in their work. Forbidden to design anything larger than a program, they respond by making that program intricate enough to challenge their professional skill.*

BDD helps developers focus on what users want. And it also helps users to figure out quickly what they really want.

Design of the Presentation

Let's put the two variations of the MVP pattern through their paces and build a sample front end for a Web and Windows presentation. The final user interface you should expect to obtain is what you already saw in Figure 7-2 for Windows and Figure 7-3 for the Web. The user interface is therefore expected to provide a detail view of a customer. The user interface features a list to let users pick out the customer whose information they want to drill down into, and it contains a few labels to display related information—ID, company name, contact name, and country.

What Data Is Displayed in the View?

In an MVP scenario, the first step to complete is defining the contract for each required view. Each page in an ASP .NET application, and each form in a Windows application, has its own interface to talk to the rest of the presentation layer. The interface identifies the data model that the view supports. Each logically equivalent view has the same interface regardless of the platform.

Let's consider the form in Figure 7-15. All you have to do is define an interface to represent all data displayed in the view.

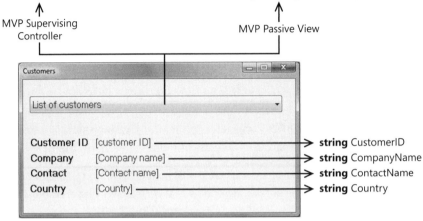

Collection<**Customer**> CustomerList   **void** AddCustomer(**string** companyName, **string** customerID)

MVP Supervising
Controller

MVP Passive View

Customers

List of customers

Customer ID	[customer ID]	→	**string** CustomerID
Company	[Company name]	→	**string** CompanyName
Contact	[Contact name]	→	**string** ContactName
Country	[Country]	→	**string** Country

FIGURE 7-15 Dissecting a view to extract an interface

Creating a Contract for the View

The view is intended to display a few properties about the currently selected customer. Each of these properties—mostly scalar values such as strings, dates, and numbers—take a member in the final interface, as shown next:

```
public interface ICustomerDetailsView
{
    string CustomerID { set; }
    string CompanyName { get; set; }
    string ContactName { get; set; }
    string Country { get; set; }
    IList CustomersList { get; set; }
}
```

As you can see, the view is expected to also display the list of available customers through a drop-down list. This poses the first issue that requires an architectural decision to be made.

How Much Logic Do You Want in the View?

The simplest approach entails that you use data binding to populate the drop-down list—be it a Windows *ComboBox* or an ASP .NET *DropDownList* control. Data binding means that you pump a collection of *Customer* objects into the *DataSource* property of the drop-down control and then select a couple of properties on the *Customer* type to decide what text is displayed in the list and the unique value that is returned when a selection is made.

```
// collCustomers is assumed to be of type Collection<Customer>.
// lstCustomers is the drop-down list control we have in the UI.
lstCustomers.DisplayMember = "CompanyName";
lstCustomers.ValueMember = "CustomerID";
lstCustomers.DataSource = collCustomers;
```

Is there anything wrong, or just debatable, in this solution? Ultimately, there's nothing wrong here. It is a perfectly functioning solution, and it works well for ASP .NET and Windows. Is it testable? Sure, it is testable; however, the topic of testability drives us to further considerations. What kind of view are we designing in this way? Is it a passive and humble view? Or is it a smarter view with a few ounces of presentation logic in it?

There's quite a bit of logic in the data binding process. Don't be fooled by how simple it is for a developer to set up a data binding mechanism. Internally, the platform's data binding engine has to load the data model, cast it to *IEnumerable*, retrieve every element in the list, and format it to display. It is a black-boxed piece of code, but it's definitely not a simple value assignment like setting the *Text* property on a *Label* control.

Using data binding makes the view (and the related presenter) much faster and more comfortable to write, but it also introduces more presentation logic in the view. After you have a portion of the model in the view (be it a part of the domain's object model or just data transfer objects), you code your way forward briskly and with ease. In a certain way, you have less bureaucracy and can code what you need without first ensuring that a particular piece of data is delivered to you through the interface. Extensions and changes are also easier to accommodate in this way and likely do not require modifications on the presenter. In a nutshell, you split the logic between the view and the presenter.

This is neither good nor bad. This is just a reasonable possibility—the Supervising Controller variation of the MVP pattern.

The more logic you have in the view, the more you should care about testing. And testing a piece of UI is a task that can hardly be automated. Going for SVC or opting for a thinner and dumber view is merely a judgment call.

If you opt for SVC, you might end up using the following (modified) interface:

```
public interface ICustomerDetailsView
{
    // Allows the presenter to update the CustomerID user interface element
    string CustomerID { set; }

    // Allows the presenter to update the CompanyName user interface element
    string CompanyName { set; }

    // Allows the presenter to update the ContactName user interface element
    string ContactName { set; }

    // Allows the presenter to update the Country user interface element
    string Country { set; }

    // Allows the presenter to get/set the currently selected Customer object
    Customer SelectedCustomer { get; set; };

    // Allows the presenter to populate the drop-down list of customers
    void SetCustomers(Collection<Customer> customers);
}
```

The combination of *get/set* modifiers in the interface members is up to you and depends on the real features you want the view to support. In this example, we assume that the presenter has no need to read what's currently displayed in the *Label* for, say, the company name. That's why we used the sole *set* modifier for the *CompanyName* member. Likewise, *SelectedCustomer* is a property that the presenter can use to know about the currently selected customer, but also to select a new customer.

Do You Want a Passive View?

If you want the least possible amount of logic in the view because you want the maximum possible testability—and also if you prefer to stuff all the logic in a single UI-less class—you take a slightly different approach.

In a passive view, you should aim to have all the code be of the same conceptual complexity of, say, a text-box assignment, like this:

```
TextBox1.Text = someValue;
```

What if you have a list to fill? In an SVC scenario, you settle on having a smarter and richer view and go with data binding. In a PV scenario, where you just want to avoid data binding, a collection is less than ideal. If you expose a collection property and link it to the *Items* property of a UI list, you invariably create a strong dependency on the platform. In fact, the *Items* collection of a Windows *ComboBox* is different from the *Items* collection of an ASP .NET *ListControl*. This means that you end up with a similar view interface:

```
public interface ICustomerDetailsView
{
    ListItemCollection CustomersList { get; }
      ⋮
}
```

The *ListItemCollection* class wraps the UI element you want to fill and exposes its *Items* collection as a custom collection. However, you need to provide a different implementation of this class for each supported platform—ASP .NET, Windows Forms, WPF, and so on. Put another way, the details of the collection belong to the view. Subsequently, the view is not as skimpy as you might desire. Here's a better approach:

```
public interface ICustomerDetailsView
{
    void AddCustomer (string companyName, string customerID);
    string CustomerID { set; }
    string CompanyName { set; }
    string ContactName { set; }
    string Country { set; }
}
```

The *AddCustomer* method takes the smallest possible amount of information you need in the view for each customer. The implementation of this method is specific to each view. The presenter simply adds customers to the view by calling the method. The method, internally, adds information to the UI list.

What if you have more customer information to pass down to a view? What if, for example, you have grid instead of a list? In this case, you can either add more parameters to the *AddCustomer* method or, better yet, use DTO, as shown next:

```
public interface ICustomerDetailsView
{
    void AddCustomer(CustomerDto customer);
}
```

The *CustomerDto* class indicates a custom class that groups all the information you need at that point. It can be as simple as in the following code snippet:

```
public class CustomerDto
{
    public string CustomerID {get; set; };
    public string CompanyName {get; set; };
      :
      :
}
```

> **Note** The bottom line is that with a Passive View approach, the view is just…passive and is at the total mercy of the presenter. When looking for data, the view is like a little baby; the presenter plays the role of the attentive mom who caringly chops the data and spoon-feeds the view.

Implementing the Contract in the View

The interface that represents the view must be implemented by the class that represents the view itself. As mentioned, the view class is the page in ASP .NET, the form in Windows Forms, the Window in WPF, and the user control in Silverlight. Here's an example for Windows Forms:

```
// This code is part of the view: therefore, it must be platform-specific.
// This is a Windows Forms implementation.
public partial class CustListForm : Form, ICustomerDetailsView
{
    public void AddCustomer(CustomerDto customer)
    {
        this.lstCustomers.Items.Add(customer);
    }

    public string CustomerID
    {
        set { this.lblCustomerID.Text = value; }
    }

    public string CompanyName
    {
        set { this.lblCompanyName.Text = value; }
    }
```

```
    public string Country
    {
        set { this.lblCountry.Text = value; }
    }

    public string ContactName
    {
        set { this.lblContactName.Text = value; }
    }
}
```

As you can see, each property in the interface is bound to a particular property on a particular UI element. For example, the *Country* property is bound to the *Text* property of a *Label* in the form named *lblContactName*. Any time the presenter assigns (or reads, if a *get* accessor is provided) a value to the property, the UI is automatically updated.

Let's have a look at the *AddCustomer* method. The presenter doesn't need to know anything about the view. It only gathers any information to stuff in the DTO and passes it down to the view. The drop-down list needs to know about the value and display members. These can also be set directly in the UI markup of the form or communicated through an additional method on the view interface.

> **Note** A passive view is not codeless, so some code still runs even in a passive view. However, this is trivial code that is almost impossible to write in the wrong way. And even if a developer does her best to sneak in a mistake, any misbehavior will be immediately caught on the first run of the code. You can skip automated testing for these views and go with manual testing without any serious risk of running into trouble.

In Windows Forms, you use the *ComboBox* control to create a drop-down list. In ASP .NET, you use a *DropDownList* control. And you use other components in other platforms. These controls running on different platforms might or might not, have the same programming interface. Here's how you rewrite the *AddCustomer* method in an ASP .NET Web form:

```
public void AddCustomer(CustomerDto customer)
{
    // In ASP .NET, you can add items to list controls only through a ListItem object.
    ListItem item = new ListItem();

    // DataTextField and DataValueField for determining what's displayed in the UI
    // can be set in the ASPX markup or defined through another method in the view.
    string dataTextField = this.lstCustomers.DataTextField;
    string dataValueField = this.lstCustomers.DataValueField;
    string formatString = this.lstCustomers.DataTextFormatString;

    // Extract properties from the DTO
    item.Text = DataBinder.GetPropertyValue(customer, dataTextField, formatString);
    item.Value = DataBinder.GetPropertyValue(customer, dataValueField, null);
    this.lstCustomers.Items.Add(item);
}
```

The *AddCustomer* method can be simplified if you make some assumptions—for example, that fields to use in the UI of the list control are fixed or received from the outside:

```
public void AddCustomer(CustomerDto customer)
{
    ListItem item = new ListItem();
    item.Text = customer.CompanyName;
    item.Value = customer.CustomerID;
    this.lstCustomers.Items.Add(item);
}
public void AddCustomer(string companyName, string customerID)
{
    ListItem item = new ListItem();
    item.Text = companyName;
    item.Value = customerID;
    this.lstCustomers.Items.Add(item);
}
```

Important The MVP pattern allows reuse of the presentation logic across platforms. However, this is not always a hassle-free process. Sometimes, you need to tweak the presentation logic a bit to make it work on different platforms. The more similar the presentation platforms are, the more likely you'll be able to minimize the amount of required changes. Finally, note that you can even reuse binaries between ASP .NET, Windows, and Windows Presentation Foundation, but you cannot do this with Silverlight. Silverlight, in fact, requires a different CLR, meaning that reusability, if there is any, applies only at the source level.

For a Silverlight presentation layer, a PV is the only viable approach. One of the reasons you might want to consider SVC is to smooth development and DTO manipulation. In Silverlight, before you can use a domain object from a shared library, you have to recompile it. Most of the time, you end up recompiling a significant share of your business layer only to use an SVC in the UI. We've found out that it is largely preferable to create a few DTOs rather than embarking on the recompilation of the domain model.

Processing User Actions

The controls in the view capture any user action and trigger an event to the view, such as a button click or a selected-index-changed. The view contains very simple event handlers that dispatch the call to the presenter that is in charge of the view.

Connecting View and Presenter

When the view is loaded for the first time, it creates an instance of its presenter class and saves that internally as a private member. Here's the typical constructor of a Windows form:

```
public partial class Form1 : Form, ICustomerDetailsView
{
    private CustomerDetailsPresenter presenter;
```

```
public Form1()
{
    // Framework initialization stuff
    InitializeComponent();

    // Instantiate the presenter
    presenter = new CustomerDetailsPresenter(this);

    // Attach event handlers
    lstCustomers.SelectedIndexChanged += new EventHandler(this.OnSelectedIndexChanged);
}

private void Form1_Load(object sender, EventArgs e)
{
    presenter.Initialize();
}

// ICustomerDetailsView interface
  :
  :

// Rest of the form
  :
  :
}
```

The implementation of the view in ASP .NET develops around the same guidelines, as shown next:

```
public partial class CustomersPage : System.Web.UI.Page, ICustomerDetailsView
{
    private CustomerDetailsPresenter presenter;

    protected override void OnInit(EventArgs e)
    {
        base.OnInit(e);
        presenter = new CustomerDetailsPresenter(this);
    }

    protected void Page_Load(object sender, EventArgs e)
    {
        if (!IsPostBack)
        {
            presenter.Initialize();
        }
    }

    // ICustomerDetailsView interface
      :
      :

    // Rest of the page
      :
      :
}
```

The view holds a reference to the presenter. And the presenter holds a reference to the view. As you can see in the preceding code, the presenter's constructor—note that the presenter class is exactly the same in ASP .NET and Windows—accepts a reference to the view. The actual object being passed is a *Form* class in Windows and a *Page* class in ASP .NET. However, the presenter is bound to the interface of the view, not to an implementation of the view—all that the presenter sees is the interface.

Building the Presenter

You compile all presenters and view interfaces in the same assembly and then reference the assembly wherever possible. (See Figure 7-16.)

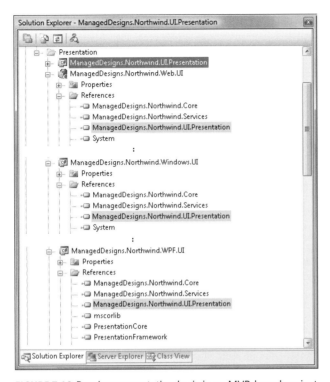

FIGURE 7-16 Reusing presentation logic in an MVP-based project

Let's have a look at the presenter class. In its simplest form, the presenter is a class with a constructor, an *Initialize* method, a helper method to update the view, and a bunch of methods to execute requested actions on the BLL. Here's an example:

```
public class CustomerDetailsPresenter
{
    private readonly ICustomerDetailsView view;

    public CustomerDetailsPresenter(ICustomerDetailsView view)
    {
        this.view = view;
    }

    public void Initialize()
    {
        // Initialize the view by filling the list of customers.
        // In a realistic implementation, this will probably refer to
        // loading just one page of the data set.
        Collection<CustomerDto> customers = this.LoadAllCustomers();
```

```
            // Populate the customer list in the view
            foreach(Customer c in customers)
            {
                view.AddCustomer(c);
            }

            // Clear the view
            ClearView();
        }

        private void ClearView()
        {
            view.CustomerID = String.Empty;
            view.CompanyName = String.Empty;
            view.ContactName = String.Empty;
            view.Country = String.Empty;
        }

        private void UpdateView(Customer customer)
        {
            view.CustomerID = customer.ID;
            view.CompanyName = customer.CompanyName;
            view.ContactName = customer.ContactName;
            view.Country = customer.Country;
        }
        :
        :
}
```

During initialization, the presenter loads customers' data from the BLL, populates the list, and clears the rest of the view. The method *LoadAllCustomers* in the snippet is a stub, and we'll return to it in a moment.

In ASP .NET, you can load items in a list and be sure that this does not affect the user interface until the page is rendered again. This is different in Windows Forms, for example. Each time you add an item to a *ComboBox*, the user interface is refreshed. In the code snippet, we call *AddCustomer* from within a loop. This means that each time we add an item to the list we refresh the user interface. As a form of optimization, you might want to disable rendering of the UI at the beginning of the loop and restore it at the end of the loop. In this case, you can add a couple of members to the view interface, such as *BeginViewUpdate* and *EndViewUpdate*.

Executing User Actions

When the user selects a customer from the list, the *SelectedIndexChanged* event is fired in the view. The view simply forwards the call to the presenter, as shown next. The code is nearly identical in ASP .NET and Windows implementations.

```
private void OnSelectedIndexChanged(object sender, EventArgs e)
{
    presenter.ShowCustomerDetails();
}
```

The presenter holds a reference to the view. The presenter doesn't really know whether the view is a Windows form or an ASP .NET page. All that it knows is that it holds an object that implements a contracted view interface. The presenter reads and writes the state of the view only through the members of the interface. For example, in our sample implementation, the presenter is not allowed to read the name of the currently displayed customer—the *CompanyName* property is write-only.

Through the view interface, the presenter collects all the information it needs to carry on the requested action. Next, it prepares the call to the BLL or resolves it internally by accessing some previously cached data. If the user action requires navigating to another view—be it another ASP .NET page or another Windows form—the presenter does anything necessary. The following fragment shows how the presenter retrieves information about the customer currently selected in the list:

```
public void ShowCustomerDetails()
{
    string id = this.SelectedCustomerID;
    if (!String.IsNullOrEmpty(id))
    {
        Customer customer = this.LookupCustomer(id);
        UpdateView(customer);
    }
}

public string SelectedCustomerID
{
    get { return view.CustomersList.SelectedItem.Value; }
}
```

To update the view, the presenter simply assigns new values to the properties exposed by the view interface. The implementation of the view interface in the actual view class will finally take care of updating properties on UI widgets.

The Presenter and the Service Layer

To carry on business operations, the presenter needs a reference to the BLL. The shape and color of the entry point in the business layer of the application depends on how you actually organized that. (See Chapter 4.)

Most of the time, if you have a service layer, the presenter gains a reference to one of these macro-services and invoke methods. As we saw in Chapter 5, the service layer is a collection of classes that implement the application logic and do that by scripting business objects, application services, and workflows. Stubs, such as *LoadAllCustomers* and *LookupCustomer*, just symbolize calls to the service layer. Here's a more detailed implementation of *ShowCustomerDetails*:

```
public void ShowCustomerDetails()
{
    string id = this.SelectedCustomerID;
```

```
if (!String.IsNullOrEmpty(id))
{
    // Grab a reference to one of the services in the service layer
    CustomerServices service = new CustomerServices();
    Customer customer = service.LookupCustomer(id);
    UpdateView(customer);
}
}
```

A service layer is simply a way to abstract the business logic for the sake of presentation. If you don't have a service layer, the presenter deals directly with the BLL and calls services, runs workflows, or scripts the domain's object model as is most appropriate for you.

> **Note** Where's the model in this sample implementation of the MVP pattern? We've seen the view and the presenter, but what about the model? As we said in "The Model in MVP" section earlier in the chapter, the model is of secondary importance in an MVP scenario compared to the view and presenter. The model refers to something—the BLL—that is part of the system. The model is not, therefore, something you add just because you're applying the MVP pattern. If you want to go with a Presenter-First development methodology, you need to make the model mockable, which basically means extracting an interface. However, in a multitier application, the entry point to the model is represented by the service layer interface or data context interface—either a custom one or one provided by the Object/Relational Mapper (O/RM), as we saw in Chapter 6, "The Data Access Layer."

Selecting the Next View

The presenter is also responsible for navigation within the application. In particular, the presenter is responsible for enabling (or disabling) subviews in the managed view and for commanding navigation to the next view.

A subview is essentially a subset of the view. It is typically a panel that can be expanded or collapsed according to the context or perhaps a child window—either modal or modeless. The presenter controls subviews through members (mostly Boolean members) on the view interface.

What about transferring control to another view (and presenter)?

In the "The MVC Controller" section earlier in the chapter, we already examined all the core code that you need to have. We did it for ASP .NET then; now let's rephrase it for Windows and expand on it a little bit.

You start with a static class that represents the application controller—that is, the central console that holds all the logic to determine the next view. Application Controller is a pattern defined by Fowler on page 379 of [P of EAA] as a centralized point for handling screen navigation and the flow of an application, as shown in Figure 7-17.

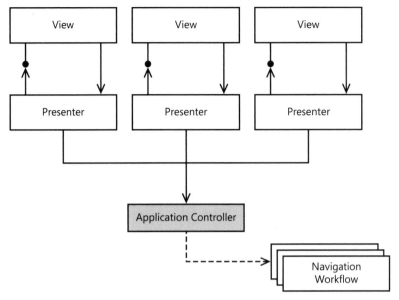

FIGURE 7-17 The application controller

Here's some sample code:

```
public static class NavigationController
{
    private static INavigationWorkflow instance;
    private static object navigationArgument;

    public static void Register(INavigationWorkflow service)
    {
        if (service == null)
            throw new ArgumentNullException();
        instance = service;
    }

    public static void NavigateTo(string view)
    {
        if (instance == null)
            throw new InvalidOperationException();
        instance.NavigateTo(view);
    }

    public static void NavigateTo(string view, object argument)
    {
        if (instance == null)
            throw new InvalidOperationException();
        navigationArgument = argument;
        NavigateTo(view);
    }

    public static object Argument
    {
        get { return navigationArgument; }
    }
}
```

The *NavigationController* class represents the shell that presenters invoke to navigate elsewhere. The *NavigateTo* method invokes an internal component that ultimately implements the workflow. The actual navigation workflow is attached to the class upon loading through the *Register* method. The *NavigateTo* method takes up to two arguments—the name of the view and, optionally, the argument for the invoked view to receive. The *NavigationController* class lives in the same assembly as presenters and view interfaces and is shared across UI platforms.

In *global.asax* for ASP .NET applications, and in *program.cs* for Windows applications, the actual navigation component is instantiated and registered:

```
// mainForm is the program's main form
MainForm mainForm = new MainForm();
ApplicationNavigationWorkflow nav = new ApplicationNavigationWorkflow(mainForm);
NavigationController.Register(nav);
```

The actual navigation workflow class—the *ApplicationNavigationWorkflow* in our example—contains the workflow to move to a given view. The class implements the *INavigationWorkflow* interface:

```
public interface INavigationWorkflow
{
    void NavigateTo(string view);
}
```

Internally, it can be as simple as a long *switch* statement, as shown here:

```
public void NavigateTo(string url)
{
    switch (url)
    {
        case "main":
            if (customersForm != null && !customersForm.IsDisposed)
            {
                customersForm.Close();
                customerForm = null;
            }
            break;
        case "customers":
            if (customerForm != null && !customerForm.IsDisposed)
            {
                customerForm.Close();
                customerForm = null;
            }
            if (customersForm == null || customersForm.IsDisposed)
            {
                customersForm = new CustomersForm();
                customersForm.Owner = mainForm;
            }
            customersForm.Show();
            break;
        case "customer":
            if (customerForm == null || customerForm.IsDisposed)
            {
                customerForm = new CustomerForm();
                customerForm.Owner = mainForm;
            }
```

```
            customerForm.ShowDialog();
            break;
    }
}
```

The *ApplicationNavigationWorkflow* class holds references to all possible forms in the application and switches to the right one as appropriate.

> **Note** This is not the only possible approach to implementing an application controller. Another possibility entails that you set up a workflow—for example, using Windows Workflow Foundation (WF)—and go through the workflow to determine the next view. In terms of design, an application controller approach—regardless of the implementation details—is beneficial because it doesn't create dependencies between views.

Note also that the navigation controller depends on the navigation workflow only through an interface—which makes it possible for you to decide at run time which workflow to load using a plug-in model or, better yet, dependency injection as we saw in Chapter 3.

Cardinality of Views, Presenters, and Application Controllers

In an MVP implementation, is it OK to have one interface and one presenter for each supported view? How many application controllers should you have? Just one? Well, it depends.

Logically speaking, each view is represented by an interface and managed by a presenter. Take a moderately complex application with dozens of views, and you'll start feeling the burden of MVP on your shoulders quite soon. As we'll see in a moment, Microsoft released an ad hoc application block (the Web Client Software Factory) to smooth out some of these issues at least in the realm of ASP .NET implementations. There's no magic though—just some designer tools to create ready-made stubs with views and presenters and a workflow to handle the navigation logic. This is to say that MVP is inherently complex and targeted to enterprise applications and to other scenarios where complexity is large enough to require precise patterns and policies.

So to get back to the original question about cardinality, most of the time you really have a one-to-one correspondence between logical views, interfaces, and presenters. A wise use of base classes and inheritance can certainly lessen the coding burden and save you some code in certain presenters. On the other hand, a presenter is the presentation logic for a particular view: if you need two different views, why should you have only one or maybe three presenters?

As far as application controllers are concerned, things can be a little bit different. An application controller is the machinery that decides about the next view based on some input, such as the view name (as in our example) or just a collection of values that denote the state of a view. If you have a large application with hundreds of views, the application controller that takes care of all possible transitions for all views can become quite a complex one. For this reason, you might want to split the navigation logic across multiple controllers at the granularity that you feel works best for you. You might even want to use an application controller for each use case, if use cases involve several views and complex navigation sequences. Needless to say, in a presentation layer with multiple navigation controllers, each presenter must receive a reference to its navigation controller upon instantiation.

Idiomatic Presentation Design

So far, we've presented a few patterns for designing the presentation layer of a software system. We focused on what patterns consist of and the principles that back them up. The advent of RAD years ago changed the approach to creating the presentation layer. Today, visual designers are too powerful and the time savings are too substantial for developers to not use them extensively.

We are not against wizards—quite the opposite. We love wizards and have personally written a few of them for internal purposes. However, we warn people about blindly using wizards without full awareness of what they do. In other words, it's okay to use wizards if they simply do the work you would have done yourself in a fraction of the time. It is not a good thing, conversely, if you use wizards because they represent the only way you know to accomplish a certain task.

Some of the presentation patterns we discussed in this chapter have been integrated in popular frameworks. Let's review a few examples.

MVP in Web Presentations

For years, the Web pushed an unnatural programming model and unusual languages—mostly script languages. ASP .NET changed things significantly because it was the first product (on the Windows platform) to enable Web programming using a true programming language. In retrospect, you can see that ASP .NET opened the doors of Web programming to quite a few C++ developers. In the long run, ASP .NET led (all) Web developers to take design seriously and consider principles such as SoC.

ASP .NET made the Web really simple but, honestly, it was not designed to let developers apply the best design patterns and practices without struggling.

ASP .NET Web forms are UI focused, built around the concept of the "page," and have a hidden page controller. The hidden page controller gets input, operates on it, and determines the output for the browser. And it shows you its own entry points in terms of postback events. You can customize the page controller to gain more testability and SoC, but you have to struggle for that.

ASP .NET certainly doesn't prevent SoC, but it makes it seductive to go the other way—to drag controls onto a form, double-click and enter code in event stubs, and code your application's logic right in place. MVP is neither prohibited, nor is it a blasphemy; however, it takes sweat and blood to write it entirely on your own. And that's why very few developers do it.

Enter the Web Client Software Factory (WCSF) and the ASP .NET MVC framework.

The Web Client Software Factory

WCSF is a software factory made of a collection of reusable components and libraries to apply proven practices and patterns to ASP .NET applications. WCSF comes with a bunch of Visual Studio 2008 templates, automated tests, and wizards that speed up development. The software factory uses the Windows Workflow Foundation and the Enterprise Library. (For more information, see *http://msdn.microsoft.com/en-us/library/cc304793.aspx*.)

Among other things, WCSF supports MVP as far as the user interface is concerned. Visual Studio 2008 templates and extensions help you to get an MVP implementation without needing to write all the code (view interfaces, presenters, and controllers) yourself. (See Figure 7-18.)

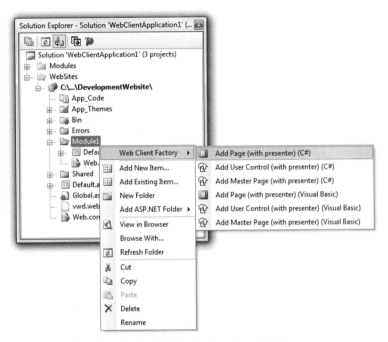

FIGURE 7-18 The Visual Studio 2008 extensions from WCSF

Another significant benefit you get from WCSF is the Page Flow Application Block (PFAB). The application block provides ready-made classes that let you orchestrate the sequence of Web pages that fulfill some process. Put another way, PFAB replaces your own handwritten application controller with a framework that is based on a WF workflow. The benefits are tangible—to apply changes, you don't touch a single line of your code; you just modify the page flow definition for the particular process. To give you an idea of the changes, have a look at the following code snippet:

```
// Method exposed by the presenter class and invoked from the UI.
// The presenter just navigates away from the current view.
```

```
public void RequestLoan(decimal amount)
{
  if (amount > MaxAmountWithoutApproval)
  {
    Response.Redirect("loan.aspx");
  }
  Response.Redirect("request.aspx");
}
```

What if at some point you need to modify this code? If you forward the request to an application controller (as we did earlier), you put yourself on the right track. But still you have to maintain the code for the application controller. PFAB offers you a workflow-based controller that you only declaratively configure. In WCSF, the preceding code turns to the following:

```
// Method exposed by the presenter class and invoked from the UI.
// The presenter just navigates away from the current view.
public void RequestLoan(decimal amount)
{
    // Pump data into the workflow
    StorePageFlow.UserData["LoanAmount"] = amount;

    // The WCSF specific workflow will redirect to the configured page
    StorePageFlow.Next();
}
```

PFAB comes with a workflow designer through which configuring the desired flow is as easy as child's play.

In summary, MVP is mostly for large and durable projects. It helps you deal well with complexity, but it might be overkill for simple projects. WCSF might help to cut down development time.

The ASP .NET MVC Framework

The ASP .NET MVC Framework is a Model2-based framework for building ASP .NET applications. It is an alternative to the classic Web forms model. Microsoft likes to illustrate the differences between the MVC framework and Web forms by calling them cars and motorcycles. We definitely agree. Both cars and motorcycles can take you somewhere, but with different speeds, levels of comfort, sense of freedom, and trunk sizes. To us, classic ASP .NET is the more comfortable car and the MVC framework is the motorcycle, which is more agile, cheaper, and hardly ever gets stuck in traffic jams.

The MVC Framework doesn't support classic postbacks and view state and doesn't consider any URLs as the endpoint to a physical server file to parse and compile to a page class. In classic ASP .NET, you almost always have a one-to-one correspondence between a URL and a server resource—whether it's a page, a data file, or an image. The only exception to this rule is when you use completely custom HTTP handlers bound to a particular path.

In the MVC Framework, well, you just have a custom HTTP handler—the routing engine— mapped to handle each and every request. A URL is seen as the means to address an action to be executed in response to a user action. The URLs employed by the pages of an MVC framework application have a custom format that the application itself mandates.

In *global.asax*, you define the URL syntax you want the routing engine to recognize for your application:

```
protected void Application_Start()
{
    RegisterRoutes(RouteTable.Routes);
}

public static void RegisterRoutes(RouteCollection routes)
{
    routes.IgnoreRoute("{resource}.axd/{*pathInfo}");
    routes.MapRoute(
        "Default",                          // Route name
        "{controller}/{action}/{id}",       // URL with parameters
        new { controller = "Home",          // Parameter defaults
            action = "Index",
            id = "" }
    );
}
```

The *MapRoute* method defines the route name and the syntax. By default, any URL is assumed to have passed the server name, the controller name followed by the action required, and optional parameters. If any parameter is missing, the default controller is assumed to be the class *HomeController* and the default action is a method named *Index* on the class. Needless to say, the syntax can be customized at will and multiple routes can be defined.

A controller is a class inherited from a framework-provided class with a few public methods. Each public method is an action that can be invoked via URL from the user interface.

```
public class HomeController : Controller
{
    public ActionResult Index()
    {
        ViewData["Title"] = "Home Page";
        ViewData["Message"] = "Welcome to ASP .NET MVC!";
        return View();
    }
    :
    :
}
```

As an example, let's consider the following URL: *http://www.contoso.com/home/about*. After parsing the URL, the framework figures out that the request is serviced by invoking the method *About* on a controller class named *HomeController*:

```
public ActionResult About()
{
    ViewData["Title"] = "About Page";
    return View("About");
}
```

Anything in the URL that follows the method token is considered a parameter for the method. If the method is expected to be passed parameters, you just edit the signature in the controller class. The method performs its tasks and renders the view.

Fresh data are explicitly passed to the view using the *ViewData* collection, as in the diagram shown in Figure 7-8. The *View* method in the code snippet uses a naming convention to locate the ASPX file to render out. If no parameter is specified, a file named after the method (*About*, in this case) plus the *.aspx* extension is searched for in the *Views* subdirectory. (Figure 7-19 provides an overall view of an ASP .NET MVC project in Visual Studio 2008.)

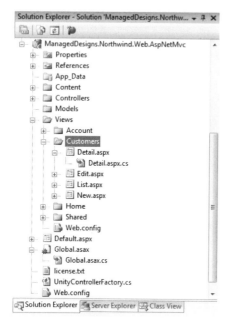

FIGURE 7-19 An ASP .NET MVC framework project

The view is pure HTML with ASP-style code blocks <% .. %> plus some macros and helper methods to quickly generate common pieces of HTML. Here's an example:

```
<h2><%= Html.Encode(ViewData["Message"]) %></h2>
```

The *ViewData* container can also be transformed into a strongly typed object. Consider the following controller method:

```
// Method invoked to get details about a customer.
// The ID is an argument in the URL.
public ActionResult Detail(string id)
{
    ViewData["Title"] = string.Format("Customer detail - Code: {0}", id);
    return View("Detail", this.GetCustomerByID(id));
}
```

The method uses a BLL method to retrieve a *Customer* object and passes that instance as an argument to the view. The code-behind class for the page might then look like this:

```
public partial class Detail : ViewPage<Customer>
{
}
```

In this case, *ViewData* stops being a generic data container to expose an instance of the type *Customer*. The view is therefore more readable. The inner *Customer* object is accessed using the property *Model*:

```
<div>
    ID: <%=ViewData.Model.Id%><br />
    Total income: <% = string.Format("{0:0.00#}",
                      ViewData.Model.CalculateTotalIncome()) %><br />
    Company name: <% = ViewData.Model.CompanyName %><br />
    <% =ViewData.Model.ContactInfo %><br />
    <% =ViewData.Model.AddressInfo %><br />
    <% =ViewData.Model.PhoneNumber %>(fax: <% =ViewData.Model.FaxNumber %>)<br />
</div>
```

There's lot more to be discovered about the MVC framework, and the topic probably deserves a book of its own. Our purpose here is much more limited: the framework allows you to build MVC-like ASP .NET applications (specifically, Model2 applications) and puts a strong accent on testability. The run-time environment that supports the framework is entirely based on interfaces and provides extensibility at all levels. Visual Studio 2008 project templates also push testability, and a sample test project is also generated and appended to any MVC project you create. For more information on the ASP .NET MVC framework, have a look at *http://www.asp.net/mvc*.

MVP in Windows Presentations

As a matter of fact, frameworks for MVC Web development have sprouted copiously in the development community—but not specifically for desktop applications. There's probably a reason for this. A Web-specific variation of MVC—Model2—has been successfully implemented in a popular framework, such as Struts on the Java platform and MonoRail on the Windows platform. So, for the Web, the question of which pattern to choose was closed quite quickly. Whatever you think of ASP .NET, if you want testability and SoC go for a Model2-based framework. In this context, the ASP .NET MVC framework is an excellent choice.

For desktop, Silverlight, and mobile applications, there's no specialization of any pattern made popular by any framework. The original MVP (in both PV and SVC flavors) is still the way to go—mostly through a handmade implementation. However, a couple of frameworks to look at for MVP development that is not limited to the Web exist. One is the twin brother of the Web client software factory we examined earlier; the other is a recently proposed open-source framework for MVP development.

The Smart Client Software Factory

SCSF is a software factory made of a set of tools that help with the development of composite smart client applications. For more information on SCSF, have a look at the following URL: *http://msdn.microsoft.com/en-us/library/cc540671.aspx*.

As far as MVP is concerned, SCSF provides a set of Visual Studio 2008 extensions to automatically generate stubs for views and presenters. There's a wizard that guides you through the creation of a view interface and a class that implements the interface. You then modify this class to call the presenter for UI actions that affect other views or business logic. The wizard also creates a presenter class for the view. The class extends the presenter base class in the framework and contains the business logic for the view. You modify this class to update the view for your business logic.

The MVC# Framework

MVC# is an MVP framework designed for the .NET platform. In spite of the name, which refers to both the root MVC pattern and the C# language, MVC# is totally devoted to simplifying the implementation of the MVP pattern in Windows applications of any type—Windows, Web, and Silverlight. For more information on MVC#, pay a visit to *http://www.mvcsharp.org*.

The main benefit of MVC# is that, as a framework, it takes on a large share of the work that is usually concerned with MVP usage and offers developers a simplified application programming interface (API).

The MVC# API, for example, automatically establishes links between a view and its presenter. It also supplies a platform-independent navigation between views that is logically equivalent to our application controller. In other words, you tell the framework the name of the view you want to reach and the framework takes you there regardless of whether the view is ASP .NET, Windows, or perhaps Silverlight.

However, the most relevant aspect of MVC# is its native support for tasks. A task is defined as a collection of related views that, when traversed in a given order, form a business process—such as booking a hotel room or posting an order to some sales system. A task mostly corresponds to the steps involved in a use case. Here's a sample task that consists of two views—one for listing all customers and one for viewing details of the selected customer:

```
public class CustomerDetailsTask : TaskBase
{
    string CustomerID;

    // This view can be activated by any name (the true value).
    // From this view, you can navigate to the view named "CustomerDetails".
    [IPoint(typeof(CustomersPresenter), true, CustomerDetails)]
    public const string ListOfCustomers = "CustomersView";

    // This view is activated only programmatically and is the last of the tasks.
    [IPoint(typeof(CustomerDetailPresenter))]
    public const string Products = "CustomerDetailsView";
}
```

The *IPoint* attribute indicates the presenter for the view. In the presenter of the *CustomersView* view, the change of selection executes the following code:

```
public class CustomersPresenter : ControllerBase<CustomerDetailsTask, ICustomersView>
{
    public void CustomerSelected(string customerID)
    {
        // Task is a property on the IController interface
        // (implemented by ControllerBase). The property is s used to reference
        // the task this presenter is working with.
        Task.CustomerID = customerID;

        // Navigate to the next view in the task
        Task.Navigator.Navigate(CustomerDetailsTask.CustomerDetailsView);
    }
    :
    :
}
```

MVC# is a recent, and extremely interesting, project that is attempting to slim down the development of MVP applications.

Note Don't get confused by the use of the word "Controller" in the MVC# hierarchy of classes. This is due exclusively to a caprice of the author of the framework—Oleg Zhukov. Regardless of the fact that your classes inherit from a class named *ControllerBase*, they ultimately are, and act as, MVP presenters.

Windows Presentation Foundation

Just like ASP .NET and Windows Forms, WPF is also well suited, as a UI platform, to implementing the MVP pattern. The same holds true for WPF's Web counterpart—Silverlight. In the end, implementing MVP in WPF and Silverlight is not an issue. Note, though, that in Silverlight you can't reuse the same assemblies with presenters and view interfaces you created for other platforms. Silverlight targets a subset of the .NET Framework and, more importantly, a different model of CLR. This is to say that your code might need further adaptation (and a new compile step, at the very minimum) to make its way to Silverlight. (An interesting article on techniques you can use to write code that runs on both WPF and Silverlight appeared in the October 2008 issue of MSDN Magazine.)

In WPF and Silverlight, however, the most attractive presentation pattern to look at is Presentation Model. Why is this so? The quick answer is that a WPF infrastructure provides strong support for two-way data-binding. Let's dig out more details.

As we saw earlier in the chapter, the PM is a variation of MVP that defines a new actor in addition to the classic view, model (BLL), and presenter. The new actor is essentially a view's model that is an object that holds all the data the view needs to display, as well as any state information. In our opinion, one of the primary reasons that prevented PM from reaching widespread use is the inherent unease of synchronizing the view with its view model. You need to write and maintain a long list of instructions that copy state from the UI elements of the view (usually, more than just one property per control) down to the view's model, and vice versa. This is just the kind of code that developers hate to write—there's no fame and honor if you write it right (it's a litany of assignments, after all) and, conversely, there's endless blame if you happen to write it incorrectly.

In Windows Forms, this created the perfect habitat for tools and libraries to thrive and possibly make some good use out of some smart and bidirectional forms of data binding. In WPF, two-way data binding comes out of the box, so synchronizing a bunch of UI controls with an existing object is no longer an issue—better yet, it's a declarative matter.

In WPF (including Silverlight), you use the XAML markup language to define the user interface. And in XAML, you can have the following code:

```
<TextBox x:Name="txtCompanyName" Text="{Binding CompanyName, Mode=TwoWay}" />
```

What this line of code says is the *TextBox* element named *txtCompanyName* has the *Text* property bound in a bidirectional way to the *CompanyName* property of some source object. At least in Silverlight, the source object can only be specified via code through the *DataContext* property of UI elements:

```
// Set the binding context
this.DataContext = viewModelObject;
```

In WPF and Silverlight, two-way data binding means that any change to the *Text* property of the UI element modifies the *CompanyName* property on the bound object. At the same time, it also means that the user interface is notified promptly of any changes that occur on the bound object and the changes are reflected in the view. This form of bidirectional data binding is perfect for successfully implementing the PM pattern.

The object that actually represents the view's model is preferably a cushion object that sits in between the view and the business layer. This approach is recommended for two reasons. One has to do with the implementation of your domain objects. If these objects throw exceptions when passed inconsistent or invalid data, you have to catch those exceptions in the presentation layer. It's a doable task, but it is far from being efficient—most exceptions can be prevented by simply validating and filtering any input data. The second reason for preferring a cushion object is that, by design, the view's model is just an object modeled after the view and the state it represents. If you accept this point, the view's model can only be a made-to-measure object.

As a final note, the PM pattern in WPF goes by a totally different name—the Model-View-ViewModel (MVVM) pattern. More significant than the name, though, is the substance.

Summary

The advent of Visual Basic 3.0 many years ago marked the definitive success of the RAD approach. This was a watershed for the presentation layer of all applications. Most user interfaces ever since have tended to be attention-grabbing, and interactivity and responsiveness became critical requirements.

Among other things, interactivity refers to the presentation's ability to offer a fully synchronized view of data, with automatic handling of master/detail views. This evolution of the user interface put the accent on the code required to obtain it—boring code that takes a long time to write. Hence, developers started looking around for alternate solutions, and they invented data binding. Data binding and RAD together triggered an unintended consequence—the development of the user interface became the last step in a project. Developing the user interface is so simple that we just don't want to spend any valuable time on it. Creating the presentation layer is a matter of attaching buttons and grids on a form—it's for newbies and new recruits.

The presentation layer, however, is no less important than the business layer and the data access layer. A nice presentation layer accounts for nothing without the core behavior of the middle tier; a powerful middle tier that is not assisted by an equally effective presentation layer will fail to complete the mission.

In this chapter, we presented the responsibilities of the presentation layer and split it in two segments—the user interface and presentation logic. Next, we went through 30 years of software design and traced the evolution of the presentation layer, from autonomous views to the MVC pattern to the latest variations of the MVP pattern.

We discussed principles and applied them through concrete code snippets and popular frameworks for Windows.

Many years ago, after building the back end and the front end of a system, developers were ready to test or to have their end users poke around the system. Today, things are different. Testability is probably the driving force behind the evolution of the presentation layer. So you often first write tests and then start coding; at the least, you use tests as a development tool. What, then, is the final step of a system? The acceptance test, which is usually run in cooperation with the customer. Preparing the UI for the final acceptance test requires care—and for this reason, the choice of the pattern for the presentation layer is critical.

Murphy's Laws of the Chapter

A lot has been said about the usability of programs, and we said a lot about the importance of delivering a system that works as expected and, more importantly, provides the features that customers really need. Making jokes about the user interface of computer programs, however, is like shooting the piano man—it can sometimes be way too easy and way too fun.

- The only thing worse than an end user without a clue is an end user who has a clue—usually the wrong one.

- When designing a program to handle all possible dumb errors, nature creates a dumber user.

- Build a system that even a fool can use and only a fool will want to use it.

For more tongue-in-cheek laws beyond the ones in this book, have a look at *http://www.murphys-laws.com*.

Final Thoughts

The pessimist complains about the wind; the optimist expects it to change; the realist adjusts the sails.

—*William Arthur Ward*

Now that you made it this far, do you feel like a better informed professional? We definitely hope so, and we certainly did work hard to put into this book the best content we could. We call ourselves architects, and we design systems for customers and help customers build and improve their own systems. Nobody has time to do it right the first time, but there is always time to fix it when it doesn't work. So we also often fix existing systems.

A number of jokes and urban legends circulate about architects being more concerned with playing golf, talking in UML, or washing their hands after hitting a curly bracket button on a keyboard. We would like to point out once again that we are born developers who are just writing software the best we can. And we wanted to share our experiences, (best) practices, patterns, and vision with you. Thanks for your trust and attention!

This book is divided into two parts: design principles and using those design principles in development. The first part on design principles is for everybody with some interest in serious software development—from any perspective, whether it is a developer, architect, tester, project manager, database expert, analyst, or customer perspective. The second part is for the development team, including database developers.

Software is one big building with many floors and rooms. Architecture is all around you, regardless of the reason why you're in the building.

Like posters on the walls of this building, we want to finish the book with some of our favorite *mantras* that everybody who happens to work with us knows very well.

Mantra #1—It Depends

It always depends. As an architect, you are never sure about anything. There's always the possibility that you're missing something. However, the role requires that decisions be made, so you must be able to evaluate all options and make an informed decision, and to do this promptly, when a decision is required. To buy yourself some time and activate your mental processes in the background, first say, "It depends," and then explain why and what the answer depends on. If you are unsure about what a point depends on, the default answer is, "It depends on the context."

Mantra #2—Requirements Are Lord Over All

The architect is just one link in the natural chain of actors in a software project. The customer says what he wants. If the customer doesn't know what he wants, someone will be there to prompt him for specifics. The analyst formalizes what the customer wants. The project manager prepares the groundwork for the formally-defined project. The architect gets the bundle of requirements and sorts them out. Developers follow the architect. The database administrator does his best to make the database support the application effectively. Note that the customer leads the chain, and what the customer wants is the law. What the customer wants goes under the name of *requirements*. Of course, only few customers know what it is they want. So requirements change.

Mantra #3—Program to an Interface

Even if you make a living out of *implemented* code, you should leverage *interfaces* wherever possible. Repeat with us: "No implementation is possible without an interface." Look around, there's always an interface that can be extracted.

Mantra #4—Keep It Simple but Not Simplistic

You know KISS (Keep It Simple, Stupid), right? This is just our customized version. Simple and concise is usually equivalent to great and well done. Aim at simplicity, but give yourself a boundary for the low end of the range. If you go below that lower boundary, your solution will become simplistic. And this is not a good thing.

Mantra #5—Inheritance Is About Polymorphism, Not Reuse

Object-oriented programming (OOP) taught us that we should write a class once and reuse it forever and extend it at will. And this is possible thanks to inheritance. Does this naturally extend to class reuse? Reuse is a much subtler concept than you might think at first. Polymorphism is the key aspect of OOP to leverage. Polymorphism means you can use two inherited classes interchangeably. As others have said, "Reuse is a nice side effect to have." But reuse shouldn't be your goal, or put another way, don't reuse a class through inheritance just to reuse the class. It's better to write a new class that more precisely fits the needs than to try to inherit an existing class that wasn't designed for the job.

Mantra #6—Not the DAL? Don't Touch SQL Then

Repeat with us: "Separation of concerns. Separation of concerns." Push data access code and details (such as connection strings, commands, and table names) to the corner. Sooner or later, you need to take care of them, but consider business and presentation logic separately from persistence. And if possible, delegate persistence to ad hoc tools such as Object/ Relational Mapper (O/RM) tools.

Mantra #7—Maintainability First

If you could pick only one attribute for your software, what would it be? Scalability? Security? Performance? Testability? Usability? For us, it would be none of the above. For us, what comes first is maintainability. Through maintainability, you can achieve anything else at any time.

Mantra #8—All User Input Is Evil

You should have heard this already. If there's a way for users to do something wrong, they'll find it. Oh, this sounds like Murphy's Law. Yes, you should have heard this one, too, already.

Mantra #9—Post-Mortem Optimization

Donald Knuth said that premature optimization is the root of all software evil. We go even further. Do not optimize the system. Instead, design it for being improved and extended at any time. But focus on pure optimization only when the system is dismissed.

Mantra #10—Security and Testability Are by Design

If you're serious about a system attribute, design for it right from the beginning. Security and testability are no exception to this rule, and there's an International Organization for Standardization (ISO) standard that specifically says so.

Appendix
The Northwind Starter Kit

There are two ways of constructing a software design. One way is to make it so simple that there are obviously no deficiencies. And the other way is to make it so complicated that there are no obvious deficiencies.

—C.A.R. Hoare

The Northwind Starter Kit (NSK) is a set of Microsoft Visual Studio 2008 projects that form a multilayer .NET-based system. Produced by Managed Design (*http://www.manageddesign.it*), NSK is a reference application that illustrates most of the principles and patterns we have discussed in this book.

Motivation for Creating NSK

Many developers know about patterns and acknowledge that they have some value. Far fewer developers actually use patterns or use them in the appropriate manner. You shouldn't feel like you have to catch up with pattern use, though. There's no need for you to find a pattern in everything you do. However, patterns are there to help. Humbly and obligingly.

When it comes to developing the user interface for an application, to achieve testability and proper separation of concerns, you look around for guidance. And, upon looking, you find the Model-View-Presenter (MVP) and Model-View-Controller (MVC) patterns. You sit down and read the definitions for them: at first sight, the description ranges from obscure to impenetrable. Then you read them repeatedly and maybe come to a rudimentary understanding. And you're happy. But then you read about another, similar, pattern to draw a comparison. And you're lost. You might come to understand the patterns from a different perspective, but the two forms of understandings might be incompatible.

It took years for us to build the considerable array of skills and knowledge we have today. Andrea started with object-oriented design back in 1998 when architecture books were a rarity, as were the opportunities to exchange ideas with fellow architects. It took much less time for Dino to grab the same knowledge a few years later—pure subliminal absorption obtained from daily chats, meetings, and interviews with experienced professionals such as Andrea. You buy books, read them, and then feel lost. You don't understand cross-references, and examples are either too simple or way too complex. We've had these experiences, so we assume many of you also have had, or still have, such experiences.

We've found that the language used in many architecture resources (books, Web sites, and so forth) is a bit too formal and can be difficult for a good share of developers to follow (or at least, this was often the case for us). Code, and especially well-written code, is what developers understand more quickly and completely. So we wrote an architecture book that uses a conversational language throughout and takes a pragmatic approach to explaining concepts.

You find a number of C# code snippets in the 300+ pages of this book. But we might not have done better in this regard than other analogous books. You might find our code snippets to be too simple or incomplete if you look at them individually. What would make a big difference is providing a nontrivial sample application. Enter NSK.

Downloading NSK

NSK is a CodePlex project. You can get the full source code from a link available on the *http://www.codeplex.com/nsk* page. Once the download is completed, you get a Visual Studio 2008 solution with more than 20 projects. To compile it, you need the .NET Framework 3.5, plus a number of other libraries and frameworks—some mandatory, some optional.

NSK Requirements

The list of requirements for successfully compiling NSK is shown in Table A-1, along with the URLs where you can get the missing bits.

TABLE A-1 NSK Dependencies

Library	Optional	More Information and Download
NHibernate 2.0	yes	*http://www.nhibernate.org*
Enterprise Library 4.0	no	*http://www.codeplex.com/entlib*
NUnit 2.4	yes	*http://www.nunit.org*
NMock2	yes	*http://sourceforge.net/projects/nmock2*
ASP.NET MVC FX	yes	*http://www.codeplex.com/aspnet*
CastleProject 1.0	yes	*http://www.castleproject.org*

NUnit is optional in the sense that the Visual Studio 2008 solution also has tests for the native MSTest environment. So you need this tool if you want to test the code using that framework. Other testing environments are welcome, provided that you adapt tests yourself.

NHibernate is optional, and to remove it you just drop the NHibernate project from the Data folder.

You need the ASP.NET MVC framework only for the one Web front end; if you remove the project, you also remove the dependency.

Finally, CastleProject 1.0 is currently required only for the MonoRail Web front end. However, a planned upgrade deals specifically with the exploitation of aspect-orientation in CastleProject. When this upgrade is implemented, CastleProject will become a required install.

The Northwind Database

NSK is entirely based on the popular Northwind database. The Northwind database no longer ships with SQL Server 2005 and newer (any version), so you'll need to download that separately provided that you don't have it installed yet.

You can download the necessary installation scripts for the Northwind database from *http://www.microsoft.com/downloads/details.aspx?FamilyId=06616212-0356-46A0-8DA2-EEBC53A68034&displaylang=en*.

Installation instructions are included on the download page.

What's in NSK?

NSK is a reference implementation of a .NET layered application. Entirely written in C#, NSK can serve as a sort of blueprint for your architecture. In NSK, you find an MVP presentation layer and a service layer implemented as vanilla .NET classes. You'll also find a domain model and a handmade data access layer, plus test projects. The data model is the popular Northwind database.

Let's briefly have a look at the projects and the architectural characteristics of the layers. Figure A-1 shows the solution window in Visual Studio 2008.

FIGURE A-1 Visual Studio 2008 Solution Explorer opened on the latest build of NSK

The solution is articulated in two main sections: source code and tests. The source code area is divided into sections for the data access layer, business layer, and presentation layer. The test area is divided into two distinct testing environments: MSTest incorporated in Visual Studio 2008 and NUnit. (See *http://www.nunit.org*.)

The Data Folder

Projects in the Data folder refer to the data access layer (DAL) of the application. The DAL is designed around a common interface—*IDataContext*, as we saw in Chapter 6, "The Data Access Layer." The Data project defines the common types in the DAL. The DbProviderBase project creates an assembly for the base class of the data context, as we saw in Chapter 6.

The DAL is designed to be injected into the business layer through a plug-in model. The Data project features a *DataAccessProviderFactory* class, which represents for a client the point of contact with the DAL. The *DataAccessProviderFactory* class uses information in the configuration file to load the currently selected DAL as a plug-in. The other four projects in the folder just offer sample implementations of a DAL for different purposes. The physical database is always Northwind.

The SqlServer project refers to a SQL Server DAL, whereas the MsAccess project implements a DAL that accesses the database through OLE DB and the Microsoft Access engine. Likewise, the NHibernate project provides a DAL entirely based on NHibernate. (See *http://www.nhibernate.org*.) Finally, the FakeProvider project represents a fake DAL used for testing purposes.

> **Note** Although NSK offers a bunch of DAL implementations, they shouldn't be considered complete. We focused on defining the interface versus other layers, and implemented at least once every DAL responsibility discussed in Chapter 6.

The Business Folder

The Business folder groups all projects that relate to the business logic layer and service layer. In terms of patterns, the project supports the Domain Model pattern and propounds a hierarchy of manually created plain .NET classes. No LINQ-to-SQL and no Entity Framework are used.

The Core project contains the implementation of the domain model. All classes derive from a common class named *DomainObject*. This does not signal a lack of persistence ignorance because this class is just part of the domain model and doesn't represent an external dependency. Domain entities perform validation of content using the Microsoft Application Validation block in Enterprise Library 4. (See *http://www.codeplex.com/entlib*.)

The domain model also implements the Special Case pattern and provides special case classes for the entity Customer. There's not a large amount of business logic in the classes, but the plain-old CLR object (POCO) design of classes and plugs for business logic methods emerge clearly. (See Chapter 4, "The Business Layer.") It should also be noted that the design of classes is different from the design of the database—we demonstrate this difference by using intermediate classes for contact and address information and by creating aggregates of entities, such as Customer->Order->OrderDetail.

The two Services projects you see in Figure A-1 reference the service layer. The project Northwind.Services defines the interfaces of the service layer for some of the entities—for example, ICustomerServices and IOrderServices. The project ManagedDesign.Northwind. Services provides, instead, a concrete implementation of the service layer classes. For example, there you find a *CustomerServices* class that implements the *ICustomerServices* interface. (See Chapter 5, "The Service Layer.")

As an example of application logic, the *CustomerServices* class has a method that calculates the discount rate of a customer when given its past orders record, for which you have a business method in the *Customer* class.

No WCF services are used yet, but using a WCF service for implementing the service layer is an implementation detail. Likewise, classes in the service layer resort to the aforementioned *DataAccessProviderFactory* class to get a reference to the DAL and operate. An approach based on dependency injection is possible. However, in this case, we also enter the realm of implementation details.

The Presentation Folder

NSK supports five different presentations: ASP.NET, Windows Forms, Windows Presentation Foundation (WPF), Castle MonoRail, and the ASP.NET MVC framework. The Presentation folder contains all these projects plus the project that creates a presentation logic assembly shared by all these presentations.

The presentation layer is based on the MVP pattern, as discussed in Chapter 7, "The Presentation Layer." All view interfaces, presenters, and data transfer objects are defined in the Presentation project. This assembly is then referenced by presentation layers that support the MVP pattern— ASP.NET, Windows Forms, and WPF. (See Figure A-2.)

The other two presentations—Castle MonoRail (which you can learn more about at *http://www.castleproject.org*) and the ASP.NET MVC framework—have their own MVC implementation (actually Model2, as we saw in detail in Chapter 7). Also, there's no possibility for sharing the presentation logic—at least, given the implementation of presentation logic in NSK. For example, if you stratify the presentation layer a little bit more and add tasks, the tasks could be shared with Web-specific presentation implementations. Figure A-3 shows the ASP.NET MVC Web front end.

FIGURE A-2 A WPF front end for NSK

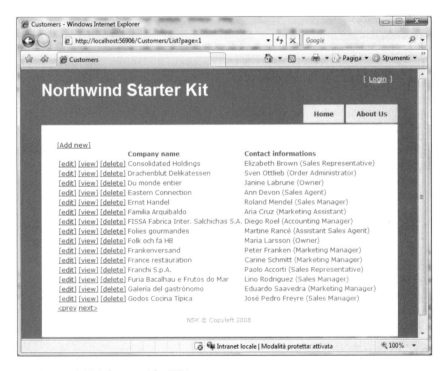

FIGURE A-3 A Web front end for NSK

Note NSK currently doesn't provide any presentation with AJAX capabilities. This is not really an architectural point. AJAX can be simply added to the ASP.NET implementation either via partial rendering or script capabilities and an AJAX service layer. (See Chapter 5.) Likewise, there's no support for Silverlight. Also, in this case, we admit that it is not for any particular reason—it's just a matter of priorities and time constraints. Note, though, that with Silverlight in the middle you have to renounce reusing any assembly compiled targeting the full .NET framework because of the binary incompatibilities between .NET and Silverlight. (See Chapter 7.)

Future Evolution of NSK

NSK is essentially a reference implementation of a .NET layered system. It will never become a full application. Why? Well, we think that NSK serves its purposes very well in this (shrink-wrapped?) form. From our perspective, the added value you can get from a full application is nearly the same you get today from a reference, and incomplete, implementation.

The focus is on architecture and design, not on the implementation of features such as the DAL or MVP (although this is important). Navigating through the source code, you'll find at least one sample of any significant feature. Don't be too surprised to find out that the implementation of some methods might be a bit naïve. Again, implementation is not our main purpose. So the actual code might be questioned, but not the method's signature or the use case.

This said, we believe that the life span of NSK will be nearly the same as the life span of the book. If we ever upgrade the book to the .NET Framework 4.0—an announced major release—we'll probably upgrade NSK too. NSK, however, has existed for a couple of years now as a standalone project. It will continue its evolution—maybe slowly—in full autonomy. Be sure to send us your feedback and suggestions.

Index

Symbols and Numbers

About the Authors

Dino Esposito

Dino Esposito is an IDesign (*http://www.idesign.net*) architect and a trainer based in Rome, Italy. Dino specializes in Microsoft Web technologies, including ASP.NET AJAX and Silverlight, and spends most of his time teaching and consulting across Europe, Australia, and the United States.

Over the years, Dino developed hands-on experience and skills in architecting and building distributed systems for banking and insurance companies and, in general, in industry contexts where the demand for security, optimization, performance, scalability, and interoperability is dramatically high. In Italy, Dino and Andrea, together, run Managed Design (*http://www.manageddesign.it*), a premier consulting and training firm.

Every month, at least five different magazines and Web sites throughout the world publish Dino's articles covering topics ranging from Web development to data access and from software best practices to Web services. A prolific author, Dino writes the monthly "Cutting Edge" column for MSDN Magazine and the "ASP.NET-2-The-Max" newsletter for the Dr. Dobb's Journal. As a widely acknowledged expert in Web applications built with .NET technologies, Dino contributes to the Microsoft content platform for developers and IT consultants. Check out his articles on a variety of MSDN Developer Centers such as ASP.NET, security, and data access.

Dino has written an array of books, most of which are considered state-of-the-art in their respective areas. His more recent books are *Programming Microsoft ASP.NET 3.5* from Microsoft Press (2008) and *Programming Microsoft ASP.NET 2.0 Applications—Advanced Topics* from Microsoft Press (2006).

Dino regularly speaks at industry conferences all over the world (Microsoft TechEd, Microsoft DevDays, DevConnections, DevWeek, Basta) and local technical conferences and meetings in Europe and the United States.

Dino lives near Rome and keeps in shape playing tennis at least twice a week.

Andrea Saltarello

Andrea Saltarello is a solution architect and consultant at Managed Designs (*http://www.manageddesigns.it*), focusing on architecture and virtualization topics.

He has spoken at events and conferences in Italy and has also taught "Operating Systems" during the "Master in Editoria Multimediale" class organized by the university "Politecnico of Milan."

In 2001, Andrea co-founded UGIdotNET (*http://www.ugidotnet.org*), the first Italian .NET User Group, of whom he is the president.

Andrea is passionate about sports and music, and grew up playing volleyball and listening devotedly to Depeche Mode, a group he fell in love with after listening to "Everything Counts" for the first time.

These days he tries to keep in shape by catching up to balls on squash or tennis courts, and he enjoys going to as many live music gigs as he can.

Andrea has a blog at *http://blogs.ugidotnet.org/mrbrightside*.

Best Practices for Software Engineering

Software Estimation: Demystifying the Black Art
Steve McConnell
ISBN 9780735605350

Amazon.com's pick for "Best Computer Book of 2006"! Generating accurate software estimates is fairly straight-forward—once you understand the art of creating them. Acclaimed author Steve McConnell demystifies the process—illuminating the practical procedures, formulas, and heuristics you can apply right away.

Code Complete, Second Edition
Steve McConnell
ISBN 9780735619678

Widely considered one of the best practical guides to programming—fully updated. Drawing from research, academia, and everyday commercial practice, McConnell synthesizes must-know principles and techniques into clear, pragmatic guidance. Rethink your approach—and deliver the highest quality code.

Agile Portfolio Management
Jochen Krebs
ISBN 9780735625679

Agile processes foster better collaboration, innovation, and results. So why limit their use to software projects—when you can transform your entire business? This book illuminates the opportunities—and rewards—of applying agile processes to your overall IT portfolio, with best practices for optimizing results.

Simple Architectures for Complex Enterprises
Roger Sessions
ISBN 9780735625785

Why do so many IT projects fail? Enterprise consultant Roger Sessions believes complex problems require simple solutions. And in this book, he shows how to make simplicity a core architectural requirement—as critical as performance, reliability, or security—to achieve better, more reliable results for your organization.

The Enterprise and Scrum
Ken Schwaber
ISBN 9780735623378

Extend Scrum's benefits—greater agility, higher-quality products, and lower costs—beyond individual teams to the entire enterprise. Scrum cofounder Ken Schwaber describes proven practices for adopting Scrum principles across your organization, including that all-critical component—managing change.

ALSO SEE

Software Requirements, Second Edition
Karl E. Wiegers
ISBN 9780735618794

More About Software Requirements: Thorny Issues and Practical Advice
Karl E. Wiegers
ISBN 9780735622678

Software Requirement Patterns
Stephen Withall
ISBN 9780735623989

Agile Project Management with Scrum
Ken Schwaber
ISBN 9780735619937

microsoft.com/mspress

Collaborative Technologies—Resources for Developers

Inside Microsoft® Windows® SharePoint® Services 3.0
Ted Pattison, Daniel Larson
ISBN 9780735623200

Get the in-depth architectural insights, task-oriented guidance, and extensive code samples you need to build robust, enterprise content-management solutions.

Inside Microsoft Office SharePoint Server 2007
Patrick Tisseghem
ISBN 9780735623682

Led by an expert in collaboration technologies, you'll plumb the internals of SharePoint Server 2007—and master the intricacies of developing intranets, extranets, and Web-based applications.

Inside the Index and Search Engines: Microsoft Office SharePoint Server 2007
Patrick Tisseghem, Lars Fastrup
ISBN 9780735625358

Customize and extend the enterprise search capabilities in SharePoint Server 2007—and optimize the user experience—with guidance from two recognized SharePoint experts.

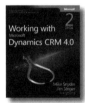

Working with Microsoft Dynamics® CRM 4.0, Second Edition
Mike Snyder, Jim Steger
ISBN 9780735623781

Whether you're an IT professional, a developer, or a power user, get real-world guidance on how to make Microsoft Dynamics CRM work the way you do—with or without programming.

Programming Microsoft Dynamics CRM 4.0
Jim Steger et al.
ISBN 9780735625945

Apply the design and coding practices that leading CRM consultants use to customize, integrate, and extend Microsoft Dynamics CRM 4.0 for specific business needs.

ALSO SEE

Inside Microsoft Dynamics AX 2009
ISBN 9780735626454

6 Microsoft Office Business Applications for Office SharePoint Server 2007
ISBN 9780735622760

Programming Microsoft Office Business Applications
ISBN 9780735625365

Inside Microsoft Exchange Server 2007 Web Services
ISBN 9780735623927

microsoft.com/mspress

For C# Developers

Microsoft® Visual C#® 2008 Express Edition: Build a Program Now!

Patrice Pelland

ISBN 9780735625426

Build your own Web browser or other cool application—no programming experience required! Featuring learn-by-doing projects and plenty of examples, this full-color guide is your quick start to creating your first applications for Windows®. DVD includes Express Edition software plus code samples.

Microsoft Visual C# 2008 Step by Step

John Sharp

ISBN 9780735624306

Teach yourself Visual C# 2008—one step at a time. Ideal for developers with fundamental programming skills, this practical tutorial delivers hands-on guidance for creating C# components and Windows–based applications. CD features practice exercises, code samples, and a fully searchable eBook.

Learn Programming Now! Microsoft XNA® Game Studio 2.0

Rob Miles

ISBN 9780735625228

Now you can create your own games for Xbox 360® and Windows—as you learn the underlying skills and concepts for computer programming. Dive right into your first project, adding new tools and tricks to your arsenal as you go. Master the fundamentals of XNA Game Studio and Visual C#—no experience required!

Programming Microsoft Visual C# 2008: The Language

Donis Marshall

ISBN 9780735625402

Get the in-depth reference, best practices, and code you need to master the core language capabilities in Visual C# 2008. Fully updated for Microsoft .NET Framework 3.5, including a detailed exploration of LINQ, this book examines language features in detail—and across the product life cycle.

Windows via C/C++, Fifth Edition

Jeffrey Richter, Christophe Nasarre

ISBN 9780735624245

Jeffrey Richter's classic guide to C++ programming—now fully revised for Windows XP, Windows Vista®, and Windows Server® 2008. Learn to develop more-robust applications with unmanaged C++ code—and apply advanced techniques—with comprehensive guidance and code samples from the experts.

CLR via C#, Second Edition

Jeffrey Richter

ISBN 9780735621633

Dig deep and master the intricacies of the common language runtime (CLR) and the .NET Framework. Written by programming expert Jeffrey Richter, this guide is ideal for developers building any kind of application—ASP.NET, Windows Forms, Microsoft SQL Server®, Web services, console apps—and features extensive C# code samples.

ALSO SEE

Microsoft Visual C# 2005 Step by Step
ISBN 9780735621299

Programming Microsoft Visual C# 2005: The Language
ISBN 9780735621817

Debugging Microsoft .NET 2.0 Applications
ISBN 9780735622029

microsoft.com/mspress

For Visual Basic Developers

Microsoft® Visual Basic® 2008 Express Edition: Build a Program Now!

Patrice Pelland

ISBN 9780735625419

Build your own Web browser or other cool application—no programming experience required! Featuring learn-by-doing projects and plenty of examples, this full-color guide is your quick start to creating your first applications for Windows®. DVD includes Express Edition software plus code samples.

Microsoft Visual Basic 2008 Step by Step

Michael Halvorson

ISBN 9780735625372

Teach yourself the essential tools and techniques for Visual Basic 2008—one step at a time. No matter what your skill level, you'll find the practical guidance and examples you need to start building applications for Windows and the Web. CD features practice exercises, code samples, and a fully searchable eBook.

Programming Microsoft Visual Basic 2005: The Language

Francesco Balena

ISBN 9780735621831

Master the core capabilities in Visual Basic 2005 with guidance from well-known programming expert Francesco Balena. Focusing on language features and the Microsoft .NET Framework 2.0 base class library, this book provides pragmatic instruction and examples useful to both new and experienced developers.

Programming Windows Services with Microsoft Visual Basic 2008

Michael Gernaey

ISBN 9780735624337

The essential guide for developing powerful, customized Windows services with Visual Basic 2008. Whether you're looking to perform network monitoring or design a complex enterprise solution, this guide delivers the right combination of expert advice and practical examples to accelerate your productivity.

ALSO SEE

Microsoft Visual Basic 2005 Express Edition: Build a Program Now!
Patrice Pelland
ISBN 9780735622135

Microsoft Visual Basic 2005 Step by Step
Michael Halvorson
ISBN 9780735621312

Microsoft ADO.NET 2.0 Step by Step
Rebecca Riordan
ISBN 9780735621640

Microsoft ASP.NET 3.5 Step by Step
George Shepherd
ISBN 9780735624269

Programming Microsoft ASP.NET 3.5
Dino Esposito
ISBN 9780735625273

Debugging Microsoft .NET 2.0 Applications
John Robbins
ISBN 9780735622029

Microsoft® Press

microsoft.com/mspress